Till Death Do Us Part

TILL DEATH DO US PART

American Ethnic Cemeteries as Borders Uncrossed

Edited by

Allan Amanik and Kami Fletcher

University Press of Mississippi / Jackson

The University Press of Mississippi is the scholarly publishing agency of the Mississippi Institutions of Higher Learning: Alcorn State University, Delta State University, Jackson State University, Mississippi State University, Mississippi University for Women, Mississippi Valley State University, University of Mississippi, and University of Southern Mississippi.

www.upress.state.ms.us

The University Press of Mississippi is a member of the Association of University Presses.

First printing 2020
∞

Unless otherwise indicated, all illustrations are courtesy of the contributors.

Library of Congress Cataloging-in-Publication Data

Names: Amanik, Allan, editor. | Fletcher, Kami, editor.
Title: Till death do us part : American ethnic cemeteries as borders uncrossed / edited by Allan Amanik and Kami Fletcher.
Description: Jackson : University Press of Mississippi, 2020. | Includes bibliographical references and index.
Identifiers: LCCN 2019053828 (print) | LCCN 2019053829 (ebook) | ISBN 9781496827883 (hardcover) | ISBN 9781496827890 (trade paperback) | ISBN 9781496827906 (epub) | ISBN 9781496827913 (epub) | ISBN 9781496827920 (pdf) | ISBN 9781496827937 (pdf)
Subjects: LCSH: Cemeteries—United States—History. | Burial—United States. | Segregation—United States—History. | Minorities—United States—Social conditions. | BISAC: SOCIAL SCIENCE / Anthropology / Cultural & Social
Classification: LCC GT3203 .T55 2020 (print) | LCC GT3203 (ebook) | DDC 393/.1—dc23
LC record available at https://lccn.loc.gov/2019053828
LC ebook record available at https://lccn.loc.gov/2019053829

British Library Cataloging-in-Publication Data available

Contents

Acknowledgments

At the outset of this project, and in the tunnel vision of my own research, I was foolishly convinced that Jews, more than other American minorities, prioritized separate cemeteries. On the other side of this book I have a far more nuanced perspective. The realization of how common and how meaningful the drive to bury apart has been for so many diverse communities treated in these pages is enlightening. However small, that finding offers a special window into the universalism that often resides in difference. At a moment when this country is so divided, I hope that the common themes across the cemetery borders that give this book its meaning might offer an example of all that we share and the mutual "American" forces that shape us. It is recognizing ourselves in others that will pave the way toward healing.

The birth and conclusion of this volume took place over the initial phase of my career. I have learned an immense amount from the process, from my coeditor, and from all of our contributors. I thank them all for their commitment and the value they saw in the work. I would also like to thank family, friends, and colleagues for their support, love, and interest along the way. In particular Dora, Oscar, Philip, and Rita Amanik, Sophia Gutherz, Marty Miller, Alec Gutherz, Alyssa Keene, Max, Laura, Seamus, and Clem Miller, Celeste Conway, and Jeffrey McEachern deserve special attention. I also could not ask for better colleagues at Brooklyn College and thank Sara Reguer, David Brodsky, Sharon Flatto, Robert Shapiro, and Beverly Bailis for their mentoring, friendship, and professional support.

—ALLAN AMANIK

Without the infinite love and support of my lifemate Myron Strong and our sons Jayvyn, Zahir, and Kasai Fletcher-Strong, this project would have soon been shelved. Their lengthy trips to the barbershop, movies, and the supermarket provided me with the space to read, think, and write. Their encouragement when the ideas wouldn't formulate or lay disorganized were the driving force of this project. And a special thank you to Myron for serving as not only a supportive spouse but also as sounding board and editor. I would also like to extend a hearty thanks to colleagues Lauren Anderson, Sarah Lirley McCune, Kristine McCusker, Lawrence Peskin, and Jamie Warner for reading, editing, and providing suggestions to strengthen and tighten my individual essay. I would also like to extend a special thanks to Director of University Press of Mississippi, Craig Gill, for reaching out and contacting me, providing that initial spark to this project. I thank my coeditor for believing in this project and serving in all capacities to complete this original, insightful, and great contribution to Death Studies that follows within these pages.

—KAMI FLETCHER

Till Death Do Us Part

Introduction

—ALLAN AMANIK AND KAMI FLETCHER

In 2013 the United States came the closest it had in decades to passing sweeping immigration reform. The Senate's so-called "Gang of Eight" not only crafted bipartisan legislation that would have allowed, by some estimates, a pathway to citizenship for upwards of eleven million undocumented immigrants in just over a decade, but they also included provisions for immigrant youth set out earlier in the Development, Relief and Education for Alien Minors (DREAM) Act.[1] It was the most comprehensive examination of the country's southern border in nearly three decades. Reflecting on that pivotal moment in US history, the Organization of American Historians (OAH) chose "Crossing Borders" as the theme for its 2014 annual conference. Scholars focused on peoples who crossed the nation's borders over time, the cultural capital that accompanied that movement, and the ways that this influx of bodies and ideas shaped the United States and its social climate. They also examined the physical and intangible borders that have framed the lives of migrants and native born, communities of faith, women and men, ethnic and racial enclaves, and their efforts at cultural pluralism, desegregation, or integration activism, to name but a few themes treated.

Less than a decade later, an exploration of cultural and political borders in the United States seems even more important. Politicians continue to battle over the fate of young immigrant "Dreamers." Iterations of "travel bans" have emerged and retreated in stubborn persistence, stoking thinly veiled prejudices while verging on religious tests to enter the United States. Threats of a wall along the dividing line between the United States and Mexico and the stationing of troops there have bookended cruel family separations for crossing that boundary. All have fanned hate and divisions that many imagined was a thing of the past. Borders, it would seem, remain a ripe lens of analysis for thinking about the American past as much as its present.

3

Till Death Do Us Part emerged from that OAH conference but has reflected over the course of its development upon seemingly new (and surprisingly dormant) divisions in American society. It takes as its subject the tendency among most Americans to separate their dead along communal lines rooted in race, faith, ethnicity, or social standing and asks what a deeper exploration of that phenomenon can tell us about American history more broadly. As much as Americans are aware of that norm, most take that ultimate border in death for granted and few would imagine that its acceptance has had any implications beyond matters of burial. The authors in this volume, however, demonstrate that the motives and means by which Americans have separated themselves in death not only reflected persistent social hierarchies shaping the nation, but also played some role in reinforcing them over time. Centered less on more traditional questions that commonly drive studies of cemeteries or the funeral industry in the United States, this book focuses instead on the physical and symbolic borders around them. Why have Americans across ethnic, racial, religious, and socioeconomic backgrounds typically preferred to keep to themselves in death? What does a deeper exploration of those divisions reveal, not only about these groups but also about core traditions and social forces that have underpinned American society since the early nineteenth century?

Comparative in scope, and regionally diverse, chapters look to immigrants, communities of color, the colonized, the enslaved, rich and poor, and religious minorities as they laid their dead to rest in locales spanning the Northeast to the Spanish American Southwest. Whether African Americans, Muslim or Christian Arabs, Indians, mestizos, Chinese, Jews, Poles, Catholics, Protestants, or various whites of European descent, one thing that united these Americans was a drive to keep their dead apart. At times that choice stemmed from internal preference. At others it was a function of external prejudice. Whether religious law, interethnic tension, racial hostility, presumptions of consumer entitlement, rights of private property, the allure of the market and exclusivity of private grounds, or bonds of communal loyalty, *Till Death Do Us Part* unearths and explores all of these concerns. The present authors consider these among other motivations as they chart the value or priority that their respective communities found in burying among their own. In the process, they seek better to understand how Americans have come to accept or expect a degree of separation in death. While burial spaces have reflected and preserved cultural and communal identity, particularly in a society as diverse as the United States, the invisible and institutional borders built around them (and into them) also tell a powerful story of the ways in which Americans negotiated race, culture, class, national origin, and religious difference in the United States during its formative century.

By design this book avoids cemeteries that one might loosely classify as public grounds in favor of those established and maintained by voluntary grassroots associations. The former might include sites like potter's fields or municipal common graves; infirmary, asylum, prison, or hospital cemeteries; or military and national graveyards. To be sure, each of these offers its own perspective on the ways in which setting graves apart has marginalized or honored the dead, be they poor or servants of the state. Nevertheless, in formulating this study we have been much more curious about grassroots divisions that play out time and again in American burying places, whether voluntary or coerced, among ethnic, racial, or faith-based communities. As Marilyn Yalom poignantly remarks in her survey of American cemeteries, "as solitary beings each of us merits a separate grave; as members of a group, we are buried together . . ."[2] Here, we seek to dig beneath that sentiment and offer an extensive exploration of various forces that underwrite it.

While group identity has been a key factor in that trend, Americans of all stripes have also buried apart in response to larger dynamics shaping American history. Their drive to keep to themselves in death stemmed from internal concerns over religious law, communal loyalty, or collective self-reliance as much as larger issues of racial prejudice or empowerment, deficiencies in America's social welfare system, or separation of church and state versus the driving altar of the market. By bringing separation to the fore of this study of American cemeteries, we hope not only to highlight those forces as they influenced American ways of death but to contemplate the less typically considered role that deathways played in their own right in shaping several core dynamics molding American society.

For this reason, too, we focus largely on the nineteenth century, when many of those forces took shape. Emancipation and Reconstruction, for instance, intended drastically to revise the relationship between black and white Americans. As Jeffrey Smith and Kami Fletcher point out, cemetery spaces both enshrined racial inequality at the same time that they offered tools for African Americans to challenge that hierarchy. Industrialization and mass migration also thread these pages. Although the nation's voracious appetite for labor attracted millions to seek out new lives, deficiencies in state social welfare required them to fend for themselves in matters of communal aid. Fearing poverty in life or a pauper's grave in death, they organized around regional or religious lines to secure land and funerary provisions.[3] As Rosina Hassoun, James Pula, and Allan Amanik highlight, internal religious law prohibiting burial beyond one's faith community led Muslim, Catholic, and Jewish immigrants in particular to keep to themselves in death. At the same time, the legal and social entitlements that some of these immigrants gained as owners of property, in some cases the first they ever owned, cast their cemeteries as sites in which to set down roots in their new home or to work out interethnic conflicts dividing denominations. Much like their native-born and middle-class counterparts who, as Kelly Arehart argues, invested their cemeteries with supposedly genteel sensibilities as a matter of social standing, these and other immigrants also introduced American ideals into their burying spaces as a means to further claims of American belonging. Finally, western expansion, hemispheric imperialism, and xenophobia at home and abroad not only reshaped the nation's geographic and political borders but, as Martina Will de Chaparro and Sue Fawn Chung explain, those endeavors recast notions of white supremacy as the United States staked its claim to newly occupied southwestern territory. That incorporation had deep implications for Spanish and Indian populations subsumed within those shifting political borders as much as Asian immigrants laboring toward its development. Catholic and Chinese deathways in the Southwest would never be the same. The essays in this volume turn on these and other developments. American cemetery spaces and the respective communities that maintained them, however, were not just reactive, the present authors argue. Rather, they also had a role in shaping social and political dynamics beyond them.

In this sense, we seek to build on a rich legacy of scholarship on America cemeteries over the decades. That work has covered a host of subjects, whether focusing on iconography or style of grounds early on, the evolution of American burying places amid urban and market growth, or ethnic cemeteries as measures of communal identity and tradition. Material culture, for instance, occupied many early historians of colonial churchyards. Reading deeply into stonework and inscriptions or changing physical material over time, studies traced the craft surrounding grave markers as well as the social and spiritual attitudes about death that they reflected.[4] The spatial evolution of American cemeteries has also been ripe for inquiry. This has been captured most dramatically by studying America's mid-nineteenth-century shift from churchyards to rural cemeteries beyond city limits. Classic studies of the Rural Cemetery Movement have closely followed grounds like Mount Auburn, in Cambridge, Massachusetts, or others that quickly followed its model developing around the nation.[5] These works detail how the move from graveyards to lush cemeteries overflowing with monuments and natural beauty could allude to ancient motifs like Greek or Egyptian culture while reflecting modern attitudes around death or horticultural science of the day. Although the rural cemetery aesthetic aimed to please the eye and soul, it also offered a window into contemporary anxieties over rapid urban expansion. Cemetery surveys over much longer periods have similarly approached American burying places as sites reflecting concerns and sensibilities of the living who created them.[6] Comparative or individual studies of ethnic grounds have also received much attention. Scholars have especially highlighted diversity and difference across various immigrant or minority cemeteries in the United States. They have approached these spaces as expressions of communal tradition and a measure of that identity's endurance in America.[7] Some have even posited immigrant burial grounds as sites of "identity and stability in a new country characterized by change."[8] As suggested by the essays in Richard Meyer's classic volume, *Ethnicity and the American Cemetery*, ethnic burial grounds also offer an instructive lens to chart the duality of "cultural retention and assimilation." They do so through the transformations that play out in ethnic cemeteries or linguistic and traditional elements that survive over several generations.[9]

Beyond these familiar approaches, recent scholars have also increasingly employed historical archaeology or local history to recover lost voices and experiences through American burying places. The restoration and preservation of African American burial grounds offer a prime example. Whether instances like the 1991 discovery in Manhattan of nearly five hundred seventeenth- and eighteenth-century African American remains, removed grounds like Love Cemetery in rural East Texas, or efforts to restore Dallas's Freedman's Cemetery, these and similar sites offer a powerful window into the history of slavery, white supremacy, and black/white relations past and present. In some instances, these grounds have spawned interactive museums allowing rich collaboration among community leaders, genealogical societies, and concerned citizens. Together they have not only unearthed entirely forgotten cemeteries or restored those falling into disrepair but have also created memorials and larger movements to remember and return these communities' stories to the historical record. Through exhibits like those centered on Manhattan's burial ground, visitors learn about black New Yorkers as people whose lived experiences extended well beyond labor to include familial bonds, African heritage and culture, the larger communities to which they belonged, and their contributions to New York's development. Restoration and recovery of grounds like Dallas's Freedman's Cemetery and accompanying sculptures teach about slavery, resistance, and that city's black community as well. A massive gateway flanked by an African king and queen serve as the entrance to the cemetery which leads visitors to a garden with statues of enslaved blacks mourning and consoling. These and other similar cemeteries serve a dual function, exposing lies of the time deeply rooted in racism and white supremacist norms while providing a means for contemporary scholars and community members to reclaim and offer a scale of justice and interracial healing.[10] That kind of approach has also extended beyond matters of race with studies employing innovative uses of forensic analysis to burial spaces in order to access otherwise marginalized voices among the poor, the infirmed, the imprisoned, or the disabled.[11]

Others have considered American cemeteries as a means to explore local history, taking up regional cemeteries to tell the tale of local cities, counties, and their residents. These works conduct far-reaching and comprehensive cemetery research to recall local collective history through bones and stones. Via personal connections to one cemetery, authors tell its history through those interred or even cemetery superintendents and caretakers. Historians have shown how these local histories offer new insights into much larger dynamics. One case highlights how local traditions at the grave played a role inspiring one of the nation's most cherished cemetery celebrations: Memorial Day.[12] Another points to late nineteenth- and early twentieth-century women's efforts to challenge their social and political status through cemeteries in the Rocky Mountain West via gendered monuments that portrayed grief, sorrow, hope, and faith as feminine.[13] They claim that this depicted death as the emotional and domestic realm of women, but ignored national gains and reinforced artificial divisions for women between public and private life. Local histories rooted in local cemeteries have shed important light on American history, often resisting larger narratives beyond them.

Till Death Do Us Part builds on all of this preceding work but does so with an eye to the borders, real and imagined, that Americans have employed to separate their cemeteries along religious, racial, ethnic, or socioeconomic lines. Although mostly limited in scope to the nineteenth century and, by and large, to ethnic and religious minorities, the essays nonetheless intersect with larger issues shaping the nation in that period. Each chapter illustrates and highlights what deeper explorations of the dead in America can tell us about American identity, nationhood, and national belonging.

In chapter 1, Allan Amanik examines the interplay among immigration, race, and religion through New York City and the nation's first Jewish rural cemeteries of the 1850s. He argues that these grounds embodied an important duality for the Jewish New Yorkers who buried within them as markers of social belonging to New York's emerging white middle class while also safeguarding Jewish particularity and continuity over time. On the one hand, recent Jewish immigrants eagerly participated in the city's sprawling Rural Cemetery Movement. They laid out lavish rural grounds and embraced the movement's spirit of universalism by setting their cemeteries in closer proximity than ever before to nonsectarian Christian counterparts. On the other hand, they made sure to cluster together behind clear physical barriers, and nearly all synagogues and Jewish fraternities prohibited Christian burial. They also all maintained old links between interment rights and intermarriage. Even as broader market, family, and aesthetic ideals wholly transformed the city's Jewish funeral sphere, most Jewish communal orders held fast to divisions in death. Aware of increasing acceptance in the United States, Jewish New Yorkers celebrated their costly new cemeteries as symbols of mobility and belonging. At the same time, they doubled down on physical and intangible divisions within them to temper that integration.

In chapter 2, James S. Pula focuses on themes of Polish migration, religion, and ethnic identity as they underwrote Polish cemeteries at the turn of the twentieth century. On one level, he fills a void of study on Polish cemeteries in the United States. On another, he follows interethnic divisions among Catholic Poles and their Irish or German counterparts, who dominated key leadership positions in the American church. Pula draws on a wide array of Polish cemeteries in the United States and Poland for comparative perspective. Considering immigrant sensibilities at these cemeteries' creation, he casts them as important bastions of ethnic and national affirmation and a fulfillment of religious law to bury apart. At the same time, he considers the limits of ethnic distinction in later generations. Although Americans of Polish descent continued in subsequent generations to bury in Polish grounds or to employ linguistic or cultural symbols, they embraced larger funerary conventions amid upward mobility and subsumed distinctively Polish norms within larger Catholic practice. Pula's study highlights spatial distinctions among Poles and other ethnic Catholics in death, but also the cemetery's role as a site to resist indifference to national Polish traditions in parish grounds, schools, or services with majority Polish parishioners led by non-Polish bishops and priests. Through a survey of legal and institutional battles that centered on parish grounds among Poles and their American ethnic Catholic counterparts, Pula's study also offers a fascinating look into the workings of ethnoreligious dissent in the United States from a little-studied vantage point.

Like Jewish and Polish immigrants, Chinese newcomers carried culturally and religiously distinctive funeral norms with them as they sought new lives and livelihoods in the United States. However, as Sue Fawn Chung points out in chapter 3, they faced added racial and legal discrimination that ultimately led to temporary burial in separate Chinese cemeteries. Chinese women and men found their dead banned from white cemetery holdings or worried that vandals would desecrate their graves. Restrictive immigration laws also prevented key rites of ancestral veneration. This led many in the American West to participate in what Chung calls the "repatriation of bones," the act of exhuming and cleaning remains, placing them in sealed tin or ceramic urns, and returning them for burial at home in Chinese villages of origin. Separate Chinese cemeteries, whether internally or externally motivated, drew on broader racial hierarchies crystallizing in nineteenth-century America as much as they helped frame them, particularly western hostility to Asian migration and labor. At the same time, rights of private property and collective association allowed Chinese immigrant associations some agency by burying apart.

Similarly unwanted in death, African Americans too were not interested in having an American identity that erased the cultural roots of their homeland. In chapter 4, Kami Fletcher contends that blacks not only rejected an American identity that sought to marginalize and enslave them but used death to gain burial freedoms and graveyard autonomy, in addition to using death as a path for self-help and wealth building. Fletcher follows the growth and development of Baltimore's African Burying Ground, illustrating how the trustees of Sharp Street Church (who owned it) used the burial ground as a call for humanity and dignity in death. Founded in 1807 as the city's first autonomous black burial ground, Fletcher argues, Baltimore's African Burying Ground pushed back against slave cemeteries and potter's fields to serve as a protected and autonomous space of interment for all "Africans and people of colour." As the burial ground grew and moved around the city, Sharp Street Church trustees fostered benevolent and burial aid societies while creating savvy ways of using cemetery grounds to invest in both individual and collective black entrepreneurship. Ultimately, the essay highlights the interplay of race, death, and burial rights and the power that American society vested in racialized burial borders, only to have them reinvented and used as catalysts for agency and resistance.

In chapter 5, Jeffrey Smith casts Bellefontaine Cemetery (the largest nondenominational nineteenth-century rural/garden cemetery in St. Louis, Missouri) as a powerful window into evolving ideas about slavery and race relations in a northern border state. Beyond parallel racial hostility at sharing burial space in nonurban or plantation settings, growing urban concentration and limited land in St. Louis forced cemetery trustees and lot holders to engage with race far more directly as they determined cemetery policies governing black and white bodies. Smith surveys various cemeteries owned by white and African American churches as well as regulations set for individual interments or lot sales to African American institutions. He traces exclusive policies governing African Americans as well as the ways in which white families physically marginalized graves of current or former slaves within their private lots. In so doing, Smith demonstrates how a study of African American interment patterns in Bellefontaine reflected as much as they reinforced living racial hierarchies taking shape in a state in transition. Although nominally the great equalizer, death and the physical and symbolic divisions within it preserved racial inequities during a moment of shifting hierarchies.

Lawn-park cemeteries provide the backdrop of Kelly Arehart's essay in chapter 6. She approaches the issue of separation in death from an otherwise uncharted perspective—that of cemetery superintendents. Arehart follows members of this emerging profession as they developed and refined American resting places from the mid-nineteenth to early twentieth centuries. She demonstrates how these superintendents created the very standards of beauty and taste to which so many Americans aspired in their cemetery spaces. Embedded in their efforts at taste-making, though, Arehart highlights the ways in which these professionals also omitted old-world traditions, worked against racial equality, and favored inflated prices that ultimately excluded the poor or working class. Either through physical boundaries, prohibitively expensive lots or, most simply, racially exclusive owners' policies, cemetery superintendents drew upon understandings of whiteness and gentility in their efforts to promote respectable middle-class cemeteries. At the same time, their cemetery oversight had a hand shaping the contours of that very ideal by creating obstacles for immigrants, people of color, or the poor to access and attain it.

As much as nineteenth-century rural/garden cemeteries created a dominant American way of death, Martina Will de Chaparro wholeheartedly questions its exclusivity and regional reach in chapter 7. Will de Chaparro surveys death and burial in nineteenth-century New Mexico amid the region's political transition from Spanish, to Mexican, to United States control. Looking especially to Albuquerque and Santa Fe, she considers the territory's multiracial and multicultural past by tracing Indian and Spanish burial practices, the role of colonialism and independence therein, and ultimately the arrival of non-Catholic "Anglo," African American, European, and Asian newcomers who all reinvented the region's burial landscape. Although preceding periods' archival and archaeological evidence suggests that New Mexicans did not segregate their dead by race and ethnicity, subsequent imperial shifts undid that situation. Within the colonial framework, concerns over public health pushed burial to new distant cemeteries and away from coveted rest in parish spaces for eternity. Wealth and influence allowed some to circumvent those laws, only further fueling a two-tier burial system. Being folded into the United States further drove religious and racial divisions as existing church infrastructure could not and would not tend to new non-Catholic populations in death. Despite New Mexico's earlier egalitarian approach, Will de Chaparro highlights the role of an expanding state and shifting imperial alignments to separate the dead by faith, national origin, race, or economic standing.

Finally, in chapter 8, Rosina Hassoun brings many of these themes forward in time through her pioneering research into Arab American cemeteries over the nineteenth and twentieth centuries. Hassoun overlays shifting approaches to burial onto three broad phases of Christian and Muslim Arab immigration to America. Like other immigrants, these newcomers buried along denominational lines, be they Catholic or Orthodox Christians or Sunni and Shi'a Muslims. They also did so in separate sections of extant grounds or in independent cemeteries established in later periods as Arab Americans gained a sense of belonging and communal numbers and means. The importance of family intersected with minority deathways. Early Arab Americans, like their Chinese counterparts, sent remains back to villages of origin to be buried among kin. Some even astoundingly transgressed religious laws against cremation when the costs of sending remains proved otherwise prohibitive. Later Christian Arabs who married non-Arab Christians could also face complications in death if denominational differences did not allow for burial in congregational holdings or if they converted and could not be buried with the rest of their family. Looking to the nation's largest Arab population centers over time, Hassoun charts a rich array of Arab American cemeteries and offers a unique lens to explore communal dynamics among Muslim and Christian Arabs as they intersected with immigration policy, socioeconomic standing, and a larger sense of rootedness to America society.

Although the question of why Americans separate their dead remains rather simple, its exploration from the vantage point of this heterogeneous mix of communities adds to our understanding of the United States writ large. This plays out particularly as each essay intersects with pivotal forces shaping the modern nation over its formative century. Whether constructions of whiteness, the rise of the middle class, migration and restriction, western expansion, idealizing the family or private rights of property, slavery and freedom, religious liberty and nonestablishment, or grassroots agency through collective association, communal cemeteries offer an otherwise underappreciated lens into all of these themes. They also played some role shaping those forces as they, in turn, shaped the landscape of the final resting places charted in these pages. In examining America and Americanness through the lens of death and, in particular, the tangible and invisible boundaries surrounding American cemetery spaces, this volume invites its readers to consider the processes of nation-building and identity from an often sentimentalized though rarely analyzed perspective. We seek to highlight the work of death, deathways, and burial in producing or traversing those forces. We seek, too, to demonstrate how a convention so easily taken for granted also proved quite influential to forces and concerns well beyond it.

Notes

1. The Border Security, Economic Opportunity, and Immigration Modernization Act of 2013 aimed at comprehensive immigration reform. The DREAM Act targeted the children (ages twelve to thirty) of undocumented immigrants who entered the country as minors, putting those with a high school diploma (or GED) and in good moral standing on a path to permanent residency and eventual full citizenship. "A Guide to S.744: Understanding the 2013 Senate Immigration Bill" Special Report, *Immigration Policy Center at the American Immigration Council,* July 10, 2013, https://americanimmigrationcouncil.org/sites/default/files/research/guide_to_s744_corker_hoeven_final_12-02-13.pdf.

2. Marilyn Yalom, *The American Resting Place: Four Hundred Years of History through Our Cemeteries and Burial Grounds* (Boston: Houghton Mifflin, 2008), 28.

3. On the interplay among immigrant aid, American social welfare, and funerary provisions see for instance John E. Bodner, *The Transplanted: A History of Immigrants in Urban America* (Bloomington: Indiana University Press, 1985), 120–31; Lizabeth Cohen, *Making a New Deal: Industrial Workers in Chicago, 1919–1939* (Cambridge, UK, and New York: Cambridge

University Press, 1990), 58–75; Daniel Soyer, *Jewish Immigrant Associations and American Identity in New York* (Cambridge, MA: Harvard University Press, 1997), 87–93; David T. Beito, *From Mutual Aid to the Welfare State: Fraternal Societies and Social Services, 1890–1967* (Chapel Hill: University of North Carolina Press, 2000); Michael K. Rosenow, *Death and Dying in the Working Class, 1865–1920* (Urbana: University of Illinois Press, 2015).

4. See, for instance, representative studies published in *Markers* over the years like Ernest Caulfield, "Wanted: The Hook-And-Eye Man," *Markers* 1 (1979–80): 12–50; Betty Willshire, "Scottish Gravestones and the New England Winged Skull," *Markers* 2 (1982): 105–14; David Watters, "The JN Carver," *Markers* 2 (1982): 115–32; Lucien L. Agosta, "Speaking Stones: New England Grave Carving and the Emblematic Tradition," *Markers* 3 (1984): 47–70; as well as Richard E. Meyer, ed., *Cemeteries and Gravemarkers: Voices of American Culture* (Logan: Utah State University Press, 1995); Douglas Keister, *Stories in Stone: A Field Guide to Cemetery Symbolism and Iconography* (Salt Lake City: Gibbs Smith, 2009); Richard Francis Veit and Mark Nonestied, *New Jersey Cemeteries and Tombstones: History in the Landscape* (New Brunswick: Rivergate Books, 2008).

5. For a history documenting the founding of Mount Auburn Cemetery, see Jacob Bigelow, *A History of the Cemetery of Mount Auburn* (Boston and Cambridge: James Munroe and Company, 1860). For more recent works, see Blanche M. G. Linden, *Silent City on a Hill: Picturesque Landscapes of Memory and Boston's Mount Auburn Cemetery* (Amherst: University of Massachusetts Press, 2007); Stephen Kendrick, *The Lively Place: Mount Auburn, America's First Garden Cemetery, and Its Revolutionary and Literary Residents* (Boston: Beacon Press, 2016); Stanley French, "The Cemetery as a Cultural Institution: The Establishment of Mount Auburn and the 'Rural Cemetery' Movement," *American Quarterly* 76 (March 1974): 37–49; Thomas Bender, "The 'Rural' Cemetery Movement: Urban Travail and the Appeal of Nature," *New England Quarterly* 47 (June 1974): 196–211.

6. See Kenneth T. Jackson and Camilo José Vergara, *Silent Cities: The Evolution of the American Cemetery* (New York: Princeton Architectural Press, 1989); David Charles Sloane, *The Last Great Necessity: Cemeteries in American History* (Baltimore, MD: Johns Hopkins Press, 1991); Robert Pogue Harrison, *The Dominion of the Dead* (Chicago: University of Chicago Press, 2003); Meg Greene, *Rest in Peace: A History of American Cemeteries* (Minneapolis, MN: Twenty-First Century Books, 2008); Yalom, *The American Resting Place*.

7. See perhaps most famously Richard E. Meyer, ed., *Ethnicity and the American Cemetery* (Bowling Green, OH: Bowling Green State University Popular Press, 1993) as well as Meyer's rich annotated bibliography highlighting similar works on "necroethnicity" in America. Sue Fawn Chung and Priscilla Wegars, eds., *Chinese American Death Rituals: Respecting the Ancestors* (Lantham, MD: AltaMira Press, 2005) offers a more recent example of this approach.

8. Jackson and Vergara, *Silent Cities*, 60.

9. Meyer, *Ethnicity and the American Cemetery*, 4.

10. Joyce Hansen and Gary McGowan, *Breaking Ground, Breaking Silence: The Story of New York's African Burial Ground* (New York: Henry Holt, 1998); Andrea E. Frohne, *The African Burial Ground in New York City: Memory, Spirituality, and Space* (Syracuse, NY: Syracuse University Press, 2015); China Galland, *Love Cemetery: Unburying the Secret History of Slaves* (New York: HarperOne, 2007).

11. See, for instance, David A. Poirer and Nicholas R. Bellantoni, *In Remembrance: Archaeology and Death* (Westport, CT: Bergin and Garvey, 1997), or Sherene Baugher and Richard Veit, *The Archaeology of American Cemeteries and Gravemarkers* (Gainesville: University Press of Florida, 2014).

12. Alan Jabbour and Karen Singer Jabbour, *Decoration Day in the Mountains: Traditions of Cemetery Decoration in the Southern Appalachians* (Chapel Hill: University of North Carolina Press, 2010).

13. Annette Stott, *Pioneer Cemeteries: Sculpture Gardens of the Old West* (Lincoln: University of Nebraska Press, 2008).

Chapter One

"A Beautiful Garden Consecrated to the Lord": Marriage, Death, and Local Constructions of Citizenship in New York's Nineteenth-Century Jewish Rural Cemeteries

—ALLAN AMANIK

Gathered crowds lined West Thirty-Fourth Street on May 3, 1880, to pay their last respects to one of America's most prominent Jewish entrepreneurs. Joseph Seligman had died about a week earlier in New Orleans on April 25. Six days later, and just two before the funeral, his body reached New York where it was "embalmed and inclosed [*sic*] in a silver-mounted iron coffin." As a glowing eulogy honored the banker, a metal casket lay-in-waiting: "two wreaths of immortelles rested at the head . . . and a broken column of the same flowers stood at the foot . . . above it six waxen candles burned dimly in the darkened room." When the service ended, "friends and mourners took a last look at the body, and the lid of the casket was closed." Soon after, 132 carriages set off for the cemetery of the Temple Emanu-El where Seligman was laid to rest following a host of funeral addresses.[1] Given the Seligman family's stature, certain genteel sensibilities necessarily outweighed traditional Jewish taboos, whether lack of immediate burial, extravagant casket and ceremony, or a body, embalmed and on view, amid flowers and flickering candles. Nevertheless, one core Jewish element still defined his committal: Seligman would rest for eternity in an exclusively Jewish cemetery.

Although far wealthier than most Jewish New Yorkers, Seligman and even Jews of meager means had something in common as far as their funerals. Nearly all of the city's Jewish residents by the mid-nineteenth century held fast to divisions in death regardless of religious observance or economic standing. They did so despite increasing access to the American mainstream. Indeed, beginning early in the 1850s New York's leading synagogues established the nation's first Jewish rural cemeteries, while fledgling Jewish fraternal orders won their independence by buying tracts in neighboring nonsectarian grounds. These moves introduced unprecedented practices into Jewish cemetery design and organization. Many even displaced conventions that Jewish New Yorkers had observed for over a century. They gave up the somber egalitarianism, for instance, that had long defined Manhattan's Jewish graveyards for a new, ornate aesthetic. They also began to sell cemetery lots for profit and in advance, allowing Jewish families to bury together for the first time in private holdings. In an equally striking departure, they buried in unprecedented proximity to Christian contemporaries and their cemeteries. In style, space, and sentiment, Jewish congregations and benevolent societies truly embraced America's emerging "way of death" as one among several new social and religious practices to mark their sense of integration into a majority culture.

And yet, despite so many innovations, Jews of all stripes retained one taboo against mixing the dead across faiths. Regulations universally banned Christian interment in consecrated Jewish ground, and most synagogues and fraternal orders upheld complex policies for interfaith families. These ranged from exclusion from Jewish cemeteries or communal circles to pragmatic compromise. Exclusionary policies, in their most extreme, refused membership and funeral rights to Jewish partners who married Christians. Softer policies agreed to bury Jewish spouses but refused their Christian partners who had not converted. Interment of children of interfaith families raised a host of other issues. No matter their stance, in upholding these funerary regulations to greater or lesser degrees, all Jewish institutions preserved an old convention to guard ritual and physical divisions among the dead. Not only this, but they continued to accept a well-worn idea that, beyond precepts of Jewish religious law, separating the dead could also limit social and communal boundary crossing among the living.

The city and the nation's first Jewish rural cemeteries therefore embodied an important duality. On the one hand, Jews touted them as symbols of mobility and integration, marking their embrace of American material culture and religiosity in death. Lush Jewish landscapes that neighbored Protestant cemeteries stood as testaments to Jewish inclusion, nearly unprecedented on either side of the Atlantic. On the other hand, Jewish New Yorkers sought to temper that very integration in American life by doubling down on physical and ritual borders in death. They did so through the separate cemeteries they maintained but also in those spaces' governing policies that were designed, in part, to discourage exogamous marriage. The clear lines that synagogues and lodges maintained between Christian and Jewish dead offered some stability in a period of social barriers otherwise in flux. While many Jews held up their new rural cemeteries

Figure 1.1 The latest of three surviving Jewish graveyards in Manhattan, between 6th and 7th Avenues on 21st Street. Dedicated by Shearith Israel in 1829, it served the congregation just over two decades before the city outlawed interment below 86th Street. The yard's aesthetic captures the somber simplicity that predated Jewish rural cemeteries. Photo taken in 2018.

Figure 1.2 The remnants of Manhattan's second oldest Jewish graveyard occupy a small triangle of land on the corner of 11th Street and Sixth Avenue. The yard was dedicated in 1805 before urban development engulfed most of its land. Photo taken in 2018.

as bastions of belonging, they also conceived of them just as strongly as engines of Jewish particularity.

Jewish preferences to separate in death had a long legacy in New York well before the Rural Cemetery Movement. Among their first acts when arriving to New Amsterdam in 1654, Jewish settlers requested a separate Jewish graveyard. As the Dutch put it: "they did not wish to bury their dead . . . in the [colony's] common burying ground."[2] Well into the nineteenth century each time that that yard or others reached their limit, wealthy Jews set about purchasing new land far from the city and away from existing churchyards. That priority even applied to the poor when the synagogue, in 1800, petitioned the city for a separate Jewish potter's field.[3] Even as Jewish undertakers began emerging in the mid-nineteenth century, one of New York's first such professionals advertised that all of his shrouds and caskets would "be prepared by members of the Jewish faith" and that even his carriages would be "driven by a Jew."[4] Among leaders and laity, most Jewish New Yorkers highly valued separation in death and burial.

That preference afforded synagogue elders immense social control. In fact, for over a century until the 1820s, New York's one Jewish congregation, Shearith Israel, also managed its only Jewish graveyards. Leaders used that monopoly to promote conformity and cohesion. In the process they laid the ground for policies that average Jewish households would reject when they embraced rural cemeteries. Most often over the eighteenth and early nineteenth centuries, trustees leveraged burial as a means to promote regular and consistent payment of dues. At times they even threatened interment rights for spotty synagogue attendance or consumption of meat not sold by the congregation.[5] Beyond punitive measures, elders also used the graveyard to promote collectivism and a sense of long communal bonds. The majority of congregants experienced this through a ban on family burial until the creation of Jewish rural cemeteries introduced family lots in the 1850s. Before that shift, trustees forbade family graves so that stature or wealth would not divide their yards. Instead they laid to rest all congregants who had met communal expectations in sequential rows defined by the order of decease.

Links between interment rights and intermarriage that carried over into Jewish rural cemeteries remained a part of that earlier system as well. Most synagogues refused to bury Christian spouses or quite literally marginalized a Jewish partner's grave with placement along the fence or the outskirts of the yard. By visually marking members' graves, trustees hoped to discourage marriage out of the community. At the same time, they aimed to preempt the complex problems of burying members of interfaith families in consecrated Jewish grounds, since too few ordained rabbis had yet settled in the United States to perform conversions in accordance with Jewish law. In the few instances where conversions for marriage did occur, some American Jewish communities still questioned their ritual validity because lay leaders had performed them. That reality persisted until the 1840s, when trained rabbis began to arrive in significant numbers. Even then, most remained reluctant to perform conversions. Finally, as eighteenth- and nineteenth-century synagogues leveraged interment rights to discourage Jewish members from marrying out of the fold, they revealed a deeper anxiety over the social fluidity the United States extended to its Jewish residents. If trustees and synagogue elders did not set stark communal and religious lines in access to basic life-cycle rites like marriage or interment, they feared, ever more porous social boundaries seemed poised to challenge communal cohesion and continuity.[6] Prior to the proliferation of New York's rural cemeteries, most of the city's synagogues replicated these policies, leaving New York Jewish households with few options or control in matters of death.

As New York City expanded in the nineteenth century, its development forever changed that dynamic. Rapid urban growth forced most religious and benevolent groups to vacate older city graveyards in favor of new, removed sites to lay their dead to rest well beyond the city. Otherwise, parks and city improvements menaced the prospect of eternal repose. City officials, religious leaders, and enterprising land speculators all understood the need for new distant burying places, and their efforts drove the boom in New York's rural cemetery economy. Following the success of Green-Wood Cemetery nearly a decade earlier, the Common Council passed an act in 1847 to encourage burial across the East River through tax exemptions for nonprofit cemeteries in Kings and Queens counties. Churches and synagogues responded fairly quickly, but so did land speculators who intended to convert cheap farmland into resalable cemeteries. As larger congregations like St. Patrick's Cathedral, the Temple Emanu-El, or St. Paul's German Lutheran Church addressed the challenges of urban interment by sculpting rural cemeteries like Calvary Cemetery (1846–48), Salem Fields (1851), or the Lutheran Cemetery (later All Faiths, 1852), private investors created their own nonsectarian properties like Cypress Hills Cemetery (1848), the Cemetery of the Evergreens (1849), or Washington Cemetery (1850).[7]

Commercial promoters targeted smaller churches and fraternal societies that lacked independent funds to purchase large holdings independently. They also sold their grounds through language of inclusion and the promise of physical security from looming urban development. Through affordable rates on smaller tracts, for instance, Cypress Hills boosters promised any group "lots at a price that would exclude no one from participating in the advantages that have hitherto been enjoyed only by incurring large expenses."[8] They also stressed its "[geographic] isolation from innovation or the inroads of improvements" in a site supposedly "perpetually secluded and protected from all danger of invasion or desecration for all time."[9] In coming years, religious and benevolent organizations transferred thousands of graves across the East River. To Cypress Hills

Cemetery alone, just a handful of churches had moved 35,000 graves by 1860.[10] Although in 1820 New York City had maintained 100 active burial grounds, by 1850 only twenty-three remained in use.[11]

As synagogue trustees imagined their own new rural cemeteries, the physical and conceptual possibilities of an entirely new burial frontier led them to innovate in death as they never had previously. Whether the introduction of family burial in response to pent-up congregant demand or new, lush aesthetics, the broader Rural Cemetery Movement allowed Jewish New Yorkers to create Jewish cemeteries without precedent or parallel. Those changes even inspired deeply controversial debates around Jewish law itself that governed disinterment. Congregants, emboldened by new ownership of cemetery parcels, sought to transfer long-departed loved ones from Jewish yards in Manhattan to newly purchased family lots in emerging synagogue cemeteries.[12] In embracing these innovations, New York Jews not only proudly drew on motifs driving the Rural Cemetery Movement but also saw that project as a means to celebrate American standing and demonstrate their fitness for inclusion.

Cemetery aesthetic marked the first innovation. Away from the somber rows of Manhattan's Jewish graveyards, Salem Fields, America's first modern Jewish cemetery, cut an entirely new model. In 1851 the Reform Temple Emanu-El fashioned twenty-five acres of Brooklyn farmland to rival any modern cemetery. "As was never before the case with a Jewish cemetery," leaders still boasted decades later, "this was designed and laid out systematically with fine roads, well-ordered pathways . . . and was stocked with plants and flowers; family vaults were built and neatly fenced in; and, in fact, all that was possible was done to make the place beautiful. To this day it presents the appearance of a lovely garden consecrated to the Lord, and the name, 'Salem Field Cemetery,' has become celebrated."[13] In 1895, an anniversary volume for Emanu-El hailed Salem Fields as "one of the most beautiful cemeteries of the many fine ones maintained upon Long Island" and dedicated an entire final chapter to twenty-eight full-page glossy photos of the most ornate mausoleums.[14]

Emanu-El trustees preened Salem Fields for decades to come. In 1877 they hired the architect Henry Fernbach to design an imposing new entrance. This came on the heels of his iconic work on projects like Stern's Department Store, the exclusive Harmonie Club, the Soho Hotel, and the New York Mutual Life Insurance Company. Of equal importance, Fernbach had also designed opulent Moorish-style synagogues for congregations Emanu-El (1868), Shaaray Tefila (1869), and Ahawath Chesed (later the Central Synagogue, 1872). These structures' grandeur not only displayed Jewish material attainment in New York, they embraced a style clearly proclaiming them as Jewish houses of worship. At the same time, their distinctive aesthetic hoped to connect the tolerance that Jews in the United States enjoyed to another idealized golden age of Spanish

Figure 1.3 Seligman family mausoleum. From Emanu-El's anniversary volume *The Rise and Progress of Reform Judaism*, 1895.

Figure 1.4 Other family lots in Salem Fields Cemetery. The ornate monuments and landscaping reflect graves in surrounding rural cemeteries like Cypress Hills. Emanu-El's celebratory volume *The Rise and Progress of Reform Judaism*, 1895.

multiculturalism during the Islamic Middle Ages.[15] Little wonder that Emanu-El also sought to infuse that spirit into its celebrated rural cemetery so closely positioned alongside universalist Christian counterparts.

Funerary innovations beyond cemetery design soon followed. After its early successes pioneering Salem Fields, Emanu-El attempted a total overhaul of Jewish funerary rite and tradition. From deathbed to grave, Samuel Adler, its recently instated rabbi, tried by 1858 to excise all rites considered "antiquated national usages" or "offensive to refined feelings."[16] These included customs such as placing the dead on the floor during ritual washing ceremonies before burial or other mourning traditions that had developed over the centuries without clear foundations in religious law. Tearing of garments, growing a beard, or abstaining from leather shoes ranked high among these practices along with "the prohibition of washing, bathing and saluting, [that] have lost, in OUR time, all meaning, are even repulsive to our feelings, and are therefore abolished." For Adler, these rites seemed less a matter of the soul's catharsis than clear challenges to modernity in Jewish funerary rite and, by extension, full Jewish access to polite American society. After all, he claimed, "deportment of man in times of deep mourning furnishes the best evidence of his clearness of mind, firmness of principle and true enlightenment." Like other reforms, these, too, drew on broader Jewish concerns over seemingly archaic practices or a desire to be perceived as steadily marching toward American gentility.

While trustees of the city's second synagogue, B'nai Jeshurun, did not revise central funeral traditions, they did follow Emanu-El's lead by elevating their new cemetery as a symbol of American modernity and inclusiveness. They not only set up a dedicated garden on their Beth Olom Cemetery to grow specialized trees to ornament family lots but broadcast their new rural holdings as the epitome of civic achievement. "It is our happy privilege to be citizens of a republic," they opened their cemetery regulations, "in which perfect equality of rights, civil and religious, is fully carried out, both in law and in fact, and in which the security of person and property is as sacredly respected as the safeguard of a mighty people can render it."[17] Trustees contrasted these protections with a far less celebratory view of Jewish counterparts throughout the ages whose "security of person and property was so long denied to them." In particular, they heralded new family lots as one of the ultimate signs of stability and belonging. Convinced of a promising future in New York and the United States broadly, B'nai Jeshurun leaders claimed that Jews could now lay down their most decisive roots: burying loved ones without fear of disturbance or unrest. If the specter of desecrated graves had menaced the Jewish dead in other periods or settings, America, they asserted, would embody something entirely different.

Much of that optimism drew on the Rural Cemetery Movement's broader gestures at religious and racial inclusion.[18] Investors in Cypress Hills Cemetery, New York's first nonsectarian ground, avidly endorsed a universalist ideal. "It is our ambition and our hope," they wrote in 1858, "to see all religious denominations . . . orders of benevolence, and national and industrial societies, meet together on this common ground, and by proximity and good will, acknowledge that all men are brethren, having a common origin and a common destiny."[19] That early call attracted congregations spanning several denominations like St. Stephens Protestant Episcopal Church, the Duane Street Methodist Episcopal

Church, the West Presbyterian Church of Manhattan, and the Madison Avenue Baptist Church. Many fraternal lodges also bought tracts in the cemetery like the Independent Order of Odd Fellows, the Free Sons of Israel, and even the nativist Order of United American Mechanics.[20] Although the cemetery did maintain a separate section for African Americans that the local press criticized in later decades, it did allow individuals to purchase lots among white lot holders.[21] Several black churches purchased shares by the 1850s and by 1890, despite recognized segregation, Cypress Hills was the preferred rural cemetery of African American New Yorkers.[22]

That general inclusiveness positioned Cypress Hills as a beacon for Jews as well. By 1858 at least twelve smaller Jewish fraternities and synagogues had already purchased tracts there.[23] Even as premier congregations like Emanu-El, B'nai Jeshurun, Shearith Israel, or Shaaray Tefila set up independent rural holdings, they all did so on land directly neighboring Cypress Hills. That trend stood out, especially since Jewish New Yorkers had never buried in such close proximity to Christian neighbors. Of course, they did not do so randomly. Inasmuch as the synagogues and fraternities chose to border or buy within Cypress Hills Cemetery, they opted to neighbor that ground over one far more particularistic like the Roman Catholic Calvary Cemetery. Calvary stood not only a full eight and a half miles away, but its 1848 consecration predated all Jewish cemeteries by at least three years. As Jewish New Yorkers gradually loosened taboos against proximity to Christian grounds, they chose to do so alongside a Protestant universalist ideal rather than one more closely associated with the city's "deserving poor," let alone its growing Irish and German Catholic immigrant residents.[24]

That Jews in this period approached their cemeteries in this way is not surprising. Indeed, it fit their larger efforts to prove compatibility with American society by highlighting similarities between Jewish modes and broader nondenominational or Protestant norms. Simultaneously, they responded to contemporary critiques that, in benign or more nefarious ways, cast them as perpetual religious outsiders. Mid-century visitors to synagogues across the nation commonly marveled at Jewish practice, as did newspaper interest pieces juxtaposing Judaism with Christianity in America. At best, these surveys cast Jewish continuity and religion as exotic vestiges of antiquity. At worst, they maligned Jewish practice as backward, overly self-interested, and, by the latter half of the century, increasingly racialized.[25] That rhetoric drew especially on a supposedly innate Jewish inability to Americanize given a strong aversion toward intermarriage or presumed preference for exclusivity.

New York of course was no exception, particularly in the middle decades of the nineteenth century, as new immigrants increased the city's Jewish population and surpassed other Jewish centers around the nation. Some encounters meditated on Jewish novelty, such as a visit by activist and writer Lydia Maria

Child, who wrote up her attendance at a Jewish New Year service during an 1841 trip to New York. There, she found herself often overtaken "with recollections of those ancient times when the Divine Voice was heard amid the thunders of Sinai." Biblical rushes aside, she noted clear oddities in worship like physical separation of women and men, curiosities in religious garb, unintelligible use of Hebrew, or the foreign (and to her, ultimately unsatisfying) Jewish mode of prayer rendering the devotion anything but familiar.[26] Locals could be even less forgiving, particularly as they watched Jewish newcomers cluster in lower Manhattan and take up a seemingly outsized role in its aggressive and thriving Chatham Street market. Xenophobic onlookers expressed their anxieties as Jewish residents reached 25,000 by 1860. An 1858 interest piece in *Frank Leslie's Illustrated Newspaper* casually invoked these immigrants' "low stature, shining black eyes, crisp inky hair, hooked noses, stooping shoulders, and eager movements" when opening a survey of Jewish matzo production in Lower Manhattan for the Passover festival.[27] The holiday, as much as perceived physiognomy, coded these residents as Jews while stressing a larger point. Stubborn Jewish retention of distinctive religious and national traditions, the claim went, rendered them unassimilable as they insisted on keeping apart in "all social and religious intercourse as if they were in a different country." In particular, Jewish sensitivities surrounding intermarriage ranked high for this writer and others of the period, especially as it related to long-term integration. "It is by this refusal to amalgamate with the people by whom they are surrounded that they preserve themselves a distinct body," the article claims. "All other races and religions blend and coalesce with the natives of the country and in a generation or two become thoroughly and completely Americanized."[28] That sentiment still echoed decades later. In 1893 the New York *Sun* not only continued handwringing over Jewish particularity but also alluded specifically to that Jewish stigma of intermarriage in its claims that "after a few generations immigrants to this country lose their race identity and become Americans only. Generally, the Jews retain theirs undiminished, so that it is observable by all men."[29]

The dual function that New York's new rural Jewish cemeteries quickly came to represent at mid-century emerged within that context. Although replete with policies to discourage marriages between Christians and Jews, the cemeteries remained nonetheless highly visible symbols of material, social, and spiritual integration. Indeed, they encapsulated the drive among aspiring middle-class Jewish New Yorkers to counter denigrations of their separateness, even (or perhaps especially) in a matter as sensitive as laying the dead to rest in cemeteries that visually and physically hugged those of their Protestant counterparts. And as Adler excised overtly national or supposedly outmoded elements from Jewish funeral rituals to align more closely with American standards, he drew on a broader logic that measured Jews' supposed racial otherness in direct proportion to their adherence to wider "cultured" norms. As historian Matthew Frye Jacobson has explained of the period's sensibilities, "when Jews [were] of the 'better' type . . . the observing eye need not scout their Jewishness."[30] Those developments said nothing of the more subtle American innovations that coursed through the cemeteries' rows, such as new market options giving households the ability to bury among family or to own cemetery parcels in their own right.

And yet, like so many other religious innovations among American Jews of the period, their grounds retained distinctive practice as much as they fit Jewish particularity into American sensibilities. Despite so many innovations overtaking the city's Jewish funeral sphere, New York Jews held fast to several older taboos. Whether synagogues or fraternal lodges, advocates of tradition or proponents of Reform, all retained the prohibition against mixing the dead across faiths. So too, although intermarriage was still a rare occurrence, most synagogues regardless of denomination continued to leverage interment rights to safeguard communal cohesion and to offer a specific strategy to negotiate marriages between congregants and Christians.

The most conservative bodies, like Shearith Israel, carried over long-standing graveyard policies when addressing those issues in their new cemeteries and family lots. Trustees refused to sell holdings to any who had converted to Christianity, married out of the faith, or fell behind in payment of dues. Newer synagogues like Anshe Chesed, Rodeph Shalom, and B'nai Jeshurun also followed that model in cemetery regulations. Rules over new and much-desired private lots proved especially effective. Typically, they contained stipulations that "the owner . . . has no right to sell the same to any person not of the Jewish faith and will not be allowed to bury any person . . . unless . . . of the Jewish faith."[31] Policies also typically refused family lot sales to any members "who shall have married out of the Jewish Faith."[32] Combined with synagogue membership policies that created a hierarchy for congregants with non-Jewish spouses, the policies governing family lots and Jewish rural cemeteries reinforced old institutional and communal dynamics thoroughly established over the previous century.

Less conservative congregations crafted more forgiving policies, particularly for interfaith families. Nevertheless, even these synagogues preserved stark ritual lines that would not compromise consecrated Jewish ground by allowing Christian interment. Emanu-El, for instance, offered immense freedom over its family holdings. It even allowed owners and their heirs to use lots without retaining active membership in the congregation. The entitlement associated with private property ownership did not outweigh core ritual laws, however. Rules still allowed only Jews to be buried in Salem Fields, and that provision extended to subdivided tracts. Deeds to individual families or Jewish fraternal orders specifically stated, "the sale or assignment to a person or persons who are not of the Jewish faith is illegal, and of no effect."[33] Moderate congregations like Shaaray Tefila, whose members ignited their own battle with trustees to follow Emanu-El's liberal approach to affiliation, also still safeguarded Jewish exclusivity. Their rules refused owners the right to bury any "who has apostatized from the Jewish Faith, no male who shall not have entered into the Covenant of Abraham, nor a suicide." They also specifically refused "Persons who have married out of the Jewish Faith, and who up to the time of their decease, shall have continued out of the pale of the Synagogue."[34] On the one hand, this approach continued to punish certain congregants for leaving the fold; on the other, it encouraged those few who had intermarried to retain communal ties by at least allowing a system that could include spouses who had converted to Judaism.[35] To be sure, that stance did not seek to tear down social or religious divisions between Jewish and Christian New Yorkers. Rather these policies responded to otherwise insurmountable porous lines between them.[36] Still, the retention of ritually exclusive cemetery spaces was a point that none would compromise.

Jewish fraternal lodges also maintained those connections, still seeing a link between interment rights and intermarriage as an effective tool to guard communal boundaries. Some did so implicitly, like the Jonathan Lodge, No. 14 of the order *Kesher Shel Barzel* (Band of Iron), which required all potential members be "an Israelite, and not removed out of the pale of Judaism."[37] Others, like the Noah Society, extended that spirit to members' families through stipulations that "every candidate as well as his wife and children must profess the Jewish faith" in order to merit interment rights, religious and financial funeral provisions, and material awards to widows and surviving children.[38] The Noah Society refused to bury non-Jewish relatives from its inception in 1849 and continued that policy well into the twentieth century. Other orders like the B'nai B'rith extended membership rights to intermarried members but would not bury Christian partners in society holdings.[39] Although primarily organized around American fraternalism rather than religious practice, these Jewish lodges respected ritual laws as much as their synagogue counterparts. They too mandated intrinsic separation from the Christian dead, even as some skirted that line burying within larger nonsectarian cemeteries. Nevertheless, they upheld communal and social barriers governing the dead in order to retain a clear limit over Jewish and Christian interactions among the living.

Beyond old ritual boundaries still drawn within new Jewish cemeteries, physical divisions also set them apart from neighboring Christian counterparts. Although most of New York's major synagogues set up independent holdings directly bordering Cypress Hills, they clustered together and never developed past an old roadway called the Plank Road, later renamed Cypress Hills Street.[40] Smaller synagogues bought subdivisions within the first congregations' cemetery, concentrating holdings within that shared Jewish acreage. Even into the

1860s and 1870s, as congregations and others set up new cemeteries like Mach-
pelah or Union Field, they followed that trend and developed behind Cypress
Hills Street among the pioneering Jewish cemeteries. Jewish grounds concentrated to such a degree in this area that despite the subethnic, denominational,
and institutional divisions within them, New Yorkers beyond Jewish circles simply conceived of these holdings as one overarching Jewish ground. Maps even
flattened the array of rural parcels to a simple designation: "Jewish Cemetery."[41]

Smaller Jewish lodges followed a similar pattern. Those that pioneered buying land in Cypress Hills Cemetery itself like the Noah Benevolent Society or
branches of the Independent Order Free Sons of Israel or Free Sons of Judah
typically did so on the cemetery's outskirts. Their choice of peripheral land may
have reflected a hesitance to bury too deeply within larger non-Jewish ground.
Later in the 1850s, when far more Jewish lodges buried in Cypress Hills, their
holdings threaded tracts around the cemetery's main entryway called Via Dolorosa. Not only did they bury close to one another; their parcels rested barely half
a mile away from Salem Fields, Beth Olom and Shearith Israel's cemeteries on
just the other side of Cypress Hills Street.[42] And even if a Jewish association like
the Maimonides Benevolent Society opted in 1853 to procure land independent
of Cypress Hills or the major congregations, it still settled on parcels closely
neighboring Jewish peers. Indeed, it is no coincidence that land that ultimately
became Maimonides Cemetery rested just outside of Cypress Hills Cemetery in
a lot between early holdings of the Noah or Aryeh lodge to the north and to its
west that array of Jewish orders laced throughout the roads surrounding the Via
Dolorosa. Jewish societies and congregations may have buried in or near larger
nonsectarian grounds but, no matter their location on either side of Cypress
Hills Street, they pushed spatial and ritual limits only so far by favoring close
spatial proximity to other Jewish institutions.

In all, this array of Jewish approaches to new rural cemeteries spoke to a
period of transition over the second half of the nineteenth century and Jewish
efforts to find a means of navigating a nearly unprecedented process of social
inclusion. Unlike their counterparts in central Europe, Jews in the United States
did not have to weather a process of formal and arduous civic emancipation
to gain a foothold in society. They faced few legal restrictions on residence or
employment, and even as some elite circles or institutions closed their doors
to prominent Jewish patrons to counter "what they saw as the dangerous lev-
eling of social distinctions," by the latter half of the nineteenth century Jews
nonetheless enjoyed broadly increasing interaction, acceptance, and mobility
in New York and the wider United States.[43] As Eric Goldstein has pointed out,
"while these opportunities made Jews ebullient, they also raised anxieties about
what borders were to remain between them and the rest of society. Much of
this anxiety stemmed from the tension between Jews' impulse for integration

and their desire to maintain a distinctive Jewish identity."[44] Goldstein's work highlights the useful tool that American Jews in this period found in positive racial conceptions of their Jewishness as an avenue to celebrate peoplehood and particularism without challenging their credibility as committed and integrated Americans. So too, as certain religious practices seemed to wane, or barriers of leisure culture and sociability frayed between Christians and Jews, that rhetoric, even if only briefly, validated an internal Jewish elevation of shared ancestry and an effort to carefully preserve it.

The duality with which Jews in New York approached their new cemeteries (and other American cities that soon followed their example by adopting the rural cemetery model) fits well within that dynamic. Indeed, the cemeteries truly served in this period as a tangible tool for Jews to navigate a social landscape in flux. They could claim some ground in the mainstream, infusing their new cemeteries with varied American ideals centered on the family, collective association, or a sense of security and common bonds in America. To borrow B'nai Jeshurun's rhetoric, they embraced the Rural Cemetery Movement's promise of universalism and integration, entrusting their dead to eternity alongside Protestant peers. In that act they forever rejected the possibility that present or future generations might violate that trust. At the same time, they also declared their investment in the city they had come to embrace by doing their part to beautify old farmland beyond the city in union with fellow New Yorkers. Jews, too, would enshrine an imagined rural past within the hinterland of that urban behemoth they called home. In that sense, the cemeteries served as powerful sites to validate a Jewish belonging within larger local and regional identities. In more ways than one, they could counter derisive ideas of Jews or Judaism as somehow locked in the past, overly self-interested, or in other ways perpetually non-American.

Nevertheless, despite the innovative spirit infusing these new Jewish cemeteries, the grounds themselves also marked a line in the literal and metaphorical dirt of Jewish distinctiveness that few if any would willingly cross. By way of death and the ritual and institutional separation preserved within these cemeteries and their governing policies, Jewish communal leaders and members fully accepted interment rights tied to an effort to discourage boundary-crossing among the living. Indeed, the preservation of separation in death remained an important strategy to counter perceived challenges to Jewish cohesion or continuity well beyond any cemetery's gates. This stood out especially in that near universal retention of bans on Christian interment within consecrated Jewish grounds and the survival of that well-worn union between interment rights and intermarriage. Those mandates persisted despite the lapse of so many other policies as synagogues and fraternities reinvented Jewish cemeteries and their governance for a new era. That phenomenon spoke to sensitive taboos in death as much as to the accepted role of the cemetery to temper wider Jewish integration. Although new rural cemeteries celebrated and even encouraged Jewish access to American society, they could not counter deeper ritual law prescribing division in death and, by extension, the maintenance of certain social divisions in life.

Notes

1. "Simple Ceremonies at His Home and at the Grave. The Funeral of Joseph Seligman the Banker," *New York Times*, May 4, 1880, 3.

2. David de Sola Pool, *Portraits Etched in Stone: Early Jewish Settlers, 1682–1831* (New York: Columbia University Press, 1952), 7.

3. Pool, *Portraits Etched in Stone*, 120.

4. *Asmonean*, September 21, 1855, 177.

5. See entries April 10, 1752, and September 14, 1757, in "The Earliest Extant Minute Book of the Spanish and Portuguese Congregation Shearith Israel in New York, 1728–1760," *Publications of the American Jewish Historical Society* 21 (1913): 66–67, 74–75; David de Sola Pool and Tamar de Sola Pool, *An Old Faith in the New World: Portrait of Shearith Israel, 1654–1954* (New York: Columbia University Press, 1955), 248; Hyman B. Grinstein, *The Rise of the Jewish Community of New York, 1654–1860* (Philadelphia: Jewish Publication Society of America, 1945), 349.

6. For some instances of Jewish and Christian marriages in the eighteenth century as well as synagogue elders' refusal to perform conversions, see Malcolm Stern, "The Function of Genealogy in American Jewish History," in *Essays in American Jewish History to Commemorate the Founding of the American Jewish Archives under Direction of Jacob Rader Marcus* (Cincinnati, OH: American Jewish Archives, 1958), 95; Grinstein, *Rise of the Jewish Community*, 382; Jacob Rader Marcus, *United States Jewry, 1776–1985*, 4 vols. (Detroit: Wayne State University Press, 1989), 1: 137–38; Pool, *Portraits Etched in Stone*, 325. On nineteenth-century debates over how to treat children of interfaith unions in New York and other Jewish centers, see Edwin Wolf and Maxwell Whiteman, *The History of the Jews of Philadelphia from Colonial Times to the Age of Jackson* (Philadelphia: Jewish Publication Society of America, 1957), 261, n. 131; Charles Reznikoff and Uriah Zevi Engelman, *The Jews of Charleston: A History of an American Jewish Community* (Philadelphia: Jewish Publication Society of America, 1950), 152; Grinstein, *Rise of the Jewish Community*, 320–21.

7. Kurt T. Kraska, *The History of Cypress Hills Cemetery and its Permanent Residents* (New York: Woodhaven Cultural and Historical Society, 1980); John Rousmaniere and Kenneth Druse, *Green Oasis in Brooklyn: The Evergreens Cemetery, 1849–2008* (Kittery Point, ME: Seapoint Books, 2008). On Calvary, http://www.calvarycemeteryqueens.com/default.asp. Officials of the St. Paul's German Lutheran Church purchased 225 acres in 1852 in Middle Village, Queens, for ground first known as the Lutheran Cemetery. It later took the name All Faiths Cemetery; see http://www.allfaithscemetery.org/history.htm. On the Evergreens, see "The Evergreens Cemetery," http://www.theevergreenscemetery.com/. All websites accessed June 6, 2013.

8. Cypress Hills Cemetery, *Catalogue of Proprietors* (New York: Printed for the Cemetery, 1858), 6.

9. Cypress Hills Cemetery, *Catalogue of Proprietors*, 12.

10. Kraska, *The History of Cypress Hills Cemetery*, 4.

11. Rousmaniere and Druse, *Green Oasis in Brooklyn*, 45.

12. For a deeper exploration of these matters and their implications for communal social structures, see Allan Amanik, *Dust to Dust: A History of Jewish Death and Burial in New York* (New York: New York University Press, 2019).

13. Myer Stern, *The Rise and Progress of Reform Judaism, Embracing a History Made from the Official Records of Temple Emanu-El of New York, with a Description of Salem Field Cemetery, Its City of the Dead, with Illustrations of Its Vaults, Monuments, and Landscape Effects* (New York: M. Stern, 1895), 32.

14. Stern, *The Rise and Progress of Reform Judaism*, 32.

15. Annie Polland and Daniel Soyer, *Emerging Metropolis: New York Jews in the Age of Immigration, 1840–1920* (New York: New York University Press, 2012), 77–79.

16. "Temple Emanu-El, New York," *American Israelite*, April 9, 1858, 318.

17. "The Beth Olom Cemetery," *Asmonean*, May 6, 1853, 25.

18. Sloane, *The Last Great Necessity*, 75–83; Aaron Sachs, "American Arcadia: Mount Auburn Cemetery and the Nineteenth-Century Landscape Tradition," *Environmental History* 15 (April 2010): 213.

19. Cypress Hills Cemetery, *Catalogue of Proprietors*, 12.

20. Kraska, *The History of Cypress Hills Cemetery*, 4. I.O.O.F lodges included Pilgrim and Sincerity lodges; see "List of Lot Holders in the Cypress Hills Cemetery," in Cypress Hills Cemetery, *Catalogue of Proprietors*, 69.

21. "Where the Color Line Exists: No Equal Rights in Some of the Cemeteries," *Brooklyn Daily Eagle*, December 7, 1890, 3.

22. Congregations included the African Methodist Episcopal Zion Church, the St. Phillips Protestant Episcopal Colored Church of Manhattan, and societies that had buried in the Citizens' Union Mount Pleasant Cemetery, a ground established in 1851 as another nonsectarian cemetery without any "rule which excludes any person from sepulture within its borders, on account of complexion," but "designed more particularly as a burial place for the colored." On AME Zion, see http://projects.ilt.columbia.edu/seneca/village2c.html. On St. Phillips, see Kraska, *The History of Cypress Hills Cemetery*, 4; "List of Lot Holders in the Cypress Hills Cemetery," in Cypress Hills Cemetery, *Catalogue of Proprietors*, 69. On Citizens' Union, see Carolee R. Inskeep, *The Graveyard Shift: A Family Historian's Guide to New York City Cemeteries* (Orem, UT: Ancestry, 2000), 39–40.

23. These ranged from subsequent lodges of the Independent Order Free Sons of Israel—the larger national fraternal network that the Noah Society launched—to smaller Jewish burial and relief groups. "List of Lot Holders in the Cypress Hills Cemetery," in Cypress Hills Cemetery, *Catalogue of Proprietors*, 69.

24. Inskeep, *The Graveyard Shift*, 31–32; Rhona Amon, "The Cemetery Belt," reprinted from *Newsday* (2006) by Juniper Park Civic Association, accessed January 29, 2018, http://www.junipercivic.com/HistoryArticle.asp?nid=76#.Wm-J5K2ZPMV.

25. Hasia R. Diner, *A Time for Gathering: The Second Migration, 1820–1880* (Baltimore, MD: Johns Hopkins University Press, 1992), 181–85.

26. Lee M. Friedman, "Mrs. Child's Visit to a New York Synagogue in 1841," *Publications of the American Jewish Historical Society* 38 (1948–49): 176–77, cited in Howard B. Rock, *Haven of Liberty: New York Jews in the New World, 1654–1865* (New York: New York University Press, 2012), 205–6; Karla Goldman, *Beyond the Synagogue Gallery: Finding a Place for Women in American Judaism* (Cambridge, MA: Harvard University Press, 2000), 110–11.

27. "The Jewish Passover of 1858," *Frank Leslie's Illustrated Newspaper*, New York City, April 10, 1858, 296, cited in Diana L. Linden, "An Introduction to the Visual and Material Culture of New York City Jews, 1654–1865," in Rock, *Haven of Liberty*, 293.

28. "The Jewish Passover of 1858," 296.

29. Quoted in Matthew Frye Jacobson, *Whiteness of a Different Color: European Immigrants and the Alchemy of Race* (Cambridge: Harvard University Press, 1998), 178.

30. Jacobson, *Whiteness of a Different Color*, 174.

31. Appendix C, "Sale of private cemetery plots and related material from the minutes of Anshe Chesed," in Grinstein, *Rise of the Jewish Community*, 500.

32. December 15, 1852, Letter Book 1825–51, Trustee Minute Book, 1850–52, 62; article 5, section 4, Resolutions, for Beth Olom Cemetery, Board of Trustees Minutes, 1840–1852, Congregation B'nai Jeshurun, JTS.

33. Article 9, "Rules and Regulations for the Salem Fields Cemetery, as adopted by the Board of Trustees of the Emanuel Congregation," printed on the back a deed to Bruder Verein No. One, May 5, 1862, Records of the Brothers in Unity (Bruder Verein #1) 1890–1978, RG 1634, YIVO Institute for Jewish Research, NY; article 4, section 3, "Extracts of the Statutes of Salem Field Cemetery" on the back of "Deed of Cemetery Lot 807," April 1 1853, Goldstein Family Papers, P-259, AJHS.

34. "The Cemetery Question: To the Electors of the Congregation Shaaray Tefilla," *Asmonean*, August 29, 1856, 158.

35. "The Cemetery Question," *Asmonean*; Grinstein, *Rise of the Jewish Community*, 318.

36. While records do not preserve rates of intermarriage, the practice seems low and, at least in New York, few conversions of Christian spouses occurred in the period. Still, by the 1870s, communal leaders and the press spilled much ink over the issue. Grinstein, *Rise of the Jewish Community*, 380; Eric L. Goldstein, *The Price of Whiteness: Jews, Race, and American Identity* (Princeton: Princeton University Press, 2006), 11–31.

37. Article 5, "Membership," section 2, *By-Laws of Jonathan Lodge, No. 14, K.S.B.* (New York: A.G. Levy, 1871), 9, Kesher Shel Barzel Records, 186?–1905, I-28, box 1, folder 2, AJHS.

38. Article 6. "Members and Their Admission," *Constitution and By-Laws of the Noah Benevolent Widows' and Orphans' Association* (New York: Rode and Brand, 1889), 16, Noah Benevolent Society Records, I-186, box 28, folder:"1906 Constitution," AJHS.

39. Grinstein, *Rise of the Jewish Community*, 380.

40. B'nai Jeshurun and Shearith Israel joined forces to buy their own twelve acres alongside Emanu-El's Salem Fields; see Meeting Minutes of the Board of Trustees entry May 11, 1851, 16; B'nai Jeshurun Records, Trustee Minute Book 1850–1852, JTS. B'nai Jeshurun later sold a portion of its holdings to Shaaray Tefila and Emanu-El regularly sold subdivisions of Salem Fields to smaller congregations and some Jewish fraternal orders.

41. One survey of New Lots in 1873 labeled a larger mass "Cypress Hills" and the cluster of congregational holdings under an umbrella category, "Jewish Cemetery"; F.W. Beers, New Lots. Kings Co. L.I., scale 120 rods to the inch, NYPL Digital Gallery, accessed January 28, 2018, http://digitalgallery.nypl.org/nypldigital/id?1527276.

42. See roads and lot sections designated in Cypress Hills Cemetery, *Catalogue of Proprietors*, 69.

43. Naomi Cohen, *Encounter with Emancipation: The German Jews in the United States, 1830–1914* (Philadelphia: Jewish Publication Society, 1984); Ira Katznelson, "Between Separation and Disappearance: Jews on the Margins of American Liberalism," in *Paths of Emancipation: Jews, States, and Citizenship*, eds. Pierre Birnbaum and Ira Katznelson (Princeton, NJ: Princeton University Press, 1995); Quote from Goldstein, *The Price of Whiteness*, 14.

44. Goldstein, *The Price of Whiteness*, 15–16.

Selected Bibliography

ARCHIVES

Congregation B'nai Jeshurun (New York) Records, Jewish Theological Seminary Archives
    (JTS), New York.
Goldstein Family Papers, American Jewish Historical Society (AJHS), New York.
Kesher Shel Barzel Records, AJHS, New York.
Noah Benevolent Society Records, AJHS, New York.
Records of the Brothers in Unity (Bruder Verein #1), YIVO Institute for Jewish Research, New
    York.

NEWSPAPERS

The American Israelite
The Asmonean
The Brooklyn Daily Eagle
The New York Times

OTHER SOURCES

Amanik, Allan. *Dust to Dust: A History of Jewish Death and Burial in New York*. New York:
    New York University Press, 2019.
Cohen, Naomi. *Encounter with Emancipation: The German Jews in the United States, 1830–1914*.
    Philadelphia: Jewish Publication Society, 1984.
Cypress Hills Cemetery, *Catalogue of Proprietors*. New York: Printed for the Cemetery, 1858.
Diner, Hasia R. *A Time for Gathering: The Second Migration, 1820–1880*. Jewish People in Amer-
    ica 2. Baltimore: Johns Hopkins University Press, 1992.
"The Earliest Extant Minutes of the Spanish Portuguese Congregation Shearith Israel in New
    York, 1728–1786," *Publications of the American Jewish Historical Society* 21 (1913): 1–81.
Friedman, Lee M. "Mrs. Child's Visit to a New York Synagogue in 1841," *Publications of the
    American Jewish Historical Society* 38 (1948–49): 173–84.
Goldman, Karla. *Beyond the Synagogue Gallery: Finding a Place for Women in American Juda-
    ism*. Cambridge, MA: Harvard University Press, 2000.
Goldstein, Eric L. *The Price of Whiteness: Jews, Race, and American Identity*. Princeton, NJ:
    Princeton University Press, 2006.
Grinstein, Hyman B. *The Rise of the Jewish Community of New York, 1654–1860*. Philadelphia:
    Jewish Publication Society of America, 1945.
Inskeep, Carolee R. *The Graveyard Shift: A Family Historian's Guide to New York City Cemeter-
    ies*. Orem, UT: Ancestry, 2000.
Jacobson, Matthew Frye. *Whiteness of a Different Color: European Immigrants and the Alchemy
    of Race*. Cambridge, MA: Harvard University Press, 1998.
Katznelson, Ira. "Between Separation and Disappearance: Jews on the Margins of American
    Liberalism." In *Paths of Emancipation: Jews, States, and Citizenship*, edited by Pierre Birn-
    baum and Ira Katznelson, 157–205. Princeton, NJ: Princeton University Press, 1995.
Kraska, Kurt T. *The History of Cypress Hills Cemetery and Its Permanent Residents*. New York:
    Woodhaven Cultural and Historical Society, 1980.

Linden, Diana L. "An Introduction to the Visual and Material Culture of New York City Jews, 1654–1865." In Howard B. Rock, *Haven of Liberty: New York Jews in the New World, 1654–1865.* New York: New York University Press, 2012.

Marcus, Jacob Rader. *United States Jewry, 1776–1985.* 4 vols. Detroit: Wayne State University Press, 1989.

Polland, Annie, and Daniel Soyer. *Emerging Metropolis: New York Jews in the Age of Immigration, 1840–1920.* New York: New York University Press, 2012.

Pool, David de Sola. *Portraits Etched in Stone: Early Jewish Settlers, 1682–1831.* New York: Columbia University Press, 1952.

Pool, David de Sola, and Tamar de Sola Pool. *An Old Faith in the New World: Portrait of Shearith Israel, 1654–1954.* New York: Columbia University Press, 1955.

Reznikoff, Charles, and Uriah Zevi Engelman. *The Jews of Charleston: A History of an American Jewish Community.* Philadelphia: Jewish Publication Society of America, 1950.

Rock, Howard B. *Haven of Liberty: New York Jews in the New World, 1654–1865.* New York: New York University Press, 2012.

Rousmaniere, John, and Kenneth Druse. *Green Oasis in Brooklyn: The Evergreens Cemetery, 1849–2008.* Kittery Point, ME: Seapoint Books, 2008.

Sachs, Aaron. "American Arcadia: Mount Auburn Cemetery and the Nineteenth-Century Landscape Tradition." *Environmental History* 15 (April 2010): 206–35.

Sloane, David Charles. *The Last Great Necessity: Cemeteries in American History.* Baltimore: Johns Hopkins University Press, 1991.

Stern, Malcolm. "The Function of Genealogy in American Jewish History." In *Essays in American Jewish History to Commemorate the Founding of the American Jewish Archives under Direction of Jacob Rader Marcus,* 69–98. Cincinnati: American Jewish Archives, 1958.

Stern, Myer. *The Rise and Progress of Reform Judaism, Embracing a History Made from the Official Records of Temple Emanu-El of New York, with a Description of Salem Field Cemetery, Its City of the Dead, with Illustrations of Its Vaults, Monuments, and Landscape Effects.* New York: M. Stern, 1895.

Wolf, Edwin, and Maxwell Whiteman. *The History of the Jews of Philadelphia from Colonial Times to the Age of Jackson.* Philadelphia: Jewish Publication Society of America, 1957.

Chapter Two

"Death Is Not a Wedding": The Cemetery as a Polish American Communal Experience

—JAMES S. PULA

"Cemeteries are far more than merely elements of space sanctioned off and set aside for the burial of the dead," concluded Richard E. Meyer, "they are, in effect, open cultural texts, there to be read and appreciated by anyone who takes the time to learn a bit of their special language."[1] The study of cemeteries for their cultural ingredients is not new, but it enjoyed a reawakening and broadening of interest beginning in the second half of the twentieth century with the publication of seminal works by researchers such as Meyer, Robert Pogue Harrison, Blanche Linden, Martha Norkunas, Richard A. Kalish, and David K. Reynolds.[2] Despite the renewed attention to the topic, and the fact that Poles were the second largest ethnic group to arrive on America's shores during the Great Migration[3] between 1870 and 1920, almost nothing has been written about Polish American cemeteries and burial customs. Richard Meyer's *Ethnicity and the American Cemetery* and *Cemeteries and Gravemarkers: Voices of American Culture* do not mention them and his extensive bibliographies do not list a single title relative to Poles. Likewise, Richard A. Kalish and David K. Reynolds's *Death and Ethnicity: A Psychocultural Study* contains nothing at all about Poles. Marilyn Yalom's *The American Resting Place: Four Hundred Years of History through Our Cemeteries and Burial Grounds* includes only one Polish cemetery in a little over one page that is more a generalized descriptive vignette than analysis. Even Helen Sclair's "Ethnic Cemeteries: Underground Rites," which explores Chicago burial grounds, contains surprisingly little on the group considering their proportional significance in that city's population.[4] Among those scholars who focus their research on "Polonia," the Polish American community, there has also been a lack of attention to the topic. For the most part, Poles appear only tangentially in studies that deal with death and grieving customs such as the work of Helen Stankiewicz Zand, Deborah Anders Silverman, and Sophie Hodorowicz Knab.[5] In each of these cases the focus of the research is on death and mourning customs with nary a word about the cemetery.

This chapter will attempt to fill the void in the literature on Polish Americans by exploring how the immigrant experience, interacting with the new reality of the American urban environment, influenced the adaptation of Polish death, mourning, and burial customs and the creation of distinct ethnic cemeteries that functioned both as barriers to separate and segregate the ethnic community and as a proud affirmation of its continuing existence. In the first instance, the chapter will discuss the transmission of Polish customs to the United States, emphasizing those that were retained or adapted to American conditions. Next, it will analyze the ethnic elements of Polonia's cemeteries during the immigrant generation and explain how and why these began to change in succeeding generations. This chapter will also discuss how the various ethnoreligious influences interacted to create self-imposed boundaries that shaped or precluded interactions with other groups and influenced the creation of a markedly Polish ethnic death ideology.

Since the chapter focuses on Polish Catholics, it begins by explaining how religious requirements influenced cemetery formation, and with it the erection of barriers prescribing who could be admitted to the burial ground. Catholicism influenced Polish Americans in two ways. First, it imposed a religiously sanctioned barrier that enforced as rigidly as any physical wall a separation of Catholics from non-Catholics both in their worship and in the self-segregation of their cemeteries. Second, since Polish Catholics arrived in the United States with a history of looking to the Church to protect their ethnic traditions in their partitioned homeland, they were often aggravated by the control of the Church in America by an unambiguously indifferent or openly hostile ecclesiastical hierarchy. This, coupled with the Poles' vision of American democracy, led to serious conflicts over issues of property rights, including the ownership of cemeteries and their preservation as ethnic symbols. While Catholic canon law enforced immutable metaphysical barriers, Polish ethnic assertion superimposed an ethnic barrier further separating Polish Catholics not only from non-Catholics, but from other Catholics as well.

Finally, the chapter will explore the influence of industrial America and the gradual assimilation of succeeding generations on death, mourning, and burial customs as well as the physical configuration of traditional Polish American cemeteries. In this respect, the influence of religious and ethnic imperatives in the creation of cemetery barriers changed over time through the interaction of increasing contacts with the dominant society, changes in the socioeconomic environment of the United States, and eventually, expanding intermarriage.

Of course, notions of death, mourning customs, burial rites, and cemeteries are intrinsically linked. To understand the connection and thereby the role of the cemetery in differing cultures requires some appreciation of the ethnic social customs and traditions that determine its functions and limits. As a basis for constructing this chapter, I reviewed the relevant extant literature, including that noted above, sources for Polish customs and cemeteries, and visited cemeteries in Kraków, Warsaw, and Zakopane in Poland. I also explored ten historically Polish American cemeteries in Connecticut, Illinois, Indiana, Pennsylvania, and New York to conduct field research. To collect information I sent surveys to and consulted with twenty-nine priests, funeral directors, and researchers in Connecticut, Florida, Illinois, Indiana, Michigan, New York, Pennsylvania, and Wisconsin. Based on the information obtained from these sources, this chapter will explore the death, burial, and cemetery customs of Catholic Polish Americans along with the ethnoreligious requirements for burial grounds, the cultural significance of those graveyards, and the effects of generational assimilation on the design of the cemeteries themselves.

The Establishment of Polish American Parishes, Cemeteries, and Ethnoreligious Boundaries

Although there were Poles in what would become the United States as early as the Jamestown colony of 1608, the arrival of sizable numbers did not begin until the 1870s. Between 1870 and 1920, hundreds of thousands of people migrated from the lands of partitioned Poland[6] to the United States, most being Catholic or Jewish. Once in America these two groups might be found in the same secular organizations, but for the most part they established their own ethnic organizations and cemeteries based on their religious beliefs. If one counts only ethnic Poles, an average of nearly 100,000 arrived each year.[7] With few exceptions the original Polish ethnic communities and cemeteries were established by the immigrant generation arriving during this time.

Naturally, Polish immigrants brought with them "cultural baggage" learned in the families, communities, and churches of their homeland, a major element of which was Catholicism. The Polish state adopted Christianity in 966 when King Mieszko I accepted the religious authority of the Papacy, perhaps more in an attempt to halt the invasions of Christian crusaders into his realm than from any strong religious conviction. Yet conversion to Christianity did not produce a singular set of practices because the historic Poland of Mieczko's time was an amalgam of many local and regional groups, each with its own customs and traditions. In the sixteenth century, when Western Europe was being torn by the passions of religious warfare, King Zygmunt August of Poland refused to constrain non-Catholics, commenting, "I am the king of the people, not the judge of their consciences."[8] One could be a Pole regardless of religious belief as long as one was loyal to the monarch. Poland thus emerged as a multiethnic, multireligious state, creating variations that were later magnified by foreign rule in the three partitions.[9] Because of the multicultural nature of the Kingdom of Poland, the later Polish-Lithuanian Commonwealth, and the period of the partitions, "Polish" culture was in many ways a mélange of various Slavic and other East European traditions. This meant that immigrants brought with them many distinct regional traditions not necessarily shared by all, or even a majority of their fellow Poles. Some survived the transoceanic voyage, some did not.

Despite the disparity in origins and customs created by historical circumstances, most Polish immigrants retained a jealously guarded sense of their culture and traditions. To a large extent this was the product of three-quarters of a century of foreign occupation. To a greater or lesser extent, the Polish language and culture had been repressed in each of the partitions, with only the Austrians allowing at least some semblance of cultural expression and political representation. Through this period of foreign occupation Polish Catholics had come to view their local Roman Catholic parish as an ally in the struggle to maintain their ethnic identity. In times of repression, they could worship as they pleased, sing traditional songs, and celebrate ethnic holidays within the safety of the church walls. Local parishes generally supported "underground" political meetings, schools, theater groups, musical productions, and other clandestine activities designed to preserve what the people called "Polskość"—a sense of "Polishness," the maintenance of Polish history, culture, language, and traditions.[10]

Because of the symbiotic relationship between the Polish people and the Roman Catholic Church in Poland, immigrants arriving in the United States expected to find this same reflection of religious conviction and group identity within the Church in America. They quickly found otherwise. "Their" church was quite different from that in Poland, where the religious hierarchy was comprised of fellow Poles. In America the Church was dominated by Irish bishops, with a smattering of Germans, virtually all of whom had, at best, no interest in Polish culture or historical traditions, and at worst were openly hostile to both. One of the more egregious examples of this anti-Polish attitude was the response of Cardinal John McCloskey of New York to a request by Poles to erect a church of their own: "A pig shanty is sufficient for the Poles as a church."[11] After experiencing Bismarck's *kulturkampf*[12] and similar attempts by the other partitioning powers to denationalize them, Polish immigrants were particularly sensitive to these hostile attitudes.

In the early years of Polish migration during the 1870s, Poles initially lacked sufficient numbers to establish their own communities, parishes, and cemeteries. Poles more often than not attended German Catholic churches since the

earlier arrivals were numerically dominated by those from the German parti-
tion, and later from Austrian Galicia, both of which provided residents with
at least some fluency in conversational German. Given the experiences of the
partitions, this was not ideal, but rather a necessity dictated by numbers, their
attachment to Catholicism outweighing their reluctance to remain temporarily in a German-dominated parish. Naturally, in these cases burials took place
in the cemeteries associated with those parish churches. As soon as sufficient
numbers were present to form a new parish, Poles inevitably broke from their
German coreligionists to found their own churches so they could preserve
their ethnic customs. In this typical process, the religious barrier that separated
Poles from other groups in both the old country and the new acquired another
dimension that created a likewise formidable barrier between Poles and their
erstwhile coreligionists in America based on ethnic identity.

Separation was not an easy process. It could be quite painful since this
implied not only leaving behind any relatives already buried in the German
cemetery, but also the financial contributions previously made to support the
original German church. This could lead to friction and at times even legal
actions. One example of this was the conflict between parishioners of St. Stanislaus, Bishop and Martyr, Parish in New York City and the German Allgemeine
Verein. When Poles decided to found their own parish, the Allgemeine Verein
provided a loan for the purchase of land and construction of the church but
then refused to turn over the deed once the loan was repaid and also laid claim
to the money the church raised through banquets, concerts, and other fundrais-
ers. In the resulting legal action, *Church of St. Stanislaus v. Allegemeine Verein*,
the New York State courts found that title to the property and funds rightfully
rested with the Polish church and its parishioners, a decision that served as a
legal precedent for cases as recently argued as 2008.[13]

Aside from the land and the church building itself, the most contentious
property issue that developed was control of the parish cemetery.[14] Once a
Polish Catholic parish was established, creation of a cemetery was subject to
religious requirements that created very specific and immutable boundaries.
Roman Catholic canonical law states that "Deceased members of the Christian
faithful must be given ecclesiastical funerals according to the norm of law"[15]
and requires that "Ecclesiastical funerals, by which the Church seeks spiritual
support for the deceased, honors their bodies, and at the same time brings the
solace of hope to the living, must be celebrated according to the norm of the
liturgical laws."[16] The Catholic requirement that the deceased be interred in consecrated cemeteries, combined with the Polish sensitivity to preserving their
own sense of Polskość, meant that there was very little cooperation with other
ethnic groups, much less the general society, in forming or maintaining cemeteries. For the most part, except in the very early years when Poles tended to

Figure 2.1 Czech headstone with Latin-style cross.

worship in German churches, Poles were buried in Polish Catholic cemeteries, which required the consecration of the Catholic hierarchy. In this way, the duality of religious requirement and ethnic preference combined to form an impervious ethnoreligious barrier creating uniquely Polish cemeteries in America.

There were of course some exceptions, at least to the ethnic portion of this equation. Two of these are St. Adalbert's and Resurrection Cemeteries in Chicago, where Poles and Czechs combined to purchase large tracts of land, but even within these the land was originally divided into Polish and Czech sections. Figure 2.1 shows the headstone of Anna and Jan Viskočil in the Czech section of Resurrection Cemetery.[17] The inscription is in Czech. The Latin-style cross atop the modified tablet style stone closely resembles those also in general use among Poles as seen in figures 2.4 (on the left), 2.9 (on the left), 2.16, and 2.17. Although these were joint enterprises of the two groups, within the geographic boundaries of the cemeteries there existed separate sections for the burial of Poles and Czechs, thus maintaining the ethnic barrier.

Although the process for creating a cemetery under Roman Catholic canon law is relatively straightforward, this often became a divisive issue reflecting, and in some ways fueling, the often-contentious relationship between Polish American parishes and the Irish-dominated ecclesiastical leadership. The Roman Catholic hierarchy exerted strict control over its parishes including demanding title to all property and the right to assign priests. This conflicted with the Poles' concept of how *their* Church ought to operate. In Poland, there was a tradition called *ius patronatus*—a long-established "right of patronage"—whereby an affluent family might endow a local parish and in return receive some voice in the appointment of the local pastor and in parish affairs. Since the typical Polish parish in America began through lay initiative, the Poles, relying for justification on both the Polish precedent of lay involvement and their own understanding of American democracy, sought for themselves some control over parish property and finances. The Irish hierarchy in America would have none of it. This dichotomy of perspectives, along with other emotional issues such as the refusal of the Irish to nominate Polish priests to bishoprics, greatly increased intrareligious friction and in the process reinforced the ethnic barrier Poles found essential to protecting their culture and traditions.

Most of the Poles' grievances involved their desire for a voice in parish governance. The complaints of parishioners were articulated emphatically in the Chicago newspaper *Kuryer Polski* (The Polish Courier):

> The founders and benefactors of Polish churches in America are not priests nor American bishops. THE FOUNDERS AND BENEFACTORS OF POLISH CHURCHES IN AMERICA ARE THE POLISH PARISHIONERS. Polish parishioners give their hard-earned pennies for the founding and support of the churches. . . . But the priests and bishops are only the servants of the church. Therefore the bishops and priests should honor the founders and benefactors of the church, not tyrannize them. In the old country, the founders and benefactors had a voice not only in the running of church affairs, but in the selection of the pastor. Here in America, the founders and benefactors of the Polish churches, that is, the Polish people, should certainly have the same rights and privileges.[18]

Three factions developed within Polonia because of these ethnoreligious tensions. Some people remained completely loyal to the Church, while others agitated for change within the Church. In this respect, historian J. David Greenstone found that "the Poles were the most ethnically assertive among the Roman Catholic immigrant groups."[19] So frustrated did Bishop Ignatius F. Horstmann of Cleveland become that he once famously lamented, "Why is it that only the Poles cause trouble?"[20]

Trouble there was, and plenty of it. The third faction that emerged were those
who became so dissatisfied that they broke from the Roman Catholic Church
to form an entirely new denomination, the Polish National Catholic Church
(PNCC), which adhered to most Roman Catholic theology but refused to rec-
ognize the Pope as head of the church, substituted Polish for the traditional
Latin in the Mass, and promoted local control of parish affairs including the
assignment of priests and control of property including cemeteries. The new
church attracted tens of thousands of Polish immigrants who preferred to worship in parishes reflecting the familiar customs of their ethnic homeland. Naturally, over time the more nationalistic PNCC also tended to preserve Polish
burial, mourning, and cemetery customs to a greater extent than did Roman
Catholic parishes. This was in some respects a reflection of the idea of "democracy," which Polish immigrants expected to find in "their" church in America,
as well as the application of the familiar *ius patronatis*.[21] In the process this created yet another barrier that strictly separated Roman Catholic from National
Catholic cemeteries, one Polish community from another.

In the United States this ongoing ethnic conflict exerted a strong centrifugal
influence resulting in practical complications for the Roman Catholic Church.
A major cause of this "trouble" was the control of ethnic cemeteries and the
provision of suitable Polish burial rites. While canon law strictly prohibited any
of the "National Catholics" from being buried in Roman Catholic consecrated
cemeteries, and forbade burial rites to any individuals interred in lay property,
by doing so it risked losing the loyalty and financial contributions of its parishioners. One example of the controversies this sometimes created was the case
of St. Casimir's Parish in South Bend, Indiana. In 1904 the parishioners, with
the approval of the Bishop of Fort Wayne, raised money to purchase land for
a cemetery. As was customary, once the land was purchased by the parish or a
lay group, individual plots were then sold to members. However, in accordance
with Roman Catholic law the bishop expected the deed to be turned over to his
control. When the parishioners demurred, the bishop responded by refusing to
bless the new cemetery, thereby denying it the required consecration to become
a Catholic cemetery. In response, over 300 parishioners who had made financial contributions for the purchase of the land met in March 1906 and voted
to incorporate as owners of the cemetery. Hearing this, the bishop forbade the
pastor from performing the burial sacraments. Despite the impasse, burials
continued during the next two years with neither the Poles nor the bishop willing to concede. Eventually, parishioners began threatening to leave the Roman
Catholic Church entirely and affiliate with the Polish National Catholic Church.
Under this pressure, the bishop finally turned a blind eye as the pastor, Rev.
Anthony Zubowicz, performed burial rites and individually consecrated graves
of the deceased, rather than the whole cemetery, in an attempt to circumvent

the letter of canon law. However, when the priest was transferred to another parish in 1914 and the bishop refused to consult parishioners on a replacement, a thousand people turned out to prevent the entry of the new priest into the church despite the presence of some two dozen police officers charged with maintaining the peace. After twenty-eight arrests and a series of legal actions, a compromise priest arrived, but many of the parishioners left to form St. Mary's Polish National Catholic Parish.[22]

Even when the faithful remained faithful, serious problems could nevertheless arise. A case in point took place at St. Mary, Our Lady of Częstochowa, Parish in New York Mills, New York. In 1932 the St. Casimir's Polish Men's Society and the Society of St. Stanislaus, two lay organizations closely aligned with the parish, jointly pledged their resources to purchase property for a cemetery with future decisions made by majority vote of a governing body consisting of representatives of each group.[23] They purchased the land, opened the cemetery, and interments began. All might have gone well except that Monsignor Charles F. McEvoy, Chancellor of the Diocese of Syracuse, found out that burials were being conducted at the new cemetery whose deed had not been turned over to the Church. McEvoy wrote to Rev. Aleksander Fijałkowski, the parish pastor, to inquire if he knew anything about the situation and to remind him that "In case such a cemetery is organized and managed solely by laymen, the burial of Catholics may *not* be allowed in it."[24]

Fijałkowski attempted to respond diplomatically, characterizing the cemetery as a "gift," which clearly was not the intent of the societies.[25] Perhaps Fijałkowski hoped that by making it appear that the land was being "given" to the parish he might forestall any further complications, but McEvoy would not be put off. He responded citing Church requirements and ordering that since "this plot is not as yet a cemetery; hence, no burials are to be made there until the organization is complete. If people insist that their dead be buried there at the present time before such organization, then no church services can be given in such cases."[26] Although Fijałkowski continued attempts to defuse the growing crisis, leaders of the two societies fired off a defiant letter to the diocesan administrator demanding that the diocese pay for the cost of the land and the societies' expenses if it expected the land to be turned over to diocesan control. With little subtlety, the letter noted that "The Polish people look with great resentment at the attitude your Grace takes . . . and your unchanged attitude will cause dissension which may prove very detrimental to your interests."[27] The issue finally exploded in 1937 when the societies filed a legal action to clarify title to the cemetery.[28] Following lengthy litigation the court certified the societies' ownership. The incident established a legal precedent in New York: lay ownership of cemetery land was supported by law, if not by the Church.[29]

Despite this precedent, most Polish Roman Catholic cemeteries remained under the control of the Church hierarchy; truly independent cemeteries were rare. Conversely, cemeteries in the Polish National Catholic Church were, because of the nature of the Church, independent in the sense that the property was owned and administered by the parish itself. The PNCC was the only successful Catholic schismatic movement in the United States. Over time, some dissenting groups of Lithuanian and other Roman Catholics were accepted into the PNCC, including twenty-six Italian parishes. Although the death, burial, and cemetery rites of the groups differed according to their ethnic traditions, this was an interesting reduction of ethnic boundaries to accommodate similarly independent religious beliefs.[30] With these exceptions aside, and recognizing that in a few cases such as St. Adalbert's and Resurrection Cemeteries noted above, Polish American cemeteries generally resulted in a consciously constructed border that segregated Polonia from other communities because of the interplay of Roman Catholic canon law and the ethnic assertiveness of Polish immigrants. Because of this separation the cemeteries also came to function in America as emotional expressions of ethnic pride, both within the religious group and vis-à-vis the general community.

The Transfer of Death and Burial Customs

Immigrants arriving in the United States brought with them the death, mourning, burial, and cemetery customs familiar to them from their homeland. Contemporary scholars of the death ideology often begin with a discussion of the role of death in society: how a given culture's view of death shapes the part that it plays in the society. Is it something to be feared? Something to be embraced as a final reward? Or is it simply something to be accepted as a natural part of the life-cycle? For Polish Americans the traditional view has been what folklore scholar Deborah Silverman has referred to as "a measure of stoic resignation."[31] And so it appears to have been for Poles throughout the ages—a realization that death is something that will occur regardless of any of life's other considerations.

In many lands to which Christianity spread the local populace often retained their pre-Christian customs, which they adroitly camouflaged behind the rhetoric and terminology of the new religion. In Poland, death was sometimes personified as "a tall, thin woman draped in white." In fact, the Polish word for "death" (śmierć) is a feminine noun.[32] Often named Marzanna, she was usually portrayed carrying a scythe while coming to the home three nights in a row, knocking on the door or window each time, to advise of the impending death.[33] As early as the fifteenth century, every spring people in northeastern Poland would weave sheaves of straw or grain into a representation of Marzanna that

would then be ceremonially thrown into a river or lake. The drowning of Marzanna ("Topienie Marzanny") was done in the belief that it lessened the chance
of a death in the village that year or of the coming of sickness or plague. As
Christianity became more influential, and the clergy more insistent on the
elimination of earlier customs, the traditional Marzanna for a time merged
with Judas, although no doubt in the eyes of the celebrants the intent remained
the same.[34] Despite these folkways, it was acknowledged that realistically these
remedies at most only briefly postponed the inevitable—no one could escape
death.[35] By the nineteenth century, Marzanna enjoyed a resurgence of popular-
ity as a folk figure, resulting in her appearance in the United States along with
the mass migration. In early Polish funerals in the United States, mourners wore
white and white flowers were the preferred means of honoring the deceased,
certainly a reflection of the Marzanna tradition, along with the stoic view of
death's inevitability.

The occasion of death in a family called for specific actions to be taken. Since
under Catholic theology only those who were baptized and had received the
sacraments could enter into Heaven, it was important in Poland that a priest
be called to hear a dying confession. Upon his arrival, family members would
go to another room so the confession could be heard in the privacy one would
enjoy in a church confessional. If the priest arrived after death had occurred,
the Sacrament of Extreme Unction would be performed as the best available
substitute for the actual confession and absolution. By this act God was asked
to forgive whatever sins or other faults the deceased might have had to ease the
way of the spirit into Heaven. This custom was transferred to the United States,
where in the immigrant generation the sick were usually treated in the home
and the deceased viewed in their own living room.[36]

Once death arrived, other customs prescribed how the deceased was to be
remembered and what was to be done by the family, friends, and neighbors. An
old proverb cautioned that "Jakie życie, taka śmierć" (as you live, so you will
die). In Poland a gradual death through illness was considered natural and thus
preferred. Death that came without warning, such as through some accident,
was considered to be punishment for sins. If a person fell into and out of a coma
it was ascribed to the influence of Satan.[37] Interestingly, once imported into the
United States this traditional view underwent a 180-degree change in meaning.
Perhaps because of the necessity of multiple family members working to support the household in urban, industrial America, the original interpretation
quickly gave way to the more common American expression that it was better
to go quickly or in one's sleep than to linger on in ill health—directly the opposite of the Old World belief.

In Poland, at the moment of death, clocks had to be stopped so they would
not disturb the soul at rest. A lit candle was placed between the hands of the

deceased, a custom that originated in pre-Christian times to light the way for
the departed into the world beyond. Since the twelfth century this has traditionally been the Catholic *gromnica*, a type of ceremonial candle used in baptism,
confirmation, and other Church ceremonies. Any mirrors in the home had to
be covered lest someone see the reflection of the dead because that was a sure
sign that another death was coming. Drapes or shades would be placed across
the windows and a black mourning cloth attached to the front of the house to
signify that someone had died, but it was important at the same time to open
the doors and windows so that the soul might begin its journey. This would be
done briefly, but to leave them open too long gave the spirit an opportunity to
re-enter and risk losing another person to death. In the evening food and drink
were left near the deceased as nourishment for his or her travels.[38]

In one form or another, one can see all of these reappearing in Polish communities in the United States. During the immigrant generation it was customary to place a lit candle in the hands of the deceased, or at least close beside the
casket. The practice of covering mirrors continued, while the black mourning
cloth denoting death was continued. The custom of leaving food out for the
dead developed into feeding the living in both Poland and among the immigrants in the United States, so that friends and neighbors brought food to the
home of the deceased to ease the burden on the family and so that visitors could
be offered a meal or refreshment. This was particularly important when the
deceased was presented for viewing in the family's home as it was in the immigrant generation.[39]

Because of the lack of widespread embalming methods, the dead in rural
Poland were usually buried within twenty-four hours, which necessitated some
preplanning.[40] One item often procured was the coffin which, especially in the
mountain regions of southern Poland, was handcrafted by the family ahead of
time or by a professional woodcrafter. Traditionally it was hexagonal in shape
(width and height), wider at the shoulders and narrower at the feet. Those who
could afford to do so put money aside for a coffin and a new set of clothes in
which to be buried, and it was not unheard of for people to obtain a coffin and
keep it in the attic of their cottage until need for it arose.[41] Photographs of Polonia funerals from the last two decades of the nineteenth century often include a
coffin that resembled the Polish versions.[42]

When the time for burial came, the casket was always carried out feet first on
the shoulders of the bearers on its way to the interment.[43] A cross led the procession, followed by a priest, the coffin, and then the mourners. If the family could
afford it, the event might also include musicians or even a choir.[44] In Poland the
procession would normally pause at a roadside shrine or at the outskirts of the
village for a final farewell speech on the way to the cemetery. This would feature an entreaty by a relative or member of the community asking forgiveness

Figure 2.2 Latin crosses and crucifix typical of Polish Catholic cemeteries.

for any offenses the deceased may have committed. During the first generation in America this was normally the procedure, although since the religious
ceremony was usually performed in a church the tradition of pausing en route
to the burial was discarded in favor of the hearse passing by the home of the
deceased on the way to the cemetery and a priest's final prayers in a cemetery
chapel before interment, replacing the supplications at the edge of the village.[45]

In pre-Christian Poland relatives would bury useful objects with the dead,
a practice continued under Christianity with the placing of a rosary or hymn
book in the hands of the deceased and possibly including in the coffin anything
including a favorite pipe and tobacco for men, a special piece of jewelry for
women, or perhaps even a bottle of vodka to ease the journey.[46] This continued
in the United States, with a common custom being to place some of the palms
obtained on Palm Sunday into the casket of anyone who passed away during the
succeeding year, while family photographs or other personal items were often
enclosed in the coffin along with religious items.

When death occurred, it was important to link the family's mourning with
the surrounding community, for in small rural villages a death affected many

people.[47] In Poland this was accomplished by placing a black cloth on the door and other devices readily observable. In the United States, where most Poles worked in industries and mines and resided in larger ethnic enclaves that were in some way akin to the East European agricultural villages in terms of human networks, it was equally important to notify community members of the tragedy. In the immigrant generation the black cloth was often replaced on the front door by a wreath, but a standard form of notification became the newspaper obituary. Beginning in the immigrant generation, these usually bore the initials Ś.P., often separated by a cross (Ś†P). This was an abbreviation for Świętej Pamięci which literally means "sacred memory" and served as a notification that the person was deceased. The same construction of letters could also be found on some early gravestones.[48] An example of this are the Furgoł family markers in Holy Trinity Cemetery in Utica, New York, that appear in figure 2.2, which also illustrates traditional forms of Latin crosses and the crucifix that are typically found in Polish and Catholic cemeteries along with Polish inscriptions.

Obituaries normally contained the notation "Zmarł opatrzony Św. Sakramentami" (The deceased received the Holy Sacraments) as a reassurance to relatives and friends that the departed had been appropriately prepared for entry into Heaven.[49] Such notices frequently included symbols of various organizations in an attempt to inform supporters of those groups that one of their own was deceased. Members would be expected to don their organizational regalia and to come in a group to pay their respects during the wake (czuwanie), at the church ceremony, and at the graveside during the burial ritual. Usually comrades also served as pallbearers and played other parts in the formal ceremonies, acting as an extended family would in the small rural village in the old country. Members of Polish American organizations normally wore colorful ribbons and badges to identify themselves as members of the societies. The reverse of these symbols was printed in black with silver writing so they could be turned over for use at wakes and funerals.[50]

In nineteenth-century Poland, the deceased was placed in the largest room in the home for relatives and friends to come and offer their prayers for the departed and condolences to the family. This was an important social coping mechanism by which the family could share feelings with their loved ones and friends. In nineteenth-century rural Poland, it was also, as researcher Rebecca Crandall explained, "a vehicle for strengthening the sense of community, cohesion, and solidarity within the group."[51] People came to the home of the deceased, brought food, and were in turn offered refreshments. Within the small rural Polish village it brought people together in a common mourning that cemented interpersonal bonds and promoted community solidarity. If anything, this function was perhaps more important in the larger urban setting of industrial America where opportunities for community functions and socializ-

Demonstracyjny pogrzeb jednego ze strajkujących robotników w N. Y. Mills, N. Y.   Demonstration Funeral one of the strikers of New York Mills, N. Y.

Figure 2.3 Example of a funeral being used for political purposes.

ing were less than in the small village. In urban America population density was much greater, promoting a certain sense of anonymity; people from the same family or neighborhood often worked in different industries or different facilities of the same industry and, given the varied work schedules, it was difficult to arrange community-wide activities. In the wake that occurred following death, family, friends, members of organizations, fellow parishioners, and even casual acquaintances had an opportunity to interact with a common purpose. Most often this happened, as in Poland, in the home of the deceased.

Prior to transferring the deceased to the cemetery, a Catholic Mass of Christian Burial would be said. In the immigrant generation the normal Latin used in that service was often supplemented with prayers, readings, and a eulogy in Polish. In the case of prominent community personalities, or members of large religious or lay organizations, the procession from the home to the church for the funeral mass could become a major community event. At times it might even take on political significance either for general ethnic community pride or on such occasions as that seen in figure 2.3. This photograph depicts the funeral cortege of Jan Chrzan, a member of Local 753 of the United Textile Workers of America. Although his death was of natural causes unrelated to the strike of Polish workers taking place against the A. D. Juilliard Company in New York Mills, New York, in 1916, it was used by the community to rally support for their cause. Headed prominently by the symbolic American flag to the right, followed by a community band, the casket can be seen to the left in the lowered American-style rather than the Polish form at shoulder height. Note that the men appear to be dressed in dark clothing while those women who are present are in white, perhaps a remnant of the early Polish tradition. Especially interesting is the double Polish and English caption at the bottom. The strikers very astutely printed this and other photographs on postcards, with the captions, and sold them to raise money for the support of the strikers.[52]

Regardless of the size of the procession or the mass, with the conclusion of the religious rite the remains of the deceased were ready for transport to the burial site. The proper place of burial for a Polish Catholic was in the parish cemetery, the ground of which, as early as the Rome Synod of 1059, was officially recognized by the church as requiring consecration.[53] The graveside service followed typically Catholic customs, with a priest saying a prayer over the grave, then blessing the coffin, sprinkling holy water upon it, and throwing a handful of symbolic dirt over the casket. During the immigrant generation, and even into the second or third generations, obituaries often ended with the phrase "Ziemia obca niech mu będzie lekka" (May the foreign soil rest lightly upon him). This same phrase was used at the graveside, and whenever possible relatives coming to the United States would bring a small amount of Polish earth with them to sprinkle over the grave so the departed might rest content beneath native soil.[54]

Following the graveside services it was traditional for the priest and mourners to sing an appropriate funeral hymn. In Poland this was usually "Witaj, Królowo nieba" (Hail Queen of Heaven).[55] In English translation by Robert Strybel, its words are:[56]

> Hail our Queen of Heaven and Mother of Mercy,
> Hail our hope in sorrow and all adversity.
> We, the banished sons of Eve, are calling out to Thee,
> Sighing and weeping in this prison valley.
> O our Mediatrix, direct Thy gaze so merciful
> Upon our hearts unworthy, ever so pitiful.
> Deign to show us Thy womb's fruit
> Glorious and most blessed,
> When it's time we leave this world
> Miserable and wretched.
> Hail Mary full of grace, piety and devotion
> Let all sinners, me amongst them, obtain our salvation.

In the United States this tradition persisted among the first generation, and often the second as well. The hymn refers to Mary, the mother of Christ, who is considered the patron saint of Poland.

In Poland, once the graveside rites were concluded, the participants adjourned to the home of the deceased for a *stypa*, a post-funeral meal that served as closure for the death and burial rituals as well as a time for family and community to remember positive attributes of the deceased. Relatives, friends, and neighbors brought food and drink and an extra place was always set for the soul of the deceased that the departed might partake. Music and singing livened the occasion as mourning transformed into fond remembrance, an indication of public closure, and it was not unusual to find dancing at the stypa as well.[57] This was an accepted transformative occasion by which, through the means of remembering the deceased, the mourners could move beyond the stage of public grief, to resume their lives and the life of the community.

The stypa continued in the United States, but in a very different form. Unlike in Poland, where it was an occasion to move beyond mourning to the celebration of the deceased's life, and for the survivors a return to everyday activities, it became a much more somber occasion in America during the immigrant generation as reflected in the saying "Starość nie radość, śmierć nie wesele" (Old age is not joy, death is not a wedding).[58] Sociologist Helen Zand explained that in the United States, "Bereavement was more real" because "the widowed wife or husband had not the clan, the community and the land to count on as in Europe; death of the provider or of the mother was often prelude to tragedy and felt as such."[59] Music, singing, dancing, or any kind of merriment was usually lacking because, in addition to the grief of losing a loved one, the economic consequences resulting from the lost income of the deceased could be ruinous to an immigrant family only barely making ends meet. To address the economic problem, early Polish immigrant organizations in the United States began to assess dues that were placed into an insurance fund.

The stypa also marked the beginning of traditional remembrance ceremonies. Early Polish folk culture emphasized a strong relationship between nature, life, and the afterlife. There were ceremonies at the time of the winter solstice in which empty places were set at the table as an invitation for the departed to return. Another custom, dating at least to the first extant description in 1267, was the practice of taking eggs to the graves of deceased relatives. Since the egg was the symbol of life and people in the pre-Christian era believed that the dead lay under the ground ensuring that seeds would germinate and produce a bountiful crop, it was important to keep the deceased happy by periodically bringing them offerings of food and drink along with the symbolic eggs. Failure to do this would anger the dead, leading to crop failures. During the fifteenth century, long after the official conversion of the nation to Christianity, the clergy made a concerted effort to stop this custom, but in some places it continued into the nineteenth century, while in most it simply adapted to become part of the accepted Christian Easter ceremonies.[60] The immigrant generation pursued both of these overlapping customs, leaving eggs at the graveside as well as featuring eggs prominently at Easter and Christmas.

Aside from the symbolic offering of the egg, other holidays provided the opportunity to remember the deceased. In addition to the Christmas Eve *wigilia* (a ceremonial dinner in which an empty place is set at the table for "visitors") and the commemoration of All Saints Day, which celebrates the memory of those who have achieved salvation in the eternal life, Poles also observe All Souls Day. Called *Zaduszki* (for the souls), this is a time when relatives meet to honor the deceased, clean and decorate graves, and light candles symbolizing that memories of the deceased remain in people's hearts.[61] All three of these traditions arrived with the immigrants and remained popular in Polish American communities.

The Polish Ethnic Cemetery Comes to America

While most of the death, mourning, and burial customs discussed involve the interaction of people with family, friends, and the surrounding community as they move through the mourning process toward the resumption of normal life activities, the other important element in this procedure is the cemetery itself. Richard Meyer defines cemeteries as "outdoor, spatially delineated repositories of cultural artifacts."[62] He continues: "The monuments in our cemeteries speak to us in many ways—through their shape, their size, their composition (type of material), and even their positioning with regard to one another and the cemetery site as a whole."[63] This is especially true of traditional Polish cemeteries. In early times the very poor in Poland simply filled a grave and decorated the top with flowers or shrubbery. Most would outline the grave in stones or wood with the plants inside the created boundaries directly over the grave. A wooden or stone marker recorded the deceased's name along with a cross. People of even modest means normally would outline the grave in stone with an engraved headstone which could be as elaborate as the taste and budget of the family allowed. These tended to be very personalized and to differ between the geographic and cultural regions. In general, stone grave markers were preferred, although in the mountainous regions of the south the distinctive *górale* (mountaineer) culture, where woodworking was both an employment and a unique folk art, cemeteries were distinguished by the often elaborate wood carvings that adorned the graves.[64] These patterns can be clearly seen in photographs from three of the nation's most well-known historic cemeteries—Powązki in Warsaw, Rakowice in Kraków, and Cmentarz Zasłużonych (Remembrance Cemetery) at Pęksowy Brzyzk in Zakopane, the latter reflecting the culture of the Tatra Mountains. As religiously sanctioned burial grounds, these were open to any of the Catholic faithful while at the same time they erected a metaphysical barrier between that community and the multiplicity of other Poles with differing religious traditions.

Located in the Wola district on the western side of Warsaw, Powązki Cemetery opened in 1790 and contains monuments and grave markers carved by

Figure 2.4 Powązki Cemetery in Warsaw, Poland.

some of the most well-known craftsmen of the nineteenth century. Figure 2.4 shows typical stone sarcophagus graves with personalized gravestones in a variety of artistic forms. The headstones are mostly of a block style, although individuals were free to choose whatever form they chose. The graves are decorated in traditional fashion with urns containing candles reminiscent of the early custom, flowers, and other remembrances. The trees have grown up over the decades and remain because to cut them might upset the dead, and for the pleasant pastoral scene they present. Cemeteries in Poland are not only places to remember deceased loved ones; they are locations where one can meditate or simply escape for a stroll in the pastoral setting.

Rakowicki Cemetery, established in Kraków in 1803, contains the remains of both ordinary citizens and some of Poland's most famous humanists, artists, and political leaders. Special sections are devoted to participants in Poland's long history of revolutions against occupying powers, the remains of Poles who were conscripted into the armies of all three of the imperial occupying powers in World War I, and those of Allied airmen shot down over the country during World War II. Figure 2.5 shows a portion of the military section of the cemetery with a monument to the soldiers of the 1939 campaign in World War II. While this is a much more modern section of the cemetery, note that the graves reflect the traditional Polish construction with headstones supported by a stone framework outlining the grave, the Latin cross, and flowers planted within. Traditional Polish cemeteries quite often contain separate sections for the burial of those who fell in defense of the nation.

The headstones in Powązki and Rakowice are predominantly of a block or occasionally tablet form topped with a romanesque arch, much like the pre-

Figure 2.5 Rakowicki Cemetery in Kraków, Poland.

Figure 2.6 Cmentarz Zasłużonych in Zakopane, Poland.

dominant basic styles of early Polonia cemeteries but quite different from those in the Tatra Mountains along Poland's southern border. Established in 1848,[65] Zakopane's Cmentarz Zasłużonych (Remembrance Cemetery) is an exceptional cultural reflection of the górale traditions, notably the woodcarving that even today distinguishes the region's architecture, handicrafts, and daily life. Figure 2.6 provides examples of the intricate wood carvings that adorn the graves. Note also the traditional stone facings on the graves that are filled with flowers and plants, as well as religious symbols, the nooks containing urns with candles, and the peaked-roof effect that mirrors traditional mountaineer homes. All of these are cultural elements of Polish cemeteries as they existed at the time of the Great Migration. The inscription over the gate to the Remembrance Cemetery provides a valuable insight into how Poles perceive the burial ground beyond the simple resting place of their deceased family members: "Ojczyzna to ziemia i groby. Narody tracąc pamięć tracą życie" (The fatherland is its soil and its graves. In the loss of memory a nation loses its life").[66]

Speaking of immigrant communities in the United States, William D. Pattison observed that "Cemeteries have, especially in earlier decades, served to make a symbolic show of independence and pride on the part of foreign sub-communities."[67] Given the experience that Poles brought with them from Europe of having their culture and traditions repressed, they were especially concerned with fostering group consciousness, and the ethnic parish cemetery was one public manifestation of this. The mere existence of an "ethnic" cemetery delivered a strong message of group identity to ecclesiastical authorities and to the general public alike. Sending a message of permanence by its very nature, the Polish cemetery not only informed the surrounding community that Poles were there, but that they were there to stay. Thus, it formed a voluntary self-imposed barrier for the preservation of ethnic identity.

To a large degree, the early Polonia cemeteries did in fact reflect a distinctly Polish flavor. Those established by the immigrant generation, roughly the years from 1870 through 1920, reflect some noticeable similarities between the traditional cemeteries in Poland and those established in the United States. Founded in 1872 in Niles, Illinois, St. Adalbert Cemetery served the early Polish community in the northern and downtown areas of Chicago. By 1900 this area included what were then the two largest Polish parishes in the world—St. Stanisław Kostka and Holy Trinity.[68] Figures 2.7 and 2.8, taken in the older section of St. Adalbert Cemetery, clearly illustrate some of the similarities of these early Polonia cemeteries with those of traditional Poland. The trees, the closely sited row of mausoleums with their angel statuary and floral urns, the stone sarcophagi, and the granite borders enclosing some of the gravesites all reflect parallels with their European antecedents as seen in figures 2.4 and 2.5 above. In figure 2.8, the sarcophagus of Rev. W. Zaleski, the chalice indicates that the deceased was

Figure 2.7 Mausoleums in St. Adalbert Cemetery, Niles, Illinois.

Figure 2.8 The chalice indicates the resting place of a priest.

Figure 2.9 A typical cherubic angel in Holy Cross Cemetery, Utica, New York.

a priest. In addition to Catholic religious symbols such as a crucifix, angels, and an occasional statue of Christ, the gravestones contained traditional Polish elements: a high percentage of statues and inscriptions relating to Mary, who is considered the patron saint of Poland; Polish inscriptions; and engravings of flowers and other elements of nature. In fact, research has shown that the extent of the use of statuary in Polish cemeteries and sepulchers was quite unique in Europe, and this tendency can clearly be seen in early Polonia cemeteries.[69]

Although the design of statuary in Polish American cemeteries varies somewhat, so does that in Poland. In style, statuary in Polish cemeteries was greatly influenced by the forms of the Renaissance, which persisted long after that era closed.[70] In terms of both Catholic and Polish preferences, this can be seen in later periods as well, although there are various traditional styles from which to choose. The monument on the left in figure 2.9, located in Holy Trinity Cemetery, Utica, New York, is a basic obelisk style capped by the plain Latin cross frequently used in the immigrant generation, when more extravagant sculptures were beyond the means of the average person. The stone on the right is

Figure 2.10 A cement memorial reflecting the
wooden mountaineer sculptures.

capped by a small cherubic angel, a symbol often used to denote innocence (the
cherub) or spirituality (an angel). Polonia cemeteries tend to contain a high
percentage of angels and cherubs, which are also typically Catholic symbols.[71]
There were no specific prescribed forms for crosses, angels, or other such symbols, each family being free to select its own style; thus, some are quite simple
while others are much more ornate. Some typical examples also appear in figures 2.2, 2.7, and 2.9.

Figure 2.11 Southern mountaineer sculptures featured nature scenes.

One can also see reflected in Polonia cemeteries some of the distinctive elements of Polish regional subcultures. For example, Chicago is home to a large and active górale community from the southern mountain regions of Poland. This influence can clearly be seen in figure 2.10 from All Saints Polish National Catholic Cemetery in northwest suburban Chicago which contains several monuments and grave markers of similar motif. Although crafted from stone, the design clearly imitates a tree trunk and the wooden carvings found in cemeteries such as those in Zakopane. The angel and crucifix on the top are standard Catholic religious symbols, while the squirrel, the nest of birds, and the flowers recall analogous features of nature found on górale cemetery carvings (see the closeup in fig. 2.11). This particular example also contains photographs of three of the interred, a feature that was not particularly common in Polish cemeteries. In some cases, such as figure 2.12, the low stone walls surrounding graves were even carved to resemble tree trunks, leaves, and foliage.

All Saints Cemetery is also an excellent example of a Polish National Catholic cemetery. Unlike in the Roman Catholic Church, PNCC cemeteries are owned and operated by the individual parishes, with each having its own specific regulation. Once land is purchased it is blessed by the diocesan bishop, although this is relatively *pro forma* as the bishop does not have direct authority over the cemetery and it is acceptable for the parish priest to officiate at the blessing. It is also the parish priest, with the approval of the parish committee or board, who makes the specific arrangements for the burials, although in some cases there

Figure 2.12 A cement grave siding made to resemble wood.

is a separate cemetery committee. Most PNCC cemeteries are simply named after the designation of the parish and contain an altar to be used for special services such as those on All Souls Day or Memorial Day (the former an especially Polish occasion and the latter reflecting assimilation into American culture). Parishioners may purchase cemetery plots ahead of time or as needed and many of the parish members include the PNCC symbol on their headstones. An example of this can be seen in figure 2.13 from St. Joseph's PNCC cemetery in Middleport, Pennsylvania. The captions read, from left, "Truth, Work, Struggle." The book signifies the word of God, the sun denotes freedom and fervor, the cross indicates suffering and consecration, and the palm connotes peace. In larger metropolitan areas where there may be more than one parish in close proximity, the parishes may cooperate in the purchase and operation of a single cemetery. In Scranton, Pennsylvania, the PNCC cathedral purchased a large tract of land and then sold portions of it to other groups, thereby creating a large complex of cemeteries including those of a Russian Orthodox parish, an independent Italian parish, and even a Roman Catholic parish, the latter being unusual since the two groups have traditionally maintained a rigid separation.[72] In this sense the cross-denominational cooperation promoted by the PNCC Scranton cathedral is an exception to the boundaries that generally exist between Polish Roman Catholics and National Catholics, as well as between Poles and other ethnic groups.

Cemeteries reflect the values of the cultural environment. Those in Poland are considered public spaces, normally with a pastoral ambiance often includ-

Figure 2.13 Polish National Catholic Church symbolism in Middleport, Pennsylvania.

Figure 2.14 Typical pastoral Polish cemetery arrangement in Michigan City, Indiana.

ing trees, shrubbery, grass, open spaces, and benches. They usually include some provision for people who wish to linger during their visit to pray, meditate, or simply rest in a pastoral setting. This same concept can be observed in most Polonia cemeteries. An excellent example of this is seen in the All Saints Polish National Catholic Cemetery, noted above, which contains a community hall and picnic grove. Another example appears in figure 2.14, taken in St. Stanislaus Cemetery in Michigan City, Indiana. It includes the typical features of trees, shrubbery, flowerbeds, benches, and spaces set aside for walking. This example features a statue of Christ holding a young child looking out over flowers, shrubbery, and benches so as to be facing those who might stop to meditate.

All of these similarities illustrate the close cultural tie between Polish cemeteries and those established by their diaspora in the United States.

The Effects of Assimilation on Polish Traditions

The vast majority of second- and third-generation Polish Americans obtained jobs in the factories and mines of industrial America, where they worked side by side with people from other ethnic groups and members of the dominant culture. Gradually, through working and interacting with these people in labor unions, local taverns, and some social events, they began a slow transformation into what became the typical working-class "American." While not strictly assimilation, since they tended to retain much of their European cultural heritage, at least in habit if not original intent, there was nonetheless an unmistakable adaptation of many of the original death, mourning, and burial customs through the influence of this cultural interaction.

By the end of the immigrant generation, the black mourning cloth denoting death was replaced by a wreath on the door, and the traditional Polish use of white in mourning was replaced by the more traditional dark mourning clothing used in the United States. Similarly, floral arrangements became less standardized and more colorful, again reflecting American influences. Marzanna herself, the original prototype for equating white with death, quickly faded from view in most immigrant communities, although she did occasionally appear, if only in a maimed memory divorced from its original meaning. In the large Polish American community around Buffalo, New York, the program for the annual occasion notes that originally Marzanna "was the name of the ancient pagan goddess of Death," but goes on to describe a somewhat different purpose, noting that "children would make a straw effigy dressed and throw it into a nearby river and rejoice in winter's departure and the advent of warmer weather."[73] This is accompanied by the recitation of the rhyme:

> Już wiosenne słonko wzbija się po niebie,
> W tej wezbranej rzece utopimy ciebie.
> As the spring sun rises in the sky of blue,
> In this swollen river we are drowning you.

In Seattle, Washington, with a much smaller Polish ethnic community, a "Drowning of Marzanna" ceremony is attached to the annual Seattle Beer Week and appears to be more of an occasion to indulge in Polish food and drink than any serious recollection of folklore from the past. It is described by its website as "the drowning of the effigy of a witch named Marzanna" that is accompanied by "a large assortment of bottled and draft Polish beer" along with "pierogies and other Polish foods."[74] Clearly the original meaning of the custom has been entirely lost. In Buffalo it remains at least somewhat linked to a cultural past in a community that makes explicit efforts to recall its ancestral traditions and promote its ethnic identity to the general western New York population. In Seattle much more assimilation has taken place, to the point where remembering Marzanna is little more than a superficial attempt to add a Polish element, no matter how badly the recollection is tortured, to an otherwise broad-based community festival. In this instance, what had been an element of an ethnic cultural border has been used instead as a means of eliminating any perceived boundary to promote participation in the broader community.

Outward mourning customs also underwent change. The use of the traditional hexagonal casket was impractical and costly in America and did not survive the immigrant generation. Similarly, pallbearers quickly discarded the Polish tradition of carrying the casket on their shoulders for the perhaps more practical American custom of carrying it at the waist. The practice of covering mirrors did not generally disappear until after World War II, while in the more traditional Polish families clocks are stopped at the time of death even today. The significance of breaking a mirror morphed from a sign of impending death to mean simply ten years of bad luck. By the end of the second generation, the custom of placing the candle in the hands of the deceased was largely replaced by lighting a devotional candle in church and locating one on the grave. The frequent appearance of candles within Polish cemeteries continues to this day, especially on All Souls Day or other holidays. The custom of bringing food to the home of the mourners, which was particularly important when the deceased was presented for viewing in the family's home as it was in Poland and among the immigrant generation, continued even after the use of funeral homes began to become popular in the late 1930s.[75]

In the immigrant generation, voluntary associations levied dues to pay a death benefit to the families of deceased members. Over time, the selling of this insurance led to some of the richest ethnic organizations of the first and second generation and attempts by existing insurance companies in the 1930s to restrict these competing businesses.[76] By the third and fourth generations, with the economic circumstances and socioeconomic mobility of working-class Polish Americans rising to parity with other Americans, the transition to professional funeral homes began to occur. With this, the wake became less of an opportunity to socialize over refreshments and more of a shorter, formal occasion for "paying respects" to the deceased without the weightier social connotations.

Similarly, by the third generation the traditional stypa was seldom held in the home anymore but moved to a church hall, restaurant, or some other facility, but it still marked the end of the formal death and burial rituals for the family and friends of the deceased.[77] Yet even then the tradition of bringing food to the home of the deceased continued as a way to show support for the family and eliminate the necessity of cooking when the bereaved had more pressing issues demanding their time.[78]

In the immigrant generation, the Mass of Christian Burial was offered in the traditional Latin supplemented with prayers, readings, and a eulogy in Polish. Except for especially large parishes, this generally began to disappear after the 1940s. Even following the Second Vatican Council (1962–65), when Latin was replaced by the vernacular,[79] except for specifically Polish language masses held in the larger communities, Polish American parishes in 2016 routinely used English for the mass, occasionally including a reading or prayer in Polish if requested by the family, but little else from earlier tradition.

Today, gravesite rites are normally conducted in English unless a family member requests a prayer or reading in Polish from the priest or a layperson. The traditional Polish hymn "Witaj, Królowo nieba" (Hail Queen of Heaven) has disappeared, but relatives sometimes request the singing of "Serdeczna Matko" (Beloved Mother).[80]

Serdeczna Matko, Opiekunko ludzi.	Beloved Mother, guardian of our nation.
Niech Cię płacz sierot do litości wzbudzi.	O hearken to our supplication.
Wygnańcy Ewy do Ciebie wołamy.	Your loyal children kneeling we beseech you.
Zmiluj się zmiluj, niech się nie tułamy.	Grant us the graces to be loyal to you.
Do kogóż mamy, wzdychać nędzne dziatki.	Where shall we seek our solace in distress?
Tylko do Ciebie ukochanej Matki.	Where shall we turn, whom guilt and sin oppress?
U której serce otwarte każdemu.	Thine open heart, our refuge e'er shall be.
A osobliwie nędzą strapionemu.	When trials assail us on life's stormy sea.

Like the former hymn, this also refers to Mary, the patron saint of Poland. It became popular during the early nineteenth century, when the occupying powers prohibited the singing of "Boże coś Polskę" (God Save Poland), which had become Poland's de facto national hymn. Because of its religious significance,

"Serdeczna Matko" remained popular even after the regaining of Polish independence in 1919.

Today, the two-day commemoration of All Saints Day (Dzień Wszystkich Święty; November 1) and All Souls Day (Dzień Zaduszny; November 2) is a national holiday in Poland.[81] Research by sociologist Eugene Obidinski found that of all the customs practiced in Poland, the three adaptations most commonly still practiced by Americans of Polish heritage were, in rank order, the wigilia (Christmas Eve dinner), the święconka (blessing of the Easter foods), and the stypa (post-funeral meal).[82] The first two could be argued to contain the remnants of ancient traditions honoring the deceased, while the latter is clearly focused on the transitional event between death and the resumption of life.[83]

The Affects of Assimilation on Polish Cemeteries

Another feature of Polish customs that underwent change was the cemetery itself. Erwin Panofsky noted that there are three levels of meaning from which a piece of material culture may be viewed: its natural (original) meaning, the meaning that can be derived from its artistic or literary context, and its "iconological interpretation." To understand the latter requires delving into the intrinsic meaning that can only be "apprehended by ascertaining those underlying principles which reveal the basic attitude of a nation, a period, a class, a religion or philosophical persuasion."[84] In this sense, the historical, religious, and cultural traditions of Polish American cemeteries have already been described, as has their appearance in cemeteries of the immigrant generation. But did these transferred cultural elements continue to be reflected in later generations? Did the barriers they enforced continue to be immutable or did they, too, undergo a process of assimilation?

Naturally, direct Polish influences on Polish ethnic cemeteries in America were strongest during the formative years of the immigrant generation. In the years following World War II, generally considered as the beginning of the third generation, the traditional Polish American cultural elements within the cemetery began to give way to the forces of assimilation. This is quite evident from looking at the dates of the various gravestones, their general style, and their inscriptions, not to mention cemeteries founded after the immigrant generation. Increasingly, newer gravesites lacked Polish inscriptions and folk art, which tended to be replaced by the assimilated practices of the general Catholic population. Yet, some aspects of Polish cultural traditions remained. Figure 2.15 shows the tombstone for Józef and Marya Tuman, installed in 1946 in Sts. Stanislaus and Casimir Cemetery in Whitesboro, New York. They were members of the immigrant generation with the inscriptions preserving the Polish

Figure 2.15 The lyre identifies members of the Polish Singers Alliance of America.

words "żona" (wife) and "mąż" (husband), although interestingly without the Polish diacritical marks. This gradual linguistic assimilation can also be seen in the husband's given name, Józef, which also lacks the accent mark over the o. The headstone uses the Polish abbreviation UM ("umarł" or "died") for the date of death and also preserves the wife's maiden name, which was not always the case during those generations. At the top is a lyre, symbol of the parish Lyra Singing Society, as well as the Polish Singers Alliance of America, to which they both belonged. Symbols like these also frequently appeared in death notices in newspapers during the first two generations and were used to personalize many of the resting places of the immigrant and second generations, but became less frequent in the third generation.

Figure 2.16 shows the Niemiec family gravestone, also erected in Sts. Stanislaus and Casimir Cemetery, in 1962. Surrounded by typically Polish flowers and other foliage, in addition to the usual Catholic religious symbols, the stylized block stone also contains in the top center a bas relief of Christ reminiscent of the statuary found in Polish cemeteries. Though of a much more modern design, some of these elements recall their Polish antecedents. The stone in figure 2.17, also from that cemetery, was raised in 1981 to mark the final resting place of Stanley and Winifred Pula. Although its modern design is typical of any American Catholic cemetery, and it is engraved with a standard Catholic cross and floral arrangement, it preserves the original spelling of the last name with the Polish letter ł rather than the English letter l adopted in the United States.

A third photograph from the same cemetery (see fig. 2.18) illustrates several elements typical to cemeteries founded in the interwar period (the second gen-

Figure 2.16 In this later headstone, separate sculptures are replaced by carvings.

Figure 2.17 The Latin cross appears as a carving and the original Polish Ł is preserved.

eration). Since this cemetery was founded in 1932, one rarely sees the more elab-
orately carved gravestones or stone sarcophagi that typify the earlier cemeteries.
Similarly, there are no mausoleums. The larger vertical and horizontal markers
are inscribed with family names. Family plots in the cemetery range from a size
designed to accommodate two burials to those large enough to contain eight

Figure 2.18 A newer Polish cemetery lacks the ornate statuary of older cemeteries.

Figure 2.19 Here the Polish ojciec (father) and spelling (Ł rather than L) are preserved.

coffins. The smaller stones, some rectangular and others triangular in shape, contain the names and dates of individual people consigned within the family plots. Figure 2.19 illustrates a typical example of one of these in a raised-top inscription form that contains the Polish word *Ojciec* (father), the name of the deceased spelled with the Polish letter ł, and the birth and death dates separated by a cross typical of Polish cultural styles.

At the top of the hill in the center of figure 2.18, there is a small grouping of taller monuments just to the left of a large cross. The cross contains the name of the cemetery, the parish it is affiliated with, and its date of founding. The tall monuments are those of priests who died while serving the parish, or who were originally from the village. Many cemeteries set aside a special place for clergy in this manner, although it is not universal. Likewise, just beyond the section reserved for priests is a small area reserved for remembering veterans of the armed forces. Over time, as families tended to move about geographically with the changing socioeconomic climate following World War II, extended family plots became less prevalent as the dispersed population tended to be buried as individuals or married couples in whatever cemetery was associated with the parish they attended in adulthood. This arrangement can clearly be seen in the newer section of this cemetery where, on the reverse side of the hill, the normal plot size is sufficient only for two burials and the gravestones are of a more modern American design; this can be seen in the background in figure 2.16.

While the "Polishness" of Polish Catholic cemeteries has faded over the generations as assimilation takes place, an interesting development in some of the larger Polish communities is the reestablishment of these ethnic preferences in sections where burials of immigrants from the post–World War II generation are interred. An excellent example of this is Resurrection Cemetery in the southwestern suburbs of Chicago, where one of the largest mausoleums in the world serves the dual purpose of religious expression and encouragement of Polish ethnic pride. Designed in a New Formalism motif, the three stories of the mausoleum are surrounded on all sides by 22,381 square feet of stained glass, the largest such work in the world, consisting of 2,248 panels of *dalle de verre* glass depicting scenes from the Bible, Catholic religious history, and more modern representations such as jet aircraft, a satellite dish, and an atomic explosion. The inside walls are decorated with Polish and Polish American ethnic statuary, inscriptions, and a large number of sgraffito panels by artist Józef Sławiński depicting scenes and famous personages from Polish and Polish American history.[85]

Believed to be one of the largest cemeteries in the world in terms of size, Resurrection contains more than 150,000 burial sites, including a more modern section in which a large proportion of the graves appear—judging from the dates on the headstones and the fact that a high percentage remain at this writing unoccupied—to have been reserved by people who came to the United States during the Cold War migrations or the Solidarity exodus following the declaration of martial law in Poland in December 1981. Figure 2.20 shows the Morawa family gravestone, which, although its design is quite modern in concept, is an excellent example of traditional Polish cemetery representations transferred to contemporary America. The central image of Christ is typical of Polish and early Polonia statuary, though of metal rather than stone, while

Figure 2.20 Recent immigrant grave markers reflect a modernization of earlier styles.

the image etched on the stone at the right is that of the Polish-born Pope John Paul II and to the right appears Our Lady of Częstochowa, a famous Polish iconographic depiction. Both are explained in Polish underneath the portraits. The abundant flowers, the glass vessels for placing candles on the grave, and the other features are typically Polish. In the background to the right the same display of Polish ornamentation can clearly be seen on the Szwajnos family stone. Aside from the clearly Polish ethnic imagery of the gravestones, the obvious expense of the monuments also speaks to the relative affluence of the newer immigrant generation.

Conclusions

Richard Francaviglia asserts that "Cemeteries are deliberately created and highly organized cultural landscapes" that "serve both functional and emotional purposes." He concludes that "the cemetery in the United States is a microcosm of the real world, and binds a particular generation of men to the architectural and perhaps even spatial preferences and prejudices that accompanied them throughout life."[86] This is certainly true for Polish American burial grounds that are themselves historical artifacts chronicling the influence of immigrant cultural heritage and the adaptions of succeeding generations as barriers are gradually reduced through assimilation.

During the immigrant generation between roughly 1870 and 1920, Poles brought with them to the United States both vestiges of pre-Christian traditions adapted to the Christian era and strongly Roman Catholic customs adjusted to their own culture over some 900 years of adherence to Church law. Because of the unique experience of a century of partitions, Catholicism had, for most ethnic Poles, become synonymous with Polish patriotism, forming a metaphysical barrier between them and the occupying powers that was perhaps stronger than physical separation. Similarly, it ingrained in them a resistance to denationalization by the partitioners that they quickly turned against the Irish-dominated Church hierarchy in the United States that often opposed Polish cultural expression. These conflicts led to serious disagreements that were based not only on the Polish experience in the old country but also on their expectations of American democracy. This conflict was usually internal to the Roman Catholic Church, but it sometimes led to friction and legal actions over issues of property ownership and cemetery creation. In its extreme it led to the formation of the Polish National Catholic Church as an outlet for those most insistent on retaining Polish religious traditions and local parish control. This process also resulted in the establishment of a very rigid religious border between Roman and National Catholics, both of which maintained cemeteries exclusively for the use of their own parishioners. Thus, the Polish American community was not only separated from the general American population by mutually erected ethnic and religious barriers, it also erected internal barriers emanating from issues of ethnoreligious dissent.

Although a number of Polish death, mourning, and burial customs crossed the Atlantic to the ethnic communities established by the mass migration, what we see happening in Polonia in most cases is a relatively rapid adaptation to or assimilation with the broader Catholic and American society. This is especially evident by the end of the second generation, when increasing incomes allowed for more options, and interaction with non-Poles began to relax the original metaphysical barriers dictated by Polish custom and the immigrant generation's fear of denationalization began to fade. By the end of the first generation, the use of black replaced white for mourning, the coffin was carried at the waist rather than on the shoulders, the use of standard "American" coffins replaced the individually crafted variety in Poland, and the stypa transitioned from a time of celebrating the life of the deceased with stories, music, and even dancing to a much more somber occasion. By the end of the second generation, financial parity with other Americans saw the use of professional funeral homes for the wake and initial church services almost completely replaced the use of the home for those rituals. Similarly, the stypa moved from the home to a restaurant or other facility as a continuation of mourning rather than a transition to normal life.[87] In most cases, these all signaled the lessening of barriers between Polish Americans and the "average American," a definite result of the early stages of the assimilation process. By the fourth and fifth generations, those Polish customs that did survive were nearly indistinguishable from Catholic services held in other ethnic communities except for the abundance of flowers in the funeral home, the occasional Polish-language inscriptions accompanying the arrangements, and a prayer in Polish if one was requested by the family (and assuming the priest had the linguistic ability to comply). Much less frequent was the occasional display of photographs of ancestors from Poland.[88] By this time, due not only to gradual assimilation but also to increasing intermarriage as the generations passed, cemetery configurations became dynamic, so that barriers that existed between Poles and other groups were largely symbolic rather than any serious impediment to interpersonal or intergroup relations. Non-Poles began to attend historically "Polish" parishes in larger number and thus began to be buried in the parish cemetery with increasing frequency.

The primary barrier created by the cemetery in Poland was religious—the requirements of Catholic canon law that the cemetery must be consecrated and that only Catholics in good standing could be buried there. Within the confines of this religious prescription, Polish Catholic cemeteries were considered public space in the sense that walkways, trees, shrubbery, benches, and various bucolic elements combined to make them places where one could linger, meditate, or simply relax in one's own thoughts. While most cemetery plots followed similar construction, usually this was due to cultural norms since there was a great deal of individual independence in selecting the form of grave, the style of the grave-stone, and other accoutrements. Modified block and tablet styles predominated for headstones, while graves tended to be outlined in stones or contained within a sarcophagus depending on the preference and financial ability of the family. A significant diversion from the general norms can be seen in the górale culture in figure 2.6, where individual expression is seen in many forms, especially incor-porating elements of the unique mountaineer culture.

Polish American cemeteries actually reflected *more* boundaries than their European antecedents, because they not only retained the Catholic religious barriers but also served to insulate the immigrant community from other eth-nic groups and the broader population. For an emigrant population particu-larly fearful of denationalization, Poles brought with them to the United States a strong feeling of distrust of outside forces and the coping mechanisms they had honed during generations of foreign occupation. One of these methods was the erection of barriers, both real and metaphysical, between themselves and other peoples. In the United States this manifested itself in the development of very insular ethnic communities where one might live an entire lifetime without ever acquiring English fluency by patronizing Polish bakers, butchers, grocers, tav-erns, newspapers, and even funeral homes. As part of this separation, Poles were particularly anxious to form ethnic Catholic parishes reflecting their own traditions, including the establishment of a Polish parish cemetery. Both the church and the cemetery were at once expressions of ethnic pride and barriers separating the group from nonmembers.

The Polonia cemetery itself was created as a purposeful barrier delineating the religious "in-group" from "the other," those who did not share its communion. But it was also both a symbolic and a real barrier separating Polonia from other groups in the seeming perpetuity that death itself implies. Only Catholics could be buried in the Polish ethnic cemetery, and for the most part only Poles or their close Slavic coreligionists were members of the parish and thus eligible for interment. While the religious barrier survived, the ethnic barrier began to be porous following World War II; socioeconomic mobility increased, the third and fourth generations intermarried with other groups more frequently, new immigrant groups arrived to supplement the original Polish residents in established parishes, and, in recent years, the erosion of traditional urban Polish ethnic communities coupled with the increasing closure of Catholic churches has led to a much greater ethnic mixture within individual parishes. The forces of assimilation and increased opportunity due to better education have dramatically changed former Polish parishes into mixed parishes or even those in which other groups now predominate. The former ethnic barriers are largely illusory today except in the remaining vestiges of the material culture found in the older cemeteries.

Cemeteries are in a sense historical artifacts in themselves, a record of historical progression. This process of assimilation can easily be traced in any older Polish American cemetery of even moderate size. During the immigrant and first generations, these burial grounds reflect rather faithfully the design and stylistic elements of traditional cemeteries in Poland including larger family plots, the use of mausoleums, sarcophagi, statuary and floral urns, the stone grave covers, stone borders enclosing gravesites, and other Polish cultural elements reflective of their old country precursors. Beginning in the 1930s these similarities begin to diminish, producing very distinct divisions in cemeteries that trace their origin to the nineteenth century. Newer cemeteries, or more recent post–World War II sections of older cemeteries, are characterized much more by gravestones that clearly resemble traditional American models, largely without the ornate statuary, carvings, or Polish inscriptions. The newer burials also reflect the process of cultural exchange in not only their distinctly "American" look, but the number of non-Polish surnames reflecting the increasing intermarriage as generations pass, as well as the increasing diversity of historically Polish parishes as demographic changes occur.[89]

In the immigrant and second generations, physical and social barriers relating to death and burial were erected because of religious requirements, the social segregation of immigrants by the dominant group, and the self-imposed separation necessary to preserve familiar traditions in the face of societal pressures. Although the religious strictures remained intact over time, the maintenance of ethnic spatial divisions began to diminish; yet, the preservation of such features

as Polish lettering into the third and fourth generations, usually among people
who no longer speak the language, reflects a symbolic importance in maintaining the spiritual communal bond with the immigrant ancestors and as a source
of ethnic identity, no matter how diluted that may have become. In this respect,
Polish cemeteries in the United States are indeed repositories of cultural traditions, but also reflections of the historical processes of cultural assimilation.
While canon law still supports the original religious barriers under which these
cemeteries were founded, to a greater or lesser extent, depending on the cemetery, original ethnic barriers have largely disappeared. To the extent that the
newer immigration has in some areas erected grave markers that have revived
the use and feeling of traditional Polish cemetery elements, these have not created even metaphysical barriers but instead are merely regarded as the individual preferences of those families. Today the religious barriers remain but
ethnic impediments are largely a thing of the past, with the "Polish" identity
of the cemeteries increasingly permeable but retaining its utility as a means of
emphasizing envisioned group identity.

Notes

The author wishes to especially thank Dominic Pacyga, Theodore L. Zawistowski, Steven
Sass, Delphine Michalik, and Gina Trzepacz-Timpano for their assistance in his research.

1. Richard E. Meyer, ed., *Ethnicity and the American Cemetery* (Bowling Green, OH:
Bowling Green State University Popular Press, 1993), 3.

2. In addition to Meyer's *Ethnicity and the American Cemetery*, see Richard E. Meyer,
ed., *Cemeteries and Gravemarkers: Voices of American Culture* (Logan: Utah State Univer-
sity Press, 1992); Robert Pogue Harrison, *The Dominion of the Dead* (Chicago: University of
Chicago Press, 2003); Blanche M. G. Linden, *Silent City on a Hill: Picturesque Landscapes of
Memory and Boston's Mount Auburn Cemetery* (Amherst: University of Massachusetts Press
and the Library of American Landscape History, 2007); Martha K. Norkunas, *Monuments and
Memory: History and Representation in Lowell, Massachusetts* (Washington, DC: Smithsonian
Institution Press, 2002); and Richard A. Kalish and David K. Reynolds, *Death and Ethnicity:
A Psychocultural Study* (New York: Baywood, 1981).

3. Great Migration is a term used by historians in reference to the massive European immigration to the United States between roughly 1870 and 1920.

4. Marilyn Yalom, *The American Resting Place: Four Hundred Years of History through Our
Cemeteries and Burial Grounds* (Boston: Houghton Mifflin, 2008); Meyer, *Cemeteries and
Gravemarkers*; Meyer, *Ethnicity and the American Cemetery*; Kalish and Reynolds, *Death and
Ethnicity*; Helen A. Sclair, "Ethnic Cemeteries: Underground Rites," in Melvin G. Holli and
Peter d'A. Jones, *Ethnic Chicago: A Multicultural Portrait* (Grand Rapids, MI: W. B. Eerdmans,
1995).

5. See Helen Stankiewicz Zand, "Polish American Folkways (Cures—Burials—Superstitions),"
Polish American Studies 17, no. 3–4 (1960): 100–104; Deborah Anders Silverman, *Polish-Amer-
ican Folklore* (Urbana and Chicago: University of Illinois Press, 2000); Sophie Hodorowicz
Knab, *Polish Customs, Traditions, and Folklore* (New York: Hippocrene Books, 1993).

6. Poland, once a large and influential European nation, eventually fell victim to a combination of its neighbors Austria, Prussia, and Russia. In three partitions of its lands in 1772, 1793, and 1795, the Polish state was erased from the map, its lands and peoples becoming subject to the rule of the three partitioners. Thus, by the beginning of large-scale Polish migration to the United States, there had been no independent Polish state for seventy-five years.

7. Since they were usually counted as immigrants from Austria, Germany, or Russia, determining the exact number of Polish arrivals is an exercise in frustration. Probably the closest one can come are the estimates of the 1900 and 1910 census reports for the language spoken and the excellent work of Helena Z. Lopata, "Polish Immigration to the United States of America: Problems of Estimation and Parameters," *Polish Review* 21, no. 4 (1976): 85–107.

8. Mieczysław Kasprzyk, "Poland: The Rise to Power," http://conflicts.rem33.com/images/Poland/early_polska.htm.

9. The two largest groups to emigrate from former Polish lands were Jews and Roman Catholics. Since there is another chapter in this book examining the Jewish American cemetery, this chapter will be limited to addressing Polish Catholic cemeteries.

10. James S. Pula, *Polish Americans: An Ethnic Community* (New York: Twayne Macmillan, 1992), 38–39; William Galush, "The Polish National Catholic Church: A Survey of its Origins, Development and Missions," *Records of the American Catholic Historical Society of Philadelphia* 83, no. 3–4 (1973): 131; William Galush, "Faith and Fatherland: Dimensions of Polish-American Ethno-religion, 1875–1975," in Randall M. Miller and Thomas D. Marzik, eds., *Immigrants and Religion in Urban America* (Philadelphia: Temple University Press, 1977), 85–86.

11. Wacław Kruszka, *A History of the Poles in America to 1908: Part III, Poles in the Eastern and Southern States* (Washington, DC: Catholic University of America Press), 183; Frank Renkiewicz, "The Polish Immigrant in New York City: 1865–1914" (master's thesis, University of Notre Dame, 1958), 52; Anne M. Gurnack, Richard Hunter, and Renee Bradley, "The Battle Over the Deed to St. Stanislaus Bishop and Martyr Church in New York City: A Landmark Court Case," *Polish American Studies* LXVII, No. 1 (Spring 2010): 45–56.

12. The German term *kulturkampf,* or "culture struggle," has been used by historians to refer, among other things, to the attempts by Chancellor Otto von Bismarck to enforce Germanization on ethnic minorities following the unification of Germany. Poles in particular reacted very strongly against this forced ethnic denationalization.

13. Anne M. Gurnack, Richard Hunter, and Renee Bradley, "The Battle Over the Deed to St. Stanislaus Bishop and Martyr Church in New York City: A Landmark Court Case," *Polish American Studies* LXVII, no. 1 (Spring 2010): 45–56.

14. Janusz Kowalski, "The History of the Cemetery in the Parish of St. John the Baptist in Peplin in the Diocese of La Crosse in the State of Wisconsin," unpublished manuscript provided by Rev. Kowalski; Stanisław A. Elbert, *Księga Pamiątkowa Złotego Jubileuszu 50—tej rocznicy założenia parafji Świętego Piotra* (Stevens Point, WI, 1926), 109.

15. Can. 1176 §1, "Code of Canon Law," http://www.vatican.va/archive/ENG1104/__P4A.HTM.

16. Can. 1176 §2, "Code of Canon Law," http://www.vatican.va/archive/ENG1104/__P4A.HTM.

17. My appreciation is extended to Dominic Pacyga for his generous sharing of time and expertise with me on a joint visit to Resurrection Cemetery.

18. Galush, "Polish National Catholic Church," 133. Capital letters were used in the original.

19. J. David Greenstone, "Ethnicity, Class, and Discontent: The Case of Polish Peasants Immigrants," *Ethnicity* 2 (1975): 7.

20. Galush, "Faith and Fatherland," 89.

21. Eventually, after its firm establishment in America, the PNCC spread back across the Atlantic to found parishes in Poland but did not enjoy the same success there because the Church in Poland was already controlled by Poles.

22. Genevieve Stachowiak Szymarek, "The St. Joseph Polish Catholic Cemetery Association of St. Joseph County, Indiana," http://www.rootsweb.ancestry.com/~instjose/%20Szymarek-Ladewski%20Books/St%20Joseph%20Polish/stjosephpolisholdsection.htm; "St. Casimir's Parish, South Bend," https://en.wikipedia.org/wiki/St._Casimir_Parish,_South_Bend.

23. *Pamiętnik złotego jubileuszu Towarzystwa Krakusów Polskich pod op. Kazimierza, Kr. przy Parafji M. B. Częstochowskiej* (New York Mills, NY: St. Casimir's Society, 1961), n.p.; "Historical Information," manuscript in the St. Mary's Parish Archives; letter, Stephen Podkowinski to Rev. Peter W. Gleba, February 13, 1985, St. Mary's Archives; "Rules and Regulations enacted by St. Stanislaus and St. Casimer Societies of New York Mills, N.Y. for St. Stanislaus and St. Casimer Cemetery," in the possession of the author; *Pamiętnik srebrnego jubileuszu parafji Rzymsko Katolickiej Matki Boskiej Częstochowskiej w New York Mills, N.Y.* (New York Mills, NY: St. Mary's Parish, 1935), n.p.

24. Letter, Msgr. Charles F. McEvoy, Chancellor, Diocese of Syracuse, to Rev. Alexander Fijalkowski, September 9, 1932, Archives of the Diocese of Syracuse.

25. Letter, Fijałkowski to McAvoy, September 10, 1932, Archives of the Diocese of Syracuse.

26. Letter, Msgr. McEvoy to Rev. Fijałkowski, September 23, 1932, Archives of the Diocese of Syracuse.

27. Letter, Walenty Mądry, et al., to Msgr. Daniel Doody, Diocese of Syracuse, October 17, 1932, Archives of the Diocese of Syracuse.

28. Affidavit of Complaint, John Chrabaszcz, as President of St. Stanislaw B. M. Society of New York Mills, N.Y., and John Dubiel, as President of St. Casimer Society of New York Mills, N.Y., Plaintiffs, vs. Saints Stanislaw and Casimer Cemetery Association, Inc., et al., January 9, 1937, State of New York, Supreme Court, County of Oneida. The cemetery association's deed was recorded in Liber 930, page 92.

29. Another interesting example of legal action was Ignatowski v. St. Mary's Polish Catholic Cemetery Co. Et Al., heard in the Superior Court of Pennsylvania. In this instance Frank Ignatowski brought suit against the priest, the cemetery, and the archbishop because his mother had purchased a cemetery lot prior to her death but when he attempted to inter her remains he was required to bury her in a vault determined by the priest. He chose to bury her elsewhere and sued to recover financial damages since he believed he was prohibited from burying his mother by the application of rules devised by the priest and cemetery committee. The court disagreed, finding that the cemetery had the right, according to the original sale, to make whatever reasonable regulations might be required for the safe and secure burial of remains consigned to the cemetery. See 174 Pa. Super, 53–56, http://pa.findacase.com/research/wfrm DocViewer.aspx/xq/fac.19530714_0040413.PA.htm/qx.

30. Emails from Theodore Zawistowski to the author, March 2, 2016, and May 2, 2016.

31. Silverman, *Polish-American Folklore*, 56.

32. Silverman, *Polish-American Folklore*, 56.

33. Knab, *Polish Customs*, 257. This, like other customs, varied from region to region with different characteristics, but this version appears to have been the most prevalent.

34. Knab, *Polish Customs*, 84, 86, 89. References to this custom date at least to the writings of the fifteenth-century historian Jan Długosz.

35. Knab, *Polish Customs*, 257–58.

36. Silverman, *Polish-American Folklore*, 59.

37. Knab, *Polish Customs*, 259–60; "Funeral Traditions in Poland," http://www.polishforums .com/society-culture-38/funeral-traditions-poland-31624/ (accessed January 31, 2014).

38. Silverman, *Polish-American Folklore*, 58; Knab, *Polish Customs*, 265, 269; Zand, "Polish American Folkways," 101.

39. Silverman, *Polish-American Folklore*, 58; Knab, *Polish Customs*, 265, 269; Zand, "Polish American Folkways," 101; Igor Pietkiewicz, "Burial Rituals and Cultural Changes in the Polish Community—a Qualitative Study," *Polish Psychological Bulletin* 43, no. 4 (2012): 296–97; Rebecca L. Crandall, "Death and Ethnicity in Herkimer, New York: The Growth and Development of the Ethnic Funeral Home, 1905–1947," in James S. Pula, ed., *Faces in the Crowd: Ethnic Portraits* (Utica, NY: Center for Historical Research, Utica College, 2002), 129; interview by author with Rev. Arthur Hapanowicz, May 29, 2011; "Funeral Traditions in Poland," http:// www.polishforums.com/society-culture-38/funeral-traditions-poland-31624/ (accessed January 31, 2014); Martha A. From, "Polish Americans," http://www.stjoenj.net/polish.html (accessed January 31, 2014). As Igor Pietkiewicz noted, the rituals described here are mostly those of the rural areas that then contained the bulk of the population. As urban areas emerged, many of these customs became "rather uncommon" (Pietkiewicz, "Burial Rituals," 296). Since the vast majority of the Great Migration of Poles between 1870 and 1920 came from the rural areas, these traditions were the most influential on those immigrants.

40. "Death Rituals and Expectations," http://www.stjoenj.net/polish.html (accessed March 11, 2014); Pietkiewicz, "Burial Rituals," 300.

41. Robert Strybel, "American Ways Filter into Polish Burial Customs," *Am-Pol Eagle*, April 1, 2010; "Funeral Traditions in Poland," http://www.polishforums.com/society-culture-38/ funeral-traditions-poland-31624/ (accessed January 31, 2014); Pietkiewicz, "Burial Rituals," 295.

42. Pietkiewicz, "Burial Rituals," 301; "Funeral Traditions in Poland," http://www.polishfo rums.com/society-culture-38/funeral-traditions-poland-31624/ (accessed January 31, 2014).

43. Knab, *Polish Customs*, 271; Pietkiewicz, "Burial Rituals," 301; "Funeral Traditions in Poland," http://www.polishforums.com/society-culture-38/funeral-traditions-poland-31624/ (accessed January 31, 2014).

44. Knab, *Polish Customs*, 273.

45. "Funeral Traditions in Poland," http://www.polishforums.com/society-culture-38/funeral -traditions-poland-31624/ (accessed January 31, 2014); Silverman, *Polish-American Folklore*, 59.

46. Knab, *Polish Customs*, 268.

47. Pietkiewicz, "Burial Rituals," 290; J. Hunter, "Bereavement: An Incomplete Rite of Passage," *OMEGA* 56, no. 2 (2007): 153–73; Dorota Simonides, *Mądrość ludowa. Dziedzictwo kulturowe Śląska Opolskiego* (Wrocław: Polskie Towarzystwo Ludoznawcze, 2007).

48. Eugene Obidinski and Helen Stankiewicz Zand, *Polish Folkways in America: Community and Family* (Lanham, MD: University Press of America, 1987), 111; Silverman, *Polish-American Folklore*, 59; Zand, "Polish American Folkways," 102.

49. Obidinski and Zand, *Polish Folkways*, 112; Zand, "Polish American Folkways," 103.

50. "Funeral Traditions in Poland," http://www.polishforums.com/society-culture-38/ funeral-traditions-poland-31624/ (accessed January 31, 2014).

51. Crandall, "Death and Ethnicity," 117. Pietkiewicz, "Burial Rituals," 295, correctly notes that "Whereas in rural areas individual death was a collective event for the whole village, in urban areas it usually involved only small groups of people (such as family and friends of the deceased) and—unless a famous person has died—a discreet funeral which would not disturb anyone."

52. See James S. Pula and Eugene E. Dziedzic, *United We Stand: The Role of Polish Workers in the New York Mills Textile Strikes, 1912 and 1916* (Boulder, CO: East European Monographs, 1990).

53. Sławoj Tanaś, "Cmentarz jako przedmiot zainteresowań geografii turyzmu," *Turyzm* 14, no. 2 (2004): 74.

54. Pietkiewicz, "Burial Rituals," 302; "Funeral Traditions in Poland," http://www.polishfo rums.com/society-culture-38/funeral-traditions-poland-31624/ (accessed January 31, 2014).

55. Crandall, "Death and Ethnicity," 129; Zand, "Polish American Folkways," 102. The Polish version may be found in Feliks Rączkowski, *Wielbij duszo moja Pana śpiewnik kościelnu* (War-saw: Instytut Wydawniczny Pax, 1956); the English translation by Eugene Zdrojewski is avail-able at http://eugenezdrojewski.blogspot.com/2013/03/witaj-krolowo-nieba.html.

56. From http://www.poloniamusic.com/Religious_Witaj_Krolowo_nieba.html.

57. Pietkiewicz, "Burial Rituals," 303.

58. Silverman, *Polish-American Folklore*, 56, 60; Stacy Lonati Ross, "Cuisine as an Expres-sion of Mourning and Customs," *Chicago Tribune*, October 12, 2004. See also Pietkiewicz, "Burial Rituals," 290; Wojciech J. Burszta, *Antropologia kultury: tematy, teorie, interpretacje* (Poznań: Zysk i S-ka, 1998).

59. Obidinski and Zand, *Polish Folkways*, 111.

60. Pietkiewicz, "Burial Rituals," 291, 303.

61. Obidinski and Zand, *Polish Folkways*, 131.

62. Meyer, *Cemeteries and Gravemarkers*, 2.

63. Meyer, *Cemeteries and Gravemarkers*, 9.

64. Pietkiewicz, "Burial Rituals," 302; Jagoda Urban-Klaehn, "Polish Cemeteries: History, Styles and Regional Differences," http://www.polishsite.us/index.php/customs-and-religion/ saints-and-patrons/355-polish-cemeteries-history-styles-and-regional-differences.html.

65. Tanaś, "Cmentarz," 81.

66. Tanaś, "Cmentarz," 87.

67. William D. Pattison, "The Cemeteries of Chicago: A Phase of Land Utilization," *Annals of the Association of American Geographers* 45, No. 3 (September 1955): 251.

68. Matt Hucke and Ursula Bielski, *Graveyards of Chicago: The People, History, Art, and Lore of Cook County Cemeteries* (Chicago: Lake Claremont Press, 1992), 71. Back of the Yards was the area surrounding the Chicago stockyards where many Polish immigrants worked in the late nineteenth and early twentieth centuries.

69. Jeannie Łabno, *Commemorating the Polish Renaissance Child: Funeral Monuments and Their European Context* (Surrey, UK: Ashgate, 2011), 84; Jan Białostocki, *The Art of the Renais-sance in Eastern Europe: Hungary, Bohemia, Poland* (Ithaca, NY: Cornell University Press, 1976), 45; Andrzej Wyrobisz, "The Arts and Social Prestige in Poland Between the Sixteenth and Seven-teenth Centuries," in J. K. Fedorowicz, Maria Bogucka, and Henryk Samsonowicz, eds., *A Repub-lic of Nobles: Studies in Polish History to 1864* (Cambridge, UK: Cambridge University Press, 1982), 167. Wyrobisz maintains that Polish sepulchral sculpture "is a phenomenon which has no exact equivalent anywhere else in Europe." Białostocki concludes that "judged by German, Dutch or French standards, the abundance of sepulchral monuments is astonishing." Łabno notes that the statuary and gravestones were typically inscribed with motifs, reliefs, and sometimes either heraldic insignia for the nobility or *gmerk mieszczański* (a townsman's mark, meaning a trade emblem). These can often be seen in early Polonia cemeteries such as the lyre in figure 2.14.

70. Łabno, *Commemorating the Polish Renaissance*, 87. Łabno argues that the exceptional religious and ethnic tolerance of Poland during the Renaissance produced a "cross-fertiliza-tion" of Lithuanian, Polish, Ruthenian, Catholic, Orthodox, and Protestant cultural norms and hence death and burial traditions. She also notes the appeal of "melancholic" and the "sorrow-ful" images which supports Silverman's explanation of the Polish American view of death as "stoic resignation."

71. For a basic explanation of the symbolism of cemetery statuary, see Pam Reid, "Cemetery Art and Symbolism," *Cemetery Studies* (2000), http://www.angelfire.com/ky2/cemetery/reid.html.

72. Email, Theodore Zawistowski to the author, March 2, 2016. The author is indebted to Prof. Zawistowski for sharing his intimate knowledge of the PNCC as well as for reading and offering comments on the draft for this chapter.

73. For the preceding and the following rhyme, see http://www.poloniamusic.com/Poloni aBuffalo.html.

74. See http://www.seattlebeerweek.com/events/41-Drowning-of-Marzanna-Festival#sthash.okL1blAM.dpuf.

75. Knab, *Polish Customs*, 278; Silverman, *Polish-American Folklore*, 59; Pietkiewicz, "Burial Rituals," 296–97; Crandall, "Death and Ethnicity," 129; Rev. Arthur Hapanowicz, interview by author, May 29, 2011.

76. Frank Renkiewicz, "An Economy of Self-Help: Fraternal Capitalism and the Evolution of Polish America," in Charles A. Ward, Philip Shashko, and Donald E. Pienkos, eds., *Studies in Ethnicity: The East European Experience in America* (Boulder, CO: East European Monographs, 1980), 85.

77. Knab, *Polish Customs*, 271.

78. Silverman, *Polish-American Folklore*, 58; Knab, *Polish Customs*, 265, 269; Zand, "Polish American Folkways," 101; Pietkiewicz, "Burial Rituals," 296–97; Crandall, "Death and Ethnicity," 129; Hapanowicz interview, May 29, 2011; "Funeral Traditions in Poland," http://www .polishforums.com/society-culture-38/funeral-traditions-poland-31624/ (accessed January 31, 2014); Martha A. From, "Polish Americans," http://www.stjoenj.net/polish.html (accessed January 31, 2014).

79. "Welcome to Vatican II," http://vatican2voice.org/.

80. Several English translations exist. The one reproduced here is from http://www.yagelski .com/sbox/music/serdecznamatko.txt.

81. Pietkiewicz, "Burial Rituals," 291, 303. Another manifestation of the same concept of All Souls Day melded with other ethnic traditions is the Mexican *Dia de los Muertos* (Day of the Dead).

82. Obidinski and Zand, *Polish Folkways*, 131.

83. Pietkiewicz, "Burial Rituals," 302; "Funeral Traditions in Poland," http://www.polishfo rums.com/society-culture-38/funeral-traditions-poland-31624/ (accessed January 31, 2014).

84. Erwin Panofsky, *Meaning in the Visual Arts* (London: Penguin, 1993), 57.

85. Nate Lielasus, "A Treasure Trove of 20th-Century Art: Resurrection Cemetery Mauso-leum," https://chicagomodern.wordpress.com/2012/04/17/a-treasure-trove-of-20th-century -art-resurrection-cemetery-mausoleum/. I am greatly indebted to Dominic Pacyga for his information on this cemetery and for personally showing me its many facets.

86. Richard V. Francaviglia, "The Cemetery as an Evolving Cultural Landscape," *Annals of the Association of American Geographers* 61, no. 3 (September 1971): 501. For a similar conclu-sion, see W. Lloyd Warner, *The Living and the Dead: A Study of the Symbolic Life of Americans* (New Haven, CT: Yale University Press, 1959).

87. Knab, *Polish Customs*, 271.

88. Delphine Michalik, interview by the author, September 14, 2015; email from Steven Sass to the author, August 19, 2015; Gina Trzepacz-Timpano, interview by the author, July 20, 2015; email, Conrad Kaminski to Steven Sass, August 29, 2015.

89. In the fourth and fifth generations (roughly 1960–2010), there is a definite increase in the number of Polish burials appearing in non-Polish cemeteries, due primarily to increasing intermarriage and the economic mobility that has caused people to move about for jobs, often into regions with no Polish church or cemetery. Much more assimilation can also be seen in Polish cemeteries during this same period, with is a growing number of non-Polish names in

historically Polish cemeteries. Again, this is due to intermarriage and the fact that traditionally "Polish" parishes have become more integrated as older barriers between immigrants and the dominant group have disappeared, newer groups arrive, and the closure of Catholic churches forces people into those that remain.

Bibliography

Affidavit of Complaint, John Chrabaszcz, as President of St. Stanislaw B. M. Society of New York Mills, N.Y., and John Dubiel, as President of St. Casimer Society of New York Mills, N.Y., Plaintiffs, vs. Saints Stanislaw and Casimer Cemetery Association, Inc., et al., January 9, 1937, State of New York, Supreme Court, County of Oneida. The cemetery association's deed was recorded in Liber 930, page 92.

Białostocki, Jan. *The Art of the Renaissance in Eastern Europe: Hungary, Bohemia, Poland.* Ithaca, NY: Cornell University Press, 1976.

Burszta, Wojciech J. *Antropologia kultury: tematy, teorie, interpretacje.* Poznań: Zysk i S-ka, 1998.

Code of Canon Law (Roman Catholic), Can. 1176 §1 and §2. "Code of Canon Law." http://www .vatican.va/archive/ENG1104/__P4A.HTM.

Crandall, Rebecca L. "Death and Ethnicity in Herkimer, New York: The Growth and Development of the Ethnic Funeral Home, 1905–1947." In James S. Pula, ed., *Faces in the Crowd: Ethnic Portraits.* Utica, NY: Center for Historical Research, Utica College, 2002.

"Death Rituals and Expectations." http://www.stjoenj.net/polish.html (accessed March 11, 2014).

Elbert, Stanisław A. *Księga Pamiątkowa Złotego Jubileuszu 50—tej rocznicy założenia parafji Świętego Piotra.* Stevens Point, WI: {PUBLISHER,} 1926.

Francaviglia, Richard V. "The Cemetery as an Evolving Cultural Landscape." *Annals of the Association of American Geographers* 61, no. 3 (September 1971).

From, Martha A. "Polish Americans." http://www.stjoenj.net/polish.html (accessed January 31, 2014).

"Funeral Traditions in Poland." http://www.polishforums.com/society-culture-38/funeral-traditions-poland-31624/ (accessed January 31, 2014).

Galush, William. "Faith and Fatherland: Dimensions of Polish-American Ethno-religion, 1875–1975." In Randall M. Miller and Thomas D. Marzik, eds., *Immigrants and Religion in Urban America*, 84–102. Philadelphia: Temple University Press, 1977.

Galush, William. "The Polish National Catholic Church: A Survey of its Origins, Development and Missions." *Records of the American Catholic Historical Society of Philadelphia* 83, no. 3–4 (1972): 131–49.

Greenstone, J. David. "Ethnicity, Class, and Discontent: The Case of Polish Peasants Immigrants." *Ethnicity* 2 (1975): 1–9.

Gurnack, Anne M., Richard Hunter, and Renee Bradley. "The Battle Over the Deed to St. Stanislaus Bishop and Martyr Church in New York City: A Landmark Court Case." *Polish American Studies* LXVII, no. 1 (Spring 2010): 45–56.

Hapanowicz, Rev. Arthur, interview by author, May 29, 2011.

Harrison, Robert Pogue. *The Dominion of the Dead.* Chicago: University of Chicago Press, 2003.

"Historical Information." Manuscript in the St. Mary's Parish Archives, New York Mills, NY.

Hucke, Matt, and Ursula Bielski. *Graveyards of Chicago: The People, History, Art, and Lore of Cook County Cemeteries*. Chicago: Lake Claremont Press, 1992.

Hunter, J. "Bereavement: An Incomplete Rite of Passage." *OMEGA* 56, no. 2 (2007): 153–73.

Ignatowski v. St. Mary's Polish Catholic Cemetery Co. et al., Superior Curt of Pennsylvania, 174 Pa. Super, 53–56. http://pa.findacase.com/research/wfrmDocViewer.aspx/xq/fac.19530714_0040413.PA.htm/qx.

Kalish, Richard A., and David K. Reynolds. *Death and Ethnicity: A Psychocultural Study*. New York: Baywood, 1981.

Kaminski, Conrad. Email to Steven Sass, August 29, 2015.

Kasprzyk, Mieczysław. "Poland: The Rise to Power." http://conflicts.rem33.com/images/Poland/early_polska.htm.

Knab, Sophie Hodorowicz. *Polish Customs, Traditions, and Folklore*. New York: Hippocrene Books, 1993.

Kowalski, Janusz. "The History of the Cemetery in the Parish of St. John the Baptist in Peplin in the Diocese of La Crosse in the State of Wisconsin." Unpublished manuscript provided by Rev. Kowalski.

Kruszka, Wacław. *A History of the Poles in America to 1908: Part III, Poles in the Eastern and Southern States*. Washington, DC: Catholic University of America Press.

Łabno, Jeannie. *Commemorating the Polish Renaissance Child: Funeral Monuments and Their European Context*. Surrey, UK: Ashgate, 2011.

Lielasus, Nate. "A Treasure Trove of 20th-Century Art: Resurrection Cemetery Mausoleum." https://chicagomodern.wordpress.com/2012/04/17/a-treasure-trove-of-20th-century-art-resurrection-cemetery-mausoleum/.

Linden, Blanche M. G. *Silent City on a Hill: Picturesque Landscapes of Memory and Boston's Mount Auburn Cemetery*. Amherst: University of Massachusetts Press and the Library of American Landscape History, 2007.

Lopata, Helena Z. "Polish Immigration to the United States of America: Problems of Estimation and Parameters." *Polish Review* 21, no. 4 (1976): 85–107.

Meyer, Richard E. ed. *Cemeteries and Gravemarkers: Voices of American Culture*. Logan: Utah State University Press, 1992.

Meyer, Richard E. *Ethnicity and the American Cemetery*. Bowling Green, OH: Bowling Green State University Popular Press, 1993.

Michalik, Delphine. Email correspondence with the author and interview by the author, September 14, 2015.

Norkunas, Martha K. *Monuments and Memory: History and Representation in Lowell, Massachusetts*. Washington, DC: Smithsonian Institution Press, 2002.

Obidinski, Eugene, and Helen Stankiewicz Zand. *Polish Folkways in America: Community and Family*. Lanham, MD: University Press of America, 1987.

Pacyga, Dominic. Email correspondence with the author and conversations with the author.

Pamiętnik srebrnego jubileuszu parafji Rzymsko Katolickiej Matki Boskiej Częstochowskiej w New York Mills, N.Y. New York Mills, NY: St. Mary's Parish, 1935.

Pamiętnik złotego jubileuszu Towarzystwa Krakusów Polskich pod op. Kazimierza, Kr. przy Parafji M. B. Częstochowskiej. New York Mills, NY: St. Casimir's Society, 1961.

Panofsky, Erwin. *Meaning in the Visual Arts*. London: Penguin, 1993.

Pattison, William D. "The Cemeteries of Chicago: A Phase of Land Utilization." *Annals of the Association of American Geographers* 45, no. 3 (September 1955): 245–57.

Pietkiewicz, Igor. "Burial Rituals and Cultural Changes in the Polish Community—a Qualitative Study." *Polish Psychological Bulletin* 43, no. 4 (2012): 288–309.

Pula, James S. *Polish Americans: An Ethnic Community.* New York: Twayne Macmillan, 1992.

Pula, James S., and Eugene E. Dziedzic. *United We Stand: The Role of Polish Workers in the New York Mills Textile Strikes, 1912 and 1916.* Boulder, CO: East European Monographs, 1990.

Rączkowski, Feliks. *Wielbij duszo moja Pana śpiewnik kościelnu.* Warsaw: Instytut Wydawniczny Pax, 1956.

Reid, Pam. "Cemetery Art and Symbolism." *Cemetery Studies*, 2000. http://www.angelfire.com/ky2/cemetery/reid.html.

Renkiewicz, Frank. "An Economy of Self-Help: Fraternal Capitalism and the Evolution of Polish America." In Charles A. Ward, Philip Shashko, and Donald E. Pienkos, eds., *Studies in Ethnicity: The East European Experience in America.* Boulder, CO: East European Monographs, 1980.

Renkiewicz, Frank. "The Polish Immigrant in New York City: 1865–1914." Master's thesis, University of Notre Dame, 1958.

Ross, Stacy Lonati. "Cuisine as an Expression of Mourning and Customs." *Chicago Tribune*, October 12, 2004.

"Rules and Regulations enacted by St. Stanislaus and St. Casimer Societies of New York Mills, N.Y. for St. Stanislaus and St. Casimer Cemetery." In the possession of the author.

Sass, Steven. Email to the author, August 19, 2015.

Sclair, Helen A. "Ethnic Cemeteries: Underground Rites." In Melvin G. Holli and Peter d'A. Jones, eds., *Ethnic Chicago: A Multicultural Portrait.* Grand Rapids, MI: W. B. Eerdmans, 1995.

Silverman, Deborah Anders. *Polish-American Folklore.* Urbana and Chicago: University of Illinois Press, 2000.

Simonides, Dorota. *Mądrość ludowa. Dziedzictwo kulturowe Śląska Opolskiego.* Wrocław: Polskie Towarzystwo Ludoznawcze, 2007.

"St. Casimir's Parish, South Bend." https://en.wikipedia.org/wiki/St._Casimir_Parish,_South_Bend.

St. Mary, Our Lady of Częstochowa Parish, correspondence, Archives of the Diocese of Syracuse, NY.

St. Mary, Our Lady of Częstochowa Parish Archives, New York Mills, NY.

Strybel, Robert. "American Ways Filter into Polish Burial Customs." *Am-Pol Eagle*, April 1, 2010.

Szymarek, Genevieve Stachowiak. "The St. Joseph Polish Catholic Cemetery Association of St. Joseph County, Indiana." http://www.rootsweb.ancestry.com/~instjose/%20Szymarek-Ladewski%20Books/St%20Joseph%20Polish/stjosephpolisholdsection.htm.

Tanaś, Sławoj. "Cmentarz jako przedmiot zainteresowań geografii turyzmu." *Turyzm* 14, no. 2 (2004).

Trzepacz-Timpano, Gina. Interview by the author, July 20, 2015.

Urban-Klaehn, Jagoda. "Polish Cemeteries: History, Styles and Regional Differences." http://www.polishsite.us/index.php/customs-and-religion/saints-and-patrons/355-polish-cemeteries-history-styles-and-regional-differences.html.

Warner, W. Lloyd. *The Living and the Dead: A Study of the Symbolic Life of Americans.* New Haven: Yale University Press, 1959.

"Welcome to Vatican II." http://vatican2voice.org/.

Wyrobisz, Andrzej. "The Arts and Social Prestige in Poland Between the Sixteenth and Seventeenth Centuries." In J. K. Fedorowicz, Maria Bogucka, and Henryk Samsonowicz, eds., *A Republic of Nobles: Studies in Polish History to 1864.* Cambridge, UK: Cambridge University Press, 1982.

Yalom, Marilyn. *The American Resting Place: Four Hundred Years of History through Our Cemeteries and Burial Grounds*. Boston: Houghton Mifflin Company, 2008.

Zand, Helen Stankiewicz. "Polish American Folkways (Cures—Burials—Superstitions)." *Polish American Studies* 17, no. 3–4 (1960): 100–104.

Zand, Helen Stankiewicz. "Polish Immigration to the United States of America: Problems of Estimation and Parameters." *Polish Review* 21, no. 4 (1976): 85–107.

Zawistowski, Theodore. Emails to the author, March 2, 2016, and May 2, 2016.

Chapter Three

An Ocean Apart: Chinese American Segregated Burials

—SUE FAWN CHUNG

Prior to the mid-twentieth century, in the United States the Chinese were usually segregated in life and in death. This mirrored the power structure of the American community and did not begin to change until after the 1965 civil rights movement. The arrival of the Chinese coincided with an era of heightened Americanization—the drive to make immigrants blend or melt into the dominant American society. Although many ethnic groups suffered from growing racism and discrimination, the animosity was more intense for the Chinese, who provided "cheap labor," were physically and culturally distinctive, often were not Christians, and had no political power because they could not be naturalized citizens. For the first time the passage of discriminatory federal, state, and local legislation targeted a specific immigrant group—the Chinese—and made their lives more difficult, thus ignoring the welcoming message on the Statue of Liberty.[1]

This study examines some of the reasons for Chinese American segregation in life and death. Their traditional Chinese beliefs and practices, particularly their respect for ancestors and accompanying rituals of burning paper images of money and other goods, bi-annual grave cleanings, and annual food offerings to the deceased, differed from Western funerary customs.[2] Their desire to be buried in the place of their birth led to the unusual practice of exhumation and cleansing of the bones to be shipped to Guangdong, China, for reburial. For many their hesitancy in being buried in their adopted homeland because of the danger of the cemetery being moved, abandoned, taken over, or destroyed weighed heavily in their decision to subscribe to the costly reburial practice. In their minds it was better and safer to have their final resting place across the Pacific Ocean. However, the Sino-Japanese wars of the 1930s and the estab-lishment of the People's Republic of China in 1949, especially their new burial policies, halted the reburials. The shortage of cemetery space in China in recent decades led to a new phenomenon of third reburials as descendants brought remains back to the United States.

Coming to America and the Rise of Racism

The Chinese became aware of economic possibilities in North America begin-ning in the sixteenth century. At that time, Chinese sailors with their seafaring skills had manned Spanish and Portuguese ships along the Pacific Coast and built ships in Mexico and present-day Baja California. Documents indicated that as early as 1781 a Chinese man had settled in present-day Los Angeles, Cali-fornia. In 1788 Captain John Meares began a trade in lumber between Macao and the Pacific Northwest and brought to Vancouver Island approximately fifty Chinese laborers who felled trees and shaped them into spars and ship's tim-bers.[3] In his diary Meares notes that one of the Chinese seamen, Acchon Ach-ing, fell to his death from a tree and was buried in an unmarked grave on the shore, which was not uncommon for that period. This was the first recorded Chinese death on the Pacific Coast. Other trading ships brought more Chi-nese in the hopes of establishing trade relations. Captain James Colnett, who arrived in 1789, brought a crew that included Chinese carpenters, blacksmiths, bricklayers and masons, tailors, shoemakers, seamen, and a cook.[4] Due to the

Table 3.1: Places of Origin in Guangdong		
District Association	1866	1876
Ningyang (Ning Yung)	15,000	75,000
Yanghe (Young Wo)	11,500	12,000
Sanyi (Sam Yup)	10,500	11,000
Siyi or Gangzhou (Sze Yup or Kong Chow)	9,000	15,000
Hehe (Hop Wo)	8,500	34,000
Renhe (Yan Wo)	3,800	4,300
TOTALS:	58,300	151,300

Note: By 1876 most of the Chinese came from the Siyi (4 Districts) region (now called Wuyi or 5 Districts) and the Sanyi (3 Districts, which includes Yanghe but at the time had enough members to form their own association. Source: Chart based on information from Eastern Slope (July 14, 1866) and Lorraine Barker Hildebrand, Straw Hats, Sandals, and Steel: The Chinese in Washington State (Tacoma: Washington State American Revolution Bicentennial Commission, 1977), 7. Names are transliterated from Chinese characters in pinyin with Americanized version in parentheses.

growing United States–China trade, a few individuals sought opportunities on the East Coast of the United States by opening teashops and hand laundries or becoming domestic servants, but the major influx of Chinese settlers began with the gold rush on the West Coast and the building of railroads throughout the western parts of the continent.

There were numerous "push and pull" factors in Chinese migration.[5] The major "push" factors included the harsh political policies of the Manchus, who had been ruling China since 1644; the economic disruption resulting from the Opium Wars (1839–44, 1858–60); the numerous peasant rebellions (especially the Taiping Rebellion, 1850–64); the Manchu order to burn forests where rebels hid in South China; the Chinese–Western trade imbalance of the late eighteenth and nineteenth centuries; the rise in the value of silver in relation to copper coins (used by the common people), resulting in a twenty percent increase in taxes; and the growth of land tenancy as farmers became unable to pay taxes and rents.[6] Although the Manchus had forbidden emigration overseas, in 1859 the governor of Guangdong responded to the increased demand for Chinese workers abroad and independently legalized it. In 1868 the Burlingame Treaty between the United States and China allowed the Chinese to immigrate to the United States without reprisals in either country.[7] Clan leaders, especially in South China, encouraged members to go abroad so that they could send money home to enhance the clan's and their immediate family's property ownership and prosperity.[8] Merchandising firms sent relatives abroad to market goods and increase their profits. Poverty drove many to emigrate in search of wealth and jobs that were not available at home.

The attractions of the United States were numerous. Emigration from southeastern China was a centuries-old practice but when gold was discovered in 1848 at Sutter's Mill in California and the western railroads were being built beginning in the 1850s, the Chinese were lured to the American West. This was especially important in the poorer rural counties in Guangdong. Letters from relatives about their newfound wealth in the United States and the wealthy returned relatives and neighbors encouraged many to leave. Chain migration of relatives and fellow villagers left their homes in southeastern Guangdong, especially from the Four Counties (Siyi—Taishan, Kaiping, Xinhui, and Enping), and to a lesser degree, the Three Counties (Sanyi—Nanhai, Panyu, and Shunde) and Zhongshan. They sent funds back to their birthplace for schools, hospitals, and other clan, community, and county improvements that made the county and their relatives competitive in the modern economy. For example, Chin Gee Hee (1844–1929; aka Chen Yixi), a prosperous merchant and labor contractor in Seattle, Washington, provided the funds and leadership in the construction of one of China's three major railroads—the Sunning (older name for Taishan) Railway Company, founded in 1906. The railroad allowed Taishan to prosper through the transportation of goods to the port towns until its destruction by the Japanese during the Sino-Japanese War (1931–45).[9] The overseas Chinese established educational facilities, often teaching Western subjects, and supported political causes, including the 1911 Republican (*Xinhai keming*) revolutionary movement and the Nationalist Movement (1912–49), that were a great help to the prosperity of several Guangdong counties.

The discovery of gold in California in late 1848 brought more than 25,000 Chinese in 1852—a tenfold increase from the previous year, which continued to grow with the population numbering 72,472 in California by 1890.[10] Many of these men had been brought to the American West by labor recruiters. The Dutchman Cornelius Koopmanschap (1828–1882) and Sisson, Wallace and Company (connected to the Central Pacific Railroad Company) were the largest Chinese labor recruiters, with offices in China and San Francisco in the mid- to late nineteenth century.[11] Chinese had their own labor recruiters, such as Hung Wah and Company, that searched Guangdong's countryside for able-bodied men and often persuaded men tilling the soil to leave for the promise of wealth abroad.[12]

Table 3.2: Chinese Population in the United States, California, Nevada, Oregon, Washington, and Idaho, with Approximate Percent of Total Population, 1860–1890

Location	1860	1870	1880	1890
United States	34,933 (0.1%)	63,199 (0.2%)	105,465 (0.2%)	107,488 (0.2%)
California	34,933 (9.2%)	49,277 (8.8%)	75,132 (9.8%)	72,472 (6.0%)
Nevada	33 (0.5%)	3,162 (7.4%)	5,416 (8.7%)	2,833 (6%)
Oregon		3,330 (3.7%)	9,510 (5.8%)	9,450 (1.9%)
Idaho		4,274 (28.5%)	3,379 (11.6%)	2,007 (2.4%)
Washington		234 (0.1%)	3,186 (4.7%)	3,260 (0.9%)

Note: In the late nineteenth century, California had the largest Chinese population but Idaho, in 1870, had the largest percentage. The Chinese Restriction/Exclusion Acts of 1882, 1892, and later led to a decline of the Chinese population in the United States. These total figures for the Chinese were inaccurate because many Chinese were not counted but they represent the approximate population. *Source:* United States Bureau of the Census, *Characteristics of the Population of the United States, 1860 to 1890.*

At first the Chinese were welcomed in California; but when the number of Chinese immigrants dramatically increased between 1852 and 1890, the anti-Chinese movement grew rapidly. The decreased availability of easy gold, related economic downturns, growing unemployment, widespread belief in the European pseudo-scientific theory of the superiority of the white race and inferiority of the colored races, disdain for non-Christians, and the rise of labor unions fed into the developing racism.[13] The Chinese reaction to American prejudice was seen in an 1871 letter written by Chung Sun of Los Angeles, California:

I left the loved and ever venerated land of my nativity to seek in [the United States] that freedom and security which I could never hope to realize in my own [country], and now after some months' residence in your great country, with experience of travel, study, and observation. I hope you will pardon me for expressing a painful disappointment. The ill treatment of [my] own countrymen may perhaps be excused on the grounds of race, color, language, and religion, but such prejudice only prevail[ed] among the ignorant.[14]

By 1890 the Chinese had settled in every state and territory in the United States and worked primarily in the service industries as domestics, laundry workers, cooks and restaurant owners, boarding house operators, and merchants, because railroad construction and mining had declined.[15] Most of the men and a few women settled in urban and rural enclaves known as Chinatowns. Between 1880 (50.6 percent) and 1890 (43.3 percent), many Chinese lived in rural California.[16] Other western states had a higher percentage living in rural areas. Rural Chinese found it easier to purchase land for an all-Chinese cemetery than those living in urban areas, where the cemetery usually was adjacent to other ethnicities and outside of the European American burials.

Mining was one of the major occupations for the Chinese prior to 1890. Some southern Chinese had been involved in gold and tin mining, so the announcement of the discovery of gold in California got the attention of these men and their relatives. Those who were farmers were skilled in digging irrigation channels and creating reservoirs, both of which were needed in placer mining (using water to excavate and recover heavy metals like gold from alluvial placer deposits in streams and riverbeds). Expensive mining equipment that was used in hydraulic mining (use of high-pressure jets of water to dislodge rocks or sediments, often resulting in the destruction of hillsides) was not required in placer mining. Many Chinese who went into placer mining as individuals or in small, organized groups were disappointed as the gold was depleted in California's Mother Lode.[17] In 1870 the Chinese constituted 25 percent of all the miners in the American West. In the 1870s, Gold Hill/Coloma Township, El Dorado County, California, had approximately 202 Chinese, 157 of whom were miners; and in 1875 Island Mountain, Elko County, Nevada (population 100), most of the town's fifty Chinese were engaged in mining.[18] The mines at Lava Beds, California (near present-day Oroville), which thrived between 1873 and 1882, had around 8,000 Chinese miners by November 1873 but many succumbed to an epidemic that killed 700 that month and caused 3,000 more to be very sick.[19] The attraction was the twenty- to thirty-dollars-per-day per miner profit that this Chinese-dominated mining community was able to produce during peak production times. Mining was potentially dangerous work, especially when the workers faced equipment failures, blasting difficulties, bandits, diseases, and wild animals. The most danger came from the mob violence of anti-Chinese agitators who resented the Chinese presence, with their different culture and customs, strange appearance, and ability to find gold in abandoned placer sites and thus make a living in times of economic downturns.[20] The total number of deaths related to mining in the nineteenth century is unknown because coroners and others seldom kept records on Chinese deaths.

San Francisco was often the point of entry and therefore had the largest concentrated, urban Chinese population, but as mining towns "boomed" with new mineral discoveries, the population in ephemeral mining Chinatowns rivaled or exceeded the approximately 2,000 in San Francisco. For example, in 1863 Tuolumne County's Chinese Camp had an estimated 35,000 Chinese employed as wage earners in nearby hydraulic mining companies as the mining industry transitioned from small or independent miners to large-scale mining operations.[21] In 1870 the mining town of Tuscarora, Nevada, had 119 people, 104 of them Chinese;[22] shortly after the 1870 census the Chinese population rivaled that of San Francisco with an unofficial estimate of two to three thousand. By the 1870s to 1880s mining was depleted in this region, so the Chinese moved into other occupations, such as farming (also called "gardening," because the acreage was small), ranching, cooking, lumbering, merchandising, railroad construction, laundries, and domestic work.[23] The Tuscarora Chinese cemetery was adjacent to the main cemetery, bounded by a fence, and had an altar for offerings.[24] It was not maintained and only the weathered wooden boards of the altar are visible today. Chinese elsewhere experienced similar situations.

The next major occupation was railroad construction, which began with Chinese building the Panama Rail Road (beginning in 1850); the Sacramento Valley Railroad (incorporated in 1853); the Marysville-Benicia line (beginning in 1854 when 150 Chinese workers went on strike for their wages); the California Central Railroad (1858); San Francisco–Marysville Railroad (1859), which had 250 Chinese under the supervision of Sing Yat; and the San Jose Railroad (incorporated in 1860).[25] They also worked with the Irish on the San Francisco–San Jose line that opened in 1863. In 1864 the Central Pacific Railroad (CPRR), its successor, the Southern Pacific Railroad (SPRR), and its rival, the Union Pacific Railroad (UPRR) became the largest employers of Chinese railroad workers in the late nineteenth century.[26] The death toll on the CPRR might be indicative of those who worked on the other rail lines.

An estimated twelve to fifteen thousand Chinese worked for the CPRR before its completion in 1869. The cost in Chinese lives was tremendous but the total is unknown. On January 5, 1870, the *Elko Independent* reported six carloads of deceased Chinese destined for San Francisco and then probably to China. According to the *Silver State* (Winnemucca, Nevada) in March 1870, two designated Chinese funeral cars were on a siding near the present-day Bridge

Street grade crossing preparing the deceased for their final trip home. The bones were boxed, labeled with the name of the individual, and listed the date of death and association (tang) name, which were then shipped to Hong Kong via San Francisco.[27] On June 30, 1870, the *Sacramento Reporter* (California) stated that 20,000 pounds of bones (an estimated twelve hundred deceased Chinese, or one in ten Chinese workers) were en route to China.[28] Although the official claim was only five hundred deceased workers, these reports indicated that the number was much larger by 1870.[29] From the mid-nineteenth until the turn of the twentieth century, many Chinese were employed in interstate and intrastate standard- and narrow-gauge railroad lines and the related lumbering, support, and transportation activities, but the dangerous aspects of many of these jobs led to the deaths of thousands of Chinese. It was not unusual to read in the newspapers about a Chinese worker killed in an accident while working on the railroads, dying during a natural calamity like an avalanche or an epidemic like smallpox, being blown up in a nitroglycerin accident while constructing tunnels or roads, or being murdered by an angry mob. Anti-Chinese riots probably accounted for a high percentage of deaths.

Anti-Chinese activities spread throughout the western states between 1850 and 1890. The mining community was the most vociferous, and as early as 1848 Mariposa County, California, prohibited the Chinese from mining there. Other mining towns followed. Chinese visibility and cultural distinctiveness contributed to the prejudice and racism that followed. In 1870 the Chinese were 28 percent of the population in Idaho, and a decade later the Chinese constituted almost 9 percent of the total population in both California and Nevada. Harassment and mob violence were commonplace and often resulted in the deaths of Chinese immigrants. By the 1870s the nascent labor union movement gained support of newspapers and popular magazines.[30] Politicians jumped on the bandwagon when they realized that the Chinese could not vote and their anti-Chinese rallying cry could attract new voters and supporters. Mob violence increased. Between 1870 and 1890 there were at least 153 riots against the Chinese, for example, the Chinese massacres in Los Angeles in 1871 and in Rock Springs, Wyoming, in 1885.[31]

Numerous discriminatory regulations and legislations were passed in an effort to expel or drive away the Chinese or prohibit further immigration. The 1850–55 California and other western states' tax on foreigner miners, although originally not directly aimed at the Chinese, had the Chinese supplying much of the state and county income in the West in the 1850s through 1870s.[32] Politicians had to be careful of this source of revenue but knew that they could gain popular support with anti-Chinese slogans. Nevertheless, violence became commonplace. Cabins were burned and the fleeing Chinese inhabitants shot. Entire Chinatowns were set on fire. In Truckee, California, a logging town with

Table 3.3: Population in the United States and People of Chinese Descent			
	Total US population	Chinese origin	Percentage
1840	17,069,453	not available	n/a
1850	23,191,876	4,018	0.02%
1860	31,443,321	34,933	0.11%
1870	38,558,371	64,199	0.17%
1880	50,189,209	105,465	0.21%
1890	62,979,766	107,488	0.17%
1900	76,212,168	118,746	0.16%
1910	92,228,496	94,414	0.10%
1920	106,021,537	85,202	0.08%
1930	123,202,624	102,159	0.08%
1940	132,164,569	106,334	0.08%
1950	151,325,798	150,005	0.10%
1960	179,323,175	237,292	0.13%
1970	203,302,031	436,062	0.21%
1980	226,542,199	812,178	0.36%
1990	248,709,873	1,645,472	0.66%
2000	281,421,906	2,432,585	0.86%
2010	308,745,538	3,794,673	1.20%

Note: The Chinese population does not begin to increase until immigration laws changed in the 1970s, allowing for new immigrants to add to the growing number of American-born children of Chinese descent. *Source:* United States Bureau of the Census, *Characteristics of the Population of the United States, 1840–2010.*

a large number of Chinese working in the woods, an anti-Chinese faction set fire to Chinatown in 1875, 1878, and 1886.[33] During this time a more nonviolent faction devised the so-called peaceful "Truckee Method" of boycotting employers of Chinese workers and Chinese-owned businesses, and expelling the Chinese from town with economic strangulation, thus avoiding the violence of earlier mob actions. Large-scale violence did not diminish until the early twentieth century.

Attacks against Chinese women usually were directed against prostitutes and confined within the Chinese community. Few married women were able to enter the United States because the 1875 Page Law essentially required Chinese women to prove that they were not prostitutes if they wanted to immigrate. Those who were able to immigrate found life in the United States harder than that in China, where family and servant support were common. Most Chinese men lived in a "bachelor" society despite the fact that 30 to 40 percent were married. Their wives usually lived in China or sometimes in an American urban

Chinatown if the husband was in a rural community.[34] The absence of home life probably contributed to early deaths of the men. With the absence of wives and children in the nineteenth and early twentieth centuries, the men turned to their associations (*tang*) and close friends to perform the burial customs and practices and, for those who were wealthy enough, to have their bones disinterred and reburied in their home villages.

In 1882 Congress passed the first of several Chinese exclusion acts, and the Immigration Act of 1924 essentially closed the door for most new Chinese immigrants. Between the 1890s and 1950 the Chinese were able to evade the restrictions through the "paper sons/daughters/wives" practice as well as through illegal entries into the United States through Canada, Mexico, and (until it achieved territorial status in 1898) Hawai'i.[35] The Chinese population dropped drastically as the men returned to China or died by the 1920s. The exclusion laws led to decreases as seen in the population chart in table 3.3. Between 1900 and 1970 the number of Chinese Americans was very small. In 1943 the Chinese exclusion acts were repealed. However, the "open door" for Chinese immigration did not occur until after 1965–70 with the passage of new immigration laws and the recognition of the People's Republic of China in 1979.

Traditions and Adaptations

Chinese Americans were steeped in thousands of years-old traditions that evolved in China. Of primary importance was reverence for the ancestors who theoretically protected descendants who showed filial piety in funerary rituals.[36] They believed that there was a strong connection between ancestors and descendants, and that living people have two souls: the *hun*—an emanation of the *yang*, the light, male, active principle—which gives people their intelligence or spark of life—and the *po*—derived from the *yin*, the dark, female, passive principle—which animates the body. In death these become the *shen*—the spirit that ascends to heaven—and the *gui*—the spirit that returns to or remains on earth. If the *shen* and *gui* are content, then there will be prosperity in the future generations, but if not, the unhappy ancestors would cause trouble and bring disaster to future generations. As Confucius (551–479 BC) wrote, "When the parents are alive, serve them according to the *li* (rituals); when they are dead, bury them according to the *li* and make offerings to them according to the *li*."[37] Song Dynasty (960–1279) Confucian philosopher Zhu Xi (1130–1200) gave specific instructions for the preparation and laying out of the body, but there was no strict adherence to these steps, which varied from region to region and changed over time.[38] Some of the basic steps were 1) to give public notification of the passing; 2) for the family members, to wear white (the color of mourning); 3) to ritually bathe the deceased and place the body in an airtight coffin; 4) to install an ancestral tablet; 5) to arrange for a funeral procession that included professional wailers, loud music to scare off evil spirits, and perforated white squares of paper to confuse the evil spirits as to the location of the cemetery; 6) to hire ritual specialists, who were usually Buddhist and/or Daoist priests; 7) to burn paper images of spirit money, clothing, houses, and other objects to be used in the other world; 8) to offer food and drink at the gravesite; and 9) to hold a simple, plain meal banquet to thank the participants for their support.

Chinese funerary rituals had many unique features. The process of preparing the corpse was not unlike the American practice, but the washing and cleansing was done in the belief that the body had to be rid of any evil spirits that might have attached themselves. In the home, association hall, or mortuary, incense and candles, often placed in the four corners of the coffin, purified and added fragrance to the air. Coins placed on the four corners of the coffin were to be used in the afterlife. Coins, pearls, or other objects were placed in the mouth and other orifices kept the spirit in the body. A yellow silk scarf or paper covered the face as protection against evil spirits. These formalized practices date back at least to the Han Dynasty (206 BC–220 AD) in China.

Chinese American funeral practices were altered because of the American situation. The most obvious difference was the absence of wives, children, and members of the extended family in funerals because of discriminatory state and federal Chinese exclusion acts that prohibited the immigration of Chinese laborers, thus reducing the predominantly male Chinese American population until the Repeal of Chinese Exclusion Acts in 1943.[39] Kinsmen, men from the same village, district, or county, and men belonging to the same organizations (*tang*—literal meaning "meeting hall") acted in place of the family. Usually a Chinese American funeral association, often connected directly to the district association (*huiguan*), occupational guild (*gongsuo*) or clan association (*huiguan, fang, kongsi*), fraternal organization (usually *tang*), or specialized burial organization handled the details of the funeral. Like the mutual aid societies of European immigrants, these organizations were concerned with protecting members, caring for widows and aged members, supporting educational and welfare institutions, acting as the mediator between the American community and Chinese community as well as within the Chinese community, sponsoring recreational and holiday activities, and promoting links between one's birthplace and adopted homeland, often through publications such as magazines, newspapers, and newsletters.

The status of the deceased in the community determined the character of the funeral. Prominent community leaders had elaborate funerals that might include professional mourners and wailers, Daoists and/or Buddhist priests or even Christian ministers. Next came the marching band to scare off evil spirits, numerous large paper wreaths, firecrackers, and a procession of individuals, some of whom tossed perforated white pieces of paper to confuse the evil spirits as to where the deceased was to be buried. Close friends had white (instead of the American black) armbands. Horse-drawn wagons gave way to automobiles, whenever possible, a photograph or painting of the individual was prominently displayed as the procession began at the home of the deceased, stopped at his place of work and association headquarters, traveled through Chinatown, and ended at the cemetery.

Chinese funerals welcomed all, so often there were large crowds. One of the earliest reported Chinese funerals in California occurred in January 1851, when 150 attended the funeral procession and burial of a well-known but unnamed Chinese.[40] During these early decades, the local press was more concerned with the funeral than the individual involved because, as one reporter noted, "The ceremonies were of the most heatheniah [sic] description to Christian appreciation."[41] Seven years later, when San Francisco had a large Chinese population, the funeral of a wealthy Chinese Zhigontang (Chinese Free Masons) officer and merchant had a thousand attending the ceremony.[42] In 1871 the funeral of Wong Halgson, president of the large Ningyang huiguan (regional association), there were 150 carriages, fifty professional mourners, and five wagon loads of provisions and flowers.[43] In 1903 Thomas A. Edison, Inc. made a film of Colonel Tom Kim Yung (1858–1903)'s elaborate funeral procession in San Francisco (dated September 23, 1903) that is available online.[44] In later years some Chinese American funerals attracted several thousand participants, including non-Asians.

Because the Taishan immigrants were the most numerous, their district association was the most active in buying cemetery plots that had to conform to *fengshui* ("wind and water"—a mystical combination involving mathematics, astronomy, philosophy, religion, cosmology, geography, and the natural features such as a hillside or river nearby) principles.[45] As seen in the Lin Yee Chung Chinese Cemetery in Honolulu, Hawai'i, gravesites with a hillside at the rear for protection and a body of water (stream, ocean, lake) in front or nearby were most propitious. Geographer Andrew Briggs studied the Chinese cemeteries in Oregon and concluded that they followed *fengshui* principles.[46]

At the gravesite funerary objects were buried inside or near the coffin. Archaeologists have found coins to be spent in the next world, favorite objects such as ceramic vases and opium pipes, eyeglasses if one had needed them, and a yellow silk cloth covering the face. In Portland's Lone Fir Cemetery, two-thirds of the ceramic shards unearthed were Chinese and the remaining ones were western, indicating a degree of acculturation.[47] For some, in life it was more convenient to buy western teapots and dishware and these became personal favorites so they were buried with the deceased. Popular rumors circulated that the Chinese used gold or silver coins in their burials and this led to numerous raids of Chinese cemeteries for grave goods. In the late nineteenth century, the deceased's clothing and paper representations of objects to be used in the afterlife were burned in a special burner at the cemetery, but in recent decades paper objects representing clothing, homes, money, food, cars, televisions, computers, and cell phones were burned.[48] However, many Chinese cemeteries, such as the one in Los Angeles's Evergreen Cemetery, and Auburn, California's Chinese Cemetery, had brick or concrete "burners" that were used for this part of the funerary rituals. This kind of practice was unacceptable in non-Chinese cemeteries, especially since the burning could—and sometimes did—start a fire in the nearby fields.

The services were solemn. There were a variety of prayers, poems, and writings that could be read. A common closing comment in traditional Chinese burials demonstrating the strong link between the past, present, and future was, "May future generations be blessed with official emoluments [meaning wealth and a prosperous future]."[49] At the end of the readings, or sermon if the person was Christian, everyone approached the coffin, bowed three times to show respect, and said a few words. Then they tossed in the white armbands and a handful of dirt. Family members usually threw in a flower and a handful of dirt. Some also tossed in a bottle of wine and other objects for the heavenly spirits. Once the grave was closed, food (often a whole roast pig, an unseasoned whole chicken, and/or a whole fish along with symbolic fruits and flowers) and wine were offered to the deceased for his afterlife. Native Americans and town pranksters often enjoyed partaking of the food and wine left at the gravesite. Late nineteenth-century Chinese often sent guards to prevent the food and wine from being stolen. In this way the decease made his/her final farewells to the community.

A coin wrapped in white paper was given to each participant to purchase something sweet to have sweet memories of the deceased and to take away the bitterness of the funeral. In recent decades a coin and a small piece of candy are given away since the price of candy bars has risen beyond the five to twenty-five cents that were usually given. At the gravesite or at a nearby restaurant, food and drink usually were offered to the mourners. A specific ten or more course menu of "plain white" dishes was served. Prior to the twentieth century, cigars (often made by the Chinese who had a near monopoly on the industry in the late nineteenth century) were offered to the male participants.[50] Often many European Americans attended, curious about the different custom and desirous of the food and drink. The mourning period for the family ranged from seven to one hundred days and family members were not allowed to visit the homes of friends and neighbors because it would bring the latter bad luck. Seven days after the death of a family member, the soul of the departed would return to his/her home. A red plaque with a suitable inscription often was placed outside the house to ensure that the soul did not get lost.

An average person had just of few of these elements in his/her funeral. The wife of a prominent community leader might have the same type or slightly lesser funeral as her husband, but ordinary women usually had no special treatment. Some Chinese men who wanted their wives buried in the home village generally sent the bodies in coffins to Guangdong at great expense. The unfortunate aspect of this was that, because the husbands and children were in the United States, frequently the gravesites were unattended since the community often did not remember the women. As in the case of men, funds were provided for flowers and Qingming ("Clear and Bright") Festival, but the gravesites of the forgotten women were usually neglected.[51] By the turn of the twentieth century, many husbands and wives wanted to be buried together, as seen in many of the gravesites in Chinese cemeteries in Colma, California. Young children often were quietly buried and only those from wealthy families would be exhumed for reburial. Young female children had a simple burial and were not candidates for reburial since they did not contribute to the continuation of the family line. Those who died a violent death, were social outcasts (including prostitutes and criminals), or suffered a premature death or serious illness were buried away from the main part of the cemetery and were less likely to be exhumed and reburied.[52] As in life, one's status in the community was important in death.

Burial practices usually followed Confucian traditions since the Chinese often followed the "Three Religions" of Daoism, Confucianism, and Buddhism, but a mixed ceremony of beliefs, including Christianity, could be held. As early as 1879, Wong You, a Christian, was buried in St. Louis, Missouri, with a Christian service. When the 1892 Chinese Exclusion Act classified religious persons as "laborers prohibited from immigration," some Chinese employed Christian ministers to perform the burial services.[53] Second- and third-generation Chinese Americans, having been raised and educated in the United States, usually had Christian burials, did not continue the practice of exhumation, and probably included only a few of the traditional customs, such as the banquet for participants following the funeral services.

If the person was Buddhist, the individual might be cremated. Carson City, Nevada's Chinese cemetery had its own crematorium and handled Chinese from the outlying region.[54] A Buddhist priest or several priests would preside over the ceremony in front of the typical elaborate and colorful altar of deities, flowers, fruit, and incense. Although the common American belief was that all Chinese were Buddhists, few Chinese cemeteries had Buddhist deities. The Bakersfield, California Chinese Cemetery on Terrace Way was established on five acres in the early 1900s and was the only one known to have a shrine with a Buddha statue on the grounds. In 1956 the few whose bones still remained in this cemetery were relocated to a small cemetery on Sixth and Tulare Streets. Cremated remains of Buddhists usually were placed in niches instead of in the

Figure 3.1 In the 1850s and 1860s, Chinese grave markers were made of wood and the information on the deceased was written in Chinese with a Chinese brush. As in later cases, the person's name, birthplace and, if known, date, and death date were listed. Family (clan) name was listed before the first name since the family was more important than the individual in Chinese tradition. Unfortunately, the wood did not last long, so these markers have disappeared.

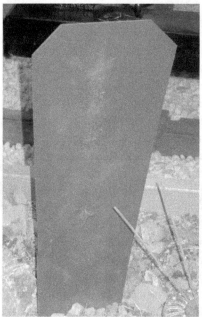

Figure 3.2 Sometimes the markers were made of more permanent materials, such as stone or marble. In the 1860s and 1870s, this marker, found in the Virginia City Chinese cemetery, was made of metal and the inscription engraved on it. The engraving has faded but can be restored. In the 1870s–1880s Virginia City reputedly had some two thousand Chinese residents in this rich mining town. The Chinese cemetery, as usual, was separate from the town's main cemetery. Joss (incense) sticks would be placed in front or nearby during the spring and fall festivals remembering the deceased. Photo taken in Virginia City, 2015.

Figure 3.3 Many of the late nineteenth- and early twentieth-century markers have photographs of the deceased husband and wife, as seen in this marker in the Chinese cemetery in Colma, California, of Hun Wong and his wife Joe [pinyin Zhou] Shee [indicated a married woman]. Although the last name of Wong is prominently displayed, the family name of Zheng is written in Chinese; this may be because he was a "paper son" (entered under another family's name) or the immigration official's mistake. Photo taken in Colma, California, 2010.

ground and probably were not repatriated. Daoist priests also performed death rituals and it is believed that the two festivals, described below, connected with cemeteries derived from Daoist beliefs from the Zhou Dynasty (1046–256 BC) and earlier times.

Early markers were usually made of wood or stone and Chinese characters listing the deceased's name, place of birth, date of birth, and date of death were written. Mid-nineteenth-century flat iron slabs with Chinese characters written in graphite were used in Virginia City, Nevada, where approximately two thousand Chinese lived between 1870 and 1880. By the late nineteenth and throughout the twentieth centuries, both English and Chinese often were used but a few had only one or the other language.[55] Unlike the rural Valhalla Cemetery in St. Louis, Missouri, where the markers were made of wood or other temporary materials, the headstones in many northern California cemeteries were written

in the good calligraphic hand of a scholar or learned individual and then transferred onto the stone or marble marker.[56] Family lineage could be traced since
relatives often were buried near each other or in the same cemetery. Many of
the headstones resembled American ones in their simplicity, but sometimes a
photograph of the deceased and his wife and basic information about them was
included. More elaborate markers, similar to some found in China and Southeast Asia, were large and had a U-shaped or rectangular area for flowers and
food. In general the tombstone had three columns: the right side had the birth
date; the left side, the death date; and the middle, in larger characters, the name
of the individual. At the top the birthplace or family name often was listed. If
a man had more than one wife, all could be buried in the same, but larger, plot
and the basic information was given.

Most of the early Chinese immigrants wanted to have their final resting
place in China. The repatriation of bones was alien to Americans, and local
newspapers often focused on this Chinese practice. Traditional Chinese believe
that spirits (or ghosts) hover over the place where bones are buried and are not
happy until the deceased is reburied in the place of one's birth or in a proper
cemetery. A popular four-character saying was, and still is, "*Luo ye gui gen*"
(Fallen leaves return to their roots), indicating the desire of the more traditionally minded Chinese Americans to have their bones exhumed and repatriated
to their home village across the Pacific.[57] Since the sending of coffins to China
was expensive, those who wanted to be repatriated had to be buried in a shal-
low grave from three to twenty years (usually seven years). An identification
marker, often a brick or a slip of paper in a sealed bottle, was placed in the coffin. The person's name, home county and village in Guangdong, date of birth
(if known) and death, and often the place of death was listed. For example,
the brick in the coffin of a prominent merchant in the railroad town of Carlin,
Nevada, read: (first line) Taishan [County], Daiyuan [Village], died May 1924
[exact day unclear]; (second line in the center and with characters larger than
the other lines) Yu Weiyuan [in Cantonese, Yee Wei-yuan], 59 years old [born
1866]. Therefore if he had been exhumed, Mr. Yu would have been reburied
in Daiyuan, Taishan, Guangdong province. Additional information might be
included but this data was the basic requirement.

Burial and exhumation practices at the cemetery involved digging a shal-
low grave of about eighteen inches instead of the usual six feet and leaving the
deceased alone for three to twenty years.[58] Decomposition of the flesh made it
easier for the specialized bone cleaner to do his job of cleaning the bones in a
ritual bath. The bones were placed in correct anatomical order in a sealed tin
or ceramic urn, the size of which was determined by the longest bones. The
deceased was then ready for the long journey home via San Francisco and the
Tung Wah Hospital in Hong Kong, where the containers were stored until there

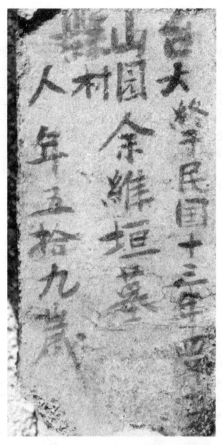

Figure 3.4 Those who were to be reburied in their birthplace in Guangdong usually had some means of noting their identity. In Carlin, Nevada, twelve coffins were uncovered in 1996 and at least two had identification bricks, a common way to identify the deceased. In coffin 11 was Yee Wai Yuan (pinyin Yu Weiyuan) (ca. 1865–1924) of Dayuan village, Taishan (Toisan), Guangdong province. This information comes from the horizontal writing at the top of the brick. On the right is his death date of 1924 and on the left, his death age of fifty-nine. No English is written since this brick was to be read in Hong Kong at the Tung Wah Hospital and Reburial Center. The reburial container of metal is then sent to the home village. Photo taken in 1996.

was a sufficient number to be sent to one's native village for final burial.[59] Once the containers arrived in the village, the local priest tossed a duck with a string around its neck into the river to recapture the spirits of the deceased individuals, and brought them back to the temple holding the containers by the river. The reuniting of the bones and spirit allowed the individual to be buried in his or her final resting place. If no one in the village claimed the remains, a special gravesite was set aside for the burial of these individuals. A Charity Cemetery still exists in Xinhui, Guangdong.

A major problem with repatriation was the absence of close relatives in the village to perform the annual ceremonies related to reinforcing the links between past and present generations and cleaning the gravesites. Another was the distance between the gravesite and home of the descendants in the United States that made attention to the deceased almost impossible. In recent decades relatives solved the latter problem by exhuming the deceased to be reburied in cemeteries in the United States near the homes of the relatives.[60]

There were additional problems. In order to create space in the cemetery, a bone house was built to house the bone containers and the burial space sold to another person. In some rural areas, the bone house was a target for rowdy teens and others to destroy. In 1890 the Chinese population of the railroad town of Elko, Nevada, was 100 but by 1910 it had dropped to 27 men and declined rapidly thereafter. Those who died around the turn of the twentieth century and wanted to be reburied in Guangdong had their exhumed bones housed in a small wooden building located in the Chinese section of the public cemetery on a hill near the Presbyterian Church in the public cemetery. One day European American teenage pranksters not only broke into the bone house but also opened the containers and scattered the bones.[61] These men never made it back to China. A few wanted to remain in Elko. Unfortunately, most of the markers are illegible due to the passage of time, but two were still readable: Ng Kee Fong (aka Ah Lee), 1852–1913, and Chow King Sing, 1848–1917. Of the two, Ng had been a merchant belonging to the influential Ng (also spelled Ung, Eng, Wu) clan of northeastern Nevada and southern Idaho. Chinese cemeteries might have a mixture of final burials and temporary burials. Just outside of the Forestvale Cemetery in Helena, Montana, where approximately two hundred Chinese were buried between 1890 and 1955, most were exhumed for reburial, but a few remained.[62] Among those who remained were forty-one-year-old Yut Quay, a gardener who died of gangrene December 18, 1900; China Baby Kee, two months old, who died from the flu; and Lee Sing, forty-four, who was killed in a railroad accident in 1904. The baby normally would not have been exhumed, but the two adults should have if they had paid the exhumation fee and were not disreputable individuals. The Lin Yee Chung Chinese Cemetery, established in 1851 in the Manoa Valley in Honolulu, Hawai'i, regularly sent bones back to China until the Sino-Japanese War of 1931–45, when the procedure was halted. The elaborate bone house still contains approximately one hundred ceramic urns, suitcases, and boxes awaiting reburial.[63]

Local or regional American newspapers occasionally mentioned train carloads of deceased Chinese bones were being returned to China for burial.[64] This publicity popularized the misperception that all deceased Chinese were repatriated and not permanently buried in the United States. Turn-of-the-twentieth-century records challenged the popular image of all deceased Chinese being

Figure 3.5 Usually the disinterred Chinese bones were placed in specially made metal boxes (the size determined by the longest bone in the body) and shipped to Guangdong to be reburied in one's native village. In Honolulu, ceramic containers were sometimes used and stored in Oahu's largest "bone house" at the Manoa Chinese Cemetery, as seen here for four different individuals, Chong and Ng on the right and Cheng and Yuen on the left. Note that the sizes of the urns are different because the largest bone determines the size of the container. They remain there because the shipment of disinterred bones was interrupted by the Sino-Japanese War (1931–45) and the establishment of the People's Republic of China (1949–). Photo taken in Honolulu, ca. 2000.

exhumed and repatriated. In the late nineteenth century. some American morticians refused to handle Chinese burials, but a few changed their minds because of the profitability involved. This was seen in the 1904–19 records of Ross Burke Funeral Home in Reno, Nevada, which at first refused to handle deceased Chinese, then took care of seventeen deceased who were born in China.[65] Fourteen were buried in the Reno area, one coffin and one disinterred person were shipped to China via San Francisco, and one was sent to Sacramento. Nothing is known about these individuals who were not listed in the census manuscripts. All were men. The reasons for the refusal to handle deceased Chinese in European American mortuaries primarily were American racism and prejudice and the perceived oddities of Chinese burial customs.

As a part of their labor contract, the importing companies or agencies, usually headed by European Americans or Chinese contractors, agreed to return the workers' bodies or bones back to their home villages, or the Chinese paid fees to specific associations to have their bodies or bones returned to China.[66] In Canada and the United States, the clan or county association was in charge and operated through a special association (*tang*) handling these shipments by charging members a set fee. In May 1880 one had to pay $50 to their association, in this case, the Hop Sing Tong, for this privilege.[67] As a secret fraternal brotherhood, the Hop Sing Tong was open to men regardless of place of birth or family name, but one had to be sponsored by a current member, swear an oath of secrecy, and agree to obey rules of conduct. In return the member enjoyed the benefits of the mutual aid offered. Often it was a major organization in rural and small Chinatowns while the Chinese Consolidated Benevolent Association (CCBA; in Chinese, Zhonghua huiguan) dominated urban communities.

District associations and family associations had a funeral organizational arm (*tang*, "association") to handle the funeral arrangements from the time of death until the reburial in China and the clan and/or district association meticulously noted the information in a record book.[68] Members of various associations (district and clan associations as well as fraternal societies) had a fund to cover the costs whether the person was rich or poor. David Chuenyan Lai, in looking at the records of Victoria, British Columbia's CCBA records, found that the association charged departing Chinese a fee for the hospital in Victoria and indigent burials, which was mandatory before a shipping company could sell them a return ticket to China.[69]

A wealthy man, especially a merchant or herbal doctor, often had money to support an elaborate funeral. Often individuals contributed to a fund that guaranteed their burial expenses in the United States and reburial back in their native village. Friends made monetary gifts to the family and relatives or association to help defray the expenses. Indigent Chinese depended upon the goodwill of the community or members of their association. Local or state governments often levied a fee for the exhumation and fees were charged for the shipment of bones to China. Because there were few wives in the American West prior to 1943, when the Repeal of Chinese Exclusion Act was passed, clan members and/or fraternal associations adopted the traditional role of immediate family members and assumed the responsibility of payments.

Figure 3.6 Chan Get Chor (1875–1971), seated on the right, and his wife, Shin (Sun) Shee next to him, are photographed with their children: Jane, Frances, May, Harry, and John Chan. Mr. Chan was a calligrapher in Chinatown, and a supporter of his wife's cousin Sun Yatsen (1866–1925), who was the first president of the Republic of China. Photograph taken ca. 1919 in San Francisco or Locke, California. Courtesy of the Chan Family.

Figure 3.7 Marker in Colma, California, for Chan Get Chor of San Francisco, who was born (right-hand line) in Guangdong, Zhongshan (also called Heungshan) province (on the right) and the name of the village (present-day Pushan) on the left, with his name in larger characters in the center. This is an example of a basic marker (essential information only) in Chinese and English that was typical of many Chinese American markers. Photo taken in 2000.

Eventually the CCBA oversaw the activities and required a departure fee to cover mortuary expenses.[70] In Victoria, British Columbia, in 1894 the exit fee was nine dollars: three to the CCBA (also known as the Chinese Six Companies), three to the district association (based on the birthplace of the individual), and three for the temporary burial, exhumation, and reburial in Guangdong.[71] Why the Hop Sing charged fifty dollars and the Canadian CCBA only three is unknown, unless the fees from San Francisco were more because of government taxes, fees, and other expenses. If relatives did not claim the remains in the home village, the final resting place was a county charity cemetery.[72] Around 1909 the CCBA in San Francisco delegated the task to the Taishan funerary association to handle all shipments. After World War II and the establishment of the People's Republic of China (which had no formal relations with the United States until 1979), few bones, if any, were disinterred and returned to China for final burial.

Burial in one's birthplace was not always an option. Descendants might decide otherwise. Get Chor Chan (1875–1971) of San Francisco, who is buried in Colma, California, was the principal of a Chinese language school in San Francisco's Chinatown, president of one of the Zhongshan associations, community calligrapher, and activist for Sun Yatsen's 1911 revolutionary cause. He immigrated as a child in the 1880s. When his first wife died in 1905, he sent her body to Zhongshan County to be buried; and when his second wife died around 1940, he did the same.[73] Both women had been born in Zhongshan. He wanted to be buried next to them, but his descendants opted to have him buried near San Francisco where they lived and could perform the Qingming ("Clear and Bright") remembrance custom.

Segregation in Life and Death

The Chinese often lived in urban and rural Chinatowns, which allowed them to mutually protect themselves against the non-Asian population and to continue many of their centuries-old traditions while adjusting to life and work in the American West. Housing and business segregation was common, especially in San Francisco's Chinatown, where the Chinese were forced to live in ten square blocks near the center of town until the civil rights movement.[74]

The European American community deemed that this segregation in death, as in life, was necessary for "others," which included ethnic and religious minorities. As Jacob Long titled his article, "Deaths and Burials: The Final Frontier for Segregation," separation was necessary.[75] The prevailing belief was that inferior people had to live in separate ghettos and be buried away from the superior white Anglo-Saxton Protestant population in separate cemeteries or segregated sections of cemeteries.[76] The differences between a Western funeral procession and burial were so different from the Chinese ones in religious practices and customs that funeral directors could use the excuse to enforce the separation.

Prior to the mid-1960s the Chinese had two main choices: to be buried in China or to be buried permanently in the United States. The more conservative Chinese did not like being buried in the American West because Americans lacked tradition, the concept of filial piety, and had no ghosts or ancestral spirits.[77] Americans did not believe in the strong connection between the spirits of the otherworld and the living. If they wanted to be buried in China and could not afford to have the coffin shipped, they had to opt for the temporary burial, exhumation, and reburial in an American segregated cemetery or a Chinese association owned cemetery. They also were afraid of what might happen to the cemetery in the future because many cemeteries were relocated or abandoned. Those who were more Americanized wanted to be buried in the United States, often because they felt that America was their home and sometimes because they had descendants, relatives, and loved ones living in the United States. If the cemetery was large enough, they were confident that traditional rituals or modified ones could be carried out.

Most nineteenth cemeteries allowed only European Americans to be buried within their boundaries. One common exception was the loyal Chinese servant who was buried with the family in the family's private cemetery. Chinese had to establish separate, but often nearby, cemetery plots. In Carson City, Nevada, the state's capital, the Chinese cemetery was built adjacent to the city's main Lone Mountain Cemetery, and in the 1930s over thirty grave markers were still visible.[78] Men like Yee Bong, a restaurant owner who was born in Virginia City in 1860 and one of the oldest continuous residents of Carson City, were undoubtedly buried there. It was one of the few cemeteries in the region with a crematorium, but most Chinese were not Buddhist and therefore would not have been cremated. In the 1990s the land was considered abandoned and sold to George Foley, a private developer with political connections, without the need to exhume the remains of the Chinese. Foley built a medical complex on top of the cemetery. This act of gentrification was common as Chinese-only cemeteries disappeared from the American landscape because of a lack of maintenance and protection from federal and state governments.

Some American cemeteries had sections reserved for different minority groups, including Chinese. In the early development of some small localities, the local cemetery was the final resting place of all residents, which was the case in Bakersfield in the 1870s.[79] In 1878 Bakersfield city officials began work on present-day Union Cemetery, which disallowed Chinese and Native American burials, who would be buried in the earlier cemetery now known as the "Chinese Cemetery." In 1907 A. S. Morton supervised the disinterment and shipping of bones to China, and other non-Chinese morticians participated in this practice, thus ending the Chinese domination of the practice. The bone containers, which were made of metal or ceramic, were individually made to the size of the deceased's largest bone. In the 1930s the Chinese cemetery had a few markers and two burners for the spiritual (paper) offerings to the ancestors in the spring and fall. The Bakersfield Chinese population declined, and after World War II the cemetery property was sold several times until, in the 1950s, the prime property was subdivided into housing units with streets. This is typical of what happened to many late nineteenth-century abandoned Chinese private cemeteries.

Popular longtime residents often were buried in the segregated section of the public cemetery. Ah Sam (d. 1933), a longtime resident of Warren, Idaho, "honorary mayor," and popular personality in the community, was buried in the European American cemetery instead of the Chinese one.[80] When Quong Kee, a former Central Pacific Railroad cook in Elko and owner of numerous restaurants, died in Bisbee, Arizona, in 1938, his friends in Tombstone, Arizona, where he had operated the famous Can Can Restaurant for years, brought his remains back to Tombstone, had an elaborate funeral attended by all of the community leaders, and buried him in Boot Hill next to the Chinese Free Masons association leader, Mrs. Ah Sam (also known as China Mary, 1839–1906).[81] They are the only two Chinese in Boot Hill.

In some places, like Nevada's rural mining town of Tonopah (founded in 1900), a select few Chinese who were regarded as "Americanized" could live outside of Chinatown, but had to be buried in a segregated section of the public cemetery. This was the case of labor contractor, restaurant owner, train crew supervisor, and borax mining boss Billy Min Chung Ford (1850–1922), who adopted an American first and last name and educated his six children in the public school so that they were even more Americanized. Like many of the early Chinese who quickly adapted to American society, he adopted an American name, wore Western clothing, married an American-born Chinese woman, and named his children after famous Americans such as James Butler Ford (after the founder of Tonopah), Bessie Ford (because it was too hard to say Betsy Ross), and George Washington Ford. He chose to be permanently buried next to his wife, Lilly Sue Loy Lee Ford, and near friends in the Chinese section of the public cemetery.[82] Two prominent and wealthy residents of John Day, Oregon, herbalist and physician Dr. Ing Hay (aka Wu Yunian and Doc Hay, 1862–1952) and merchant and car salesman On Lung (aka Liang Guanyin and Leon, 1863–1940), partners in Kam Wah Chung and Company, ignored their wives and children living in China and chose to be permanently buried in their adopted homeland at Rest Law Cemetery, overlooking the town from a hillside to the north of town.[83] The hillside had correct *fengshui* (geomancy). The same practice occurred in Portland, Oregon, where the Chinese could live outside of Chi-

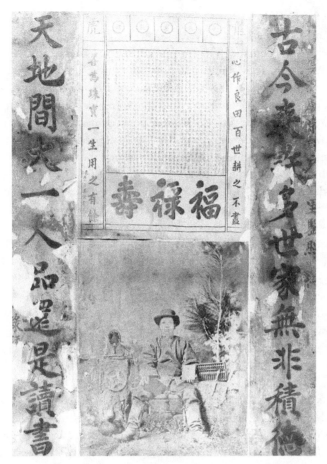

Figure 3.8 This late nineteenth-century advertisement for geomancy services circulated in Chinese communities in the West. The Daoist geomancer determined the propitious fengshui ("wind and water") for cemeteries, houses, and buildings. The tools of his trade are shown.

natown but had to be buried in Lone Pine Cemetery's Chinese section between 1854 and 1948.[84] In the Congressional Cemetery in Washington, DC, Range 99 was reserved for Chinese burials, but most were repatriated to China and like several empty Chinese cemeteries, later became a public place for mediation.[85]

In some instances the Chinese burial association, clan/regional association, or secret fraternal brotherhood purchased their own cemetery because of religious beliefs and practices. A geomancer determined the location of the privately owned cemetery and the orientation of the burials so that the spirits would be pacified. This was preferable to American public cemeteries because traditional rituals could be carried out, geomancy rules followed, and when the process of the exhumation of bones was done, there would be no objections. An example of the regional association's ownership of a cemetery that followed the principles of geomancy was seen in Carlin, Nevada, one of the major rail-road centers for the transcontinental railroad.[86] One of the tasks assigned to the Chinese was scouting for the best route across Nevada, and while doing this job some discovered the natural springs that were perfect for growing produce in the future town of Carlin, established in December 1868. Fourteen Chinese railroad workers settled there, and when Carlin expanded its roundhouses and other facilities, more Chinese moved there. Around the 1870s the funerary association connected with the Ningyang (Cantonese, Ning Yung) District Association (under the general Siyi "Four Counties" umbrella) purchased land for the burial of their members from Taishan, Guangdong province. Decades later the land was sold for back taxes, which was common in the American West. In 1997, when the new European American owner decided to build his retirement home on the land, he discovered first one then another coffin.[87] In accordance to the law regarding the discovery of human bones, he contacted the sheriff. This became one of the only fully excavated turn-of-the-century Chinese cemeteries. Local volunteer archaeologists guided by professional archaeologists eventually uncovered twelve coffins and one empty grave. The Smithsonian, National Geographic Society, and various bio-archaeologists, including Professor Ryan William Schmidt, UNLV doctoral candidate John Joseph Crandall, and others studied these remains before their reburial in the public cemetery in Carlin at the town's expense.[88] These studies have resulted in a better understanding of Chinese burial practices and provided insights into the lives of these men. For example, evidence of injury was found among eight men, and was likely fatal for two of them. Robust skeletons and degenerative joint changes also attested to the strenuous labor these men performed. Some of the broken bones were not healed properly, suggesting the limited availability of health care. In order to ease the pain from the broken bones, some of these men had been opium smokers (denture evidence). The artifacts, such as American and Chinese coins, a yellow silk cloth, false and real queues, shoes, an opium pipe, American and Chinese ceramic shards, and other objects demonstrated the preservation of Chinese traditions modified by the American situation. The queues, for example, had to be preserved if the individual wanted to return to China, where the Manchu government required the hairstyle. A man was subject to immediate execution if he did not have a queue (the Manchu hairstyle required of all Chinese men), so a false queue was needed if the man had an American male haircut. Three of the fancy American-made coffins with late nineteenth-century decorations had identification bricks, indicating a desire to be exhumed and reburied. Two of these men were merchants and probably leaders of the community. One additional Chinese man chose to be buried in the nearby public

Figure 3.9 Chung Kee (1850–1909) was a labor contractor, gardener (owned a small farm growing vegetables and fruits), and father of six children who were born in Hawthorne, Nevada. His gravesite, with some family members in front, was typical of rural Nevada cemeteries with a simple fence around it. This was in a segregated cemetery that was located in 2001 using sophisticated electronic equipment because the boundaries and markers have disappeared. Courtesy of the Kee Family.

cemetery, indicating that he did not have ties to Taishan and wanted to remain permanently in Carlin. The men in the Carlin Taishan cemetery were forgotten; but another nearby cemetery, located in the mining town of Tuscarora, had the bodies exhumed and shipped to China for reburial. Many of these *tang*-owned cemeteries in small towns and out-of-the way locations were sold for back taxes or other reasons and became sites for city parks, schools, medical buildings, parking lots, and, as in the case of the Carlin cemetery, a private home.

Some forgotten cemeteries became incorporated into other properties. In 1909 Chung Kee died of natural causes and was buried near his cousins. A typical wooden fence surrounded his gravesite in the Chinese cemetery in Hawthorne, Nevada, where he had been a merchant, labor contractor, farmer, and friend of the local Paiutes.[89] The Chinese cemetery was very small, and when his wife and six children moved to Tonopah, Virginia City, and then Reno, the cemetery was forgotten and the markers and wooden fences around the gravesites disappeared over time. When his oldest son and later his granddaughter searched for the cemetery using family photographs and talking to Hawthorne family friends, the graves could not be found. With the help of archaeologists

Figure 3.10 Evergreen Cemetery with its burners and altars was the earliest Chinese cemetery (1888) in Los Angeles, California. It underwent a 2010 restoration by Chinese Historical Society of Southern California with Barton Choy as the restoration architect. This photograph dates from before 1923. Courtesy Huntington Library, San Marino, California.

and others professionals in 2008, the graves were eventually located near the present-day US Army Ammunition Depot—almost a century after Chung Kee's death. A similar situation occurred in Cumberland, Courtenay, British Columbia, Canada, when descendants searched for the burials of Chinese ancestors. Because of the growing awareness of multiculturalism and diversity, the people and governments are striving to keep their forgotten cemetery site maintained and open.[90]

Like many cities, Los Angeles had set aside a section of the cemetery at Fort Moore Hill in the 1870s for the Chinese. By the 1880s the prestigious city-owned Evergreen Memorial Cemetery, in the Boyle Heights neighborhood on the edge of Los Angeles, relocated the Chinese cemetery and a pauper's gravesite in one section. Those without funds were buried without any charge but the Chinese were charged ten dollars per burial between 1877 and 1924.[91] In 1888 the Chinese erected a shrine with an altar platform, twelve-foot-tall kilns, and memorial stones that fell into disrepair over time. In 1923 a new Chinese cemetery was built at East 1st Street in the vicinity of the shrine. Norman Martin, superintendent of the County Department of Charities at the time, offered the community two dollars per deceased to be reburied in the new Chinese Evergreen Cemetery because he wanted the job done quickly. Not everyone was moved. In 2006 the Metropolitan Transit Authority, now the owners of the property, were constructing a new line and discovered numerous skeletal remains—902 determined to be Chinese. Grave goods, including rice bowls, jade bracelets, and other artifacts, were found. With the help of the Chinese Historical Society of Southern California and members of the Chinese community, the Chinese remains were reburied in Evergreen near the restored Chinese shrine (burner) in 2010.[92] However, there have been warnings about cemetery owners like Glenn Wong, who did not care for Evergreen and Woodlawn Chinese cemeteries and has been charged with administrative desecration, failure to keep records, unlawful burial of multiple bodies in a single plot, and other violations, with the most obvious being bones scattered on top of the grounds.[93] Similar charges have been levied against owners of several other cemeteries where other minorities have been buried. The Evergreen Cemetery is an example of what occurred elsewhere as cemeteries were relocated, individuals reburied only to be forgotten, and gentrification took place.

The movement of cemetery locations, sometimes more than once, also was problematic. In San Francisco, beginning in 1854, the Chinese were buried in Lone Mountain Cemetery at California and Geary Streets, a segregated cemetery that included, for example, a Masonic section. In 1867 it was renamed Laurel Hill Cemetery, which was forced to close. The City of San Francisco banned cemeteries within city limits so between the late 1890s and 1940, most cemeteries were relocated to Colma, San Mateo County, California.[94] A different reason for relocation was seen in the Yreka Chinese Cemetery, Siskiyou County, California. In 1877 a fire destroyed the European American cemetery, which had a Chinese section. In August 1877 a new site was selected for the segregated Chinese cemetery on Butcher Hill near the Montague Highway, because the practice of burning paper objects and the deceased's clothing had caused the fire.[95] The Chinese had been banned from burials in the original Foothill or Pioneer Cemetery because of the practice of burning paper objects. The Chinese did not object to the change of venue because the hill fit the *fengshui* requirements.

Heritage preservation, and as a corollary the preservation of Chinese cemeteries, has risen to the foreground in recent decades. One of the outstanding examples is the Chinese cemetery in Barkerville, British Columbia, Canada, which was founded in 1862 when gold was discovered in the Cariboo Mountains. By the mid-1860s the town boasted a population of five thousand, half of whom were Chinese. The Zhigongtang (Chinese Free Masons) was the primary organization in town and undoubtedly was involved in the establishment of the Chinese cemetery, which fell into disrepair over the past century. In 2016 two hundred Chinese organizations contributed a total of $100,000 for the renovation of this forgotten cemetery as a tribute to the Chinese pioneers of Barkerville, a national historic town.[96]

Figure 3.11 In the late nineteenth century, the Chinese observed the Qingming (Bright and Clear) Spring Festival by honoring the deceased by offerings of wine and other festive foods, such as a roasted chicken, and with joss (incense) sticks burning to give a fragrant aroma.

Eventually, by 1976 the federal government mandated integrated cemeteries.[97] Chinese Americans could be buried in whatever cemetery they or their families selected, such as the Forest Lawn Cemeteries in Southern California—as long as the cemetery was not restricted. Gue Gim Wah (1900–1988), who became famous as President Herbert Hoover's western cook at Wah's Café in the mining town of Prince, Nevada, wanted to be buried in nearby Pioche's cemetery and the local citizens granted her that wish. Some early Chinese were able have their final resting place in an "all-white" cemetery.

One of the main reasons to have a separate Chinese cemetery in the United States was the need to perform the funerary rituals connected with the Qingming ("Clear and Bright") Festival that reinforced the link between the living and the dead.[98] The celebration of the festival was seen in almost all Chinese cemeteries since the 1860s. At the present time, in Colma, California, and nearby Daly City, San Jose, and South San Francisco, there are numerous Chi-

Figure 3.12 Edwin Chew, MD, performs the kowtow (bowing) and offering of food to his first-generation Chinese American parents during the Qingming Festival in 2008 in Marysville, California. Courtesy of Lucky Owyang.

nese cemeteries, including Cypress Lawn Funeral Home, Woodlawn Memorial Park, Hoy Sun Memorial Cemetery, Old Hoy Sun Ning Yung Cemetery (for those from Taishan), Acme Memorial, and the Chinese Cemetery.[99] All celebrate the important Qingming Festival in the spring, usually in early April. The graves are cleaned and fresh flowers, food, and drink offerings are made to the deceased. Descendants would bow three times, usually on a mat or blanket as Song Dynasty Confucian disciple Zhu Xi prescribed, as a sign of respect to the ancestor. In Colma, California, Chinese community organizations offer free lunches to visitors who pay homage to their ancestors buried in the aforementioned Chinese cemeteries in the town.

During the fall the *Chongyang* (occurring on the fifteenth day of the seventh lunar month, or August) Festival, also called the Hungry Ghosts Festival or the *Yulan pen* if one is Buddhist, the cemeteries are cleaned again. In order to appease the restless spirits, paper money and paper representations of clothing, computers, cell phones, and other objects are burned for use in the other world. Most modern Chinese Americans often find this festival too embedded in superstitions and therefore do not celebrate this traditional festival.

This centuries-old tradition, different in its finer points depending on local Chinese traditions, is still continued in many Chinese and overseas Chinese cemeteries. For many years, those who could afford to traveled to Guangdong during *Qingming* Festival to sweep the graves and honor the ancestors, but in recent years, the remains have been exhumed and reburied in a cemetery in the United States near the home of the relatives so that the ceremony could take place nearby. In Stockton, California's Chinese cemetery, about two hundred people participated in the *Qingming* rituals between the 1990s and early 2000s, partially due to the Chinese Consolidated Benevolent Association's restoration of the cemetery.[100]

Conclusion

As early as the 1850s segregated cemeteries for the Chinese were established. For over a century the European American community believed in segregation in life as well as in death. Many of the early Chinese immigrants were poor and physically different looking, so European Americans believed that the "inferior" Chinese, with their strange rituals and beliefs, had to be separated from the general population. The Chinese were agreeable to a separate cemetery or segregated section of a cemetery that allowed them to continue their traditions, have noisy, colorful funeral processions, celebrate their ancestors in death, and disinter the bones to be buried across the Pacific in their birthplace in Guangdong. The disappearance of the segregated Chinese-only cemeteries due to back taxes, forgotten burial sites, ecological and geographical changes, encroachment of the land, government policies, land reuse, and other factors has resulted in a concern about those who remained buried in identifiable cemetery locations. Knowing that their American cemeteries could be forgotten, destroyed, or reused, the Chinese preferred that their final resting place be across the Pacific Ocean in their native land. The exhumation of bones and shipment back to China was halted with the Sino-Japanese War (1931–45); when the process was resumed, fewer and fewer bones were sent back due to the People's Republic of China government policies and other complications until the official American recognition in 1979. Second and later generations of Chinese Americans, educated in American schools and living in American society, distanced themselves from all but the most significant traditions and wanted to have the final resting place of their relatives and themselves in the United States. They adopted many American customs, such as the wearing of black instead of white, having a Christian service, and using American funerary rites. However, they often maintained the practice of handling out coins and or candy to participants and holding the "plain" banquet at the end of the burials.

For the sake of simplicity, they might go to the graves to place flowers on *Qingming* Festival but only a few still leave food and drink and bow three times as a gesture showing reverence at the gravesite. If the parents did not follow many or any of the Chinese funerary traditions, their children simply adopted the different American ones.

The trend away from reburial in China has been helped by recent problems in China. China has a graveyard space problem and the government requires citizens who died after June 1, 2014, to be cremated. The cost of being buried in a major cemetery in Beijing in 2015 was US$62,000. One alternative is to be cremated and placed in a 3D virtual box for US$1,700.[101] For Chinese Americans it meant that bringing their relatives to the United States for burial or reburial was more reasonable. The *Qingming* and *Chongyang* rituals easily could be performed in the United States due to the rise of multiculturalism and the acceptance of nonmainstream rituals. The growing post-1970 ethnic Chinese population in the United States, especially those from outside of Guangdong and those from Southeast Asia, wanted to continue the traditions in segregated sections of American cemeteries but even this trend is disappearing.

The Chinese remain the largest of the Asian American groups in the United States; in 2000 the total Chinese population was 2,564,190 and by 2010 grew to 3,535,382. At the same time an appreciation for diversity, globalization, and transnationalism, as well as Chinese cultural traditions, have resulted in the drive to preserve modified Chinese funerary practices and segregated cemeteries.

Notes

Based on Sue Fawn Chung and Priscilla Wegars, eds., *Chinese American Death Rituals: Respecting the Ancestors* (Walnut Creek, CA: Altamira Press, 2005). See especially Wendy Rouse, "'What We Didn't Understand': A History of Chinese Death Ritual in China and California," 19–47; Paul G. Chace, "On Dying American: Cantonese Rites for Death and Ghost Spirits in an American City," 47–80; Sue Fawn Chung, Fred P. Frampton, and Timothy W. Murphy, "Venerate These Bones: Chinese American Funerary and Burial Practices as Seen in Carlin, Elko County, Nevada," 107–46; Terry Abraham and Priscilla Wegars, "Respecting the Dead: Chinese Cemeteries and Burial Practices in the Interior Pacific Northwest," 147–74; Linda Sun Crowder, "The Chinese Mortuary Tradition in San Francisco Chinatown," 195–240; and Roberta S. Greenwood, "Old Rituals in New Lands: Bringing the Ancestors to America," 241–60. I am indebted to the updates on "Chinese Cemetery Studies" on the University of Idaho website managed by Terry Abraham and the reading of a draft of this manuscript by Priscilla Wegars.

1. "Give me your tired, your poor, / Your huddled masses yearning to breathe free, / The wretched refuse of your teeming shore." Inscribed on the Statue of Liberty. See also Bill On Hing, *Making and Remaking Asian America through Immigration Policy, 1850–1990* (Stanford, CA: Stanford University Press, 1993).

2. For a general background, see Marilyn Yalom, *The American Resting Place: Four Hundred Years of History Through Our Cemeteries and Burial Grounds* (Boston: Houghton Mifflin, 2008).

3. Thomas R. Cox, *Mills and Markets: A History of the Pacific Coast Lumber Industry to 1900* (Seattle: University of Washington Press, 1974), 5; Donald MacKay, *The Lumberjacks* (Toronto: McGraw-Hill Ryerson, 1978), 227.

4. George I. Quimby, "Culture Contact on the Northwest Coast, 1785–1795," *American Anthropologist*, New Series, 50:2 (April-June 1948): 249.

5. In immigration, people are pushed out of a country because of social, economic, and/or political dislocations. They relocate to a new site or country. They are attracted or pulled into another country or site for economic gain, political and religious freedom, environmental changes, and other factors.

6. Chen Guoqing and Zhang Keping, eds., *Zeng Guofan Quanji* [The Complete Works of Zeng Guofan] (Xian: Xibei Daixue Chubanshe, 1994), 523, details some of the economic considerations.

7. The Burlingame Treaty of 1868 promised the Chinese the right to free immigration and travel within the United States, allowed for the protection of Chinese citizens in the United States in accordance with the most-favored-nation principle, and gave the citizens of the two nations reciprocal access to education and schooling when living in the other country. All of these articles served to reinforce the principle of equality between the two nations. Americans violated the terms of the treaty in succeeding years.

8. Based on a field excursion to the Siyi (Four Counties of Taishan, Enping, Kaiping, and Xinhui) area under the leadership of Professor Jinhua Selia Tan and Wuyi (Five Counties) University in 2014. The four counties added one redrawn county recently to make it five counties (Wuyi).

9. Chin Gee Hee is the Americanized spelling of his name, which in the Chinese pinyin system of transliteration is Chen Yixi. The Japanese destroyed the rail line in 1938 during the Sino-Japanese War of 1931–45. Prior to 1949 there were only three rail lines in China.

10. Census manuscripts, 1850–1890; on migration, see Elizabeth Sinn, "Pacific Ocean: Highway to Gold Mountain, 1850–1900," *Pacific Historical Review* 83:2, Special Issue: Conversations on Transpacific History (May 2014): 220–37.

11. On Koopmanschap, see *San Francisco Bulletin*, July 26, 1869; Andrew Gyory, *Closing the Gate: Race, Politics, and the Chinese Exclusion Act* (Chapel Hill: University of North Carolina Press, 1998), 31–35; Elizabeth Sinn, *Pacific Crossing: California Gold, Chinese Migration, and the Making of Hong Kong* (Hong Kong: University of Hong Kong Press, 2013); Sue Fawn Chung, *Chinese in the Woods: Logging and Lumbering in the American West* (Urbana: University of Illinois Press, 2015), chapter 2.

12. There are numerous tales of this type of recruitment. For example, see William Harland Boyd, *The Chinese of Kern County, 1857–1960* (Bakersfield, CA: Kern County Historical Society, 2002).

13. For a background, see John Kuo Wei Tchen and Dylan Yates, eds., *Yellow Peril!: An Archive of Anti-Asian Fear* (New York: Random House, 2014). One of the best summations of the racial theory is Kay Anderson, *Vancouver's Chinatown: Racial Discourse in Canada, 1875–1980* (Montreal: McGill-Queen's University Press, 1991).

14. Quoted in George Kraus, *High Road to Promontory: Building the Central Pacific (Now Southern Pacific) across the High Sierra* (New York: Castle Books, 1969), 221.

15. For a general overview of Chinese American history, see Roger Daniels, *Asian America: Chinese and Japanese in the United States since 1850* (Seattle: University of Washington Press,

1988); Sucheng Chan, *Asian Americans: An Interpretive History* (Boston: Twayne, 1991); Yong Chen, *Chinese San Francisco, 1850–1943: A Trans-Pacific Community* (Stanford, CA: Stanford University Press, 2000); Madeline Hsu, *Dreaming of Gold, Dreaming of Home: Transnationalism and Migration between the United States and South China, 1882–1943* (Stanford, CA: Stanford University Press, 2000); Erika Lee, *The Making of Asian America: A History* (New York: Simon and Schuster, 2015).

16. Based upon calculations from the US Census Manuscripts, 1880–1890.

17. Sue Fawn Chung, *In Pursuit of Gold: Chinese American Miners and Merchants in the American West* (Urbana: University of Illinois Press, 2011), for more information.

18. Chung, *In Pursuit of Gold.*

19. Randall Rohe, "Chinese Mining and Settlement at the Lava Beds, California," *Mining History Journal* (1996): 51–60.

20. The definition of *placer site* is the mining of stream bed (alluvial) deposits for minerals. The equipment required is relatively inexpensive, with a gold mining pan and rocker or long tom as basic equipment.

21. On Tuolumne, see Anne Bloomfield, *Chinese Camp: Cultural Resources Inventory* (Sonora, CA: Tuolumne County Historic Preservation Review Commission, 1994).

22. Sue Fawn Chung, Fred P. Frampton, and Timothy W. Murphy, "Venerate These Bones: Chinese American Funerary and Burial Practices as Seen in Carlin, Elko County, Nevada," in Chung, Sue Fawn, and Priscilla Wegars, eds., *Chinese American Death Rituals: Respecting the Ancestors* (Walnut Creek, CA: Altamira Press, 2005), 107–46.

23. For a general background, see Erwin G. Gudde, *California Gold Camps: A Geographical and Historical Dictionary of Camps, Towns, and Localities Where Gold Was Found and Mined; Wayside Stations and Trading Centers* (Berkeley: University of California Press, 1975).

24. Personal observation, 1990.

25. Lucy M. Cohen, "The Chinese of the Panama Railroad: Preliminary Notes on the Migrants of 1854 Who 'Failed,'" *Ethnohistory* 18:4 (Autumn 1971); 309–20; www.panamarailroad.org/history1.html; Scott Alan Carson, "Chinese Sojourn Labor and the American Transcontinental Railroad," *Journal of Institutional and Theoretical Economics* 161:1 (March 2005): 89. See also Wendell Huffman, "Iron and Steel: How the Comstock Determined the Course of the Central Pacific Railroad," *Nevada Historical Society Quarterly* 50:1 (2007): 3–35; "Iron Horse Along the Truckee: The Central Pacific Railroad Reaches Nevada," *Nevada Historical Society Quarterly* 38:1 (1995): 19–36. For San Francisco–Marysville Railroad, see *San Francisco Bulletin*, October 13, 1859.

26. Central Pacific Railroad Company, Payroll Record for June 1864 had two Chinese names that are the earliest extant documented Chinese employees. California Railroad Museum, Sacramento. On microfilm.

27. J. P. Marden, "A History of Winnemucca," typewritten mss, Humboldt County Library, Winnemucca, Nevada. Also available at www.cpr.org.

28. Many railroad workers died but there are no estimates of the numbers. The *Sacramento Reporter* (June 30, 1870) noted that a train carrying the accumulated bones of 1,200 Chinese workers, who had paid their one-dollar "burial" fee, passed through Sacramento on their way to their final resting place in their home village in China. This meant that one in ten workers died if only this train was counted. There undoubtedly were more deaths.

29. See http://www.cinarc.org/Work-Data.html/ and www.cinarc.org/Death.htm/.

30. Denis Kearney and his cry to end "cheap Chinese labor" inspired much of the violence in this period and later. See Jean Pfaelzer, *Driven Out: The Forgotten War Against Chinese Americans* (New York: Random House, 2007).

31. Detailed in Scott Zesch, *The Chinatown Wars: Chinese Los Angeles and the Massacre of 1871* (New York: Oxford University Press, 2012); Isaac Hill Bromley, *The Chinese Massacre at Rock Springs, Wyoming Territory, September 2, 1885* (Boston: Franklin Press, 1886).

32. Mark Kanazawa, "Immigration, Exclusion, and Taxation: Anti-Chinese Legislation in Gold Rush California," *Journal of Economic History* 65:3 (2005): 779–805. This also applies to other states like Oregon and Washington.

33. Chung, *Chinese in the Woods*, chapter 4; Pfaelzer, *Driven Out*.

34. A gender balance was not reached until 1970. At the height of the Chinese population in Nevada in 1880, there were 5,102 men and 314 women. This imbalance was characteristic of the bachelor society and not unusual in the American West. See Chung, *Chinese in the Woods*, 54.

35. "Paper relations" are individuals who claimed to be related to a Chinese man legally in the United States who was a merchant or citizen by birth. Often they paid for that status in order to immigrate to the United States but they always knew their real family name. Estelle T. Lau, *Paper Families: Identity, Immigration Administration, and Chinese Exclusion* (Durham, NC: Duke University Press, 2006); Elliott Young, *Alien Nation: Chinese Migration in the Americas from the Coolie Era through World War II* (Chapel Hill: University of North Carolina Press, 2014). Young does not deal with entry through Hawai'i, which was also common between 1882 and 1898.

36. Norman A. Kutcher, *Mourning in Late Imperial China: Filial Piety and the State* (Cambridge, UK: Cambridge University Press, 1999), details this process. For a general background on Chinese cemeteries, especially in Los Angeles and El Paso, Texas, see Chou Li, "Heritage and Ethnic Identity: Preserving Chinese Cemeteries in the United States," *International Journal of Heritage Studies* 21:7 (2015): 642–59; and Juwen Zhang, "Falling Seeds Take Root: Ritualizing Chinese American Identity through Funerals," diss., University of Pennsylvania, 2001. Guangdong and its neighboring provinces of Guangxi and Fujian have several minorities, including the Kejia (aka Hakka), whose funerary traditions are different. They also settled in the American west but in smaller numbers prior to 1949.

37. Kongfuzi (Confucius), *Lunyu* [Analects], reprinted Taipei: Yiwen yinshuguan, 1970, 2, p. 2b. For an elaboration on the concept of *li*, see Mu-chou Poo, "Ideas concerning Death and Burial in Pre-Han and Han China," *Asia Major*, 3rd ser., 3:2 (1990): 25–62.

38. Ebrey, *Chu Xi's Family Rituals*, 70–152. See Sylvia Sun-Minnick, "Chinese Funeral Customs," *Golden Notes* 27:3 (Fall 1981), pamphlet, for variations in the funerary practices.

39. There are numerous works on federal and state legislation against the Chinese; see, for example, Erika Lee, *At America's Gates: Chinese Immigration During the Exclusion Era, 1882–1943* (Chapel Hill: University of North Carolina Press, 2003), and Hing, *Making and Remaking Asian America*.

40. "Chinese Funeral in California," *Farmer's Cabinet* [Amherst, NH], January 2, 1851; Sylvia Sun Minnick, "Chinese Funeral Customs," *Golden Notes* [Sacramento County Historical Society] 27:3 (Fall 1981): 1–15; and Zhang, "Falling Seeds Take Root."

41. "Chinese Funeral of Prominent Woman," *Daily True Delta* [New Orleans, LA], April 1, 1858.

42. "A Chinese Funeral Feast in Oroville," San Francisco *Daily Evening Bulletin*, April 20, 1858.

43. *Hartford Daily Courant* [Hartford, CT], December 27, 1871, from a San Francisco newspaper dated December 26, 1871. This is one of the early accounts that included the name of the deceased Chinese.

44. . From the Library of Congress; for the link, go to www.sfmuseum.org/loc/chinfuner.htm. The process for an ethnically Chinese from Southeast Asia is also described in detail

in Linda Sun Crowder, "Chinese Funerals in San Francisco Chinatown," *Journal of American Folklore* 115:450 (Fall 2000): 451–64, and in her chapter, "The Chinese Mortuary Tradition in San Francisco Chinatown," in Chung and Wegars, *Chinese American Death Rituals.*

45. Chuen-yan David Lai, "A Feng-shui Model," 506–13; Rouse in Chung and Wegars, *Chinese American Death Rituals.*

46. Andrew Ryall Briggs, "*Feng Shui* and Chinese Rituals of Death across the Oregon Landscape," M.A. thesis, Portland State University, 2002.

47. Nicolas J. Smits, "Roots Entwined: Archaeology of an Urban Chinese-American Cemetery," *Journal of Historical Archaeology* 42:3 (2008), 116.

48. For more information, see Janet Lee Scott, *For Gods, Ghosts, and Ancestors: The Chinese Tradition of Paper Offerings* (Seattle: University of Washington Press, 2007). Also see Terry Abraham and Priscilla Wegars, "Respecting the Dead: Chinese Cemeteries and Burial Practices in the Interior Pacific Northwest," in Chung and Wegars, *Chinese American Death Rituals.* For photographs of some burners, see http://webpage.uidaho.edu/special-collections/papers/burners.htm.

49. Timothy Y. Tsu, "Toothless Ancestors: Felicitous Descendants—The Rite of Secondary Burial in South Taiwan," *Asian Folklore Studies* 59:1 (2000): 13.

50. "Chinese Funeral in California."

51. On Qingming, see Yalom, *The American Resting Place*, 38, 250–52.

52. Roberta S. Greenwood, "Old Rituals in New Lands: Bringing the Ancestors to America," 252–53, in Chung and Wegars, *Chinese American Death Rituals.*

53. On Wong You, see C. Fred Blake, "The Chinese of Valhalla: Adaptation and Identity in a Mid-western American Cemetery," in Richard. E. Meyer, ed., *Markers X: Journal of the Association for Gravestone Studies* 10 (1993): 53; and Zhang, "Falling Seeds Take Root."

54. Patricia Ebrey, "Cremation in Sung China," *American Historical Review* 95:2 (April 1990): 406–28.

55. I am indebted to Candace Wheeler, PhD, for this information on metal markers that were on display at the Virginia City State Historical Preservation office and museum in 2014–16.

56. Blake, "The Chinese of Valhalla," 53–90. I am indebted to Professor Fred Blake for giving me a tour of Honolulu's cemeteries and bone houses.

57. Marlon K. Hom, "'Fallen Leaves' Homecoming: Notes on the 1893 Gold Mountain Charity Cemetery in Xinhui [Guangdong province]," *Chinese America: History and Perspective*, 2002, 36–50.

58. Linda Sun Crowder, "Mortuary Practices in San Francisco Chinatown," *Chinese America: History and Perspectives*, 1995, 33–46; Jonathan Richards, "Chinese Exhumations in Queensland, 1880-1930," in Gordon Grimwade, Kevin Rains, and Melissa Dunk, eds., *Rediscovered Past: Chinese Networks* (East Ipswich, AU: Chinese Heritage in Northern Australia, 2016), 76–84.

59. Communication with Professor Jinhua Selia Tan of Wuyi University, Guangdong, in Taiwan in 2013. See also Elisabeth Sinn, *Pacific Crossing*, 236.

60. This is detailed in Greenwood in Chung and Wegars, *Chinese American Death Rituals.*

61. James William Hefferon, "Bad Eye last of the CP Chinese workers left in Elko, Nevada," oral history of James William Hefferon, recorded and edited by John Eldredge, February 1, 1986, http://www.nps.gov/gosp/research/hefferon.htm, accessed March 19, 2001; no longer available in 2014. Hefferon left Elko in 1941. See also Charles Paul Keyser, "Reminiscences of Elko—circa 1890," Northeastern Nevada Museum, mss 4-6-30, dated October 1958.

62. On the Forestvale Cemetery, see Marga Lincoln, "Remembering China Row: Even in Death the Chinese Were Excluded," *Independent Record* (Helena, MT), May 24, 2015, based

upon Christopher W. Merritt, "The Coming Man from Canton, Chinese Experience in Montana (1862–1943)," diss., University of Montana, Missoula, 2010.

63. Yalom, *The American Resting* Place, 250. Chung and Neizman in Chung and Wegars, *Chinese American Death Rituals.*

64. See, for example, Jay P. Marden's account, "History of Winnemucca," based on the Winnemucca *Silver State*, mss, Humboldt County Library, Winnemucca, Nevada. Also available at www.cprr.org/Museum/Winnemucca_Marden.pdf.

65. Ross Burke Funeral Home, Reno, Nevada, records, Microfilm F849.C3 #48, 3 reels, Nevada State Library and Archives, Carson City, Nevada. See also the records of O'Brien Rogers Funeral Home, Reno, Nevada, for the period 1911–39, which handled thirty-three deceased Chinese, in the Nevada State Library and Archives.

66. *Humboldt Register* (Unionville, Nevada), 1870 statement quoted in Marsden, "History of Winnemucca."

67. Hop Sing Tong, National Archives and Records Administration, Immigration and Naturalization Service (INS), Record Group 85, Partnership Papers 12500/03–04, Box 1, Hop Sing Tong file (in Chinese and English).

68. In the 1970s while I was working in San Francisco Chinatown, I was able to survey one of these books in Chinese for those who were born in Taishan. What happened to the book after the death of Harding Chin, who was the director, is unknown.

69. David Chuenyan Lai was able to study the CCBA records in Canada. Those in San Francisco are not open to the public or scholars.

70. The Chinese Consolidated Benevolent Association (CCBA) originally consisted of six regional associations (hence the popular name "Six Companies") in San Francisco. The first of the six *huiguan* was established in 1849–51. The six *huiguan* united formally in 1882 and expanded to every major city and town in North America for social, economic, and political reasons. The CCBA acted as the intermediary between the Chinese community and the American community and government agencies. Its rival, the Zhigongtang (Chee Kung Tong or Chinese Free Masons) often challenged its power and was the most influential organization in rural towns. There is an abundance of literature on both organizations; see for example, Him Mark Lai, "Historical Development of the Chinese Consolidated Benevolent Association/ Huiguan System," *Chinese America: History and Perspective* (San Francisco, 1995), 13–51; Sue Fawn Chung, "The Zhigongtang in the United States, 1860–1949," in Wen-hsin Yeh and Joseph Eshrick, eds., *Empire, Nation, and Beyond: Chinese History in Late Imperial and Modern Times* (Berkeley: University of California Press, 2006), 231–49.

71. Hom, "'Fallen Leaves' Homecoming," 39.

72. I visited the Charity Cemetery in Xinhui with Marlon Hom and others in 2014.

73. Oral interview with Get Chor Chan of San Francisco in 1965.

74. Yong Chen, *Chinese San Francisco, 1850–1943.*

75. Jacob Long, "Deaths and Burials: The Final Frontier for Segregation," *First Coast News*, April 30, 2014.

76. The American racism expressed in cemeteries can be seen in segregated African American cemeteries; see Charlotte King, "Separated by Death and Color: The African American Cemetery of New Philadelphia, Illinois," *Historical Archaeology* 44:1 (2010): 125–37.

77. America was regarded as a "land without ghosts." See R. David Arkush and Leo O. Lee, trans. and eds., *Land without Ghosts : Chinese Impressions of America from the Mid-nineteenth Century to the Present* (Berkeley: University of California Press, 1989).

78. In the 1930s historian Thomas Chinn of San Francisco visited the cemetery and noted that there were over thirty markers still visible in his essay, "Observations 1935–1942," *Chinese Historical Society of America* 7 (1972): 6–8. This indicated that the bodies were not exhumed.

When a medical complex was under construction, the coffin and skeletal remains of one individual was uncovered but the owner of the property would not allow archaeologists to search for others.

79. This information on Bakersfield is based upon Gilbert Gia, "What Happened to the Chinese Cemetery?" 2002, www.gilbertgia.com.

80. Samuel I. Couch, "Topophilia and Chinese Miners: Place Attachment in North Central Idaho," diss., University of Idaho, 1996, 203.

81. On Quong Kee, see Opie Rundle Burgess, "Quong Kee: Pioneer of Tombstone," *Arizona Highways* 25:7 (July 1949): 14–16; Lawrence W. Cheek, "A Place Called Bisbee," *Arizona Highways* 65:2 (February 1989): 4–11.

82. Sue Fawn Chung, "Between Two Worlds: Ah Cum Kee (1876–1929) and Loy Lee Ford (1882–1921)," in Kriste Lindenmeyer, ed., *Ordinary Women, Extraordinary Lives: A History of Women in America* (Delaware: Scholarly Resources, 2000), 179–95; and "The Anti-Chinese Movement in Tonopah, Nevada," *Chinese America: History and Perspectives 2003* (San Francisco: Chinese Historical Society of America, 2003), 35–45. Recent scholarship has challenged the old Robert Park Chicago School of Sociology that the Chinese did not make efforts to adapt, acculturate, and assimilate. The Billy Min Chung Ford family and the better known See Fong family (see Lisa See, *On Gold Mountain*, New York: St. Martin's Press, 1995) were examples of late nineteenth-century families that acculturated and moved in the direction of assimilation or, to use another definition of Americanization, being integrated into American society and culture while retaining some ethnic distinctiveness as seen in food, language, filial piety, dress, and funerary rituals.

83. http://www.bendbulletin.com/lifestyle/3318763-151/john-days-chinese-heritage#.

84. Nicolas J. Smits, "Roots Entwined," 111–22.

85. I am indebted to Ted Gong of Washington, DC, for this information. Like many "empty" Chinese cemeteries because of the repatriation of the deceased, Range 99 has become an area of mediation and contemplation.

86. Carlin, Nevada's *Siyi* (Four Counties, Guangdong) cemetery studies include Ryan William Schmidt, "The Forgotten Chinese Cemetery of Carlin, Nevada: A Bioanthropological Assessment," M.A. thesis, University of Nevada, Las Vegas, 2001; and Ryan P. Harrod and John J. Crandall, "Rails Built of the Ancestor's Bones: The Bioarchaeology of the Overseas Chinese Experience," *Journal of Historical Archaeology*, 49:1 (February 2015): 148–61.

87. Thomas Gardner, "Nevadan unearths link to past in backyard: 13 graves," *Deseret News* (Utah), November 27, 1997.

88. See, for example, Schmidt, "The Forgotten Chinese Cemetery of Carlin, Nevada."

89. Oral interview with the late Shirlaine Kee Baldwin, who enlisted the help of archaeologists Fred P. Frampton and Susan Silver to find the gravesite in 2008. Silver sent me a copy of their unpublished report.

90. Drew A. Penned, "Cumberland Digs Deep into Genealogy to Keep Chinese, Japanese Cemeteries Open," *Comoros Valley Echo*, Cumberland, Courtenay, British Columbia, October 7, 2014.

91. David Pierson, "Reminders of Bigotry Unearthed," *Los Angeles Times*, March 15, 2006.

92. "Chinese Laborers Finally Rest in Peace," *Los Angeles Times*, September 5, 2010. For more details on Evergreen Cemetery, see Chou Li, "Heritage and Ethnic Identity," 648–51.

93. Doug Smith and Ryan Menezes, "Evergreen Cemetery Is Awash in History and Drowning in Blight," *Los Angeles Times*, February 2, 2016.

94. Harding Chin, "Cemeteries in San Francisco, 1776–1900," and "Golden Hills Memorial Park: A Traditional Chinese Cemetery in Colma, California," n.p., n.d. Harding Chin was a good friend of H. K. Wong, who introduced us. He was in charge of the Chinese Cemetery

Association in San Francisco until his death and gave me these pamphlets. See also Tamara Venit Shelton, "Unmaking Historic Spaces: Urban Progress and the San Francisco Cemetery Debate, 1895–1937," *California History* 85:2 (2008): 26–47, 69–70.

95. *Yreka Journal*, August 22, 1877.

96. Chuck Chiang, "Barkerville's Chinese Cemetery Attracts New Investment," *Vancouver Sun*, January 22, 2016.

97. Dena Mellick, "Unearthing History in a Kirkwood Cemetery [in DeKalb County]," newspaper article dated October 29, 2014, on the Kirkwood cemetery that was integrated between as early as 1956 and 1958; www.decaturisb.com/2014/10. She gives the federal mandate date as 1976 but the National Funeral Directors Association had adopted the policy of integration as early as the 1960s with the recognition that it was hard to enforce.

98. There is an abundance of literature on Chinese festivals. See, for example, Jacqueline S. Thursby, *Funeral Festivals in America: Rituals for the Living*, Lexington, KY: University of Kentucky Press, 2006.

99. See also Shelton, "Understanding Historic Spaces."

100. Communication with Janwyn Funamura of the Stockton Confucian Center, 2014.

101. Jonathan Kaiman, "In China, a Cremation Order Has Driven Some Elderly to Desperate Acts," *Los Angeles Times*, February 2, 2016; TechNode, "Funeral Platform Yiko Tackles High Cemetery Prices with 3D Printing," https://technode.com/2015/10/02/yiko-sets-foot-stagnant-chinese-funeral-industry-3d-printed-funerary-casket/, accessed October 2, 2015.

Bibliography

"A Chinese Funeral Feast in Oroville." San Francisco *Daily Evening Bulletin*, April 20, 1858.

Abraham, Terry, and Priscilla Wegars. "Respecting the Dead: Chinese Cemeteries and Burial Practices in the Interior Pacific Northwest." In Sue Fawn Chung and Priscilla Wegars, eds. *Chinese American Death Rituals: Respecting the Ancestors*. Walnut Creek, CA: Altamira Press, 2005, 147–74.

Abraham, Terry. "Urns, Bones and Burners: Overseas Chinese Cemeteries." *Australasian Historical Archaeology* 21 (2003): 58–69.

Anderson, John. "John Day's Chinese Heritage." http://www/bendbulletin.com/lifestyle//3318763-151/john-days-chinese-heritage#.

Anderson, Kay. *Vancouver's Chinatown: Racial Discourse in Canada, 1875–1980*. Montreal: McGill-Queen's University Press, 1991.

Arkush, R. David, and Leo O. Lee, trans. and eds. *Land without Ghosts: Chinese Impressions of America from the Mid-nineteenth Century to the Present*. Berkeley: University of California Press, 1989.

Blake, C. Fred. "The Chinese of Valhalla: Adaptation and Identity in a Mid-western American Cemetery." In Richard. E. Meyer, ed., *Markers X: Journal of the Association for Gravestone Studies* 10 (1993): 52–89.

Bloomfield, Anne. *Chinese Camp: Cultural Resources Inventory*. Sonora, CA: Tuolumne County Historic Preservation Review Commission, 1994.

Boyd, William Harland. *The Chinese of Kern County, 1857–1960*. Bakersfield, CA: Kern County Historical Society, 2002.

Briggs, Andrew Ryall. "*Feng Shui* and Chinese Rituals of Death across the Oregon Landscape." M.A. thesis, Portland State University, 2002.

Bromley, Isaac Hill. *The Chinese Massacre at Rock Springs, Wyoming Territory, September 2, 1885*. Boston: Franklin Press, 1886.

Burgess, Opie Rundle. "Quong Kee: Pioneer of Tombstone." *Arizona Highways* 25:7 (July 1949): 14–16.

Carson, Scott Alan. "Chinese Sojourn Labor and the American Transcontinental Railroad." *Journal of Institutional and Theoretical Economics* 161:1 (March 2005): 80–102.

Central Pacific Railroad Company. Payroll Record for January-June 1864. California Railroad Museum, Sacramento, MS 79. Hard copies and microfilm with index.

Chace, Paul G. "On Dying American: Cantonese Rites for Death and Ghost Spirits in an American City." In Sue Fawn Chung and Priscilla Wegars, eds., *Chinese American Death Rituals: Respecting the Ancestors*. Walnut Creek, CA: Altamira Press, 2005, 47–80.

Chan, Sucheng. *Asian Americans: An Interpretive History*. Boston: Twayne, 1991.

Cheek, Lawrence W. "A Place Called Bisbee." *Arizona Highways* 65:2 (February 1989): 4–11.

Chen Guoqing and Zhang Keping, eds. *Zeng Guofan Quanji* [The Complete Works of Zeng Guofan]. Xian, China: Xibei Daixue Chubanshe, 1994.

Chen, Yong. *Chinese San Francisco, 1850–1943: A Trans-Pacific Community*. Stanford, CA: Stanford University Press, 2000.

Chiang, Chuck. "Barkerville's Chinese Cemetery Attracts New Investment." *Vancouver Sun*, January 22, 2016.

"Chinese Funeral in California." *Farmer's Cabinet* (Amherst, NH), January 2, 1851.

"Chinese Funeral of Prominent Woman." *Daily True Delta* (New Orleans, LA), April 1, 1858.

Chinese in Northwest America Research Committee. "Death: Chinese in Early Northwest America." http://www.cinarc.org/Death.htm.

Chinn, Thomas. "Observations 1935–1942." *Chinese Historical Society of America* 7 (1972): 6–8.

Chung, Sue Fawn, and Priscilla Wegars, eds. *Chinese American Death Rituals: Respecting the Ancestors*. Walnut Creek, CA: Altamira Press, 2005.

Chung, Sue Fawn, Fred P. Frampton, and Timothy W. Murphy. "Venerate These Bones: Chinese American Funerary and Burial Practices as Seen in Carlin, Elko County, Nevada." In Chung and Wegars, 107–46.

Chung, Sue Fawn. "Between Two Worlds: Ah Cum Kee (1876–1929) and Loy Lee Ford (1882–1921)." In Kriste Lindenmeyer, ed., *Ordinary Women, Extraordinary Lives: A History of Women in America*. Wilmington, DE: Scholarly Resources, 2000, 179–95.

Chung, Sue Fawn. "The Anti-Chinese Movement in Tonopah, Nevada." *Chinese America History and Perspectives 2003*. San Francisco: Chinese Historical Society of America, 2003, 35–45.

Chung, Sue Fawn. "The Zhigongtang in the United States, 1860–1949." In Wen-hsin Yeh and Joseph Eshrick, eds., *Empire, Nation, and Beyond: Chinese History in Late Imperial and Modern Times*. Berkeley: University of California Press, 2006, 231–49.

Chung, Sue Fawn. *In Pursuit of Gold: Chinese American Miners and Merchants in the American West*. Urbana: University of Illinois Press, 2011.

Chung, Sue Fawn. *Chinese in the Woods: Logging and Lumbering in the American West*. Urbana: University of Illinois Press, 2015.

Cohen, Lucy M. "The Chinese of the Panama Railroad: Preliminary Notes on the Migrants of 1854 Who 'Failed.'" *Ethnohistory* 18:4 (Autumn 1971): 309–20.

Couch, Samuel I. "Topophilia and Chinese Miners: Place Attachment in North Central Idaho." Diss., University of Idaho, 1996.

Cox, Thomas R. *Mills and Markets: A History of the Pacific Coast Lumber Industry to 1900*. Seattle: University of Washington Press, 1974.

Crowder, Linda Sun. "Chinese Funerals in San Francisco Chinatown." *Journal of American Folklore* 115:450 (Fall 2000): 451–64.

Crowder, Linda Sun. "The Chinese Mortuary Tradition in San Francisco Chinatown." In Chung and Wegars, 195–240.

Crowder, Linda Sun. "Mortuary Practices in San Francisco Chinatown." *Chinese America: History and Perspectives 1995.* San Francisco: Chinese Historical Society of America, 1995, 33–46.

Crowder, Linda Sun, and Jonathan Richards. "Chinese Exhumations in Queensland, 1880–1930." In Gordon Grimwade, Kevin Rains, and Melissa Dunk, eds., *Rediscovered Past: Chinese Networks.* East Ipswich, AU: Chinese Heritage in Northern Australia, 2016, 76–84.

Daniels, Roger, *Asian America: Chinese and Japanese in the United States since 1850.* Seattle: University of Washington Press, 1988.

Ebrey, Patricia. *Chu Xi's Family Rituals.* Princeton, NJ: Princeton University Press, 1991.

Ebrey, Patricia, ed. *Confucianism and Family Rituals in Imperial China.* Princeton, NJ: Princeton University Press, 1991.

Ebrey, Patricia. "Cremation in Sung China." *American Historical Review* 95:2 (April 1990): 406–28.

Ebrey, Patricia. "The Response of the Sung State to Popular Funeral Practices." in Ebrey, *Confucianism and Family Rituals in Imperial China,* 209–40.

Gardner, Thomas. "Nevadan unearths link to past in backyard: 13 graves." *Deseret News* (Utah), November 27, 1997.

Gia, Gilbert. "What Happened to the Chinese Cemetery?" 2002, www.gilbertgia.com.

Greenwood, Roberta S. "Old Rituals in New Lands: Bringing the Ancestors to America." In Chung and Wegars, 241–60.

Gregory, Peter N., ed. *Religion and Society in T'ang and Sung China.* Honolulu: University of Hawai'i Press, 1993.

Gudde, Erwin G. *California Gold Camps: A Geographical and Historical Dictionary of Camps, Towns, and Localities Where Gold Was Found and Mined; Wayside Stations and Trading Centers.* Berkeley: University of California Press, 1975.

Gyory, Andrew. *Closing the Gate: Race, Politics and the Chinese Exclusion Act.* Chapel Hill: University of North Carolina Press, 1998.

Harrod, Ryan P., and John J. Crandall. "Rails Built of the Ancestor's Bones: The Bioarchaeology of the Overseas Chinese Experience." *Journal of Historical Archaeology* 49:1 (February 2015): 148–61.

Hefferon, James William. "Bad Eye last of the CP Chinese workers left in Elko, Nevada." Oral history of James William Hefferon, recorded and edited by John Eldredge, February 1, 1986. http://www.nps.gov/gosp/research/hefferon.htm, accessed March 19, 2001; no longer available in 2014.

Hing, Bill On. *Making and Remaking Asian America through Immigration Policy, 1850–1990.* Stanford, CA: Stanford University Press, 1993.

Hom, Marlon K. "'Fallen Leaves' Homecoming: Notes on the 1893 Gold Mountain Charity Cemetery in Xinhui [Guangdong province]." *Chinese America: History and Perspective 2002.* San Francisco: Chinese Historical Society of America, 2002, 36–50.

Hop Sing Tong. Record Group 85, Partnership Papers 12500/03–04, Box 1, Hop Sing Tong file (in Chinese and English). National Archives and Records Administration, Immigration and Naturalization Service (INS).

Hsu, Madeline. *Dreaming of Gold, Dreaming of Home: Transnationalism and Migration between the United States and South China, 1882–1943.* Stanford, CA: Stanford University Press, 2000.

Huffman, Wendell. "Iron and Steel: How the Comstock Determined the Course of the Central Pacific Railroad." *Nevada Historical Society Quarterly* 50:1 (2007): 3–35.

Huffman, Wendell: "Iron Horse along the Truckee: The Central Pacific Railroad Reaches Nevada." *Nevada Historical Society Quarterly* 38:1 (1995): 19–36.

Kaiman, Jonathan. "In China, a Cremation Order Has Driven Some Elderly to Desperate Acts." *Los Angeles Times*, February 2, 2016.

Kanazawa, Mark. "Immigration, Exclusion, and Taxation: Anti-Chinese Legislation in Gold Rush California." *Journal of Economic History* 65:3 (2005): 779–805.

Keyser, Charles Paul. "Reminiscences of Elko—circa 1890." Northeastern Nevada Museum, mss 4-6-30, dated October 1958.

King, Charlotte. "Separated by Death and Color: The African American Cemetery of New Philadelphia, Illinois." *Historical Archaeology* 44:1 (2010): 125–37.

Kongfuzi (Confucius). *Lunyu* [Analects]. Taipei: Yiwen yinshuguan, 1970, vol. 2: 2b.

Kraus, George. *High Road to Promontory: Building the Central Pacific (Now Southern Pacific) across the High Sierra.* New York: Castle Books, 1969.

Kutcher, Norman A. *Mourning in Late Imperial China: Filial Piety and the State.* Cambridge, UK: Cambridge University Press, 1999.

Lai, Chuen-yan David. "A Feng-shui Model as Location Index." *Annals of the Association of American Geographers* 64:4 (December 1974): 506–13.

Lai, Him Mark. "Historical Development of the Chinese Consolidated Benevolent Association/ Huiguan System." *Chinese America: History and Perspectives 1995.* San Francisco: Chinese Historical Society of America, 1995, 13–51.

Lau, Estelle T. *Paper Families: Identity, Immigration Administration, and Chinese Exclusion.* Durham, NC: Duke University Press, 2006.

Lee, Erika. *At America's Gates: Chinese Immigration during the Exclusion Era, 1882–1943.* Chapel Hill: University of North Carolina Press, 2003.

Lee, Erika. *The Making of Asian America: A History.* New York: Simon and Schuster, 2015.

Li, Chou. "Heritage and Ethnic Identity: Preserving Chinese Cemeteries in the United States." *International Journal of Heritage Studies* 21:7 (2015): 642–59.

Long, Jacob. "Deaths and Burials: The Final Frontier for Segregation." *First Coast News*, April 30, 2014.

MacKay, Donald. *The Lumberjacks.* Toronto: McGraw-Hill Ryerson, 1978.

Marden, Jay P. "A History of Winnemucca." Typewritten mss, Humboldt County Library, Winnemucca, Nevada.

Mellick, Dena. "Unearthing History in a Kirkwood Cemetery [in DeKalb County]." Newspaper article dated October 29, 2014, www.decaturisb.com/2014/10.

Merritt, Christopher W. "The Coming Man from Canton, Chinese Experience in Montana (1862–1943)." Diss., University of Montana, Missoula, 2010.

Minnick, Sylvia Sun. "Chinese Funeral Customs." *Golden Notes* [pamphlet, Sacramento County Historical Society] 27:3 (Fall 1981): 1–15.

O'Brien Rogers Funeral Home, Reno, Nevada for the period 1911–39, Microfilm #1598453, 1–5, Nevada State Library and Archives, Carson City, Nevada.

Pfaelzer, Jean. *Driven Out: The Forgotten War Against Chinese Americans.* New York: Random House, 2007.

Pierson, David. "Reminders of Bigotry Unearthed." *Los Angeles Times*, March 15, 2006.

Poo, Mu-chou. "Ideas Concerning Death and Burial in Pre-Han and Han China." *Asia Major*, 3rd ser., 3:2 (1990): 25–62.

Quimby, George I. "Culture Contact on the Northwest Coast, 1785–1795." *American Anthropologist*, New Series, 50:2 (April–June 1948): 247–55.

Rohe, Randall. "Chinese Mining and Settlement at the Lava Beds, California." *Mining History Journal* (1996): 51–60.

Ross Burke Funeral Home, Reno, Nevada records, Microfilm F849.C3 #48, 3 reels, Nevada State Library and Archives, Carson City, Nevada.

Rouse, Wendy. "'What We Didn't Understand': A History of Chinese Death Ritual in China and California." In Chung and Wegars, 19–47.

Schmidt, Ryan William. "The Forgotten Chinese Cemetery of Carlin, Nevada: A Bioanthropological Assessment." M.A. thesis, University of Nevada, Las Vegas, 2001.

Scott, Janet Lee. *For Gods, Ghosts, and Ancestors: The Chinese Tradition of Paper Offerings.* Seattle: University of Washington Press, 2007.

See, Lisa. *On Gold Mountain.* New York: St. Martin's Press, 1995.

Shelton, Tamara. "Understanding Historic Spaces: Urban Progress and the San Francisco Cemetery Debate, 1895–1937." *California History* 85:3 (2008): 26–47, 69–70.

Sinn, Elizabeth. *Pacific Crossing: California Gold, Chinese Migration, and the Making of Hong Kong.* Hong Kong: University of Hong Kong Press, 2013.

Sinn, Elizabeth. "Pacific Ocean: Highway to Gold Mountain, 1850–1900." *Pacific Historical Review* 83:2, Special Issue: Conversations on Transpacific History (May 2014): 220–37.

Smits, Nicolas J. "Roots Entwined: Archaeology of an Urban Chinese-American Cemetery." *Journal of Historical Archaeology* 42:3 (2008): 111–22.

Tchen, John Kuo Wei, and Dylan Yates, eds. *Yellow Peril!: An Archive of Anti-Asian Fear.* New York: Random House, 2014.

TechNode. "Funeral Platform Yiko Tackles High Cemetery Prices with 3D Printing." https://technode.com/2015/10/02/yiko-sets-foot-stagnant-chinese-funeral-industry-3d-printed-funerary-casket/, October 2, 2015.

Thursby, Jacqueline S. *Funeral Festivals in America: Rituals for the Living.* Lexington: University of Kentucky Press, 2006.

Tsu, Timothy Y. "Toothless Ancestors: Felicitous Descendants—The Rite of Secondary Burial in South Taiwan." *Asian Folklore Studies* 59:1 (2000): 1–22.

United States National Archives and Records Administration. Census Manuscripts, Microfilm for years 1850–1930. [Hereafter abbreviated *Census Manuscripts.*]

Watson, James, and Evelyn Rawski, eds. *Death Ritual in Late Imperial and Modern China.* Berkeley: University of California Press, 1988.

Yalom, Marilyn. *The American Resting Place: Four Hundred Years of History through Our Cemeteries and Burial Grounds.* Boston: Houghton Mifflin, 2008.

Young, Elliott. *Alien Nation: Chinese Migration in the Americas from the Coolie Era through World War II.* Chapel Hill: University of North Carolina Press, 2014.

Zesch, Scott. *The Chinatown Wars: Chinese Los Angeles and the Massacre of 1871.* New York: Oxford University Press, 2012.

Zhang, Juwen. "Falling Seeds Take Root: Ritualizing Chinese American Identity through Funerals." Diss., University of Pennsylvania, 2001.

Chapter Four

Founding Baltimore's Mount Auburn Cemetery and Its Importance to Understanding African American Burial Rights

—KAMI FLETCHER

"Aint She Got No People?"
—*Afro-American*, May 14, 1910

"Aint she got no people?" was a single question thrust from a crowd of gatherers as they watched an African American woman carted off to Potter's Field in Baltimore, Maryland.[1] There were neither family nor friends in the funeral procession. There was only immediate empathy for the loneliness of the deceased for *someone* to claim and spare this woman from the Potter's Field and to give her a decent, proper, and respectable burial. The worry for the deceased also included anger at the presumed lack of predeath care preparation. The onlooker commented that with the numerous African American benevolent societies and insurance companies, Potter's Field, a burial ground for the poor, should not still be an option for "our people" in 1910. Since its inception in the late 1700s, Potter's Field represented the seemingly invisible, yet extremely oppressed life African Americans lived on Earth. Being carted off in the city's dead wagon to Potter's Field was the equivalent to being buried, as one writer of Baltimore cemetery history put it, "without roots—unknown, unmissed, and unmourned."[2] Buried four to a lot in numbered graves, decedents were separated from their kin, highlighting the importance for African Americans to assert burial rights and establish a burying ground of their own.

The onlooker's question emphasized an important point about how burial signified social connection for African Americans and, perhaps more importantly, allowed for members of the collective black community to demonstrate the social worth of every member. Understood within the context of nine-teenth- and twentieth-century black culture and life, the question points to the interconnectedness of the black community and how this connection pushed the idea for an autonomously black burial ground in Baltimore. In 1807 the original seven trustees of the African Methodist Episcopal Church (present-day Sharp Street Memorial United Methodist Church, hereafter referred to as "Sharp Street Church") established Baltimore's African Burying Ground, which actualized black autonomy in death. It gave black Baltimoreans a proper and respectable burial and spared them from the Potter's Field, which was viewed as a less than satisfactory option for interment throughout the nineteenth and twentieth centuries when it was operational.[3] The founding of Baltimore's Afri-can Burying Ground becomes a tangible cultural symbol exhibiting the impor-tance of autonomous black burial grounds, particularly in the nineteenth- and twentieth-century United States.

Sharp Street Church founded Baltimore's African Burying Ground for both its members and all African Americans in the city, both enslaved and free, because there were minimal burial options for African Americans. Whites had at least twenty-seven burying grounds from which to choose, and only three of them routinely interred African Americans: Fells Point (Methodist), St. Patrick's (Roman Catholic), and St. Peter's (Roman Catholic). Though still a church graveyard and not explicitly a public burial ground, this was the next best option because many more than just the deceased church members were buried there.[4] For example, in 1818 Sharp Street Church records listed fourteen deaths, while the city of Baltimore listed 105 interments into Baltimore's African Burying Ground.[5] By burying ninety-one free and enslaved people who were not Sharp Street Church members, Baltimore's African Burying Ground not only illustrated collective black activism for proper burial of African Americans but also challenged the necessity of Potter's Field for black Baltimoreans.

Black burial was further complicated by early eighteenth-century burial laws that privileged whites. In 1701 *An Act for the Establishment of Religious Wor-ship in this Province According to the Church of England* made the collection of vital statistics the responsibility of the parish minister recording all burials except "Negroes and Mulatoes." Colonial church officials were responsible for only white persons' interment records, which fastened a thick racialized bor-der around burial rights by denying them to black persons and people of color while simultaneously privileging white ownership of burial grounds and indi-vidual graveyards. Burial rights are an individual's legal rights to burial and entitlement to one's own burial lot, as well as the freedom to own and oper-ate burial grounds. African Americans believed that a culturally proper burial within a safe and protected burial ground was a basic human right whether enslaved or free.

Further still, while both enslaved and free African Americans in urban Baltimore were relegated to Potter's Field, the majority in rural Maryland counties were enslaved and interred, more often than not, within slave cemeteries. Therefore, the institution of slavery did more than omit the names of deceased persons of color from death ledgers. This land was purposefully separated from the white slaveholding family with visual markers of segregation, marble gravestones for white decedents within a stone gate enclosure but wooden markers for black decedents with only the trees and the creek to serve as physical boundary lines for the slave graveyard. The idea that the graveyard was owned by the very man who held one captive reinforced, like Potter's Field, the idea of African Americans unwanted and thrown away in death. Within the framework of black burial rights, they served to dismiss the idea of black burial as an act of respect performed by one's kin and sought to further dehumanize African Americans in death.

Black men and women of Baltimore fought to establish the autonomous African Burying Ground, land that carried and displayed black humanity and black freedom into the afterlife. How the burial ground started and changed throughout the nineteenth and early twentieth centuries was directly tied to the experiences and needs of the African American community. To this point the burial ground took four different forms: Phase 1: Baltimore's African Burying Ground (1807–39); Phase 2: Belair Burial Ground (1839–71); Phase 3: Sharp Street Cemetery (1871–1903); and Phase 4: Mount Auburn Cemetery (1903–present). The first phase emphasized African cultural continuity; the second eradicated delineation between free and enslaved; the third phase centered on economic growth and revenue sharing in Baltimore's collective black community; and the fourth phase sustained robust black business under Jim Crow segregation. The burial ground sprang from collective action to reject the pauper status placed upon African Americans.

Baltimore's African Burying Ground was significant and necessary because its development challenged laws and ideas about black burial rights and created a space where African Americans could be buried with dignity and integrity. The burial ground's development maps against an effort for autonomy in death that ultimately fueled cultural and financial autonomy for the collective black community. This chapter uncovers why establishing Baltimore's African Burying Ground was important to the African Americans of Baltimore. Framing the discussion around the urgent need for the African Burying Ground in Baltimore within the context of Potter's Field brings to the forefront the reality of burying grounds for African Americans before the nineteenth century—black decedents were unprotected and without burial rights. This discussion also allows for a fuller examination of how race was used as both a barrier and a privilege for burial rights during both the eighteenth and nineteenth centuries.

Furthermore, how the original seven trustees of Sharp Street Church led the charge for black burial rights will be highlighted.

PHASE 1: Baltimore's African Burying Ground (1807–39)

Prior to the founding of Baltimore's African Burying Ground, black persons were buried in both the East and West Potter's Fields, slave cemeteries, or a church graveyard—namely one of the two Catholic graveyards or the one white Methodist church graveyard where black interment was routinely documented. These burial grounds were not chosen by African Americans. Potter's Field and slave cemeteries were not even final resting places but unprotected places of last resort. In 1796 the city of Baltimore established East and West Potter's Field (to have one on each side of town), where workers buried the unclaimed dead four to a lot.[6] The bodies interred were only identifiable by a number on an "old piece of dry-goods casing."[7] Slave cemeteries established by the slaveholder on his land maintained a strict racial divide between black and white burials. The white burial ground had engraved marble headstones while the black side had wooden posts like at Morgan Hill Farm, owned by slaveholder Robert Day in Calvert County, Maryland. Slaveholder Thomas Owings, owner at the Meadows Plantation in Baltimore County, located slave burials on the plantation's outskirts within a thicket of trees along a stream.[8] As a result, burial rights became established for whites through graveyard ownership and burial site autonomy in ways in which they were constrained for blacks.

Enforced segregation through location and gravestones did more than just erect a border to visibly separate whites and blacks. The border signaled who to remember and who to forget. Tombstones etched with names, birth/death dates, and family lineage illustrated remembrance, whereas blank wooden markers were simply place holders signaling to the gravedigger that the spot was taken. The border also shaped the memory, dictating *how* the dead were to be remembered. Explaining memory, Pierre Nora said that "memory attaches itself to sites,"[9] meaning that memory was in the location of the graveyard as well as the location of the individual graves. Slave burials were to be remembered in relation to the white family's cemetery; African Americans were to be remembered in relation to whites, i.e., eternally as slaves. Landscape architect Diane Jones has said that slavery and landscape were inseparable, leaving enslaved persons to create African American cultural overlays that transformed the gravesites on the plantation into autonomous places where the soul was free, leaving the memory unshackled from slavery.[10] Therefore, a peculiar thing happened. Located on the edges of the planation but commonly found near the slave quarters amongst the woods, slave graveyards became autonomous black spaces. Enslaved blacks began to claim and even hold fast to these physical and metaphysical borders for protection and freedom. Archeologist and slave cemetery expert Lynn Rainville attributed black persons' claims of slave cemeteries to the legacy of "intellectual amber" embedded in historical African American cemeteries—black family history, black town history, and the history of black life were all preserved in the burial ground.

As common as history has made the slave cemetery, there were many Maryland slaveholders who did not formally establish these burial grounds. Within the 2009 Plantation Analysis commissioned by Prince George's County, Maryland, an archaeological dig was commenced that rediscovered 111 plantations where it was determined that thirteen had cemeteries and only two had slave cemeteries. What this clearly told us was that slave cemeteries were optional and many slaveholders simply opted out. Enslaved blacks were still buried, and still buried on the plantations where they were held captive, but with 1 percent of all 111 plantations establishing slave cemeteries, to use the Prince George's report as an example, just where on the plantation were they buried and who decided/controlled these interment spaces?

A critical eye to the border that surrounded slave cemeteries looks not just to the white slaveholders, because it was their personal property on which the enslaved were buried, but also to the black men and women who actually buried their loved ones. Death meant freedom to the enslaved and burial grounds were reminders of this freedom, which made them that much more important to black people. Perhaps the most poignant example comes from the slave narrative of brothers Lewis and Milton Clarke. In recounting a story about an enslaved man named George who was gifted a burial plot, not in the slave cemetery but in the fancy white slaveholding family graveyard, George replied, "I'm afraid that when the devil come take my master's body, the devil may mistake and get mine."[11] This statement proved that even if slaveholders initiated segregated burial, black people did not object to it because to them the burial border was a demarcation line between those who went to Heaven and those who went to Hell. Still, there were many accounts attesting to black persons interred at the foot of ole massa. Black people were after decision-making power in burial, and no matter how autonomous slave burial, the decision was shrouded in white supremacy.

Large slave plantations, common in Maryland counties, were rare in Baltimore city, leaving urban enslaved and free blacks alike buried mainly within East and West Potter's Field or at the mercy of one of the two burial grounds—St. Peters or St. Patrick's. According to early Catholic Church records in Baltimore, between 1793 and 1800 forty-eight "free mulattos," "mulatto slaves," "children of color," "French negroes," "negroes," "negro slaves," and "free negroes" were buried in either St. Peter's or St. Patrick's burying grounds.[12] In 1791 nearly a thousand black Roman Catholics rushed Baltimore's shores as refugees from the Haitian Revolution. One Mary Magdalene Harent was listed within the burial transcription as a "Mulatto from St. Domingo." Within these seven years, 69 percent of those buried were children, the oldest a fifteen-year-old Elizabeth "slave to Mr. Aubrey Jones." Only one adult male and four adult women were interred, one of whom was buried together with her ten-month-old infant. In seven years decedents were overwhelmingly children, which aligned more with mercy burials than black Catholics with rights to burial lots. Perhaps this, along with the Haitian refugees, was why St. Francis Xavier, the first African American Catholic Church in the United States, was established in Baltimore.

Therefore, when founding Baltimore's African Burying Ground in 1807, Sharp Street Church's seven original trustees used language in the deed ensuring that the burial ground would stay with the black Methodists and be utilized to benefit the collective black community. Burial numbers exponentially higher than those listed in Sharp Street Church's death ledgers suggest that they buried more than Baltimore's black Methodists in the African Burying Ground. As a result, Baltimore's African Burying Ground was not just deeded to trustees Jacob Gilliard, Richard Russell, John Sunderland, William Moore, John Mingo, Joseph Sollers, and Richard Matthew, but also their heirs and assigns. This is important because the deed was specific about the burying ground remaining in the care of the original trustees or their heirs. However, if this was not cement enough, the deed also provided a clause reverting ownership back to the original trustees of Sharp Street Church:

> whenever the . . . trustees . . . shall be reduced to the number of two by death, resignation, or any of the ceasing to be members of the said church, the surviving or remaining trustees shall and will . . . convey said premises . . . to names prescribed in a deed with James Carey to Jacob Gilliard and others for a lot of ground on which the African church has been erected.[13]

This land deed between the trustees and Francis Hollingsworth, a white merchant and devout Methodist, was never meant to revert back to the umbrella Methodist church and furthermore was not meant to inter anyone but Africans and people of color. On the surface, Hollingsworth, who sold a portion of his land to Sharp Street Church trustees, seemed motivated by Christian brotherhood, but this transaction came on the heels of black Methodists distancing themselves from white Methodists and forming the quasi-independent Sharp Street Church. Sharp Street Church was separate in worship, with an imposed white preacher as the head but operating under and subject to Methodist laws and guidelines. White and black Methodists had a strained relationship at the turn of the nineteenth century because African Methodists were now a)

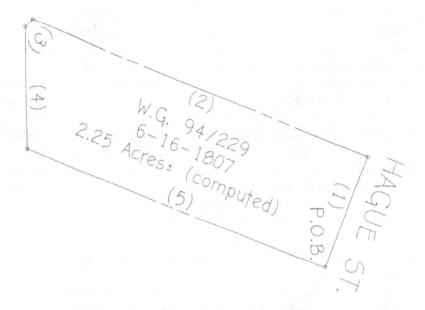

Figure 4.1 Computer-generated plat of Baltimore's African Burying Ground composed from the June 16, 1807, deed recorded by county clerk William Gibson in the Maryland Land Records book 94, page 229. Sharp Street Church purchased it for $690 from Francis Hollingsworth. Sometimes referred to as the Spring Garden Burying Ground because located within Spring Gardens section of Ridgely's Addition (South Baltimore), on the northwest side of Madeira Alley (now Madeira Street) and running along Hague Street (now Cross Street). It measures two and one quarter acres and eight square perches. 1 perch equals 16.5 feet.

segregated in seating and membership classes, b) with no decision-making power, and c) no possibility of having an ordained and autonomous black pastor over a church. In 1795 black Methodists approached Francis Asbury about their own autonomous church. This was around the time that black Methodists were becoming more and more discriminated against within the church.[14] The autonomous black church, then, resulted from white Methodists ridding people of color from church service, membership classes, and eternally through death. Hollingsworth's selling his land to African Methodists for the African Burying Ground can be read two ways: 1) it was in keeping with the segregationists' actions that plagued Methodists; 2) it was in keeping with the black autonomous spirit.

The seven trustees, who by Methodist law were in charge of any and all church-owned properties, were seeking not just to serve the Africans of Baltimore but also to obtain autonomy from the white Methodists.[15] By the time Baltimore's African Burying Ground was deeded, black Methodists had built their own church and school, establishing themselves as a spiritual and educational source for blacks in Baltimore including ownership of interment space. Death was a matter that was handled by family and religious orders, so once the African Methodists built and established their own church in 1802, it was not a surprise that five years later, in 1807, they established a burying ground. Baltimore's African Burying Ground was located within the city and, as stated specifically in the deed, "shall be for the use and benefit and serve as a burying ground for the Africans or people of colour of the precincts and the city of Baltimore belonging to and in communion with the society of Christians . . . the Methodist Episcopal Church in the United States of America."[16] The language in the deed outlined that the burial ground belonged to African Methodists and Methodists of color but was misleading. This language was used to signify ownership of the ground by the Methodists but arguably not to establish a religious border around the grounds allowing only black Methodist interment. The inclusive nature of Baltimore's African Burying Ground was seen very clearly in the numbers buried.

In addition, Baltimore's African Burying Ground was an autonomous burying ground bound not by Methodist laws and guidelines but by African cultures, customs, and norms. As illustrated by the numbers interred in 1818, for example, the African Burying Ground was a place where Africans and all people of color within Baltimore city could inter their dead according to their cultural beliefs, regardless of religious denomination. Although Methodist, many black peoples had not severed connections with their traditional African religion, merging these cultural beliefs with newly adopted Christian faith. According to the African religious scholar John S. Mbiti, African religion "is part of the [African] cultural heritage [and] has dominated the thinking of African peoples to such an extent that it has shaped their cultures, their social life, their political organizations and economic activities. . . . religion is closely bound up with the traditional way of African life."[17] This was illustrated with the twentieth-century gravesite of John Elijah Holsey Sr. (sampled not to project onto history, but instead to provide an alternate way for possibly seeing what African deathways at Baltimore's African Burying Ground looked like during this period). Holsey was born October 21, 1896, in South Carolina but moved to Baltimore to work as a caulker at the shipyard. As shown in figure 4.2, Holsey's brother visited his grave tombstone, wrapped the headstone in African cloths and hung jugs of water from the tree that shadowed it.[18] Inscribed on his headstone is "Baba Omo Kwaku–'Father of Kwaku' which means that the son buried his father. The headstone also reads in Yoruba, 'Praise God for lives forever' and acknowledges the city of Ife, Nigeria as the cradle of creation."[19]

African burial traditions are highlighted, reflecting present-day Mount Auburn Cemetery's cultural significance, specifically its ties to African cultural

Figure 4.2 Picture of John Elijah Holsey Sr.'s gravesite adorned with African fabric and bottles of water hanging on the trees behind. The grave marker reads "Baba Omo Kwaku," "Father of Kwaku" and "Praise God for lives forever." Courtesy of Dr. Diane Jones Allen.

death norms.[20] It is likely that Holsey's adorned gravesite maintains symbolism with early African American death customs practiced when Baltimore's African Burying Ground was operational. Mount Auburn Cemetery is among the fewer than 100 burial grounds nationwide where nineteenth-century African American death material culture was left and is still preserved today. This scarcity is a testament in that it provides ways of knowing and looking backward to historical African American deathways.

PHASE 2: Belair Burial Ground (1839–71)

Sharp Street Church saw itself as responsible for the burial rights of free and enslaved African Americans in and around the vicinity of Baltimore. This was illustrated clearly in the reasons for developing Belair Burial Ground. Seeking to combat the filth and disease within the city that caused mortality, in the 1830s burying grounds multiplied and were located in isolated wooded areas outside the city and called "rural cemeteries." Belair Burial Ground followed this reform with one important distinction—it sought to establish itself not as a brand new burial ground but instead as a continuation of the African Burying Ground. The trustees wanted what they described as a "more suitable place of burial," therefore disinterring all from Baltimore's African Burying Ground and rein-terring them in Belair Burial Ground.[21] Sharp Street Church trustees made it clear that Belair Burial Ground—two acres purchased for $533.33—would have more oversight and care from the church.[22] The church charged the survivors of the decedents with not taking care of the graves.[23] Sextons were employed to care for Belair Burial Ground—responsible for opening and closing graves and all general upkeep of the grounds. With this decision, Sharp Street Church answered with a resounding "Yes!" to the *ain't she got no people?* question.

Sharp Street Church determined to keep as many African Americans as pos-sible from becoming pitied Potter's Field decedents like the one witnessed by the onlooker in the chapter's opening. The solution: benevolent societies designed to help African Americans save up money for burial. The original trustees of Sharp Street Church organized and sponsored one of the earliest beneficial soci-eties in 1820.[24] Its purpose assured a decent burial and financial aid during sick-ness. By 1835 Sharp Street Church boasted of having "between thirty-five and forty benevolent institutions, both male and female, for mutual aid relief, each of which number[ed] from thirty-five to a hundred and fifty members."[25] In 1847 Sam Ware, a class leader in 1815, put forth a bill to incorporate a burial society called the "First John Mingo African Benevolent Society of Baltimore, named after John Mingo one of the original seven Sharp Street Church trustees."[26]

These benevolent and burial societies functioned like the many others dur-ing the nineteenth century. The only difference was that these organizations were founded by and for African Americans. Members pooled their money to make sure that all African Americans, not just members of these societies, had a proper burial, burial plot, and coffin. This meant that those African Americans who, on their own accord, could not afford to buy a burial lot in Belair Burial Ground could still do so and were not thrown away to the Potter's Field. In conjunction, Belair Burial Ground set aside a section of the cemetery, noted in the records as "Stranger's Ground" for those presumably not members of Sharp Street Church and too poor to pay for their own burial lot. Belair Burial Ground continued to foster activist activities that benefited the collective black community. Through this burial ground African Americans, free and enslaved, were able to maintain humanity and become free.

Sharp Street Church served as a meeting place for at least twenty benevolent and aid societies. Each offered autonomy and control over a portion of one's

Table 4.1: African American Benevolent Societies and African American Aid Societies	
1. 1st Abraham Lincoln Benevolent Society	11. Aged Men's Benevolent Society
2. Drayman Benevolent Society	12. Daughters of Paul Society
3. 1st Sharp Street Union Benevolent Society	13. Friendly Union Quarterly Society
4. Hannibal Benevolent Society	14. King Solomon Society
5. Brickmaker's Aid Society	15. Sharp Street Union Benevolent Society
6. Joseph Young Benevolent Society	16. Evening Star of Baltimore Society
7. Monumental Benevolent Society	17. Thomas Cooper Society
8. Double Beneficial Society	18. Philip Lee Benevolent Society
9. Sons & Daughters of Lincoln Benevolent Society	19. Henry Martin Benevolent Society
10. United Daughters of Ruth Beneficial Society	20. Old African Union Society

Note: List of twenty benevolent and aid societies started by and for African Americans. All of these burial societies rented out the hall inside Sharp Street Church to meet, organize, and strategize. Many of them used Christian Biblical figures and labor affiliations in their name signifying the makeup of their base, general membership. Others used "African" and "Abraham Lincoln" and names such as "Henry Martin" to illustrate their emancipated and African identity and, also, presumably, to pay homage to important black Americans. Source: Sharp Street Memorial Church Records, Reel 3114-6 Board of Trustees Cash Book, 1863–1873; classified ad, Afro-American, March 17, 1906.

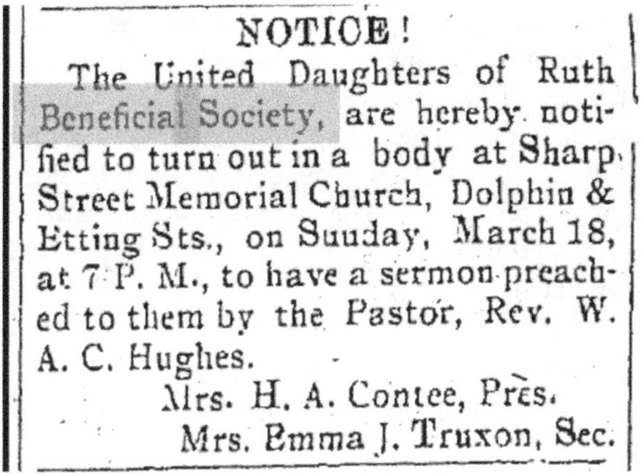

NOTICE!
The United Daughters of Ruth Beneficial Society, are hereby notified to turn out in a body at Sharp Street Memorial Church, Dolphin & Etting Sts., on Sunday, March 18, at 7 P. M., to have a sermon preached to them by the Pastor, Rev. W. A. C. Hughes.
Mrs. H. A. Contee, Pres.
Mrs. Emma J. Truxon, Sec.

Figure 4.3 Classified ad, May 17, 1906, taken out by the United Daughters of Ruth Beneficial Society, an African American burial society located at 1218 Etting Street, Baltimore. The society provided financial aid to the sick and paid financial costs for funeral and burial. At the time of this ad, 1906, the fee to join was four dollars with fifty cents monthly dues. Courtesy of the Afro-American newspaper.

life—his/her death. Around the mid-nineteenth century, benevolent societies such as the Joseph Young Benevolent Society and the Sharp Street Benevolent Society can be viewed in Sharp Street Church's financial records as collecting three and six dollars, respectively. In table 4.1, all of these societies were actively involved with Sharp Street Church. They frequently rented space in the Sharp Street Hall—a back room of the church—to hold classes and meetings and to strategize about fundraising. One dollar a month was charged for rent, and many societies rented space for three, four, and five consecutive months, while others chose to pay rent for the year. Benevolent society leaders took full advantage of Sharp Street religious services by meeting to discuss predeath care needs but also to receive a sermon by the Sharp Street Church pastor. The *Afro-American* ad (see fig. 4.3) illustrates how the president of the United Daughters of Ruth informed its members that they would have a sermon at their regular meeting.

PHASE 3: Sharp Street Cemetery (1871–1903)

Sharp Street Cemetery moved and developed during the Reconstruction Era. It moved to the southwestern portion of Baltimore County in December 1871 at the same time Hullsville, a black town, was also forming there. The institution of slavery had been abolished in Maryland in 1864. In the same year, the Rev. Benjamin Brown Sr. was assigned as the first African American senior pastor to Sharp Street Church as well as one of the first two African American preachers to be seated in the Methodist legislative body at their general conference that year. Life for African Americans in the United States as well as in Baltimore was seemingly improving. Sharp Street Cemetery was following this progress by helping to foster financial independence. Through savvy land-use ventures with sexton John F. Parker and German immigrant Peter Leiritz, Sharp Street Cemetery shifted from a service operation to a business enterprise, reaping profits while engaged in revenue-sharing with other black entrepreneurs in Hullsville and throughout Baltimore city.

Reflected in its new location, Sharp Street Cemetery restructured and became self-sustaining which allowed it to create jobs for those in the neighboring Hullsville. John F. Parker, likely a member of one of the thirteen families who founded Hullsville, was employed as sexton and later as the cemetery superintendent. As sexton he was listed receiving $320 for the year in 1882, which by 1899 had increased to $576 annually. He dug graves on a day-to-day basis and sodded frequently, filling in graves with dirt in order to even out the earth post-interment. The cemetery agent, the trustee who was responsible for actually selling burial plots, would leave written instructions on the official "Order to the Sexton" form on what type of grave to open (i.e., shoulder, grave for a child) and the time to open it. By 1885 a deal was made between Parker and the Sharp Street Church Board of Trustees allowing him to keep all profit from sodding. He was also fully responsible for his share of sodding costs, so in May of that year when the southwest corner of Sharp Street Cemetery was cleared and ploughed to grow grass, Parker paid six of the total twelve-dollar cost.[27] He then used his employed position to create a couple of side hustles: one in which he was paid fifty dollars to clear two acres of land of any trees and vegetation that would hinder the grounds from proper burials; and another in which he proposed renting out a cemetery dwelling built by himself and J. W. Henson (another Hullsville resident) specifically to the cemetery agents, to conduct lot sales and orders. Unfortunately, between his alleged alcoholism and boisterous political views, Parker became a liability to the Sharp Street Cemetery business and even to his own entrepreneurial efforts. He was issued a written grievance on January 1899 by both the trustees and the Citizens of Mount Winans for "making improper use of the cemetery to witness by using the same as a political headquarters and dispensing beer within its enclosure."[28] Combined with Parker's alleged bad management of the grounds, this caused future lot holders to start looking elsewhere, like John M. Camphor, who went and bought an eighty-one-dollar lot at Laurel Cemetery instead. This was one grievance filed against Parker, though, and appeared not to tarnish his decade-long employment with the cemetery and his influence with Hullsville and the greater Baltimore black community. Although he threatened to resign, he was never fired. At his death in 1901, Mount Washington residents petitioned with hundreds of signatures to have the flag flown at half mast in his honor.[29]

John Parker was not the only one who saw Sharp Street Cemetery as a viable business with which to partner and engage in revenue sharing. Hullsville resident Peter Leiritz had a similar story regarding revenue building. A German immigrant who came to Baltimore in 1854, Leiritz first rented unused land from Sharp Street Cemetery to build a family farm. From 1883 to 1886, Leiritz rented land to house his farm, all the while laboring elsewhere to save enough to own the land someday.[30] By November 1884, Leiritz paid forty dollars to Sharp Street Church Trustees, which equated to a year's worth of rent. At a special meeting in May 1885, Sharp Street Church Trustees decided that Leiritz's yearly rent would increase to forty five dollars per year and that he could only rent for three more years, further stipulating he uproot certain trees and vegetation to ready the ground for interment. Sharp Street bought eight acres back in December 1871 and had not cleared all the land of trees and vegetation, making it unsuitable for interments. As indicated in figure 4.4, the Sharp Street Cemetery (simply labeled "cemetery") bordered Leiritz's property that was a natural fit for their business ventures—similar to John Parker. By 1900 Leiritz owned, free from mortgage, a seven-acre farm in the town of Westport bordered by Mount

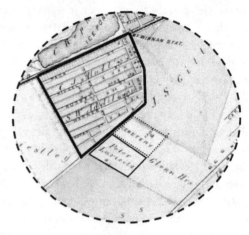

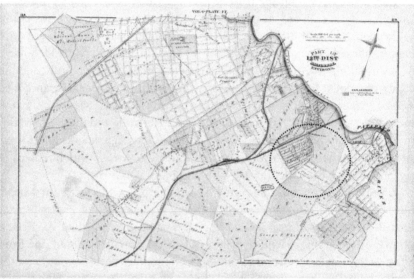

Figure 4.4 The 1876, Baltimore City, Hopkins Atlas, volume I, illustrating part of the 13th District of Baltimore, MD. The small broken-line circle on the map locates Hullsville, Sharp Street Cemetery, and Peter Leiritz's farm. The larger broken-line circle above the map is an enlarged version. The heptagonal shape is Hullsville, nineteenth century Black Town with land first purchased by philanthropist Charles J. Hull. Underneath the heptagonal shape are two rectangles. The solid lined rectangle is Peter Leiritz's farm. The dotted-line rectangle is eight-acre Sharp Street Cemetery. From Huntingfield Corporation Map, Collection of Maryland State Archives, George M. Hopkins, Cartographer, Published 1876. Courtesy of Baltimore City Archives and Maryland State Archives.

Auburn Cemetery and Hullsville.[31] In both cases, the aim was to own land and/ or dwellings in their quest for profit and stability.

Restructured with a professionalization influenced by the late nineteenth-century reform, Sharp Street Cemetery paved the way for many black people to become land owners. Unlike Belair Burial Ground and African Burying Ground before it, Sharp Street Cemetery was intentionally laid out and divided into six lettered sections—sections A–F, a total of 2,410 lots. Each of the six sections, surveyed and divided as subdivisions for housing, allowed black people to each become unconventional property owners. Everyone who purchased a lot received a deed stating the owner and its specific section and lot within the burial grounds that was signed by the president and the secretary of the Sharp Street Church Cemetery Board. Each deed was protected under an act passed during the 1832 session of the General Assembly of Maryland, which stated that the plot of land bought could be passed down to his/her heirs and assigns. As shown in figure 4.5, Isaac Downs bought two lots in section B in September 1872 and in September 1881 transferred one of the lots to his son, Lewis. In that same year and month, William Montgomery made the same transaction with his mother-in-law, Susan Nichols. Benevolent and aid societies, orphanages, and Sabbath Schools bought plots, sometimes two at a time. The tangible space of the burial lot added to the savings pinched away into the many benevolent societies. African Americans were shifting from reactively buying burial plots to participating in predeath care burial. Within the first three years of operation, Sharp Street Cemetery had sold about 20 percent of its total plots, with ten persons buying two plots at a time. Predeath burial purchases helped guarantee black people security and dignity in death. With the guarantee of their burial space, black women and men knew that their loved ones and themselves would be protected from the nameless lots in Potter's Fields. Opting to participate in predeath burial purchase allowed the black community autonomy, fostered independence, and provided true eternal rest.

Not only individuals but also an African American burial society, a religious school, and an orphanage bought lots at Sharp Street Cemetery. On January 20, 1875, Sarah Smitt purchased two lots on behalf of Baltimore's Orphan Shelter. The Sharp Street Sabbath School purchased a lot on July 14, 1880. On January 12, 1882, Mary Giles purchased two lots on behalf of the United Daughters of Ruth. The fact that these three organizations bought a total of five lots during the years of 1872 and 1885 may appear meaningless, but with forty African American benevolent and aid societies having direct ties to Sharp Street Church as early as 1835, it was not the number of lot sales but the fact that Sharp Street Cemetery maintained a relationship with these types of organizations and did so on purpose. Yes, Sharp Street Cemetery wanted to sell lots, produce revenue, and profit, but the point cannot be missed that as a burial ground

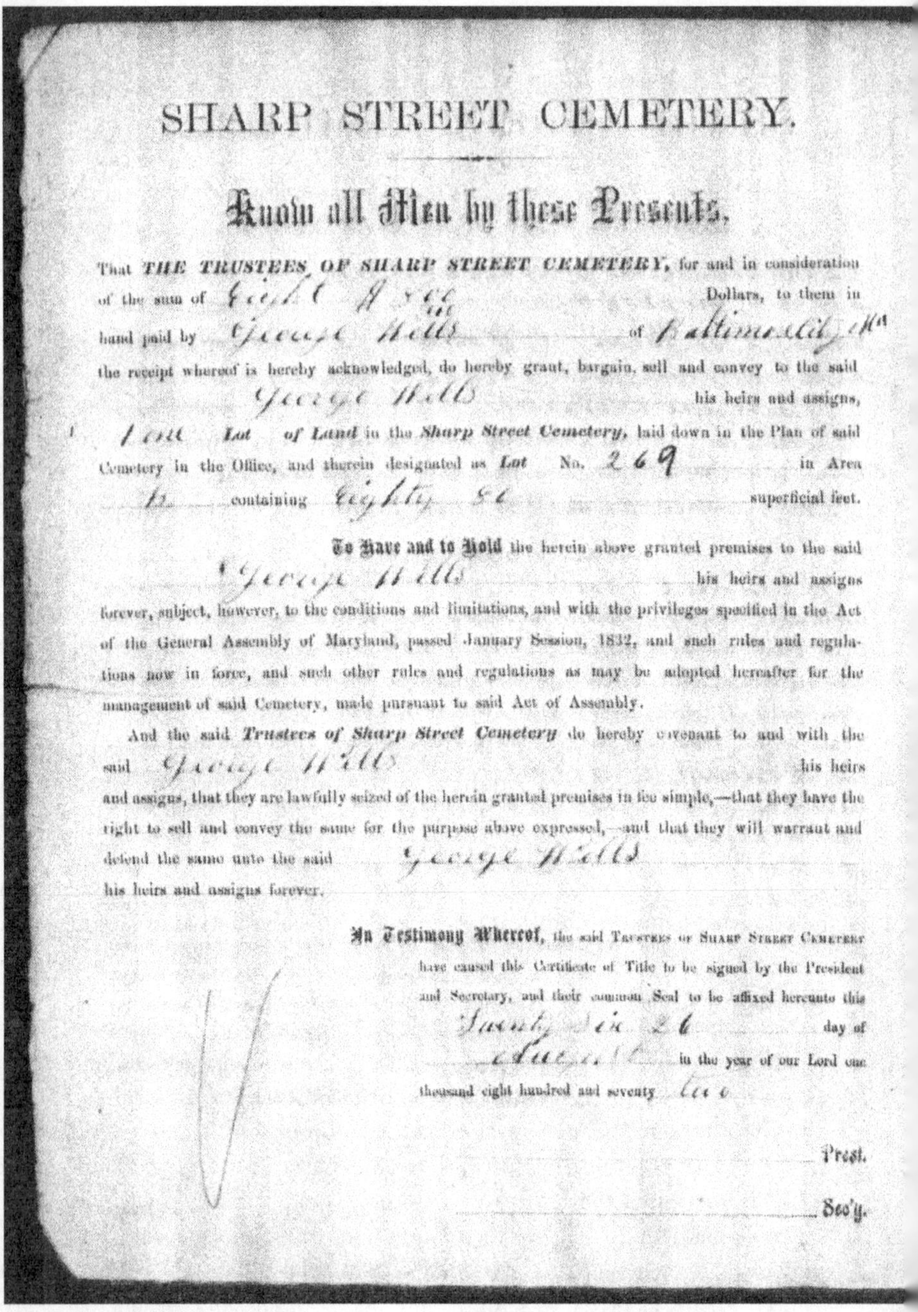

Figure 4.5 Sharp Street Cemetery deed belonging to Isaac Downs. Purchased lots 426 and 469 in section B of the cemetery for eight dollars each on September 4, 1872. Handwritten at top and at bottom left are notions that on September 26, 1881, Isaac transferred lot 426 to his son Lewis. From Sharp Street Memorial Church Records, Cemetery Lot Titles 1872–1885, Printed Forms for Deeds to Lots, Maryland State Archives, Maryland. Microfilm MdHR M 3114-1. Courtesy of Maryland State Archives.

[handwritten top margin] Stansford Lot 426 to his Son Lewis &

SHARP STREET CEMETERY.

Know all Men by these Presents,

That **THE TRUSTEES OF SHARP STREET CEMETERY**, for and in consideration of the sum of *Eight $ 8 00 each* Dollars, to them in hand paid by *Isaac Downs* of *Baltimore City Md* the receipt whereof is hereby acknowledged, do hereby grant, bargain, sell and convey to the said *Isaac Downs* his heirs and assigns, *2 care* Lot of Land in the **Sharp Street Cemetery**, laid down in the Plan of said Cemetery in the Office, and therein designated as **Lot**s No. *469 and 415* in Area *B* containing *one hundred and Sixty feet 160* superficial feet.

To Have and to Hold the herein above granted premises to the said *Isaac Downs* his heirs and assigns forever, subject, however, to the conditions and limitations, and with the privileges specified in the Act of the General Assembly of Maryland, passed January Session, 1832, and such rules and regulations now in force, and such other rules and regulations as may be adopted hereafter for the management of said Cemetery, made pursuant to said Act of Assembly.

And the said **Trustees of Sharp Street Cemetery** do hereby covenant to and with the said *Isaac Downs* his heirs and assigns, that they are lawfully seized of the herein granted premises in fee simple,—that they have the right to sell and convey the same for the purpose above expressed,—and that they will warrant and defend the same unto the said *Isaac Downs* his heirs and assigns forever.

[handwritten left margin] Isaac Downs Transfered 426 to his Son Lewis 4 Kept 415 for his Self G. W. Kilbourne Agt × 26/81

In Testimony Whereof, the said Trustees of Sharp Street Cemetery have caused this Certificate of Title to be signed by the President and Secretary, and their common Seal to be affixed hereunto this *Stewart 4th* day of *September* in the year of our Lord one thousand eight hundred and seventy *two*

_____ Presi.

_____ Sec'y.

founded to provide black people with safe and respectable burial, Sharp Street Cemetery wanted to be central to the burial aid and burial reform occurring in the city. For example, the United Daughters of Ruth Beneficial Society was one of the leading African American benevolent societies in Baltimore by the 1910s. In its published 1911 annual report, members reported paying out over $500 in sick and death benefits in 1910 and a net worth of more than $100, with an active membership roster of ninety-five women and men.[32] Furthermore, lodged within the Sharp Street Cemetery deed records was an 1883 Knights of Labor flyer for an August 1 picnic where founder Terrence V. Powderly and labor leader Henry George were scheduled to speak. The talk was given in English and German. Combined with their working relationship with Peter Leiritz, Sharp Street Cemetery was active in predeath care burial and the labor reform movement of the city, which suggests interracial efforts.

Therefore, through land ownership of their burial plot, death was used as a vehicle to freedom and cultural uplift. Whereas white supremacist practices, namely slavery and Jim Crow, barred the multitude of African Americans from land acquisition, the trustees at Sharp Street Cemetery stood ready to sell sections of their eight acres to two thousand black men and women. Sharp Street Cemetery was land designated for interment and memorial, but it was *land* none the less—land that black people could own all their own. In the United States land has historically symbolized freedom for African Americans. Land was the criteria for citizenship and political involvement. Land was the ticket to wealth building and brought prosperity that served as the promise of security for the next generation of African Americans. This burial plot of land was their legacy. It allowed these black women, men, and children to be remembered the way they wanted to be remembered in spite of the late nineteenth-century society that stereotyped and negated their full and three-dimensional lives lived with family and friends and enriched by civic clubs and community-building. Sharp Street Cemetery memorialized black people's kinship bonds and not their relationships to whites.

The cemetery eternally honored their work in the community when it went unnoticed in the larger society. With walkways named after prominent African Americans in the community, it promoted cultural uplift and racial progress. Between each section of Sharp Street Cemetery were seven walkways, and three were named after prominent African Americans in Baltimore: Peck, Brown, and Young Avenues. James Peck was pastor of Sharp Street Church (1868–69) at the time Sharp Street Cemetery (phase 3) was first developed and dedicated as "The City of the Dead for Colored People." Research suggests that Brown Avenue was named in honor of Reverend Benjamin Brown Sr., the first African American preacher of Sharp Street and first preacher in the history of the Methodist Episcopal Church to be seated in the law-making body of Methodism. Young Avenue was believed to be dedicated to Jacob Young, one of the

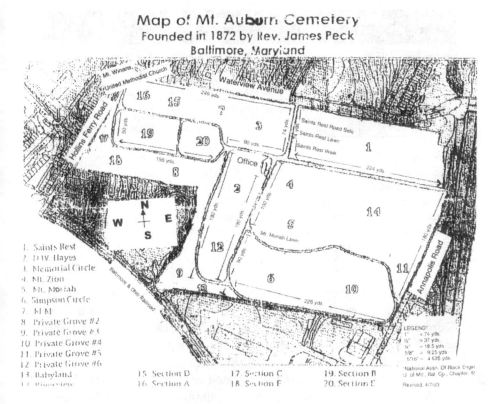

Figure 4.6 Survey of Mount Auburn Cemetery conducted by the University of Maryland, Baltimore County Chapter of National Association of Black Engineers. The surveyed land shows the twenty sections of Mount Auburn Cemetery. Sections A-E, eight acres, make up what Sharp Street Church purchased for $2,400 in December 1870 and called Sharp Street Cemetery. They purchased the rest of the land, twenty-six acres, in November 1880 for $7,743.75. This is the revised survey conducted April 7, 2003. Courtesy of Sharp Street Memorial United Methodist Church, Mount Auburn Cemetery Holding.

handful of African American preachers who petitioned the right to form the Washington Mission Conference that was the "first session of the Colored Conference of the Methodist Episcopal Church."[33]

This increase in lots led to a restructuring in staff and increase in revenue. Financial records from 1863 to 1871 list a Mr. E. Atkinson as the sexton. On May 19, 1863, he is listed as receiving a salary of $2.50. On August 8, 1864, he is listed as receiving $0.75 and $0.50 for digging graves and cemetery general maintenance. During this time period, Belair Burial Ground profited $279.60 a year with minimal repairs and service maintenance. In comparison, Sharp Street Cemetery lists John Parker with a paid salary of $320 for the year of

Table 4.2: Belair Burial Ground and Sharp Street Cemetery—Revenue and Expenses, 1867–1869

Belair Burial Ground				Sharp Street Cemetery			
Year	Revenue	Expenses	**Profit**	Year	Revenue	Expenses	**Profit**
1867	$237.96	$9.95	**$228.01**	1888	$2,813.74	$1,458.80	**$1,354.94**
1868	$229.10	$42.50	**$186.60**	1889	$2,374.59	$1,363.16	**$1,011.43**
1869	$371.75	$111.32	**$260.43**	1890	$2,925.96	$1,138.92	**$1,787.04**

Note: Revenues and expenses for three years are listed for both Belair Burial Ground and Sharp Street Cemetery. On the left, Belair Burial Ground (third phase) is a service operation having little expense and producing little revenue, not self-sustaining, but also suggesting that it was not a financial burden to Sharp Street Church. On the right is Sharp Street Cemetery (fourth phase) a business enterprise that has more expenses but produces much more revenue, suggesting it is self-sustaining. *Source:* Sharp Street Memorial Church Records, Reel 3114 Belair Burial Ground Financial Records.

1882. Furthermore, Sharp Street Cemetery received much more in revenue and extended more on expenses than Belair Burial Ground. Between 1874 and 1893, Sharp Street Cemetery received $66,783.96 in burial lot sales, lot orders, and vault rentals, which averages $3,514.95 per year. During this same nineteen-year time period, the cemetery accrued $25,288.25 in expenses inclusive to setting tombstones, sharpening/repairing tools, sexton assistants, and cemetery agents, which averages $1330.96 per year. Table 4.2 illustrates the yearly breakdown within a three-year time period. All in all, Sharp Street Cemetery was organizing into a separate business for the church.

Furthermore, as a burgeoning business, Sharp Street Cemetery implemented four rules and regulations regarding interment and vault rental at their respective prices. These regulations were just the tip of the iceberg. A key component to this rapid growth and development was not just the increase in burial lot sales and the introduction of the cemetery superintendent but the undertakers, a now present and necessary part of the cemetery. By 1885 there were twenty-four undertakers directly associated with Sharp Street Cemetery, making them a permanent fixture there. This was seen with continuous vaultage accounts. Ultimately, Sharp Street Cemetery was the true beginning of what would become Mount Auburn Cemetery, a place of racial pride and built heritage that was also a business and a financially sustaining entity.

PHASE 4: Mount Auburn Cemetery (1903–Present)

Jim Crow segregation created a border between twentieth-century black and white burial grounds that shaped how Mount Auburn Cemetery developed.

Figure 4.7 Picture of the opening entrance of Mount Auburn Cemetery in 2010. The left-hand side of the stone gate reads "MOUNT AUBURN CEMETERY" and "FOUNDED 1872 BY REV. JAMES PECK/SHARP STREET CHURCH MEMORIAL UNITED METHODIST CHURH" on the right-hand side. Rev. Peck was the head pastor of Sharp Street Church at the time of the initial establishment of this cemetery in December 1870. The founding date is listed as 1872 and not 1870 presumably to signal the year the first deeds were purchased and thus officially beginning use for burial. Photo taken September 16, 2010.

This was seen most clearly in the language used by the trustees of Sharp Street Church to advertise their new Mount Auburn Cemetery. It is noteworthy to point out that the cemetery was in the making six years before the land was deeded in July 1886 and eight years before it was resolved and named Mount Auburn Cemetery at the June 30, 1903, trustees meeting. In one of the first ads taken out in the *Afro-American* (December 19, 1903) to announce that Sharp Street Cemetery was now renamed Mount Auburn Cemetery, Sharp Street Church trustees make clear that the cemetery was fully available to African Americans. In part the ad reads: "It is now undergoing extensive improvements, which when completed, will make it one of the most beautiful cemeteries in the state that our people have access to." With the phrasing "our people" and "have access to," the ad called direct attention to the Jim Crow border that limited the geographical spaces for interring African Americans. Jim Crow segregation enforced racial segregation right down to death, creating racially bordered burial grounds where only whites could be interred or either "black sections" of white-only burial grounds. The ad then showed how Mount Auburn Cemetery planned to resist this border by swiftly building, fostering, and sustaining a cemetery that, from its foundation, was a space unequivocally for African Americans.

Arguably, having outside racial borders proved less crippling to Mount Auburn Cemetery, a burial ground founded upon the idea of black autonomous burial, one that ensured the safety, dignity, and memory of African American decedents. How can racial borders enacted to keep white decedents in white-only burial spaces affect this Afrocentric cemetery? The answer, of course, resides in white supremacy. However, Sharp Street Church trustees wasn't "studdin," as is the phrase in African American vernacular, racially bordered cemeteries especially since they had initiated and sustained a vital African American death community since the 1807 inception of Baltimore's African Burying Ground. The phrase "our people" and not just the generic "African American" expressed a closeness that black people shared with burial customs, a closeness that sheltered them from the storm of white supremacy. The phrase also signaled that Sharp Street Church leaders took full responsibility for owning and operating an Afrocentric cemetery. The "our people" was used to target exactly who they wanted in their cemetery and those they knew who wanted to be interred there. Sharp Street trustees ignored the racial biases and did what they had done since 1807—take care of their own. That self-help mentality, very common throughout the early twentieth century, allowed the trustees to focus on African Americans but also to make sure that black burial was meeting the current needs in ways to provide the best care.

In this way, perhaps, self-help worked in conjunction with black separatism allowing Mount Auburn Cemetery to build, develop, and prosper apart from the white supremacy that attacked it. The ad highlighted "extensive improvements," perpetual care, and that this new Mount Auburn Cemetery was "located on an elevation overlooking the Patapsco River"—all the components indicative of late nineteenth- and early twentieth-century cemetery reform. This period saw the introduction of the lawn-park cemetery, cemeteries constructed to resemble parks with open landscapes, uniform headstones and positioned as business enterprises. Black separatism, too, allowed Mount Auburn Cemetery to thrive as a business within a twentieth-century cash economy that was bordered by Jim Crow segregation. The separatism was not initiated by the Sharp Street Church trustees but instead created what August Meier called the Jim Crow market. With no competition, black cemeteries like Mount Auburn Cemetery cornered the market, resulting in heavy revenue flow and revenue sharing through the black Baltimore community.

As early as 1914, James F. Hall's Marble Company was based on the Mount Auburn Cemetery grounds. A one-story brick building constructed from his own hands and wallet, James Hall built a business that was later co-owned with his brother Charles. Hall, born 1877 in Tennessee, was working as a farm hand by age twenty-three; a few years later he decided to move to Baltimore, and by 1930 was an identified marble cutter who owned a farm and had in the last five years helped Mount Auburn Cemetery clear $50,000.[34]

Mount Auburn fostered and sustained other businesses and entrepreneurial ventures. It was steeped in black cultural norms but also one that saw its success connected to the growth and economic prosperity of the black community. Hullsville was first settled in 1896 by thirteen families from Sharp Street Church and was started as a result of the growing industry—Harrington & Mills Furniture Factory, Otto & Garrison's Moulding Factory, Millier's Safe Works, and a B&O Railroad yard. Seeing the industry and growth of this black town, Sharp Street Cemetery moved and rooted there. The cemetery created jobs for all involved with operating and maintaining the cemetery, most notably longtime cemetery superintendent John Parker. Between 1882 and 1888 the superintendent made a yearly salary of about $500. Moreover, Sharp Street Church started and organized a mission, Hullsville Mission, on cemetery land. With $7,500 of cemetery revenue, Hullsville Mission branched out on its own, built a new chapel, and became Mt. Winans United Methodist Church, which still stands today. The development of Mount Auburn Cemetery, including its services, goals, and daily objectives, were one and the same as that of the African American community. Mount Auburn saw its survival as one connected to its interpersonal relationship with the African American community.

Mount Auburn Cemetery was a business but stayed true to its original mission to service the burial needs of African Americans in and around Baltimore city. And because of this, Mount Auburn Cemetery found value in serving as a catalyst for wealth building in the African American community. Along with economic thrift was a self-help spirit among blacks at the time, which Mount Auburn Cemetery embraced. At the end of the nineteenth century and beginning of the twentieth, self-help among blacks was about African Americans helping themselves by helping each other. This was done by organizing church groups, benevolent societies, cooperative businesses, and most of all supporting black businesses. Black undertakers greatly benefited from this mode of thinking because, in a time where there was a segregated market due to social custom and Jim Crow laws, their clientele were members within the black community.

Conclusion

Ultimately, what came to be known as Mount Auburn Cemetery was once a simple two-and-one-quarter-acre burial ground. However, this burial ground changed and developed into a thirty-four-acre cemetery, generating revenue and serving as a cultural institution symbolizing the struggle and perseverance of African American people. The transition from the African Burying Ground to Mount Auburn Cemetery was grand but smooth. It followed the needs, social condition, and progress of the African American people. The first phase, the African Burying Ground, allowed autonomy and independence during the institution of slavery. It gave blacks the freedom to bury their own without the hand of white control. Blacks could openly and freely practice the burial rites of their African ancestry. The second phase, Belair Burial Ground, was another blow to slavery. It was fueled by benevolent and burial societies, societies organized to pay for proper burials inclusive to buying a coffin and digging a grave. The free black population in cities around the country was increasing; Baltimore was no exception. Free blacks were capitalizing on this strength in numbers, founding these societies and providing a way for their enslaved brethren to fight enslavement by buying property and controlling a part of their life: their death. Once slavery was abolished, the cemetery was transformed in its last two phrases, Sharp Street Cemetery and Mount Auburn Cemetery respectively. In these phases it became a place where African Americans asserted their citizenship, building wealth. The cemetery generated revenue for the black community by servicing black business, mainly black undertakers. Prominent African Americans in the community bought lots and were buried there, allowing it to serve as a cultural reminder of black perseverance during this long struggle for freedom.

The history of this burying ground is inclusive to the social and racial factors that developed, affected, and ultimately propelled the burying ground to develop over four phases. This first phase was not just another church graveyard but one that sought to inter all Africans and people of color in the city of Baltimore. Over its four phases, it increased in size and moved around the city. The burying ground's development was contingent upon the needs of the city and paralleled the life and culture of the African American community of Baltimore. The first phase reflected both the idea of burying grounds being located within Baltimore as well as enslaved African Americans yearning for freedom and autonomy. The second phrase is consistent with the move of burying grounds to the outskirts of town as well as a push for independence by the increasing numbers of free African Americans in Baltimore. The third and fourth phases parallel life during Reconstruction and Jim Crow segregation by first showcasing African American undertakers and their climb to success experienced during Reconstruction, and then illustrating African Americans' demand for citizenship during Jim Crow segregation with the creation of a lawn/park cemetery to showcase African Americans' historical legacy to the city.

Notes

1. Potter's Field was a burying ground established in order to combat the issue of unclaimed dead bodies that were becoming health hazards around cities. The burying grounds were called Potter's Field after its biblical namesake. Matthew 27:7 states that after Judas discarded the thirty pieces of silver he received for betraying Jesus, the priests retrieved the coins. Upon counsel, they decided to use the silver to buy the potter's field and make it into a "cemetery for foreigners."

2. Jane Bromley Wilson, *The Very Quiet Baltimoreans: A Guide to the Historic Cemeteries and Burial Sites of Baltimore* (White Mane, 1991), 99.

3. The reality of Potter's Field in Baltimore was that it was a burying ground with no physical or legal protection, and above all no respect. Generally speaking, there was a stigma attached to Potter's Field. From the 1890s through the 1930s, there were dozens of *Baltimore Sun* newspaper articles discussing the deplorable condition of Potter's Field. It said that the lots were not dug deep enough to keep dogs and mischief-making kids away. It was commonplace to have bodies that were supposedly interred in Potter's Field scattered across the city. In one case, a head was found in a cornfield that was miles away from its body still in Potter's Field. With no fence to keep desecraters out and the interred in, "body snatchers" frequently robbed the graves because they could sell the bodies to medical schools.

4. Until the establishment of public burying grounds, formal burial grounds were founded by churches that interred their members. Public burying grounds became the option but these were primarily for whites. The first of these, Green Mount Cemetery, was not incorporated by the General Assembly of Maryland until March 15, 1838; see Gerald W. Johnson and J. Hall Pleasants, *Green Mount Cemetery One Hundredth Anniversary, 1838–1938* (Baltimore, MD: Proprietors of the Green Mount Cemetery, 1938). Baltimore Cemetery followed almost fifteen years later, confirmed by Baltimore city ordinance in 1852. Neither routinely interred African Americans when established. Belair Burial Ground was founded in 1851 by three black businessmen—Frederick G. Hunt, Edward J. Richardson, and Sila M. Cochran—for the "colored people of the city and county of Baltimore"; see Clayton, Ralph and Alma Moore, "Laurel Hill Cemetery 1852–1958," *Flower of the Forest Black Genealogical Journal* (1984): 1–26. It was the first public burial ground that served as a protected and safe last resting space for any and all black women, men, and children. Yet, it would not become a real burial option for African Americans until later in the nineteenth century.

5. The Commissioner of Health of Baltimore, Maryland, *Baltimore City Health Department: The First Thirty-Five Annual Reports, 1815–1849*; Maryland Historical Society, 1953.

6. By 1920 West Potter's Field was commonly referred to as Cherry Hill Potter's Field, but by 1948 was no longer an active burying site. By the turn of the twentieth century, East Potter's Field filled up and was no longer in use. For more, see "Potter's Field Is Found," *Baltimore Sun*, August 23, 1917; "Desolate Potter's Field of Little Service Now," *Baltimore Sun*, January 5, 1908; Wilson, *The Very Quiet Baltimoreans*, 99.

7. "Batting Skulls Around Affords Amusement to Small Boys in Potter's Field," *Baltimore Sun*, November 5, 1924.

8. "Colonial Homestead: Thomas Owings' Stone Plantation House Remains Intact After Two Centuries," *Baltimore Sun*, December 6, 1981.

9. Pierre Nora, "Between Memory and History: Les Lieux de Mémoire" *Representations* (Spring 1989): 22.

10. Diane Jones, "The City of the Dead: The Place of Cultural Identity and Environment Sustainability in the African-American Cemetery," *Landscape Journal* 30 (2011).

11. Lewis and Milton Clarke, *Narratives of the Suffering of Lewis and Milton Clarke* (Boston: Bela Marsh, 1846), 118–19.

12. Mary A. and Stanley G. Piet, *Early Catholic Church Records in Baltimore, MD: 1782 through 1800* (Westminster, MD: Family Line Publications, 1989), 159–202.

13. Maryland State Land Records, Deeds, book 94, 229–32.

14. At the turn of the nineteenth century, African Methodists became marginalized and harshly discriminated against in the church: "Soon after the revolution[,] the color line was drawn ... the Whites avoided too close association with the colored members and tended to control the organization without consulting them." See James M. Wright, *The Free Negro in Maryland: 1634–1860* (New York: Longman's Green, 1921), 212. More recently, historian

Christopher Phillips writes that "the fervor of the Revolution's legacy had cooled [with] . . . black worshippers, both free and slave, seat[ed] in the rear of the church and the loft, commonly called the 'African corner,' or the 'Nigger pews.'" See Christopher Port, *Freedom's Port: The African American Community of Baltimore, 1790–1860* (Urbana and Chicago: University of Illinois Press, 1997), 125.

15. Bettye C. Thomas, "History of the Sharp Street Memorial Methodist Episcopal Church, 1787–1920," Sharp Street Memorial Church Records, Maryland State Archives, Annapolis, Maryland. Microfilm MdHR 3112–1.

16. Maryland State Land Records, Deeds, Book 94, 229–32.

17. John S. Mbiti, *Introduction to African Religion*, 2nd rev. ed. (Oxford: Heinemann International Literature and Textbooks, 1991), 10.

18. *Living History Program: Into the Future from our Past* (Baltimore, MD, June 20, 2009). Commemoration program booklet.

19. *Living History Program: Into the Future from our Past.*

20. Author's note: Although this example is from a much later period, it is absolutely representative. The records stated that in sections C and F, which contain 117 and 244 burial plots, respectively, these two sections are the oldest and were the areas of the burial ground where enslaved persons were interred. It is not for certain if they were Yoruba but it is not a large leap to conclude that if in 2000 John Holsey's brother was still adorning his grave, then surely this was happening in the nineteenth century.

21. No title, *Baltimore Sun*, September 17, 1870.

22. Maryland State Land Records, Deeds, book 289, 291–94.

23. No title, *Baltimore Sun*, September 17, 1870.

24. Edward N. Wilson, *Historical Facts About Sharp Street Memorial Methodist Church*, Sharp Street Archival Center, 7–12.

25. J. Thomas Scharf, *History of Maryland from the Earliest Period to the Present Day*, vol. III (Baltimore, MD: John B. Piet, 1879), 324.

26. "Twenty-Ninth Congress," *Baltimore Sun*, February 27, 1847.

27. Sharp Street Memorial Church Records, Book of Trustees Minutes and Financial Records 1882–1894, Maryland State Archives, Maryland. Microfilm MdHR M 3115–1.

28. Sharp Street Memorial Church Records.

29. Sharp Street Memorial Church Records.

30. Sharp Street Memorial Church Records.

31. 1900 United States Census, s.v. "Peter Leiritz," Westport, Baltimore County, Maryland, accessed through Ancesty.com; Bromley map, Baltimore County 1898, Published by George Washington Bromley, Baltimore City Archives Map Collection, bc_ba_atlases_1876-1915-0825; John W. Woods Directory, 1856–1857, Maryland State Archives, Volume 544.

32. "Union League Meeting a Success," *Afro-American*, July 15, 1911.

33. Handout from Sharp Street Archival Center, Baltimore, MD.

34. 1900 United States Census, s.v. "James Hall," Civil District No. 1, Tipton County, Tennessee, accessed through Ancesty.com; *Afro-American*, "James F. Hall Opens Two D.C. Marble Works," April 30, 1927; *Afro-American*, "Afro 'Shoe Champion, 55 Realizes Secret Ambition,'" September 6, 1930.

Bibliography

PRIMARY SOURCES

Archival Institutions

Baltimore City Archives, 201 Baltimore Street, Baltimore, MD 21202
Baltimore City Archives Health Department, BRG 19
    HRS, BCA BRG 19-1-1, Box 1
    HRS, BCA BRG 19-1-4, Box 4
    HRS, BCA BRG 19-1-19-2-4, Box 18
    HRS, BCA BRG 19-1-29, Box 28
Baltimore City Health Department Bureau of Vital Statistics, Death Record CR 48045,
    Microfilm
Baltimore City, Baltimore County Atlas Collection bc-ba-atlas-1876-1915

Lovely Lane United Methodist Museum and Archives, 2200 St. Paul Street, Baltimore, MD 21218
Sharp Street Memorial United Methodist Church Collection
    Baltimore-Washington Conference minutes, 1794–present
    Historical Facts about Sharp Street Memorial Methodist Church booklet

Maryland Historical Society, 201 West Monument Street, Baltimore, MD 21201
Books
Gary L. Browne, *Baltimore in the Nation, 1789–1861.*
Leroy Graham, *Baltimore: the Nineteenth Century Black Capital.*
Aubrey Land, *Colonial Maryland: A History.*
Commissioner of Health of Baltimore, Maryland, *Baltimore City Health Department: The First Thirty-Five Annual Reports, 1815–1849.*

Maryland State Archives, 350 Rowe Boulevard, Annapolis, MD 21402
Sharp Street Memorial Church Collection, SC4010 Collection Microfilm
    Bettye C. Thomas, "History of the Baltimore City Sharp Street Memorial Methodist Episcopal Church 1787–1920," from the One Hundred and Seventy-Fifth Anniversary.
    Cemetery Lot Titles 1872–1885, MdHR M 3114-1
    Cemetery Records 1883–1901, MdHR M 3114-3, 410
    Cemetery Lot Owners Book 1872–1893, MdHR M 3114-2
    Cemetery Records 1885–1892, MdHR M 3114-1, 413-60
    Board of Trustees Cash Book 1863–1873, MdHR M 3114-6
    Board of Trustees Minutes and Financial Records 1882–1893, MdHR M 3115-1

Sharp Street Memorial United Methodist Church, Dolphin and Etting Streets, Baltimore, MD 21217
Sharp Street Archival Center
    Trustee Minutes, 1897–1905
    Edward N. Wilson, *Historical Facts about Sharp Street Memorial Methodist Church.*
    Mount Auburn Cemetery holding
    Financial Department Records, Feb. 9, 1925–April 14, 1930

Record book of SSMED, 1894–1914
Belair Burial Ground, 1895–1902
Church Records, 1895–1904
Folder of Mt. Auburn Cemetery, Interments
Cemetery 1879–1893
Deed Books, February 20, 1888–March 24, 1972
Death Books, December 31, 1920–January 28, 1999
Cemetery ledger, 1872–1901
Cemetery ledger, 1875–1946
Order books, 1898–1909
Survey of Mount Auburn Cemetery conducted 2003

SECONDARY SOURCES

Clarke, Lewis, and Milton Clark, *Narratives of the Suffering of Lewis and Milton Clarke, Sons of a Soldier of the Revolution, During a Captivity of More than Twenty Years Among the Slaveholders of Kentucky, One of the So-Called Christian States of North America.* Boston: Bela Marsh, 1846.

Clayton, Ralph, and Alma Moore. "Laurel Hill Cemetery 1852–1958." *Flower of the Forest, Black Genealogical Journal* 1 (1984): 1–27.

Forth, Christopher. *Freedom's Port: The African American Community of Baltimore, 1790–1860.* Urbana and Chicago: University of Illinois Press, 1997.

Johnson, Gerald, and J. Hall Pleasants. *Green Mount Cemetery One Hundredth Anniversary, 1838–1938.* Baltimore, MD: Proprietors of the Green Mount Cemetery, 1938.

Jones, Diane. "The City of the Dead: The Place of Cultural Identity and Environment Sustainability in the African-American Cemetery." *Landscape Journal* 30 (2011): 226–40.

Mbiti, John S. *Introduction to African Religion,* 2nd ed. Portsmouth, NH: Heinemann, 1991.

Nora, Pierre. "Between Memory and History: Les Lieux de Mémoire." *Representations* 26 (1989): 7–24.

Piet, Mary A., and Stanley G. Piet. *Early Catholic Church Records in Baltimore, MD: 1782 through 1800.* Westminster, MD: Family Line Publications, 1989.

Wilson, Jane Bromley. *The Very Quiet Baltimoreans: A Guide to the Historic Cemeteries and Burial Sites of Baltimore.* Shippensburg, PA: White Mane, 1991.

Wright, James M. "The Free Negro in Maryland." In *Studies in History Economics and Public Law,* edited by the Faculty of Political Science of Columbia University, vol. 97. New York: Longmans, Green, 1921.

Chapter Five

Till Death Keeps Us Apart: Segregated Cemeteries and Social Values in St. Louis, Missouri

—JEFFREY E. SMITH

When noted African American antislavery minister John Berry Meachum died while preaching from his pulpit in February 1854, his burial at Bellefontaine Cemetery in St. Louis, Missouri, forced the cemetery's board to confront their views on racial segregation in the cemetery. The problem grew out of the seemingly innocuous creation of a special lot for Baptist clergy and their families who were active in St. Louis when they died. Meachum was the minister at the First African Baptist Church—a post he had held for almost three decades.[1] As such, Meachum met the criteria for burial in the Baptist Minister's Lot, so his family arranged for his interment there, and since Bellefontaine had no policy regarding the burial of African Americans, it had no choice but to allow the interment. John Berry Meachum (1789–1854) was not just any minister, however. A former slave who purchased his freedom in Kentucky, Meachum was perhaps the most prominent African American living in St. Louis who, along with his wife Mary, was a vocal and active abolitionist; notice of his death even appeared on the front page of *Missouri Republican*.[2] He also appears to be the first free African American buried in Bellefontaine.

Meachum's burial in Bellefontaine Cemetery is the tip of a much larger iceberg regarding the nuances of race relations in a city in a border state where slavery existed in the midst of a large migration of northerners. St. Louis's population grew rapidly in the decades preceding the Civil War, so that more white people from both North and South lived in closer proximity to both free and enslaved African Americans. This rapid rise in the living population meant that the number of people of both races who died and needed to be buried rose as

Figure 5.1 John Berry Meachum (1789–1854) was born into slavery in Virginia, but earned enough to purchase his own freedom by 1810. He came to St. Louis in 1815 searching for his wife, whose owner brought her to Missouri. Using his skills as a carpenter and barrel-maker, Meachum purchased freedom for his wife and children. He was ordained a Baptist minister in 1826, and rose to lead the largest African American Baptist congregation in the city and first vice president of the Western Colored Baptist Convention in 1853. This marble obelisk offers permanent confirmation of Meachum's status and material success as well.

well. While death might be the great equalizer, the living made decisions about burials, and their views on race and slavery informed those decisions. Because survivors make decisions about "eternal resting places," cemeteries reflect the social and cultural attitudes of the broader community. Unlike any other physical manifestation of segregated society, burials represent a snapshot of views at a moment in time that does not change; while segregation among the living is more fluid—housing patterns, churches, workplaces, schools, and so on change over generations—the places where the dead are buried generally do not. These cemeteries are, then, the history of race indelibly written on the landscape of cities like St. Louis. Even death and final resting places are mediated by racial views and social mores among the living. St. Louis provides a compelling case study for understanding the culture of race as reflected in burial patterns. Belle-fontaine Cemetery, the largest nondenominational cemetery in St. Louis, offers some insights, but only in the context of both urban slavery and burial patterns for free and enslaved African Americans in the city.

Just as cities underwent transformation in the decades before the Civil War, so too did cemeteries. Starting with Mount Auburn Cemetery on the outskirts of Boston in neighboring Cambridge in 1831, there evolved a new way of think-ing about burial sites that served several functions, called the "rural cemetery movement." Ironically, these rural cemeteries were a uniquely urban phenom-enon, dubbed "rural" for their pastoral settings located outside the city proper.[3] By the end of the decade, similar cemeteries opened in Philadelphia (1836), Brooklyn (1838), and Baltimore (1838), all modeled after Mount Auburn. Unlike their predecessors, founders of these new cemeteries saw them as community assets and places where people would visit on a regular basis. City residents could escape crowded and polluted cities to commune with nature in a time when Transcendentalists saw the hand of God in the natural world. Their grave-stones and monuments also served to convey a sense of collective memory, with the names of prominent community figures etched onto their grave markers. Rural cemetery design evolved into more picturesque designs starting in the late 1840s, with a focus on broad vistas and overall landscape design. When the two rural cemeteries opened in St. Louis—Bellefontaine in 1850 and its Catholic neighbor Calvary four years later—they were part of a general trend in the ways Americans thought about both city amenities and cemeteries. Bellefontaine Cemetery represented a new approach to these denominational burial grounds and city graveyards in two ways, both tied to its place in the rural cemetery movement. Like its rural cemetery counterparts in other cities, Bellefontaine was a private, chartered, and nondenominational institution for people of all faiths, despite carrying out what we associate with a sacred function.

Other cities were in similar fixes to St. Louis and responded in similar ways. Indeed, this was a key impetus behind the creation of Mount Auburn and a wave of others in growing cities, such as Laurel Hill in Philadelphia in 1836 and Green-Wood Cemetery in Brooklyn two years later. When the State of Missouri granted a charter for the Rural Cemetery Association in St. Louis January 28, 1841, and even when founders actually created the cemetery in March 1849, city fathers were at the vanguard of thinking about cemeteries and their role in a community.[4] Like other rural cemeteries, Bellefontaine was a new kind of institution in St. Louis that was more than a warehouse for bodies, but rather

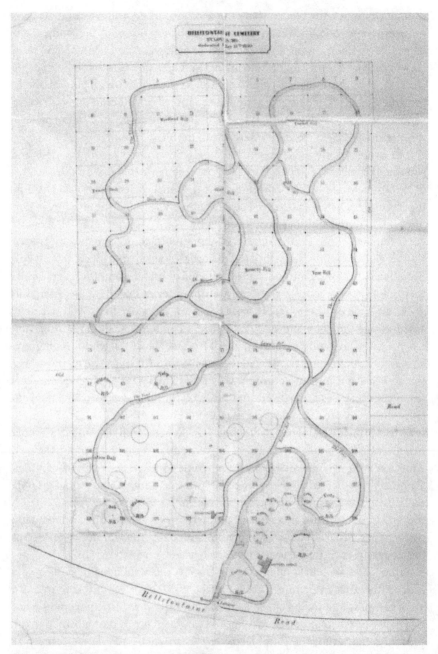

Figure 5.2 Bellefontaine Cemetery published this map in May 1850 to distribute at the dedication ceremony in May. As a way to raise money, the cemetery auctioned the opportunity to purchase the first lots on the grounds. As a result, designer Almerin Hotchkiss identified "The Tour" so purchasers could ensure that their lots were prominent from the route visitors would take. Courtesy the Missouri Historical Society.

seen as a community asset to be used by the living on a regular basis as a kind of park. The fact that people were buried there contributed to the use of such spaces. Cemeteries were to reflect romantic views not only about nature but also about the past and its people. Monuments commemorating prominent citizens lined the cemetery's central roads most viewed by visitors. These picturesque cemeteries were intended for people to visit, stroll, and meander. Bellefontaine was typical when its original design included a route called "The Tour." The Bellefontaine dedication ceremonies included a fundraising auction whereby people could purchase the privilege of being the first to select family lots. These first purchasers chose locations that were either on or within view of the Tour, ensuring their places in the city's collective memory as subsequent generations traveled the Tour.

While the literature on race and burials acknowledges segregation, it has generally focused on cemeteries for African Americans that were either slave graveyards or those founded by African American churches or societies, generally after the Civil War. More broadly, the history of nineteenth-century cemeteries falls into three general categories. The first, which has received the most scholarly attention, focuses on individual cemeteries as landscapes. These emphasize the design of the cemetery and the ways that design has changed to meet evolving priorities and views of landscapes. However, these focus almost exclusively on the landscape itself without a full analysis of the relationship between the uses of a cemetery and the city within which it is embedded. Blanche Linden-Ward's *Silent City on a Hill*, about Mount Auburn Cemetery in Boston, Massachusetts, and Christopher Vernon's *Graceland Cemetery: A Design History*, about a cemetery of the same name located in Chicago, Illinois, are good examples of these works.[5] The second broad category of cemetery histories looks at cemeteries as collections of gravestones. Virtually all of these authors are interested in artisan stonecutters in the seventeenth and eighteenth centuries. Since manufactured gravestones that were engraved locally rather than made by local craftsmen replaced these starting in the 1820s, none of them focused on the period of this manuscript. Others take a broader view of death and gravestones, including European burial sites as well. While both Linden-Ward and Vernon discuss grave markers, they tend to be in the context of enhancing the beauty of the cemetery and changing views about cemetery and landscape design. Judith Dupre's *Monuments*, Michael Ragon's *The Space of Death*, and Keith Eggener's profusely illustrated *Cemeteries* are excellent examples of works that focus on gravestone design.[6] A number of valuable works delve deeply into design history by examining cemeteries and markers in a particular region. Richard Viet's excellent examination of cemeteries in New Jersey ranks among the most insightful and useful.[7] The third category of cemetery histories focuses on specific cemeteries. Amateur historians (usually staff

Figure 5.3 Until this entrance was closed in the 1980s, this was the view that visitors saw when entering Bellefontaine Cemetery in St. Louis. Almerin Hotchkiss designed it to seem as much like a park as possible, as did designers of other rural cemetery movement sites such as Mount Auburn, Green-Wood, or Laurel Hill cemeteries.

or board members at the cemetery) often wrote these books and concentrate exclusively on the institution. Some of these are chronological in nature, while others focus on the "famous and infamous" buried there, so their appeal is primarily local. Mary Mitchell's work on Green-Wood Cemetery in New York, John Peters's book on Hollywood Cemetery in Richmond, and Carol Shepley's on Bellefontaine Cemetery in St. Louis are examples. All fill a particular niche but offer little to our understanding of the broader cultural issues of a community reflected in the cemeteries themselves.[8]

Still another body of literature helps inform the understanding of the burials of African Americans in rural cemeteries like Bellefontaine. Studies of the material culture of African American burial grounds in cities and towns emanate from the fields of archaeology, anthropology, and material culture as well as history. Some, such as Charlotte King, suggest that the material culture of African American burial patterns demonstrate a lineage between African traditions that were transplanted to the United States, a trend reflected in African American graveyards elsewhere; Keith Yanner and Steven Ybarrola also have

found death to be a last line of delineation of race in their examination of an African American cemetery in rural Louisiana.[9] But these graveyards are more complicated than mere segregation based on race. The race and status of those charged with burying people mediates the graveyard and their appearances. Garman suggests that, as early as 1720, people buried slaves in shared grave-yards, but "they seem to have objected strongly to sharing the space of death, perhaps because of the permanent nature of the latter state."[10] Slave burials, especially in urban settings, complicate the racial narrative. Angelika Kruger-Kahloula suggests that slave owners occasionally buried slaves nearby, often out of attachment as "part of the family," but still kept them in a separate and, by inference, inferior status. However, Kruger-Kahloula suggests, even cemeteries created by black communities showed a certain level of social hierarchy, not unlike white cemeteries.[11] As we shall see, the burials of slaves on owners' fam-ily lots in Bellefontaine Cemetery in St. Louis reflected similar attitudes, with slaves' graves at the opposite end of the lot and often oriented in a different direction, facing away from the white family.

Since religious groups generally succumbed to segregation in their cemeteries, as Kruger-Kahloula suggests, the burial of John Berry Meachum was particularly problematic.[12] When Bellefontaine opened in 1850 and Meachum died four years later, the city's population was burgeoning, placing new pressures of burial sites. The city almost trebled in population from 4,977 during the 1830s, and almost another fivefold by 1850 to 160,773 souls, making it the eighth-largest city in the United States.[13] The city expanded its boundaries along and away from the Mississippi River three times after its charter as a city in 1822—in 1839, 1841, and 1855. Each time it did so and reached farther into the common fields, it also enveloped burial grounds situated in what had been the countryside, away from people. The "common fields" in St. Louis grew from its colonial origins, established by French fur trader Pierre Laclede Liguest and inhabited by culturally French immigrants from New Orleans. The concept is medieval in nature, reflecting land use patterns in manorial Europe as long strips of land to be cultivated. These strips extended west of the original village to be used for farming and grazing livestock. However, people used portions of that expansive land for other purposes. During the 1810s, Methodists and Episcopalians began burying their dead in graveyards outside of town in the common fields areas. Even before St. Louis was chartered as a city in 1822, residents were figuring out that graveyards needed to be out of the way of development. This notion came from two directions. Cities in both the United States and Europe began situating cemeteries outside town for health reasons starting in the 1820s. The "rural cemeteries" created in the 1830s and 1840s were all located outside city limits, usually between one and five miles from the central city. This notion that burying bodies near the population had its roots in antiquity; the Romans placed burial grounds outside city walls for health reasons. As early as 1822, the City of New York considered banning burials in the city, and John Jay Smith, the founder of Laurel Hill Cemetery in Philadelphia in 1837, echoed similar sentiments in 1838 in his tract calling for all cemeteries to be located outside the city, noting that "It is at this day well known, and has been satisfactorily demonstrated, *that burials in cities greatly endanger the public health*; that the miasmata disengaged from burying places, may, and often have, caused frightful catastrophes, and that they not only give more virulence to prevailing maladies, but also originate contagious diseases, whose ravages have been terrible."[14] The following year Dr. Jedidiah Commins told the Ohio legislature that health concerns were central to his petition to create the Akron Rural Cemetery, noting (in the exact same words as Smith): "It is at this day well known, and has been satisfactorily demonstrated, *that burials in cities greatly endanger the public health*; that the miasmata disengaged from burying places, may, and often have, caused frightful catastrophes, and that they not only give more virulence to prevailing maladies, but also originate contagious diseases, whose ravages have been terrible."[15] And so it went in city after city. The Rev. Truman Marcellus Post echoed these sentiments in his sermon dedicating Bellefontaine Cemetery in St. Louis on May 15, 1850, observing "the burial place in the midst of the city soon becomes a nuisance, exhaling from its crowded graves the pestilence."[16]

Economics also played a role in the location of cemeteries. As the city grew, the locations of those graveyards were transformed in the public mind from merely "land" into "real estate" with monetary value and commercial uses. As cities like St. Louis grew into unincorporated areas, they enveloped burial grounds that were not considered economically efficient and profitable use of the land. Consequently, city governments assumed the task of managing those burial sites and finding alternatives for burying people in ways that did not stand in the way of economic growth. When the newly elected St. Louis City Council convened for the first time in April 1823 (after being chartered as a city by the State of Missouri the previous year), it began the task of creating a well-regulated community, dealing with the problems its members (and presumably the city's citizenry) thought were highest priorities. Its second order of business (after banning gambling tables and games of chance) prohibited burials within the city limits with stiff penalties—a twenty-five-dollar fine levied against the sexton or gravedigger, fifty dollars for the survivor who ordered or paid for it.[17] Two decades later, the ban was apparently ineffective. The city regulated all "public graveyards" with two ordinances in 1843. One mandated that sextons at cemeteries within four miles of the city had to keep records and submit weekly reports (to be published in the newspaper by the city each week) about who was buried, cause of death, and race. Further, said Ordinance 16666, in those reports "the deaths shall be set forth under the three separate heads of 'White,' 'Free Colored,' and 'Slaves.'"[18] The other placed an absolute ban on burials and new graveyards in the city: "no person or persons, congregations or societies, shall, upon any pretence [sic] whatever, establish or locate a burying ground within the limits of the city of St. Louis, nor in the common at a less distance than one quarter of a mile beyond the limits of the city."[19] Denominational cemeteries, on the other hand, were either originally or relocated outside the city limits, keeping decomposing bodies a safe distance from the living.

While most people in St. Louis buried their dead in denominational graveyards operated by the Catholic, Methodist, German Evangelical, Presbyterian, and Episcopalian churches, not everyone used them. The city council created its second City Cemetery in 1836 and placed it in the common fields southwest of town at present-day Jefferson Avenue and Arsenal Street, the site of today's Benton Park.[20] City fathers clearly saw the City Cemetery as primarily for outsiders of sorts: free blacks, slaves, individuals, or "strangers" (a euphemism for those who died poor, alone, or both) who were most likely either Protestant or those without church affiliation. The archbishop's office issued "poor tickets" for impoverished Catholics for burials that could be used in any of the Catholic burial sites at least as early as 1849, in the midst of the cholera epidemic that claimed some one in twelve that year.[21] But as the city rapidly grew in population, those cemeteries filled up, creating the need for new burial grounds. Bellefontaine Cemetery, organized in March 1849, was one response to the problem, but because people had to pay for burials there, it excluded the poorest swath of the population who still needed to be buried. The city council responded in part with its Sublette Cemetery, which served as a "potter's field" for the indigent before the Civil War, but apparently used it for less than a decade. The burial records, albeit incomplete, suggest the demographics of the city, however. The number of free blacks (about 11 percent of the burials) is disproportionately high compared to the general population, and the number of slaves (3 percent) roughly parallels the percentage of the city's population that was enslaved; among those listed as slaves was Eliza Roth, thirty-five, listed as "servant of George, free black" in October 1863. Some 30 percent of those buried were born in Ireland—including J. B. McKee, who died in early 1863 at age twenty-four, who was listed as "b Ire free black."[22]

The racial makeup of the buried population at each of these denominational graveyards reflected the congregational demographics. A few African Americans were buried in the Episcopal and Catholic cemeteries, but most were interred in either the Methodist cemeteries or those operated by the City. Before Bellefontaine Cemetery opened in May 1850, most African Americans were buried in the Wesleyan Cemetery on Grand Avenue (on the present-day St. Louis University campus), chartered in 1847 as the burial ground for Methodists from the congregations and missions that grew out of the Fourth Street Methodist Church. As St. Louis grew rapidly, Fourth Street Methodist outgrew several buildings between its first meetings in a log cabin in 1820 and 1850. Its 1822 building was the first church erected by the Methodists in St. Louis; like many, it included a segregated gallery on three sides for exclusive use of free blacks and slaves. The congregation built a larger church in 1830, and soon thereafter constructed a small church exclusively for African Americans. The Methodist Conference appointed a second white clergy to the Fourth Street Church so that this junior pastor could also minister and preach to the African Methodist Episcopal congregation.[23] Even though Fourth Street became the proslavery First Methodist Church-South when the Methodist church voted overwhelmingly to split over the issue of slavery in 1845, the two congregations remained yoked through shared clergy, tradition, and ownership of some African American congregants. Wesleyan Cemetery became the burial ground for congregants from both churches. Between 1847 and 1851, 89 percent (133 of 148) of African Americans at Wesleyan were interred in blocks 27 and 28, and all suggest a similar story: almost all the African American burials give no grave number, and the few that do are almost all in lots 27 and 28. Almost half of African American buried there (45 percent) can be readily identified as slaves.[24] While no records suggest this segregation, practice constructed boundaries of race. Several slave owners who used Wesleyan also sat on the board of directors of Bellefontaine Cemetery or owned family lots there, but chose to use Wesleyan instead, perhaps because their slaves attended the AME church. Even Bellefontaine's board president James Yeatman (1818–1901) paid three dollars for a lot for an unnamed four-year-old "female slave of J. E. Yeatman" in April 1849, along with the burial fees to local undertaker William Lynch.[25] The burial fees appear to be the last slave he paid to bury, though. Yeatman came to a different view of the peculiar institution in the early 1850s, and emancipated his slaves—first George Carr in November 1850, then three more (Arrianna, Rose Ellen, and Robert Alexander Green) on November 20, 1854.[26] In fact, Yeatman went on to become president of the Western Sanitary Commission and a vocal supporter of aid to former slaves during the Civil War.

While Bellefontaine was a cemetery carrying out a sacred function, it was a secular institution designed to fulfill the worldly functions of enhancing life on earth. The founders gathering in 1849 saw Bellefontaine as part of an evolving vision of a great metropolis. Part of this vision included social and racial relationships that segregated people according to their status on earth. The price structure of burial sites at these cemeteries separated people by socioeconomic class. Unlike the old City Cemetery, which had two prices (adults and children), Bellefontaine had separate prices for lots (which included multiple graves, as opposed to plots for individual graves), which it sold by the square foot with a minimum of 400 square feet, which came to a minimum cost of eighty dollars in 1850. Lot owners held rights that paralleled those of property owners in the city of the living, with control over landscaping, monument design, fencing, and the people buried in them. Individual graves, in designated "public lots," were less expensive, held just one body, and carried no control over the land except being allowed to place a gravestone.[27] Lot owners could select locations anywhere in the cemetery, so their lot purchases reflected property ownership patterns in life. In a similar fashion, this land use pattern within the cemetery also kept the social classes separate as well. With their lower cost and limited choice of location (one could purchase an individual grave only in the public lots) on the periphery of the cemetery, the public lots kept lower classes "in their place."

Social relationships from life were also reflected in the burial of slaves. While the number of slaves in St. Louis was shrinking by the mid-nineteenth century, a sizable number of southerners who were becoming prominent St. Louisans still owned human chattel. Just as the founding of Bellefontaine itself reflected the attitudes and values of its founders and that new generation of leadership, so

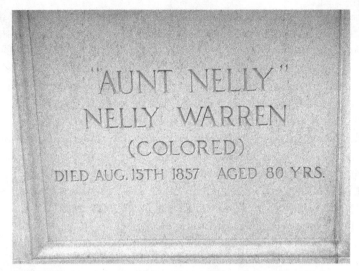

Figure 5.4 Although this marker says "Aunt Nelly" was eighty years old, the death records give her age as seventy-three, having died of "old age." Nelly Warren was born in Maryland; she is remarkable in the interment records at Bellefontaine Cemetery in that she was listed with a last name different from her owner, as this grave marker suggests.

too did the practices of the board members and the proprietors who purchased lots at Bellefontaine. When the cemetery was dedicated in May 1850, some 5,967 enslaved people lived in St. Louis; the slave population on the eve of the Civil War had dropped by almost a third to its 1840 level despite a burgeoning general population in the same period.[28] As a practical matter, many of those buried in the City Cemetery or even Wesleyan were excluded from Bellefontaine by economics as much as anything else. For many free blacks before the Civil War, even an individual plot at Bellefontaine would have been unaffordable.

Part of a slave owner's obligation was burying slaves' remains when they died. Rural owners and planters buried slaves in country burial grounds, with large plantations like Monticello or Mount Vernon having separate graveyards for slaves, but urban slave owners did not enjoy such available land. In the case of St. Louis, some opted for the inexpensive lot in the City Cemetery or a denominational cemetery. A handful of family lots in Bellefontaine have slaves buried on them, revealed in interment records, maps of family lots, or both. The first appears to be fifteen-year-old George Alexander (but with no sur-name given), identified as "Slave of L. M. Kennett" and buried on Lot 341 when he died of typhoid pneumonia in December 1853. However, George's remains are no longer on Luther Kennett's lot, apparently having been moved at a later date.[29] When three-year-old Louisa died in 1860, the interment records identi-

Figure 5.5 Wayman Crow (1808–1885), a civic leader who sat on the Bellefontaine Cemetery board of directors, purchased this lot along the east side of Bellefontaine on a bluff with a view looking down to the Mississippi River. Before using it, he had to vacate his old one all the way on the other side of the cemetery. Among the ten people buried there was Robert, a slave who died in 1870. Robert's remains are not here, though; Crow had him buried in an unmarked grave in the public lots along the north edge of the cemetery. Robert was buried there just months after Bellefontaine rescinded its ban on burying African Americans outside family lots.

fied her as "Slave of M. Weber," within burial Lot 374 showing her last name as "unknown." Four years later, when Georgiana Wagner died in August 1864, she was identified as "slave" when buried on the same lot.[30] Others appear in the burial records; some graves are marked, others not. Perhaps the most striking case is of Nellie Warren, a slave owned by the Collier family, who died at age seventy-three in 1857. They lived in the most prestigious part of town called Lucas Place just west of downtown, and had a household slave buried on the family lot. The stone monument identifies her as "Aunt Nellie" and "colored."

Moses Bailey, the last slave buried in Bellefontaine, died in November 1864 at age sixty, just two months before the new Missouri Constitution banned the peculiar institution (almost a year before the 13th Amendment was ratified in December 1865, ending slavery nationally).[31] Bailey was somewhat typical of the slave experience. He was buried on the large family lot purchased by his owner, William N. Switzer. Next to Bailey are two other slaves—Ellen, twenty-three, and Ada, twenty months, both of whose last names were listed at the time as "unknown," both noted as "slave of W. N. Switzer."[32] Their graves are all the way in the back of the large lot, in unmarked graves, as far from the family as possible; segregation followed them even to the grave. The stories of Moses Bailey, Ellen, and Ada are not unusual. Of the limited number of African Americans buried in Bellefontaine before the cemetery lifted its ban on African American burials outside family lots, almost all were either current or former slaves. Calvary Cemetery, the Catholic garden cemetery across the street, has some thirty-five African American burials, ten of whom were slaves.[33] The boundaries of race reflected those of the living—physically near yet apart, inferior status confirmed.

This handful of owners at both cemeteries appears to be the exception rather than the rule. The burial site for slaves in cities like St. Louis was selected not by the deceased, but by the slave's owner, who had to bury their slaves someplace. Because they made the decisions, their views about race informed the locations of slaves' burials. Antebellum cities like St. Louis were not necessarily segregated; owners and other whites routinely saw and interacted with slaves and free blacks more than they might have in, say, a plantation setting. Owners rented slaves to others for various tasks or duties, and used them in households. While contact was fairly constant, it was always unequal, of course. Just as owners made decisions for slaves in life, so too did they make them regarding death and burial. In other words, every one of those slaves buried on owners' lots in Bellefontaine was interred not by their own volition but a decision of their owners. Given the view in both law and society that slaves were property, it is not so striking that so few slaves are buried on family lots as it is that any are buried there at all. The number of slaves buried at Bellefontaine is about the same as at the city's Potter's Field, but is proportionately smaller by fourteenfold.[34]

There exists nothing in the record to suggest that the founders of Bellefontaine gave any thought to race, even though nine of the original founders owned slaves in 1850 and eight still owned human chattel in the slave section of the 1860 census. At no point did they address race in the published rules or set aside a special section for African Americans—at least until 1854, when Meachum's death forced their hand—and the minutes of the board of directors and executive committee are silent on the issue. Cultural mores dictated the handling of slaves, and they probably figured that free blacks could not afford a lot at Bellefontaine anyway. That all changed when noted African American antislavery minister John Berry Meachum died while preaching from his pulpit in February 1854 and was buried on Lot 410, which was set aside by local attorney and board member William McPherson for Baptist clergy who were active in St. Louis when they died, and their families. Meachum was the minister at the African Baptist Church—a post he had held for almost three decades.[35] At the board meeting on April 24, the first one after Meachum's death, founder and board member Gerard Allen proposed a ban on burying free blacks or using the Receiving Tomb (a temporary storage area for bodies awaiting burial, often because weather precluded burial), "*Provided,*" he wrote, "that this resolution shall not be so construed to prevent any lot owner from depositing the body of any colored person within his own lot." Bellefontaine saw cemetery lot owners as having certain rights of control over their lots not unlike property owners in the city of St. Louis, so it made perfect sense to grant them the same rights to control property. A discussion followed, apparently about the absolute clarity of the board's intentions, since it passed a substitute resolution: "no colored person shall be interred in the grounds of this Association or deposited in the Receiving Tomb, except slaves in the lots of their masters, unless this Board shall by special resolution authorize the same."[36] In death as in life, racial integration was acceptable in antebellum St. Louis so long as the unequal relationship was maintained. To make sure such breaches did not happen again, the board gave control of Lot 410 as trustee during his lifetime to one of its members, founder and local lawyer William McPherson.[37] The resolution remained the policy of Bellefontaine Cemetery until May 1878, when it voted unanimously "that the resolution adopted by this Board on 24 April 1854, in reference to the depositing in Receiving Tomb, and interment in the cemetery, of the remains of *Coloured Persons*, be and the same is rescinded."[38] In smaller cemeteries primarily for the impoverished or disenfranchised, borders of race were fluid and sometimes nonexistent. But in those where class distinctions were more clearly drawn, racial boundaries were consciously constructed as well. Herein lies the significance of John Berry Meachum's burial: his burial crossed an unspoken boundary of race. It was Meachum who forced the board of Bellefontaine Cemetery to formalize boundaries that were previously unspoken—and that remained unspoken but nonetheless present at almost all similar cemeteries in slaveholding cities.

The policy limiting the place of burial for African Americans in Bellefontaine changed in 1878, when the remains of Robert, a former slave of board member Wayman Crow, were moved to the public lots. Crow had purchased one of the first family lots in June 1850, Lot 15, and over the next two-plus decades buried ten people on it. But in 1878, he purchased a new and larger one (Lot 189) on a bluff overlooking the Mississippi River and, since he had to completely vacate Lot 15 in order to return it to the Association for resale, moved six of the bodies of family members to the new lot in the spring of 1879. Two more were moved to other family lots. But there was a problem with one more: "Robert (Servant)" who died in 1870—and was listed in the interment books without a last name and as "Servant of W. Crow" even though he died five years after Emancipation—had to be removed as well. By 1878 Crow apparently felt less of an obligation to keep Robert near the family, but cemetery policy through its 1854 resolution precluded moving his remains anywhere but another family lot. The

Figure 5.6 Only a handful of slaves' graves in Bellefontaine have markers. Patience, a "faithful and devoted servant," was buried on her owner's lot, but this stone is situated as far from the family as possible on the lot. Lest anyone forget her status, she is identified as a "servant," even six years after the end of slavery.

board voted in 1878 to allow the burial of African Americans in the cemetery within only months after Crow purchased his new lot. Robert was removed to the inexpensive Public Lot in 1879 and interred in a sea of unmarked graves on the northern edge of the cemetery, just a few rows from Calvary Avenue.[39]

Crow's was not the only story like this. Other descendants ordered the removals of ancestors' servants as well. Consider William Poulterer. Two of his slaves died in the mid-1850s—twenty-two-year-old Samuel (of pneumonia) in 1855 and five-year-old Pete (of whooping cough) two years later, neither with given surnames—and were buried in Wesleyan Cemetery. Poulterer purchased lot 708 in late 1857 to bury his one-year-old daughter Annie, who died of whooping cough less than a week before Pete; in January 1858, he moved the remains of the two slaves, clearly intending to use the lot for the family. Yet no one else was buried on the lot; in 1910, the heirs surrendered the lot to Bellefontaine, removed Annie's remains from the cemetery (the records are silent on where she was removed to), but had the two slaves reinterred in unmarked graves in one of the public lots, just like Robert.[40] While slave owners may have referred to servants as "members of the family" and may have even felt emotional ties to them, those bonds did not transcend time. The inferior social status of slaves did.

Figures 5.7 and 5.8 Neither Emeline Payne nor Lewis Wilson still lived with any members of the Clark family when they died in the early 1870s, but their status from slavery is still alluded to on their gravestones.

Urban slavery introduced a vexing problem for both former slaves and former owners. The new Missouri Constitution banned slavery in January 1865 but failed to address what would happen to former slaves. Some left town, of course, and others moved out of their former owners' homes and took jobs elsewhere in the city. But some continued in the employ of their former masters, and still others continued to maintain looser ties to their former owners. When Patience (no last name given) died in 1871, for example, she was buried in Lot 63 owned by her former owners, the Chambers family. Her gravestone gives only her first name (which was typical all through the slaveholding states and reflected in the interment records at every cemetery with slaves buried in them), and is far from the family at the opposite side of the lot. Benjamin Chambers, who is buried in the midst of family members, on the other hand, was listed as "killed in battle" in the Confederate army in April 1864 in Oregon County, Missouri.[41] Patience was fifty-nine when slavery ended in Missouri, and apparently stayed on as a servant for the family for the remainder of her years. It is hard to determine the nature of the relationship, but one can imagine her former owners feeling they needed help; Patience may have felt short on options and perhaps even trapped, and the family may have even felt an emotional tie to a longtime slave. At the day-to-day life level, freedom was probably a complicated notion to some urban slaves like Patience, and when she died she may have been buried with the family, but she was just as separate and unequal in death as in life.

Others undoubtedly retained some sort of ties to their former owners. Two former slaves are buried on the lot for explorer and territorial governor William Clark, for example. At the time of her death Emma Payne, fifty-nine, did not live with the Clark family but on Gay Street near Fourteenth Street when she died of marasmus in 1876. When Lewis Wilson died three years later, he was buried next to her after having been her neighbor in life on Gay Street. Unlike Patience, Wilson had an occupation identified in the city directory—a porter—after the war. Most striking are their epitaphs on the gravestones: Payne's reads "A Good and Faithful Servant" and Wilson's "Retainer of the Family."[42] Like Patience, Wilson and Payne are buried at the back of the lot, farthest away from the entrance to the explorer's lot, with its obelisk and bust flanked by pylons featuring the heads of a bear and a buffalo. Theirs are in the back, and face the opposite direction from the others, just like Patience's. Slavery may have ended, but those relationships died hard. Those relations continued even into the twentieth century. When eighty-two-year-old Henry Lewis died after being hit by a streetcar in August 1910, Phillip Chew buried him on the family lot purchased by Lewis's former owner Peter Lindell. The Chews hosted his funeral at their home on Westminster Place, a prestigious St. Louis private street that was also listed as Lewis's address in the Bellefontaine interment records. Notably, Lewis's grave is in a distant corner of the lot, far from the graves of family members.[43]

Figures 5.9 and 5.10 William Clark (1770–1838) was originally buried in a family graveyard owned by his nephew; the family purchased this lot in 1860 and moved the remains of Clark and his family here. In the early 1870s, Emeline Payne and Lewis Wilson were buried on the lot; they are situated behind the obelisk, outside the stone coping to the right, and face the opposite direction of the rest of the family markers.

Figure 5.11 Cemeteries like Bellefontaine drew their design nomenclature from park design, as this image suggests. This area sits on a hill overlooking the original tour route.

Patience. Emma Payne. Lewis Wilson. Nelly Warren. All were slaves or former ones, all buried with their current or former masters' families, all suffering the final degradation of slavery of being buried in subservience. But the story of race and burial patterns in border cities is more nuanced. The significant point is that the locations of all interments are mediated—that is, they are ultimately decided by the living. Those who purchased large family lots at places like Bellefontaine, Calvary, or other gardenesque cemeteries chose the sites of those lots within the cemeteries, ensuring that their eternal homes were in neighborhoods of their own choosing. For everyone else buried there and in other graveyards, survivors chose the locations of graves. In the case of African Americans, social conventions about race and slavery dictated those locations. After the death of John Berry Meachum, white board members at Bellefontaine Cemetery decided which African Americans could be buried in "their" cemetery. In a similar way, white church elders decided where black Methodists could worship and where in the denominational graveyard they could be buried. Only the graveyard for the most impoverished included both races, and the record is silent if they were segregated by race—and even they were identified by race and status (slave or free) in the interment records. Because burials are a "final resting place," the locations make relationships permanent, and become a lasting image of race relations in a border state, where even death kept the races apart.

Notes

1. Interment Records; Lot File 410. The Baptist Minister's Lot was available to any active Baptist clergy and their families in St. Louis. First African Baptist Church (later First Baptist Church) is the oldest continuously operating African American church in Missouri. As its founder, Meachum was minister there for three decades.

2. "John Berry Meachum," *Missouri Republican*, February 20, 1854.

3. David Charles Sloane, *The Last Great Necessity: Cemeteries in American History* (Baltimore, MD: Johns Hopkins University Press, 1991), 13–17; Keith Eggener, *Cemeteries* (New York: Norton/Library of Congress Visual Sourcebooks in Architecture, Design, and Engineering, 2010), 24–25; David Paul Schuyler, "Public Landscapes and American Urban Culture, 1800–1870: Rural Cemeteries, City Parks, and Suburbs," diss., Columbia University, 1979, 37.

4. The Rural Cemetery Association, which formally changed its name to Bellefontaine Cemetery in 1852, received a charter from the Missouri legislature in January 1841, but no one took action to organize it until eight years later, and only two of the original founders listed in the state charter participated in the organization and opening of the cemetery in 1849. The original incorporators listed were Beverley Allen, Benjamin Ayres, Lewis V. Bogy, James B. Bowlin, G. R. Budd, Pierre Chouteau Jr., Joseph B. Crockett, Wayman Crow, J. P. Doane, J. W. Farrell, A. G. Farwell, Hamilton Gamble, John Gay, William Glasgow, N. E. Janney, John Kerr, William Carr Lane, William Lynch, E. H. McCabe, William Milburn, George Morton, John O'Fallon, Trusten Polk, Nathan Ranney, S. S. Rayburn, Christopher Rhodes, John Smith, Edward Tracy, and Asa Wilgus. "An Act to Incorporate the Rural Cemetery Association," *Laws of the State of Missouri*, 11th General Assembly (City of Jefferson: Calvin Gunn, Jeffersonian Office, 1841), 192.

5. Blanche Linden-Ward, *Silent City on a Hill: Landscape and Memory in Boston's Mount Auburn Cemetery* (Columbus: Ohio State University Press, 1989); Christopher Vernon, *Graceland Cemetery: A Design History* (Amherst: University of Massachusetts Press, 2011).

6. Judith Dupre, *Monuments: America's History in Art and Memory* (New York: Random House, 2007); Michel Ragon, *The Space of Death: A Study of Funerary Architecture, Decoration, and Urbanism*, trans. Alan Sheridan (Charlottesville: University Press of Virginia, 1983); Keith Eggener, *Cemeteries* (New York: Norton/Library of Congress Visual Sourcebooks in Architecture, Design, and Engineering, 2010).

7. Richard F. Veit and Mark Nonestied, *New Jersey Cemeteries and Tombstones: History in the Landscape* (New Brunswick, NJ: Rivergate Books, an imprint of Rutgers University Press, 2008).

8. Mary H. Mitchell, *Hollywood Cemetery: The History of a Southern Shrine* (Richmond: Virginia State Library, 1985); John O. Peters, *Richmond's Hollywood Cemetery* (Richmond: Valentine Richmond History Center, 2010); Carol Ferring Shepley, *Movers and Shakers, Scalawags and Suffragettes: Tales from Bellefontaine Cemetery* (St. Louis: Missouri History Museum, 2008).

9. Charlotte King, "Separated by Death and Color: The African American Cemetery of New Philadelphia, Illinois," *Historical Archaeology* 44, no. 1 (2010): 125–37; Keith M. Yanner and Steven J. Ybarrola, "'He didn't have no cross': Tombs and Graves as Racial Boundary Tactics on a Louisiana Barrier Island," *Oral History Review* 30, no. 2: 1–28.

10. James C. Garman, "Viewing the Color Line through the Material Culture of Death," *Historical Archaeology* 28, no. 3 (1994): 78.

11. Angelika Kruger-Kahloula, "On the Wrong Side of the Fence: Racial Segregation in American Cemeteries," in Genevieve Fabre and Robert O'Meally, eds., *History and Memory in African American Culture* (New York: Oxford University Press, 1994), 138.

12. Kruger-Kahloula, "On the Wrong Side of the Fence," 136.

13. See US Census Bureau, Population Division, https://www.census.gov/population/www/documentation/twps0027/twps0027.html, accessed March 15, 2016.

14. Atticus [John Jay Smith Jr.], *Hints on the subject of interments within the city of Philadelphia: addressed to the serious consideration of the members of councils, commissioners of the districts and citizens generally* (Philadelphia: William Brown, Printer, 1838), 11.

15. Minutebook of Akron Rural Cemetery, Petition to the Ohio Legislature, 1839.

16. Scipione Piattoli, *Essay on the Danger of Interment in Cities*, was first published in the United States in 1823; "The Bellefontaine Cemetery," *Missouri Republican*, May 16, 1850.

17. *Ordinances Passed by the Mayor and Board of Aldermen of the City of St. Louis* (St. Louis: Edward Charles, 1824), 10–12.

18. "An Act to Amend an Act Concerning Bills of Mortality, in the City of St. Louis and Suburbs," Ordinance 16666, Ordinances compiled in 1846, 84, 105–6.

19. *Revised Ordinances of the City of St. Louis, Revised and Digested by the Fifth City Council, in the Year 1843* (St. Louis: Chambers and Knapp, City Printers, 1843).

20. *Ordinances of the City of St. Louis, Passed Since the Publication of the Revised Code of 1836; and, also, Such Ordinances upon Special Subjects, Now in Force* (St. Louis: Office of the Missouri Argus, 1838), 31–2. The city council closed the City Cemetery in 1865 and transformed it into City Park (later renamed Benton Park after former Senator Thomas Hart Benton) in 1866.

21. *Revised Ordinances of the City of St. Louis, State of Missouri, Digested and Revised by the City Council of Said City, in the Years 1855–56* (Thomas C. Chester, Revisor. St. Louis: George Knapp & Company, 1856); William Hyde, and Howard Louis Conard, *Encyclopedia of the History of St. Louis*, vol. 2 (New York: Southern History Company, 1899), 337. This designation of "strangers" seems harsh to us today, but it was not unusual, especially in public cemeteries. The archdiocese continues this practice today, providing free "charity burials" for impoverished Catholics.

22. The records for Sublette Cemetery are digitized by the St. Louis Genealogical Society; see http://stlgs.org/research-2/life-death/cemeteries-2/st-louis-area-cemeteries-list/city-cemetery-sublette-cemetery-c15.

23. John Emory Godbey, *History of the First M.E. Church, South, St. Louis, Mo.* (St. Louis: n.p., 1879), 16–26.

24. "List of Colored Persons in Wesleyan Cemetery, chronological order, 1847–1851" and "List of Colored Persons in Wesleyan Cemetery, chronological order, 1852–1854," St. Louis County Library, Julius K. Hunter Collection. Some are explicitly identified as "Negro of" or "servant of" someone, while others included give only a first name, suggesting they were slaves.

25. "List of Colored Persons in Wesleyan Cemetery, chronological order, 1847–1851."

26. St. Louis Circuit Court Record Book, 20:174, 24:318. George Carr was an adult, although no age was given; Arrianna was fifty-one, Rose Ellen twenty-seven, and Green eighteen.

27. *Rules and Regulations of the Bellefontaine Cemetery, with the Charter, Amendments to the Charter, and Catalogue of Proprietors, to July 1, 1862* (St. Louis: R. P. Studley and Company, 1862). This sort of pricing structure to segregate classes was typical of picturesque cemeteries like Bellefontaine. At most cemeteries, including Bellefontaine, there were even restrictions on size and height of gravestones in the public lots. Bellefontaine imposed regulations on the

installation of all grave markers to have foundations below the frost line, materials used for foundations for them, and so on. See Minutes of the Executive Committee of Bellefontaine Cemetery, October 27, 1856.

28. US Census Bureau. During the 1840s, the slave population grew just 29 percent, while the overall population of the city almost trebled; slavery was becoming less and less prevalent in St. Louis by mid-century. Ten years later, there were just 4,340 slaves in St. Louis, even fewer than twenty years previous.

29. Interment Records, Bellefontaine Cemetery; Bellefontaine Cemetery Lot File 341. Luther M. Kennett (1807–1873) was a prominent political figure in St. Louis, serving as both mayor and congressman during the 1850s. While a Whig, he also gained support from the Know-Nothing wing of the party.

30. Interment Records, Bellefontaine Cemetery.

31. However, the 13th Amendment passed the US House of Representatives in late January 1865.

32. In the interment books, some slaves have no surname listed, while others will be listed as "Unknown." Contemporary records list last names for Ellen and Ada as Switzer, the same as their owner.

33. Interment Records of Bellefontaine Cemetery; Bellefontaine Cemetery Lot File 153. The Rev. John Berry Meachum was the most notable exception; Catholic Cemeteries of the Archdiocese of St. Louis, Calvary Cemetery Burial Records.

34. The thirteen slaves buried at Sublette Cemetery constitute about 3 percent of the 343 recorded burials, whereas the seventeen slaves buried at Bellefontaine represents only 0.2 percent of the more than 8,200 burials by 1865. St. Louis Genealogical Society Cemetery Records, http://stlgs.org/research-2/life-death/cemeteries-2/st-louis-area-cemeteries-list/city-cemetery-sublette-cemetery-c15; Interment Records of Bellefontaine Cemetery.

35. Interment Records of Bellefontaine Cemetery; Bellefontaine Cemetery Lot File 410.

36. Bellefontaine Cemetery Board Minutes, April 21, 1854; Dennis L. Durst, "The Reverend John Berry Meachum (1789–1854) of St. Louis: Prophet and Entrepreneurial Black Educator in Historiographical Perspective," *The North Star: A Journal of African American Religious History* 7 (Spring 2004): 1–24.

37. Bellefontaine Cemetery Executive Committee Minutes, June 8, 1897.

38. Board Minutes, May 1, 1878; italics in the original.

39. Bellefontaine Cemetery Lot File 189; Interment Records of Bellefontaine Cemetery.

40. Interment Records of Bellefontaine Cemetery.

41. Interment Records of Bellefontaine Cemetery.

42. Interment Records of Bellefontaine Cemetery; Bellefontaine Cemetery Lot 780. It was not uncommon for marasmus to be given as a cause of death in the mid-nineteenth century. It is a severe form of malnourishment in infants and children; today, it is usually marked by a weight at least 60 percent below normal.

43. "Former Slave is Buried by Master in Bellefontaine. Henry Lewis, Aged 82, Mistreated in City Hospital, White Friends Declare," *St. Louis Post-Dispatch*, August 28, 1910. Bellefontaine Cemetery lot map, Lot 1323.

Bibliography

"An Act to Amend an Act Concerning Bills of Mortality, in the City of St. Louis and Suburbs,"
  Ordinance 16666, Ordinances compiled in 1846.

"An Act to Incorporate the Rural Cemetery Association." *Laws of the State of Missouri*, 11th
  General Assembly. City of Jefferson: Calvin Gunn, Jeffersonian Office, 1841.

Bellefontaine Cemetery Association, Archival Collections including interment records, lot files,
  and board minutes.

Dupre, Judith. *Monuments: America's History in Art and Memory.* New York: Random House,
  2007.

Eggener, Keith. *Cemeteries.* New York: Norton/Library of Congress Visual Sourcebooks in
  Architecture, Design, and Engineering, 2010.

"Former Slave is Buried by Master in Bellefontaine. Henry Lewis, Aged 82, Mistreated in City
  Hospital, White Friends Declare." *St. Louis Post-Dispatch*, August 28, 1910.

Godbey, John Emory. *History of the First M.E. Church, South, St. Louis, Mo.* St. Louis: n.p., 1879.

Hyde, William, and Howard Louis Conard. *Encyclopedia of the History of St. Louis*, vol. 2. New
  York: Southern History Company, 1899.

"John Berry Meachum." *Missouri Republican*, February 20, 1854.

Julius K. Hunter Collection, St. Louis County Library.

Linden-Ward, Blanche. *Silent City on a Hill: Landscape and Memory in Boston's Mount Auburn
  Cemetery.* Columbus: Ohio State University Press, 1989.

Mitchell, Mary H. *Hollywood Cemetery: The History of a Southern Shrine.* Richmond: Virginia
  State Library, 1985.

*Ordinances of the City of St. Louis, Passed Since the Publication of the Revised Code of 1836; and,
  also, Such Ordinances upon Special Subjects, Now in Force.* St. Louis: Office of the Missouri
  Argus, 1838.

Ordinances Passed by the Mayor and Board of Aldermen of the City of St. Louis. St. Louis:
  Edward Charles, 1824.

Peters, John O. *Richmond's Hollywood Cemetery.* Richmond: Valentine Richmond History
  Center, 2010.

Piattoli, Scipione. *Essay on the Danger of Interment in Cities*, first published in the United States
  in 1823.

Ragon, Michel. *The Space of Death: A Study of Funerary Architecture, Decoration, and Urbanism.* Trans. Alan Sheridan. Charlottesville: University Press of Virginia, 1983.

*Revised Ordinances of the City of St. Louis, Revised and Digested by the Fifth City Council, in the
  Year 1843.* St. Louis: Chambers and Knapp, City Printers, 1843.

*Revised Ordinances of the City of St. Louis, State of Missouri, Digested and Revised by the City
  Council of Said City, in the Years 1855–56.* Thomas C. Chester, Revisor. St. Louis: George
  Knapp & Company, 1856.

*Rules and Regulations of the Bellefontaine Cemetery, with the Charter, Amendments to the Char-
  ter, and Catalogue of Proprietors, to July 1, 1862.* St. Louis: R. P. Studley and Company, 1862.

Schuyler, David Paul. "Public Landscapes and American Urban Culture, 1800–1870: Rural
  Cemeteries, City Parks, and Suburbs." Diss., Columbia University, 1979.

Shepley, Carol Ferring. *Movers and Shakers, Scalawags and Suffragettes: Tales from Bellefontaine
  Cemetery.* St. Louis: Missouri History Museum, 2008.

Sloane, David Charles. *The Last Great Necessity: Cemeteries in American History.* Baltimore:
  Johns Hopkins University Press, 1991.

St. Louis Circuit Court Record Book, Missouri State Archives, 20:174, 24:318.

"The Bellefontaine Cemetery." *Missouri Republican*, May 16, 1850.

Veit, Richard F., and Mark Nonestied. *New Jersey Cemeteries and Tombstones: History in the Landscape.* New Brunswick, NJ: Rivergate Books, an imprint of Rutgers University Press, 2008.

Vernon, Christopher. *Graceland Cemetery: A Design History.* Amherst: University of Massachusetts Press, 2011.

Chapter Six

"For Interment of White People Only": Cemetery Superintendents' Authority and the Wealthy White Protestant Lawn-Park Cemetery, 1886–1920

—KELLY B. AREHART

In 1908 J. R. Gaudin, a cemetery superintendent known for his advertising prowess, presented a paper at the American Association of Cemetery Superintendents' (AACS) twenty-second annual convention. Entitled "Proper Cemetery Advertising," Gaudin revealed his secrets, telling eager superintendents not to go door to door or include boring testimonials in printed circulars. Instead, he suggested running ads in weekend editions of local papers and outlined forty-eight potential points that could be included in those ads. Most points were very mundane, such as highlighting the flowers or describing lakes and streams.[1] The last of the forty-eight suggestions was a clear message to both people of color and potential lot owners: "For interment of white people only."[2]

Gaudin's essay reveals how cemetery superintendents created cultural and physical boundaries within the cemetery that kept immigrants, people of color, and the poor out of what Longfellow called "God's Acre."[3] Through this process, cemetery superintendents were then able to situate themselves as arbiters of taste. This new role also reinforced the boundaries within the cemetery, as immigrants, people of color, and the poor had difficulties meeting the superintendents' standards.

Gaudin's suggestions targeted a demographic he identifies as "white." Based on newspaper accounts, cemetery superintendents' conference papers, and the AACS journal, *Park and Cemetery* and *Modern Cemetery*, this was a broad category. It included white Anglo-Saxon Protestants, but also Germans and Catholics who had been in the country for multiple generations and had at least some disposable income for purchasing a lot and erecting a monument. For the purposes of this essay, "people of color" is a catchall term for those considered to have been nonwhite. African Americans make up the bulk of the group, but Asian Americans are briefly discussed as well. Other groups whose whiteness was contested seem to have been lumped in with immigrants or the poor, depending on the circumstance. The term "poor" is harder to pin down, as its definition is subjective. Its use in this context is based on how cemetery superintendents and reformers used the term.

The type of cemetery for which Gaudin offers advertising advice was created fifty years before his writing and dominated cemetery planning into the 1910s. After decades of complaints about cemeteries being unkempt eyesores, Adolph Strauch designed a style of cemetery that cemetery superintendents hailed as the ideal burial place. Strauch, a landscape gardener at Cemetery of Spring Grove in Cincinnati, developed the landscape lawn plan or the lawn-park plan in 1855. He advocated for smaller monuments and headstones, carefully curated landscapes, and more open, park-like spaces in the cemetery.[4]

This lawn-park style made enforcing racial and class boundaries easy for cemetery superintendents, as the cemetery plan created tight restrictions on what was and what was not appropriate. Cemetery superintendents created arbitrary standards of taste and beauty—ones that specifically left out old-world traditions, racial equality, and those who could not afford it.

Cemetery superintendents had more power than previous generations of burial-space caretakers. The church graveyard sextons did little more than dig graves and ring church bells.[5] Their descendants, working in rural cemeteries after 1831, served as landscape gardeners with little influence beyond botanical decoration. When Strauch introduced his new cemetery layout in 1855, he also asked its board for expanded administrative powers, essentially moving the day-to-day operations from board members to a new "superintendent."[6] From this humble arrangement, other cemeteries looked to follow suit and cemetery superintendents emerged from coast to coast.

Prevaricators and Mule Drives: The American Cemetery Superintendent and His Authority

In 1886 Charles Nichols of Spring Grove Cemetery in Cincinnati conferred with like-minded cemetery superintendents and decided to create an organization that would benefit its members through "mutual education."[7] Nichols was sincere in his beliefs, as were later generations of superintendents. A member of the American Association of Cemetery Superintendents (AACS) writing twenty-two years after the organization's founding praised the other aspects of

the group's mission. The AACS's commitment to "conserving landscape gardening and rural art" made an impression on the author and he credits "noticeable improvement . . . in the appearance of cemeteries throughout the country"
to the mission of the organization.[8] These notice improvements indicate that
members of the AACS could successfully manipulate cemetery landscapes to
meet the needs of desired clientele.

It is important to note that at no point during this period was AACS numerous or diverse by any criteria. In 1897 the organization had 199 members; in 1917,
280; and by 1921, 360.[9] Geographically, 60 percent of the members were from
one of six states in 1921—Pennsylvania, New York, Ohio, Illinois, Massachusetts,
and Michigan—and this may account for the forthright and direct way the group
handled their affairs.[10] AACS members' own ethnic makeup mirrored those that
they served. The men running these cemeteries came from the ranks of white
Anglo-Saxon Protestants and German families who had been living in the United
States for many generations. Little is known about members' formal education.
Superintendents would need top-notch reading, writing, and communication
skills, but there are very few references to higher education in their writings.

Despite these shortcomings, the AACS was unapologetic about who they
were and what it was they were looking to accomplish. F. Higgins in his 1899
paper, "The Ideal Cemetery Superintendent," takes a humorous look at the five
attributes he considers essential for success. Higgins' list includes, in order, that
a superintendent be a gentleman, a prevaricator ("of marked ability"), a "mule
driver," a civil engineer, and an artist.[11]Some of his choices are expected; gentle-
manly behavior when dealing with the bereaved was a must and civil engineering
skills could enhance the landscape. Superintendents' artistic skills solidified their
role as a tastemaker and demonstrated their ability to influence their clientele.

Higgins's claims that superintendents should also be prevaricators and
mule drivers appears to be tongue-in-cheek, but reveals more than he probably intended. In his example about being a prevaricator, Higgins encourages
superintendents to outright lie to their patrons. When a widow asked why the
fictional superintendent had not tended to her husband's grave the way she
instructed, the fictional superintendent replied that instead of doing that work,
it was better that nature handle it in its own time; it's what her husband would
have wanted.[12] This example, while humorous, indicates that being in control,
even when they were in the wrong, was of tantamount importance to cemetery
superintendents. Additionally, the paper shows the superintendent's ability to
convince the widow that not following her instructions was an artistic decision
and not a mistake.

Suggesting superintendents should be mule drivers provides an insight into
labor relations in the cemetery. Higgins expects the ideal superintendent to
constantly monitor grave diggers, gardeners, the maintenance crew, and any

others who report to him. From Higgins's remarks, it seems that those who worked in the cemetery were members of groups that could not bury loved ones at their places of employment. The ideal superintendent could work with "men of almost all existing nationalities," but likely at arm's length.[13] There were limits as to who could work in a cemetery and Higgins's reference to them is frustratingly vague. While he was willing to work with men of many nationalities, he made it clear that he would not work with the "unspeakable."[14] While it is not clear as to who he was talking about, the audience who heard his paper would have known exactly to whom he was referring. This explicit reference to a group of "undesirables," show that cemetery superintendents were equally committed controlling who was in their cemeteries—above or below ground.

AACS members were so enamored of rules that, in almost every edition of *Park and Cemetery*, they published a member cemetery's by-laws. While there are some regional differences, many of the by-laws from each cemetery are the same.[15] They may have served as a constant reminder to AACS members of just how important their own by-laws were and that reading the by-laws from other cemeteries might inspire enterprising cemetery superintendents to speak to their boards about improving their rules. The constant publication of something so seemingly dull may have reinforced how important rules and order were and that superintendents were expected to internalize this way of thinking.

Undertakers, Undesirables, and Cemetery Superintendents: The Battle for Place

The superintendents' need for total control of the cemetery included monitoring everyone who came in and out and what they did while there. At an early meeting of the AACS in 1888, an anonymous member submitted a question for the group. The unknown writer asks, "What are the duties of an undertaker at a funeral after entering the cemetery?" To which a member quickly replied, "To obey the orders of the Superintendent."[16] The use of the words "obey" and "orders" are telling. The use of strong language in such a succinct answer makes it clear that even in the early days of the AACS, there was a sense of complete mastery when it came to a superintendent's cemetery.

Mr. Sargent, one of the AACS officers, provided a more comprehensive answer that echoes the anonymous answer. Sargent creates a physical barrier between the undertaker's authority and the superintendent's authority, stating that the superintendent "has sole care of everything that comes within his grounds and he is held responsible."[17] Sargent's use of "his grounds" instead of "the cemetery" encouraged a sense of ownership for members reading the proceedings.

State governments codified these barriers and superintendents' sense of ownership in the 1910s. Virginia passed a law at the very end of this period (1919) that specifically empowered superintendents with "all the powers, functions, duties, responsibilities, and authority of a constable."[18] The power included the cemetery and up to a quarter-mile away.[19] With this, superintendents finally had the legal legitimacy that reinforced their own beliefs about their power.

Despite these efforts, there were instances where cemetery superintendents did not have full control of what happened in their cemetery. In the 1896 Bloomington, Illinois, court case *Graves v. City of Blooming*, a woman hired to take care of a family's plots was assaulted by the cemetery's superintendent because she was "unseemly." He broke her wrist and she took him to court. While the judge recognized the superintendent's right to remove anyone violating the rules, the judge also ruled that the woman in question was compliant.[20] In this case, the plaintiff superintendent thought breaking a woman's wrist was a justifiable action because he found her "unseemly" and did not want her on the property. All of this poses the question, what about this woman was so offensive to the cemetery superintendent? It could have been many things, but unfortunately the historical record is silent on the matter. She may have looked poor (disheveled, soiled clothing, etc.), suspected of being an immigrant or a person of color, or some combination thereof. Regardless, the plaintiff saw this woman as so far beneath him socially that physically attacking her was within his rights.

A less dramatic, albeit chronic, challenge to a cemetery superintendent's authority was the undertaker. Despite the previously cited answer to the question from the "Question box," some undertakers flouted the rules in ways that infuriated superintendents. Cave Hill Cemetery in Louisville, Kentucky, took meticulous notes as to how the local undertakers slighted them in one way or another. In October 1899 the Cave Hill cemetery superintendent wrote Gran W. Smith & Sons threatening them that the cemetery would take them to court if they did not stop driving their hearses through the cemetery so quickly.[21] Unfortunately, it is not known if they took legal action.

Just a few years later, the cemetery superintendent at Cave Hill sent dozens of letters to undertakers and lawyers demanding that they submit their paperwork in an timely fashion. In 1905 Cave Hill's secretary wrote the superintendent that he needed to report undertakers who had not filled out the proper paperwork for burial. The secretary states that he will "take up the matter with the Undertaker's Association and see that the offence is properly death with."[22] There was probably very little the Undertakers Association could do to the offending undertaker and there is a possibility that the secretary and the superintendent knew this. Nonetheless, this letter was an effort to establish authority over those they could not control outright.

Figure 6.1 Green-Wood Cemetery is an excellent example of the rural cemetery movement. Stacy, G. (ca. 1865), Green-Wood Cemetery, Brooklyn, New York. Courtesy of Library of Congress Prints and Photographs Division.

These examples show the limitations of their influence, but also provide insights into just how powerful some superintendents imagined themselves to be and the lengths they would go to to demonstrate dominion over their cemeteries. Though this process they created rigid boundaries that cemetery superintendents would do just about anything to protect.

Establishing influence and power made it possible for cemetery superintendents to position themselves as arbiters of taste. As they built the barriers that made them the authority within the cemetery, superintendents found a way to capitalize on their newfound authority. Successful tastemakers must have the confidence to claim that identity and they must demonstrate mastery in a way that inspires confidence. Cemetery superintendents were confident in their claims as to what was and was not tasteful, but their opinions were challenged constantly. Despite this constant tug-of-war, potential/lot owners could meet the superintendents' criteria for a tasteful burial lot. A superintendent's taste-making efforts created cultural boundaries that only the sufficiently wealthy white clientele could traverse.

Superintendents had some difficulties getting the public to understand that the lawn-park plan was the most tasteful of burial settings. Potential lot owners had a hard time evaluating what it was they expected in an attractive cemetery. Many potential lot owners were familiar with the rural cemetery, with their elaborate headstones and monuments surrounding extensive botanical decorations, and were content to follow that model.[23] Meanwhile, superintendents complained about potential/lot owners and the amount of "education" that was needed to convince them. An editorial in the September 1895 edition of *Park and Cemetery* stated, "every means available to the officials [of the cemetery] should be immediately exercised to that [educating lot owners] end."[24]

An 1899 editorial expressed outright distain for those who got in the way of the cemetery superintendent:

> The public did not tell the great masters of architecture, painting what they would like. No! these great men created and made something that was pure and good and the public appreciated it, and the taste and demand increased for that which was the highest, purest and best. To this end the cemetery through its directors or super-intendent takes the place of the individual lot owner by embellishing the entire cemetery rather than the individual lots, and thus making pleasant the visits of the living by beautifying the last resting place of the dead.[25]

The author has no interest in what the public wants. He seems disgusted by the mere thought that the public has a right to an opinion at all. He implies that, like the masters before them, cemetery officials are working to create something "pure and good" that the public would learn to admire. Potential/lot owners would be so impressed that they would understand that the appearance of the cemetery was of primary importance. Is not clear as to whether this happened the way the author wanted it to, but the fact that he so badly wanted it to indicates an almost desperate desire to have his taste respected.

Funerals attracted cemetery superintendents' ire for being distasteful and for taking money "away" from the cemetery. Frederick Green presented a paper to the AACS in 1906 on rough boxes that belied a bitterness about funerals. Green shifted gears from describing the boxes in which the burial receptacle was placed before burial to railing about funerals and the American people.[26] He wrote, "Almost all good Americans like to spend their money where it will make a show and all funerals are largely show."[27] His use of "good Americans" may have been a scornful way to identify who he was talking about; the paper's audience would have known that this was a jab at potential/lot owners who think their taste was superior to all other walks of life. More importantly, the claim that "all funerals are largely for show" was a cynical dismissal of American's ability to rationally approach death.

According to papers given at AACS conventions, potential/lot owners could have benefited from a rational approach to death. In 1902 A. W. Hobert, in "Respect for the Dead and Justice to Their Descendants," examines how ephemeral funerary material culture was. He describes how the carriages full of mourners come and go, and how the flowers fade and the casket molders in the grave. He states that the family and friends think they have done all that they could for their loved one's perpetual memory, but that they have fallen short. They did not provide for the perpetual care of the lot in which the deceased was

buried.[28] This oversight communicates to the conference attendees that families mean well but are ignorant of their loved one's true needs (perpetual care)
and that the bereaved needed the guidance of the cemetery superintendent to
ensure the important things were taken care of. As evident in the sources above,
funerals were little more than a distraction that made it difficult for superintendents to assert control.

Beyond being a distraction, members of the AACS found traditional funerals
revolting. In 1893 O. C. Simonds presented a paper at the seventh annual AACS
convention. "The Object of our Association" meditates on the true purpose of
funerals and how the old practices could be abolished. Simonds goes so far as
to call funerals "relics of barbarism," a phrase that shows up in a *Park and Cemetery* editorial two years later.[29] His real objection was like Green's: funerals were
nothing more than spectacle. Simonds creates a vivid picture of the mourners
in the cemetery including "perhaps strangers and idle curiosity seekers gather
around to see how bad was the mourners feel [sic], to gaze on some celebrated
character that has attended the funeral, or to ask questions about the private
affairs of the deceased."[30]

Simonds, and possibly Green, may have objected to the typical potential/lot
owner funeral for reasons other than caring about the emotional hardships of
the bereaved. Part of their objection might have come from concerns about the
cemetery itself. In the example above, Simonds is describing throngs of people
descending on (what was likely to have been) a meticulously cared-for cemetery.[31] The number of people, who Simonds likely wanted the reader to think of
as careless, traipsing through the cemetery could damage plants, landscape features, and monuments. It is possible that Simonds was more concerned about
his hypothetical well-manicured cemetery than the bereaved when he spoke of
the barbarous nature of the funeral.

In these funerary critiques, it becomes clear that cemetery superintendents
had less control during the funeral spectacle, no matter how powerful they
claimed to be. This would have caused some duress, in part because people who
were not potential/lot owners could permeate the carefully constructed boundaries of cemeteries that the superintendents worked tirelessly to uphold.

There is another aspect of these critiques that cannot be overlooked: money.
Every dollar a bereaved family spent on the casket, the hearse, carriages for
funeral attendees, mourning clothing, the monument, and many other funerary
goods was a dollar less available for a large lot or perpetual care. Superintendent
Matthew P. Brazill makes quite clear in his 1896 paper, "The Education of Lot
Owners," what the real problem was. Potential/lot owners had "lavish funeral[s]
at the expense of a large lot" and Brazill's use of the word "expense" is telling.[32]
"Expense" drives home the point that funerals were in direct competition with
cemeteries and their superintendents.

Monument Men vs. Cemetery Superintendents: The Battle over Taste

The real battle for "taste" in the cemetery was fought over monuments that honored the dead. The lawn-park plan, to which many AACS members adhered, discouraged large monuments in every lot and warned against the use of marble and other materials that did not fare well in the elements. This plan also advocated careful planning of roads, landscape features, and planting.[33] In short, it was an orderly arrangement ideal for those who needed to be in control.

Adjusting to the lawn-park plan was difficult for many, including the potential/lot owners who superintendents tried so hard to impress. New materials now available for commemoration were more durable, customizable, and cheaper than what was available to previous generations. The use of new materials and innovative technologies in monument production created attractive, resilient markers that solved the problem of decaying monuments that plagued previous generations. These new monuments were status symbols that projected the lot owner's status in perpetuity while providing comfort to bereaved families knowing that these monuments safeguarded the memory of the deceased. As one monument company stated, "Of all the things that one purchases in a lifetime[,] the most in permanency and endurance is expected of the family memorial. Its material and construction ought to be of the most perfect character to withstand the test of time."[34] This test of time was not just about the deceased but the living who erected the memorial.

Granite's strength made it appealing, but it also made it hard to work with. Granite has a "more inert composition[, a] slower rate of deterioration," and "a lower water absorption rate" than marble, limestone, and sandstone, making the igneous rock an appealing alternative for sepulchral monuments.[35] These same properties made the stone hard to polish and carve. Those working with the material before the 1870s had two options: chisel the stone (commonly referred to as "hammering") or hand-polish it. Both options were time- and labor-intensive. Before the 1870s granite was mostly relegated to marking burial plot boundaries and cemetery curbing.[36]

A gradual reduction in cost and user-friendly carving tools created unlikely competition for stone carvers.[37] Sears Roebuck was the first to offer granite and marble sepulchral monuments in 1902, publishing special catalogs separate from their usual publication. These catalogs bragged that Sears Roebuck could furnish high-quality monuments at considerably lower prices than smaller establishments.[38] Sears Roebuck stated that they could provide "a class of cemetery work such as they will seldom if ever find in the stocks of retail marble companies" and could save the buyer up to fifty percent because Sears did not have to pay agents a commission.[39]

Figure 6.2 Cheap headstones dominated the landscape by the turn of the twentieth century. Sears headstones, Sears, Roebuck and Company, 1902. From *Special Catalogue of Tombstones, Monuments, Tables and Markers.*

However, Sears Roebuck did not offer as many choices in monument styles and ornamentation as smaller firms could. Retail dealers also purchased semi-finished stones from quarries but had the equipment and the skill to reshape or resize headstones and monuments to meet the needs of the bereft.[40] Independently operated monument companies did not produce their stones in bulk, which gave them the opportunity to offer a wider variety of options to customize the monument's carved decorations. Not all families availed themselves of this service, but for those who wanted a more personalized monument, their options were almost limitless.

Granite was not the only option in the quest for an enduring monument. Metallic plaques and monuments provided additional choices for families. The success of these products was mixed, but their introduction and marketing reinforced the importance of using durable materials to commemorate of the dead. Manufacturers relied on "science" to demonstrate the value of their products and to familiarize consumers with the properties that made metallic memorial pieces superior to marble and limestone.

Manufacturers of metallic products harped on marble's unsuitability for permanent markers. One bronze monument company stated in 1882 that "stone has proved itself an unfortunate failure as a material for enduring records, and for proof of this we simply invite an inspection of the work in any twenty-year-old cemetery."[41] This quote tacitly refers to marble stones, as granite was not an available choice for sepulchral monuments until the late 1870s and its long-term durability as grave markers was still unknown. Another metallic monument manufacturer claimed that marble was "nearly useless" for grave markers because it weathered so poorly.[42] Like granite, metallic markers solved the problem of crumbling, disintegrating monuments that slowly obliterated the memory of the dead.

The precedent of stone monuments made marketing of granite grave markers easy, but created challenges for those promoting metal commemorative pieces. Those in the market for a headstone were unfamiliar with using metals for this purpose, so manufacturers relied on "science and fact" as a means of promoting the products. Companies indicated that scientists' impartiality made individual endorsements all that more valuable as them came from "high and trustworthy sources." A zinc-monument maker stated that "those who have given the nature of Zinc a study" knew that "as soon as the film of oxidation forms it is the END OF ALL CHANGE."[43] Other companies sought endorsements. The Monumental Bronze Company published the text of a certificate from the Assayer of Metals for the State of Massachusetts: "I consider the White Bronze Monuments practically indestructible. They will not blacken or become dingy with age. Moss will not adhere or grow upon their surface as upon marble, and the color will remain unchangeable while the monuments endure. In my opinion, these monuments will outlast the stone foundation on which they stand."[44] This testimony echoes the manufacturer's claims, encouraging potential customers to take such claims more seriously. It is also possible that these claims were designed to appeal to well-educated middle-class families looking to commemorate their dead.

Cemetery superintendents did not want to share their influence with whom they called "monument men" and used a combination of cemetery regulations and derision to convince potential/lot owners that the superintendents were the arbiters of taste, not the "monument men." In maintaining their supremacy, first over undertakers, now over monument men, superintendents could continue to set the perimeters of their power.

Monument regulation was the easiest way for superintendents to control lot owners in their quest for immortality. Many AACS members agreed that each

cemetery had to make similar decisions like what percentage of a lot a monument could occupy or the best thickness and height of the headstones. Superintendents presenting papers from different cemeteries gave different answers to
these questions, but all recognized these issues needed to be addressed.

Setting the height and/or thickness of a headstone limited how much a lot
owner could lavish on an individual burial. Opinions varied, but those writing
on the subject agreed lower was better. In 1888 F. Eurich suggested that individual graves should only be marked with a "dark colored, substantial stone
sunk in the ground, level with the turf," while in 1892 Marcus Farwell, author of
the paper "Headstones and Markers," suggested the proper height for a headstone was no more than a foot and not less than six inches thick.[45] By-laws
across the country varied, but there was a collective agreement that headstones
should not be large or ornate like the marble headstones that Farwell referred
to as "old deformities" from the 1830s to the 1850s. Because there was no way to
redeem these markers, Farwell was frustrated when he had to move them from
the "ancient graveyard" to his newer cemetery.[46]

In the first decades of the twentieth century, cemetery superintendents and
their boards decided that one of the best ways to deal with overcrowding was to
limit how much of a lot a monument can occupy. As with headstones the exact
numbers differed, but typically the percentage of the lots permitted for monuments ranged from 4 to 7 percent.[47] This restriction addresses the arrogance and
ignorance some cemetery superintendents faced when dealing with potential/
lot owners.

According to Thomas Wallis, author of the paper "The Advantages of
Restricting Size of Monuments," having such a policy would protect against
small families thinking that their business would be enough that "a Cemetery
will be glad to let them up any kind of monument they may want."[48] Wallis
does not speculate as to the cause of this entitlement, but he provides other
examples where lot owners thought they were exception to the rule. In all his
examples, the cemetery superintendents held firm and were able to reestablish
their authority in these situations. In one instance, a lot owner wanted to build
a settee on his lot, but the design violated the rules and he would have to move
the bodies and buy a bigger lot. Despite his displeasure and complaints that the
cemetery's rules were "arbitrary," the gentleman moved his family and was permitted to procced with his plans.[49] The inclusion of this situation in the paper
was likely designed to reinforce other teachings about the cemetery superintendent's control over even the most wealthy and prominent lot owners.

Headstone and monument regulation was one way to control the appearance
and who could bury within the cemetery, but it was not the only way cemetery
superintendents asserted dominance. Their disparaging attitude toward monument men may have been an even more important attempt at making sure that

potential/lot owners trusted the superintendent when it came to memorializing their loved ones. This was not without its difficulties, as creating that kind of esthetic and cultural shift is difficult work.

Fanny Seavey's 1896 paper "The Cemetery As a Work of Art" recognizes that many of the potential/lot owners' failings are psychological and difficult for the cemetery superintendent to overcome. When "man's vanity and selfishness" creates a psychological need for large ornate monuments that tower over the rest of the cemetery, it was very difficult for the superintendent's "artist's" eye to elevate taste.[50] Her solution was to rid the cemetery of stones completely, which was not a viable solution.[51] Superintendents relied on other methods to convince potential/lot owners to change their ways.

Probably one of the easiest methods they employed was to express their distaste of monument men around potential/lot owners or around each other. In his 1896 paper "The Education of Lot Owners," Matthew P. Brazill encouraged AACS members to dissuade potential/lot owners from speaking to monument men about what was appropriate.[52] This issue was not resolved in the almost thirty years between Brazill's paper and S. J. Perrott's 1924 paper "Monuments, Markers and Other Cemetery Memorials." Perrott's opinion on the issue was subtler and passive-aggressive. He states that the lot owner would "profit" if they consulted the management "or advice sought of persons to possess the correct taste."[53] Perrott was of course implying that cemetery management (particularly cemetery superintendents) did possess "the correct taste" while the monument men's lack of mention indicates that they were not to be consulted.

A November 1894 editorial addressed the monument men's failings head on. The author, possibly cemetery superintendent and publisher R. J. Haight, recognized that a monument man's real function was not to elevate the tastes of potential/lot owners, but to provide the paying customer with whatever he or she desires.[54] The author even asserts, "if our cemetery memorials are bad, it is the fault of the purchaser; he gets what he wants, and all that he is willing to pay for."[55] In no way did Haight implicate cemetery superintendents in the erection of ugly or inappropriate monuments. It is as if he relinquishes power to those he would normally consider unfit to make such important decisions. While his motivations here are unknown, this may be a glimpse into cemetery superintendents' reactions when things do not go their way.

In addition to warning against unsightly monuments, Haight addresses how cemetery superintendents can salvage the broader landscape. According to the paper, it was imperative that responsible cemetery superintendents talk to lot owners about the surroundings outside their own lot. A conversation with the superintendent could put the bereaved's choices in a broader perspective. This way the family was more prudent in their monument choice and sensitive to not repeating the designs in the other nearby lots.[56]

Not all cemetery superintendents thought that a regimented approach was the best way to handle potential/lot owners. James Scorgie, who also wrote about limiting the size of monuments, recognized that being too aggressive with the public would create problems. Specifically, he referred to cemetery regulations that were "ahead of public opinion and difficult to enforce."[57] In the same article, he also stated that monumental design improved significantly between 1895 and 1920.[58] While his opinion did not resonate through other convention papers or the pages of *Park and Cemetery*, Scorgie's measured approach and patience for contemporary potential/lot owners was likely the norm for cemeteries with more moderate cemetery superintendents.

As an alternative to radical regulations likely to drive potential/lot owners away, some advocated that there might be another way to commemorate the dead—one that was mutually beneficial to the lot owner and the cemetery. Instead of a family devoting their resources to a monument, headstones, and a lot, the bereaved could instead sponsor a "useful memorial" like weather shelters, seating, or even trees.[59] This idea did not seem to influence other AACS members or the public, and its failure to do so exposed the limitations of superintendents' influence.

Cemetery superintendents' efforts to control sepulchral monuments were an extension of their attempts to create boundaries between their cemeteries and the rest of the world. In headstone and monument regulation, superintendents were able to assert their power over potential/lot owners in ways they never could beyond the cemetery walls. Monument regulations forced potential/lot owners to comply with the superintendent's vision of the cemetery rather than the family's vision of their lot. Superintendents set themselves up as arbiters of taste to separate the monument men from the potential/lot owners. Creating an artificial barrier between the monument men and lot owners isolated the lot owners and made them dependent on the superintendent for suggestions and advice.

Cemetery superintendents' control of their cemeteries was predicated not only upon expertise and enforcing the rule law, but also on how well they could create and maintain boundaries between potential/lot owners (who were white and sufficiently wealthy to afford lots) and those deemed undesirable (who were immigrants, people of color, and the poor). Superintendents found ways to separate the "undesirables" from the potential/lot owners burying their loved ones in these carefully manicured cemeteries. Superintendents created physical boundaries between the working-class sections and the rest of the cemeteries and then lamented that the families of those inhabitants were unable to meet the superintendent's expectations of refinement. Cemetery superintendents also used carefully chosen language in their advertising to convey to potential lot owners that the cemetery was restricted to sufficiently wealthy whites. When communicating in the courts or with each other, cemetery superintendents demonstrated that explicit racism and rampant discrimination were some of the many ways they maintained control of their cherished burial spaces.

According to some writers, death was the great equalizer, even if funerary culture was not. Consolation manual author Daniel C. Eddy contrasted the burial of a rich man with that of a poor man. The rich gentleman "has a splendid funeral" and was "laid down in his lot which his wealth purchased for himself." "He expired just as the poor man did," further explains Eddy, "who died without his gate, and was borne away to some rude tomb, over which the flowers were ashamed to bloom and the birds to sing."[60] As seen in Eddy's prose, there were very clear expectations about how the "poor" were to be buried: simply, cheaply, and without the funerary material culture reserved for the financially comfortable.

Cemetery superintendents writing thirty-plus years later would have agreed with Eddy's expectations as to how the poor or working-class should be buried. Cemetery superintendents relegated the working class and the poor to single-burial lots in part of the cemetery sometimes called the "potters' field" or the "pauper lot."[61] While some objected to those terms, AACS members seemed to agree that an out-of-the-way space designated for the burials of the poor and/or working class was an important, albeit irritating part of the overall cemetery design.

Many superintendents advocated that single-grave sections should be located just inside the boundaries of the cemetery.[62] The author of "The Sub-dividing of a Cemetery into Sections, Lots, and Single-Grave Sections" wanted to create boundaries between the single lots and the rest of the cemetery. He stated that the single lots should "be so located that the crowds of people going to and from the single graves will not be tempted to cross other sections and wear paths in the sod."[63] This superintendent assumed that working-class and poor lot owners would not know how to behave and as such their relatives were relegated to the outskirts of the cemetery.[64]

Cemetery superintendents' frustrations about monuments in large lots was nothing compared to scorn they heaped upon the stonework that went up in "the cheaper class of lots." Their irritation was twofold. First, those who owned these "cheaper class of lots" put up their monuments or headstones with no thought of good taste.[65] Secondly, these erections were often of poor quality and cheaply put up.[66]

While both the wealthy and those buried in the single-grave sections could have monuments, additional adornment of the lot set working-class and possibly immigrant lots apart from those of the sufficiently wealthy whites, much to superintendents' chagrin. AACS members would complain that their cemeteries were full of "jam tins, lard pails, honey pails," and sundry other items used to "decorate" gravesites.[67] Forest Hill Cemetery in Birmingham, Alabama, went so far as to change its by-laws to include a rule that states: "no trinkets, toys, shells, artificial flowers, glass cases, pickle jars, tin cans, etc. or brick, sand or other artificial material will be allowed on any lot; and such articles and material will be removed without further notice."[68] This crackdown and others like it indicates that those buried in the less desirable lots were participating in their own traditions of grave-site decorations unlike those of wealthy whites. Writing new regulations provided an opportunity for cemetery superintendents to reassert their authority over the landscape and create further distinctions between the nice, respectable parts of the cemetery (inhabited by the graves of wealthy whites) and the undesirable, chaotic, and unrefined sections of the burial space.

Cemetery superintendents relied on advertising to catch the eye of potential lot owners. One of the most important things for the ad to convey was that the cemetery in question was appropriate for sufficiently wealthy whites looking to demonstrate their position in society in perpetuity. Some of Gaudin's advertising suggestions, introduced in the beginning of the essay, were subtler that the blatant "for white people only."[69] His first suggestion was to highlight the location of the cemetery and its distance from manufacturing districts of cities. This location would make it difficult for city dwellers, including immigrants, people of color, and the poor to access the cemetery. Even when Gaudin mentioned cemetery access via streetcar, his focus was funeral cars available to those who could afford to procure them.[70]

Another ad capitalized on potential lot owners' perceived place in the social order. The short copy encouraged potential lot owners to think of the cemetery as a neighborhood, their plot as their "home" and the adjacent lots full of their neighbors.[71] The ad encourages its audience to transplant their current social order to the nearby cemetery and take comfort in knowing that the right sort of people will be their eternal neighbors.

The most direct way cemetery superintendents policed the boundaries of the cemeteries was though the courts. A 1910 case in Kentucky had a surprising verdict and forced superintendents and cemetery boards to carefully prepare for a similar incident. Joel J. Walker (white) passed away and left his cemetery plot in the Richmond Cemetery in Richmond, Kentucky, to one of his black servants. Eventually, the woman wanted to bury her child in the cemetery, and the Richmond Cemetery's board said no. The bereaved woman took them to court. The cemetery argued that it was a cemetery for white people and that they already made their contribution when they bought three and a half acres for the African American community to bury their dead. Furthermore, the cemetery offered to pay the inheritor full price for the lot. But the court was not impressed. The judge stated that there were segregation laws for most aspects of life, but none that regulated who could be buried in what cemetery.[72]

While the woman could bury her child in peace, states and cemeteries quickly closed loopholes. An Illinois law required equal pricing for lots regardless of race, but did not require that cemeteries sell to African Americans.[73] Renowned cemetery attorney A. L. Street confirmed that a cemetery could refuse to sell a lot to a black man or woman; if that man or woman already held the deed to the lot, it would be illegal to refuse them.[74]

Most immigrants were not barred from the single-grave lots in lawn-park cemeteries and, as a result, these became a popular place for some groups to bury their dead.[75] Immigrant's "old-world" customs challenged the order of the well-manicured lawn-park cemetery and the authority of the cemetery super-intendent. Cemetery superintendents constantly complained to their peers that these new Americans were guilty of backward customs, tasteless displays, and downright dangerous actions.

A cemetery superintendent writing in 1903 remarked that immigrants were foolishly devoted to the ways of their homeland. The newly arrived, and in some cases those who had been in America for a few generations, wanted cemeter-ies that were geared toward wealthy native-born whites to erect civic statues to figures from the "old country."[76] This expectation, along with the author's observation that immigrant groups did not change any of their customs and prejudices once they were settled in America, indicates that some cemetery superintendents may have found immigrant funerals and the surrounding ritu-als disorienting and a challenge to their authority.

One AACS member wrote that merely having an immigrant group bury their dead in the cemetery was disruptive. The Romani had chosen Woodlawn Cemetery in Dayton, Ohio, as their national burial space. During a weekend Romani funeral, thousands of locals descended upon the cemetery because they had never seen a "Gypsy funeral." The onlookers injured the grounds and converted the cemetery into "a place of amusement."[77] The foreignness of the funeral and the spectacle it created undermined the cemetery superintendents' efforts to maintain a sense of "decorum."

In other instances, cemetery superintendents saw immigrants as a menace to public health. In Chicago in 1891, a father buried his child, dead of diphtheria. Shortly thereafter, the father wanted to move the body elsewhere and the super-intendent would not let him because the child died of a communicable disease. The father moved the body and was arrested. He then sued the superinten-dent for malicious prosecution, arguing that only families could make decisions about disinterment. The jury agreed with the cemetery's argument that allowing families to make that kind of decision was inappropriate and that "there would be nothing to prevent ignorant persons, particularly foreigners," from digging up bodies dead of "foul disease."[78] Even though the father in this case was not foreign, the jury immediately identified foreigners as potential threats that cem-etery superintendents and other health officials had to "neutralize."

Despite cemetery superintendents' dismissive and condescending attitudes toward those who were different, it is possible that they may have been more inclusive and accepting than what the bulk of the historical record tells us. In the spring of 1918, someone anonymously asked a question that was published in *Park and Cemetery*'s "Asked and Answered" column. The curious party wanted to know if there were any objections to setting up a Jewish section in a cemetery and if there were any drawbacks to doing so. The response was overwhelming—no one objected. In his reply, William Falconer of Pittsburgh's Allegheny Cemetery made it clear that having a Jewish section was no different than having ones "for Catholics, Elks, Masons or any other Christian people" and, like any other group, the should be by themselves. He also states that the Jews "like to have their lots looking pretty nice, just like the Catholics and the Elks, and the Masons."[79]

Cemetery superintendents' ability to assert their authority in the late nineteenth and early twentieth centuries was an uneven process, but many factors made it possible for these new professionals to shape the cemetery landscape in more ways than one. The creation of the American Association for Cemetery Superintendents in 1886 provided like-minded superintendents with an organization sympathetic to their ambition. In turn, these men and women created the cultural, aesthetic, economic, and racial boundaries of white, Protestant, middle-class cemeteries. Ultimately, this process isolated sufficiently wealthy whites from sharing burial spaces with people of color, the poor, and immigrants. The AACS encouraged its members to think of themselves as more than caretakers of the wealthy whites' final resting place. Instead, those associated with the organization asserted their dominance over their clientele and the unwelcome by controlling who had access to the cemetery and what they could do within its walls. Once these conventions were firmly in place, it became easier for the superintendents to demonstrate their ability to strictly enforce who could be there—both above and below ground.

Superintendents' enforcement of cemetery rules isolated the graves of sufficiently wealthy whites from those of whoever they deemed undesirable. The poor could be buried in the single-plot section of the finest cemetery, but there was no guarantee that they would ever be surrounded by loved ones again. Some cemeteries were so desperate to avoid those they found undesirable as to create a separate cemetery to keep them far from the sufficiently wealthy whites' cemeteries. In becoming the arbiters of taste, cemetery superintendents also became gatekeepers who enforced economic and racial hierarchies that were as prevalent behind the cemetery gates as they were in the outside world.

Notes

1. J. R. Gaudin, "Proper Cemetery Advertising," *AACS Proceedings of the 22th Annual Convention*, August 1908, https://www.iccfa.com/reading/1900-1919/proper-cemetery-advertising.

2. Gaudin, "Proper Cemetery Advertising."

3. Henry Wadsworth Longfellow, "God's Acre," 1842, http://www.hwlongfellow.org/poems_poem.php?pid=73.

4. David Charles Sloane, *The Last Great Necessity: Cemeteries in American History* (Baltimore: Johns Hopkins University Press, 1991), 4–5, 97.

5. Sloane, 4–5.

6. Sloane, 106–7.

7. *Proceedings of the Second Annual Convention of the Association of American Cemetery Superintendents* (Akron, OH: Beacon Publishing, 1888), 11.

8. Frank Eurich, "The Association Of American Cemetery Superintendents | ICCFA," *AACS Proceedings of the 22nd Annual Convention*, August 1908, http://www.iccfa.com/reading/1900-1919/association-american-cemetery-superintendents.

9. R. J. Haight, "A Survey of the Association of American Cemetery Superintendents | ICCFA," *AACS Proceedings of the 36th Annual Convention*, September 1922, http://www.iccfa.com/reading/1920-1939/survey-association-american-cemetery-superintendents.

10. Haight.

11. F. Higgins, "The Ideal Superintendent of a Cemetery," *Proceedings of the Third Annual Convention of the Association of American Cemetery Superintendents* (Akron, OH: Akron Engraving Co., 1899), 12.

12. Higgins, 13.

13. Higgins, 13.

14. Higgins, 13.

15. *Modern Cemetery*, 1893, 1894, 1896, 1901, 2011; *Park and Cemetery*, 1901, 1910. Note: these works contain the monthly publications of the trade organ.

16. Question Box–Question 1," *Proceedings of the Second Annual Convention of the Association of the American Cemetery Superintendents* (Akron, OH: Beacon Publishing, 1888), 52.

17. "Question Box–Question 1."

18. Arthur L. H. Street, *American Cemetery Law: A Digest of Cemetery Laws of All the States and Important Court Decisions* (Madison, WI: Park and Cemetery, 1922), 509.

19. Street, 211.

20. Street, 509.

21. Cave Hill to Gran W. Smith and Sons, *Cave Hill Cemetery Collection*, Book 225.

22. *Cave Hill Cemetery Collection*, Book 228.

23. Sloane, 4–5.

24. *Modern Cemetery* 4 (Chicago: R. J. Haight, 1896), 110.

25. "Annual Planting or Embellishment of Cemetery Lots," *Park and Cemetery* 9–10 (Chicago: R. J. Haight, 1901), 135.

26. Frederick Green, "Rough Boxes; ICCFA," *AACS Proceedings of the 20th Annual Convention*, August 1906, http://www.iccfa.com/reading/1900-1919/rough-boxes.

27. Green.

28. A. W. Hobert, "Respect for the Dead and Justice to Their Descendants," *AACS Proceedings of the 16th Annual Convention*, http://www.iccfa.com/reading/1900-1919/respect-dead-and-justice-their-descendants.

29. O. C. Simonds, "The Object of Our Association," *AACS Proceedings of the 7th Annual Convention*, https://www.iccfa.com/reading/1887-1899/object-our-association; *Modern Cemetery* 4, 117.

30. Simonds.

31. This is an assumption, as he does not comment on the appearance of the fictional cemetery. Since the situation is hypothetical, one can assume that Simonds is describing an ideal cemetery.

32. Matthew P. Brazill, "The Education of Lot Owners," *AACS Proceedings of the 10th Annual Convention*, http://www.iccfa.com/reading/1887-1899/education-lot-owners.

33. Sloane, 107–9.

34. Muldoon Monument Company, *Muldoon Memorials* (Louisville, KY: Muldoon Monument Company, 192?), n.p.

35. United States General Services Administration, "Granite: Characteristics, Uses and Problems," http://www.gsa.gov/portal/content/111938, June 2012, Accessed November 12, 2013.

36. Donovan & Megowan, "Order Book and Ledger of Wilmington Del. Stone Cutting business," 1888–95, n.p., Hagley Library; "Ledger, May 1858–1896," Diaries Collection, Winterthur Library; George Shelley, Account Book, n.d., Connecticut Historical Society.

37. Arthur W. Brayley, *History of the Granite Industry in New England* (Boston: National Association of Granite Industries of the United States, 1913), 87.

38. Sears, Roebuck and Company, *Special Catalogue of Tombstones, Monuments, Tablets, and Markers*, (Chicago: Sears, Roebuck and Company, 1902), n.p.

39. Sears, Roebuck and Company, 1–2.

40. Muldoon Monument Company, "Muldoon Monument Company Records," n.d., Book 3, Book 7, Filson Historical Society.

41. Monumental Bronze Company, *Catalog of the Monumental Bronze Company* (Bridgeport, CT: Monumental Bronze Company, 1882), 1.

42. "Frosted Zinc Corinthian Monuments," *Mariposa Gazette*, January 12, 1877.

43. "Frosted Zinc Corinthian Monuments."

44. *Catalog of the Monumental Bronze Company*, 2.

45. F. Eurich, "An Ideal Cemetery," *Proceedings of the Second Annual Convention of the Association of American Cemetery Superintendents* (Akron, OH: Beacon Publishing, 1888), 27; Marcus A. Farwell, "Headstones and Markers," *AACS Proceedings of the 6th Annual Convention of the American Association of Cemetery Superintendents*, http://www.iccfa.com/reading/1887-1899/headstones-and-markers.

46. Farwell.

47. Thomas Wallis, "The Advantages of Restricting Size of Monuments," *AACS Proceedings of the 33rd Annual Convention*, http://www.iccfa.com/reading/1900-1919/advantages-restricting-size-monuments; James Scorgie, "The Control of Stonework in Cemeteries," *AACS Proceedings of the 34th Annual Convention*, http://www.iccfa.com/reading/1920-1939/control-stonework-cemeteries.

48. Wallis.

49. Wallis.

50. Fanny Copley Seavey, "The Cemetery as a Work of Art," *AACS Proceedings for the 10th Annual Convention*, http://www.iccfa.com/reading/1887-1899/cemetery-work-art.

51. Seavey.

52. Brazill.

53. S. J. Perrott, "Monuments, Markers, and Other Cemetery Memorials," *AACS Proceedings of the 38th Annual Convention*, http://www.iccfa.com/reading/1920-1939/monuments-markers-and-other-cemetery-memorials.

54. R. J. Haight, November 1894, *Modern Cemetery*, vol. 3–4, (Chicago: R. J. Haight, 1895), 100. http://archive.org/details/moderncemetery3418unse.

55. Haight, November 1894.

56. Haight, November 1894.

57. Scorgie.

58. Scorgie.

59. May 1895, *Modern Cemetery*, vol. IV–V, 37.

60. Daniel C. Eddy, *Angel Whispers; Or, The Echo of Spirit Voices: Designed to Comfort the Mourning Husband, Wife, Father, Mother, Son and Daughter* (Boston: Thayer & Eldridge, 1860), 205.

61. William Stone, "Care and Maintenance of Public Lots," *AACS Proceedings of the 6th Annual Convention*, September 1892, https://www.iccfa.com/reading/1887-1899/care-and-maintenance-public-lots-city-cemeteries.

62. T. McCarthy, "Cemetery Boundaries," *AACS Proceedings of the 9th Annual Convention*, https://www.iccfa.com/reading/1887-1899/cemetery-boundaries; "The Sub-dividing of a Cemetery into Sections, Lots, and Single-Grave Sections," *Park and Cemetery Landscape Gardening*, Vol. 19–20 (Chicago: R. J. Haight, 1911), 139.

63. W. N. Rudd, "The Subdividing of a Cemetery Into Sections, Lots and Single Grave Districts | ICCFA," *AACS Proceedings of the 23rd Annual Convention*, September 1909, http://www.iccfa.com/reading/1900-1919/subdividing-cemetery-sections-lots-and-single-grave-districts.

64. Rudd.

65. Brazill.

66. Rudd.

67. S. L. Landers, "Flower Container Menace," *AACS Proceedings of the 40th Annual Convention*, http://www.iccfa.com/reading/1920-1939/flower-container-menace.

68. "Rules for Forest Hill Cemetery, Birmingham, Al," *Modern Cemetery*, vol. IV (Chicago: R. J. Haight, 1896), 178.

69. Gaudin.

70. Gaudin.

71. "Neighbors in the Cemetery," *Modern Cemetery*, vol. IV (Chicago: R. J. Haight, 1896), 183.

72. "Refusing Burial to Negro Lot Holder Illegal," *Park and Cemetery and Landscape Gardening*, vol. 19–20 (Chicago: R. J. Haight, 1911), 243.

73. Street, 212–13.

74. Street, 62–63.

75. I say most because there may have been cemeteries out west that discriminated against Japanese and Chinese burials. See Street, 65–67.

76. *Modern Cemetery* 14 (Chicago: R. J. Haight, 1905), 10.

77. J. C. Cline, "Funerals," *Proceedings of the Second Annual Convention of the Association of American Cemetery Superintendents* (Akron, OH: Beacon Publishing, 1888), 41.

78. "Authority to Disinter Bodies," *Modern Cemetery*, vol. IV (Chicago: R. J. Haight, 1896), 212.

79. "Asked and Answered," *Modern Cemetery*, vol. IV (Chicago: R. J. Haight, 1896), 37.

Bibliography

PRIMARY SOURCES

"Annual Planting or Embellishment of Cemetery Lots." *Park and Cemetery* 9–10. Chicago: R. J. Haight, 1901.

"Asked and Answered." *Modern Cemetery* 4. Chicago: R. J. Haight, 1896.

"Authority to Disinter Bodies." *Modern Cemetery* 4. Chicago: R. J. Haight, 1896.

Baker, Oliver. "Account Book," 1827–1856. Connecticut Historical Society.

Beezley, Charles. *Our Manners and Social Customs.* Chicago and Philadelphia: Elliott & Beezley, 1891.

Benham, Georgene. *Polite Life and Etiquette: Or, What Is Right and the Social Arts.* Chicago and Philadelphia: Louis Benham, 1891.

Brazill, Matthew P. "The Education of Lot Owners." *AACS Proceedings of the 10th Annual Convention.* September 1896. http://www.iccfa.com/reading/1887-1899/education-lot-owners.

Bucktrout, Richard Manning. "Bucktrout Collection," n.d. Swem Library Special Collections. The College of William and Mary.

Cave Hill Cemetery Collection. Kentucky Historical Society. Frankfort, KY.

Clarke, Joseph Henry. *Practical Embalming.* Cincinnati: C. Horace Clarke, n.d.

Clatton, Joseph. "Joseph Clatton," n.d. Winterthur Library, Winterthur, DE.

Cline, J. C. "Funerals." *Proceedings of the Second Annual Convention of the Association of American Cemetery Superintendents.* Akron, OH: Beacon Publishing, 1888.

Crane & Breed. "The 'Old Reliable.'" *The Sunnyside* XXXIV, no. 6 (November 1909).

De Valcourt, Robert. *The Illustrated Book of Manners.* Cincinnati: R. W. Carroll, 1865.

Donovan and Megowan. "Order Book and Ledger of Wilmington, Del. Stone Cutting Business, 1888–1895." Hagley Library, Wilmington, DE.

Dowd, Quincey Lamartine. *Funeral Management and Costs: A World-Survey of Burial and Cremation.* Harvard Medicine Preservation Microfilm Project. Part 2; 04106. Chicago: University of Chicago Press, 1921.

Duffey, Eliza. *The Ladies' and Gentleman's Etiquette.* Philadelphia: Porter and Coates, 1877.

Dunbar, M. C. *Dunbar's Complete Handbook of Etiquette.* New York: Excelsior Publishing House, ca. 1884.

Eckels, Howard S. *Derma-Surgery: A New Science, a New Era, a New Book: With Complete Catalogue of Embalmers' Supplies.* Philadelphia: H. S. Eckels, 1900.

Eddy, Daniel C. *Angel Whispers; Or, The Echo of Spirit Voices. Designed to Comfort the Mourning Husband, Wife, Father, Mother, Son and Daughter.* Boston: Thayer & Eldridge, 1860.

Eurich, Frank, "An Ideal Cemetery." *Proceedings of the Second Annual Convention of the Association of American Cemetery Superintendents.* Akron, OH: Beacon Publishing, 1888.

Eurich, Frank. "The Association of American Cemetery Superintendents." *AACS Proceedings of the 22nd Annual Convention,* August 1908. http://www.iccfa.com/reading/1900-1919/association-american-cemetery-superintendents.

Farwell, Marcus A. "Headstones and Markers." *AACS Proceedings of the 6th Annual Convention of the American Association of Cemetery Superintendents,* August 1892. http://www.iccfa.com/reading/1887-1899/headstones-and-markers.

Foss, William. "Diaries." n.d. Maine Historical Society, Portland, ME.

Frigid Fluid Company. "Embalmers' Undertakers' and Cemetery Supplies." Frigid Fluid Company, 1920. Trade Catalogues, Hagley Library, Wilmington, DE.

Frost, S. Annie. *Frost's Laws and by-Laws of American Society: A Condensed but Thorough Treatise on Etiquette and Its Usages in America, Containing Plain and Reliable Directions for*

Deportment in Every Situation in Life, on the Following Subjects . . . besides One Hundred Unclassified Laws Applicable to All Occasions. New York: Dick Fitzgerald, 1869.

"Frosted Zinc Corinthian Monuments." *Mariposa Gazette*, January 13, 1877.

Gebhart, John C., and Advisory Committee on Burial Survey. *Funeral Costs; What They Average. Are They Too High? Can They Be Reduced?* New York: G. P. Putnam's Sons, 1928.

Gordon, Adelaide. "Funerals." *Correct Social Usage: A Course of Instruction in Good Form, Style, and Deportment, by Eighteen Distinguished Authors.* New York: New York Society of Self-Culture, 1909.

H. E. Taylor Company. *The H.E. Taylor Co., Manufacturers of Fine Casket Hardware, Burial Robes, Casket Linings, &c., &c., and Dealers in Choice Funeral Goods, of Every Description.* New York: H. E. Taylor Company, 1890.

Haight, R. J. "A Survey of the Association of American Cemetery Superintendents/ICCFA." *AACS Proceedings of the 36th Annual Convention*, September 1922. http://www.iccfa.com/reading/1920-1939/survey-association-american-cemetery-superintendents.

Haight, R. J. *Modern Cemetery* 3–4. Chicago: R. J. Haight, 1895. http://archive.org/details/moderncemetery3418unse.

Harland, Marion. *Everyday Etiquette: A Practical Manual of Social Usages.* Indianapolis: Bobbs-Merrill, ca. 1905.

Helverson Funeral Home Records. 1828–1895. Historical Society of Pennsylvania, Philadelphia.

Hirst, Thomas. *The Quiz Class.* New York: The Casket, Inc., 1921.

Hobert, A. W. "Respect for the Dead and Justice to Their Descendants." *AACS Proceedings of the 16th Annual Convention*, 1909. http://www.iccfa.com/reading/1900-1919/respect-dead-and-justice-their-descendants.

Hohenschuh, W. P. *The Modern Funeral: Its Management.* Chicago: Trade Periodical Co., ca. 1900.

Josiah Allen's Wife. "The Most Stylish Funeral in Jonesville: A STORY OF VILLAGE LIFE, WITH A MORAL." *Ladies' Home Journal* (1889–1907) XX, no 8 (July 1903): 3, 36.

Kollock, David, and Bruton. "Memo Book." October 1859–61. Historical Society of Pennsylvania, Philadelphia.

Landers, S. L. "Flower Container Menace." *AACS Proceedings of the 40th Annual Convention*, August 1927. http://www.iccfa.com/reading/1920-1939/flower-container-menace.

Longfellow, Henry Wadsworth. "God's Acre." 1842. http://www.hwlongfellow.org/poems_poem.php?pid=73.

Low, Alexander. Account book. 1790–1826. Winterthur Library, Winterthur, DE.

Marbury, Elizabeth. *Manners: A Handbook of Social Customs.* New York: Cassell, ca. 1888.

Marbury, Elizabeth. *Manners: A Handbook of Social Customs.* New York: Herbert S. Stone, 1898.

McCarthy, T. "Cemetery Boundaries." *AACS Proceedings of the 9th Annual Convention.* https://www.iccfa.com/reading/1887-1899/cemetery-boundaries.

McCarthy, T. "The Sub-dividing of a Cemetery into Sections, Lots, and Single-Grave Sections." *Park and Cemetery Landscape Gardening* vol. 19–20. Chicago: R. J. Haight.

Modern Cemetery vol. IV. Chicago: R. J. Haight, 1896.

Monumental Bronze Company. Catalogue. Bridgeport, CT: Monumental Bronze Company, 1882. Winterthur Library, Winterthur, DE.

Moore, Clara Jessup. *Sensible Etiquette of the Best Society: Customs, Manners, Morals, and Home Culture/Compiled from the Best Authorities by Mrs. H. O. Ward [pseud.].* Philadelphia: Porter and Coates, 1878.

Muldoon Monument Company. *Muldoon Memorials.* Louisville, KY: Muldoon Monument Company, 192?. Filson Historical Society, Louisville, KY.

Muldoon Monument Company. "Muldoon Monument Company Records," books 3 and 7. n.d. Filson Historical Society, Louisville, KY.

National Casket Company. *National Garments*. Springfield, OH: National Casket Company, 1923. Hagley Library, Wilmington, DE.

National Casket Company. *Catalog O*. Springfield, OH: National Casket Company, 1916. Hagley Library, Wilmington, DE.

National Casket Company. *National Specialties: A Catalogue of Undertakers' Sundries and Embalmers' Supplies*. Springfield, OH: National Casket Company, 1923. Hagley Library, Wilmington, DE.

"Neighbors in the Cemetery." *Modern Cemetery* 4. Chicago: R. J. Haight, 1896.

Nichols, James White. Diary. 1847–46. Winterthur Library, Winterthur, DE.

"Refusing Burial to Negro Lot Holder Illegal." *Park and Cemetery and Landscape Gardening* 19–20. Chicago: R. J. Haight. 1911.

Perrott, S. J. "Monuments, Markers, and Other Cemetery Memorials." *AACS Proceedings of the 38th Annual Convention*, 1931. http://www.iccfa.com/reading/1920-1939/ monuments-markers-and-other-cemetery-memorials.

"Question Box–Question 1." *Proceedings of the Second Annual Convention of the Association of the American Cemetery Superintendents*. Akron, OH: Beacon Publishing, 1888.

Rayne, M. L. *Gems of Deportment and Hints of Etiquette: The Ceremonials of Good Society, Including Valuable Moral, Mental, and Physical Knowledge, Original and Compiled from the Best Authorities, with Suggestions on All Matters Pertaining to the Social Code*. Detroit: Tyler & Co., 1880.

Rudd, W. N. "The Subdividing of a Cemetery into Sections, Lots and Single Grave Districts." *AACS Proceedings of the 23rd Annual Convention*, September 1909. http://www.iccfa.com/ reading/1900-1919/subdividing-cemetery-sections-lots-and-single-grave-districts.

"Rules for Forest Hill Cemetery, Birmingham, Al." *Modern Cemetery* 4. Chicago: R. J. Haight. 1896.

Sargent, Lucius Manlius. *Dealings with the Dead*. Boston: Dutton and Wentworth, 1856.

Scorgie, James. "The Control of Stonework in Cemeteries." *AACS Proceedings of the 34th Annual Convention*, 1927. http://www.iccfa.com/reading/1920-1939/ control-stonework-cemeteries.

Sears, Roebuck and Company. "Special Catalogue of Tombstones, Monuments, Tablets and Markers." Chicago: Sears, Roebuck and Company, 1902. Winterthur Library, Winterthur, DE.

Service and Research Department, Champion Company. *Champion Materia Morticia*. Springfield, OH: Champion Chemical, 1928. Winterthur Library, Winterthur, DE.

Simms, Thomas. "Funeral Customs." *Christian Advocate* (1866–1905), October 20, 1887.

Simonds, O. C. "The Object of Our Association." *AACS Proceedings of the 7th Annual Convention*, August 1893. https://www.iccfa.com/reading/1887-1899/object-our-association; *Modern Cemetery* 4.

Smith, Charlotte Maria. "Charlotte Smith Diary," n.d. Connecticut Historical Society.

Sterns, Samuel. *The American Oracle*. New York: Hodge and Campbell, Berry and Rogers and T. Allen, 1791.

Street, Arthur L. H. *American Cemetery Law: A Digest of Cemetery Laws of All the States and Important Court Decisions*. Madison, WI: Park and Cemetery, 1922.

Stone, William. "Care and Maintenance of Public Lots." *AACS Proceedings of the 6th Annual Convention*. September 1892. https://www.iccfa.com/reading/1887-1899/ care-and-maintenance-public-lots-city-cemeteries.

Taylor, Francis. "Diary of Francis Taylor." 1786–99. Filson Historical Society, Louisville, KY.

Wallis, Thomas. "The Advantages of Restricting Size of Monuments." *AACS Proceedings of the 33rd Annual Convention*, 1926. http://www.iccfa.com/reading/1900-1919/ advantages-restricting-size-monuments.

White, Annie Randall. *Polite Society at Home and Abroad: A Complete Compendium of Information upon All Topics Classified under the Head of Etiquette.* Chicago: Monarch Book Company, 1891.

Woman of Fashion, A. *Etiquette for Americans.* Chicago: New York: Herbert S. Stone, 1898.

SECONDARY SOURCES

Ariès, Philippe. *The Hour of Our Death.* New York: Knopf, 1981.

Benson, Susan Porter. "Gender Generation, and Consumption in the United States: Working Class Families in the Interwar Years." *Getting and Spending: European and American Consumer Societies in the Twentieth Century.* Strasser, Susan, Charles McGovern, and Matthais Judt, eds. Washington, DC: German Historical Institute, 1998.

Brayley, Arthur W. *History of the Granite Industry in New England.* Boston: National Association of Granite Industries of the United States, 1913.

Conway, Steve. "Death, Working-Class Culture and Social Distinction." *Health Sociology Review* 21, no. 4 (2012): 441–49.

Faust, Drew Gilpin. *This Republic of Suffering.* New York: Knopf, 2008.

Grier, Katherine C. *Culture & Comfort: Parlor Making and Middle-Class Identity, 1850–1930.* Washington, DC: Smithsonian Institution Press, 1997.

Halttunen, Karen. *Confidence Men and Painted Women: A Study of Middle-Class Culture in America, 1830–1870.* New Haven, CT: Yale University Press, 1982.

Harding, Vanessa. *The Dead and the Living in Paris and London, 1500–1670.* New York: Cambridge University Press, 2002.

Hemphill, C. Dallett. *Bowing to Necessities: A History of Manners in America, 1620–1860.* New York: Oxford University Press, 2002.

Howard, June. "What Is Sentimentality?" *American Literary History* 11, no. 1 (Spring 1999): 63–81.

Kasson, John F. *Rudeness & Civility: Manners in Nineteenth-Century Urban America.* New York: Hill and Wang, 1990.

Litten, Julian. *The English Way of Death: The Common Funeral since 1450.* London: Robert Hale, 1991.

McCall, Walter M. P. *American Funeral Vehicles: 1883–2003.* Hudson, WI: Iconografix, 2003.

McPherson, Thomas A. *American Funeral Cars & Ambulances since 1900.* Glen Ellyn, IL: Crestline Publishers, 1973.

Merish, Lori. *Sentimental Materialism: Gender, Commodity Culture, and Nineteenth-Century American Literature.* Durham, NC: Duke University Press, 2000.

Piervittori, R. O. Salvadoria, and A. Laccisaglia. "Literature on Lichens and Biodeterioration of Stonework." *Lichenologist* 26, no. 2 (April 1994): 171–85.

Rosenow, Michael. *Death and Dying in the Working Class, 1865–1920.* Chicago: University of Illinois Press, 2015.

Sandberg, Mark B. *Living Pictures, Missing Persons: Mannequins, Museums, and Modernity.* Princeton, NJ: Princeton University Press, 2003.

Sloane, David Charles. *The Last Great Necessity: Cemeteries in American History.* Baltimore: Johns Hopkins University Press, 1991.

Stabile, Susan. *Memory's Daughters: The Material Culture of Remembrance in Eighteenth-Century America.* Ithaca, NY: Cornell University Press, 2004.

United States General Services Administration. "Granite: Characteristics, Uses and Problems." http://www.gsa.gov/portal/content/111938.

Chapter Seven

"In the Grave We Are All Equal": Northern New Mexican Burial Grounds in the Nineteenth Century

—MARTINA WILL DE CHAPARRO

Over just three generations in the course of a half-century, New Mexicans witnessed their land change hands from Spanish to Mexican to United States control. In contrast to other communities considered in the present volume, "Anglo-" or "Euro-" Americans defined New Mexico by its difference, segregating its inhabitants entirely from the national body politic during decades of debate over statehood.[1] Though rapaciously claimed as a territory of the United States in 1848, even after occupying troops withdrew, the nation long delayed admitting New Mexicans to full citizenship. Relegated to territorial status for fully sixty-three years, the marginalized New Mexicans were subject to federal laws but lacked a national political voice; even that of Santa Fe's legislature could be silenced by a veto from Congress.[2] The twin buttresses of Manifest Destiny—whiteness and Protestantism—intersected in New Mexico, home to a majority minority "brown" and Catholic population that was besmirched by the "jaundiced racial perspectives" of the conquering Anglos.[3] Thus the territory remained a place apart, snubbed in part for its otherness for a full six decades before finally admitted as the forty-seventh state in 1912.

Long before the bloody US conquest, however, New Mexico was multiracial and multicultural, home to communities of tremendous ethnic and cultural diversity. Burial practices mirrored this diversity provided that the dead had been Catholics, the only sanctioned religion for over two centuries of Spanish and then Mexican rule. Shielded by the mantle of their faith, corpses reposed in sacred ground, typically beneath the parish church. Within these increasingly crowded floors, the dead's proximity to sacred images, oratory, and music as well as the prayers of the pious promised untold spiritual benefits. In their wills, the dying requested interment close to the baptismal font or within a chapel dedicated to a favorite manifestation of the Virgin, for they believed that a stray drop of holy water or prayers to Mary might permit their immortal souls a quicker release from purgatory. Though no grave markers indicated where individuals had been interred within the church, the dead thus remained a part of the Communion of the Saints, the community of the faithful living and dead within Catholic theology. Rather than individualism, a collective identity governed deathways for much of the period in question. The resultant relative egalitarianism, however, was itself predicated on one's residence, which in turn might well be closely entwined with one's ancestry and ethnic identity. The parish where one had lived and prayed typically became the repository for one's remains. Still, New Mexican burial practices remained somewhat democratic until the late nineteenth century, when economic, population, and political pressures led to more discernable socioeconomic distinctions even in death.

Population Diversity and Shifting Demographics

Within New Mexico's colonial and Mexican-era boundaries resided about twenty different Pueblo Indian tribes, Mescalero Apaches, Jicarilla Apaches, Navajos, the descendants of Spaniards who had settled in central Mexico, and the mixed-race descendants of these same peoples, referred to sometimes as "mestizos" (the offspring of Spaniards and Indians) or "coyotes" (the progeny of Indians and mestizos). Not including the jurisdiction of El Paso in the south, Fray Francisco Atanasio Domínguez estimated New Mexico's population in 1776 to be 18,344 souls, of whom less than a third possessed Spanish ancestry.[4] After 1779 the Hispanic population grew dramatically, eclipsing the Pueblo population, which was disproportionately devastated by the smallpox epidemic of 1780–82.[5] Those designated as *españoles* or "Spaniards" by contemporaries, however, included many different racial admixtures; in fact, "Spanish" typically denoted a cultural rather than an ethnic or "national" identity as we might conceive of it today.[6] About 2.6 percent of the population in 1790 could claim some African ancestry, but this category gradually disappeared, especially as caste labels lost their importance over the course of the nineteenth century. Indeed, after independence, "vecino" became the most commonly used identifier. Literally meaning "neighbor," this term shifted meaning over time to embody "both a cultural and a civic identity, rather than caste or race," according to John Nieto-Phillips.[7]

Mexican independence (1821), which proclaimed the equality of all citizens, reduced the use of caste designations; new laws decreed, for example, that official documents could not classify people according to their racial origins. Within a decade of freeing themselves from Spanish rule, the nation's leaders banned slavery and sought civil equality, backing up the lofty rhetoric with policies. Though reality often left much to be desired, Mexico's path diverged significantly from that taken in the United States, where racial mixing made the dominant white society anxious, threatening its conception of the nation and driving both de jure and de facto segregation. In Mexico, by contrast, liberal thinkers embraced the idea of a multiracial society and even elevated the notion of the mixed-race individual or mestizo through what Claudio Lomnitz and others refer to as "mestizophilia."[8] Olivia Gall contends of these early nineteenth-century Mexican liberals: "following a theoretical egalitarianism, they constitutionally erased the racial differences that survived in practice, by confusing nationality (a notion regarding citizenship), mestizaje (a racial and cultural category) and liberalism (an economic and political system)."[9]

Though decreeing full citizenship and equality before the law did not translate into practice, it did signal a notable shift from the early colonial period, when two polities officially existed. The Indian and Spanish republics—the "república de indios" and the "república de españoles"—had formally (if only briefly) segregated Indians and Spaniards into separate communities, each with its own political hierarchy. María Elena Martínez explains this model as "the result of a Spanish political ideology that initially justified the colonial enterprise on the basis of the need to convert the indigenous people, of the crown's desire to deter the emergence of colonial lordships, and of the royal interest in reproducing a population of tributaries."[10] These practical considerations were paired with the Spanish appreciation for the Indians' "limpieza de sangre," or "purity of blood," a concept rooted in religion rather than race, which esteemed the Americas' natives as untainted by Jewish or Muslim blood. Thus, even the officially mandated—but seldom enforced—segregation of the early colonial period differed fundamentally from the racial segregation that came to define the United States. In any event, the "two republics" model did not succeed and, long before independence, these distinctions had ceased to be meaningful in daily life, especially in peripheral areas like New Mexico. The termination of Indians' special legal status after independence, however, was consequential, as it signaled the loss of formal protections, including the right to hold communal lands. Many native communities across Mexico would lose their lands as a result.

New Mexico's Pueblo Indians remained in their ancestral communities along the Rio Grande even after independence while most "Spaniards" resided in or near one of four *villas* or Spanish towns: Albuquerque, Santa Fe, Santa Cruz de la Cañada, and El Paso del Río del Norte.[11] Due to space limitations, this chapter focuses on northern New Mexico and especially Albuquerque and Santa

Fe, where the surviving documents are richest. New Mexico's other principal settlements were those of the "genízaros," detribalized and Hispanicized Indians not of Pueblo origin. James Brooks estimates that "between 1700 and 1880 . . . some five thousand members of plains or pastoral Indian groups entered New Mexican society as indios de rescate [rescued Indians], indios genízaros, criados [servants incorporated into Spanish families and raised as Catholics], or *huérfanos* [orphans], primarily through the artifice of 'ransom' by colonial purchasers."[12] Illegal though it was, Indian slavery flourished under the guise of redeeming war captives, with traders and tribes deliberately preying upon Navajos, Apaches, Utes, and Comanches.[13] Some of these captives became fully part of New Mexico's Spanish society over time, accepting Catholicism and being adopted into families.[14] Others, after serving out their peonage, petitioned for land to establish their own settlements, founding Abiquiú, Ranchos de Taos, and Belén, among others. These peripheral villages quite deliberately served as buffers from periodic raids by nomadic Indians.[15]

By 1850, in the first years of the Territorial period, New Mexico's population hovered near 62,000 in a landscape that included parts of modern Arizona, Nevada, and Colorado. Many people retained their tribal identities and distinctive languages. Others claimed a Spanish identity that subsumed the mixed-race categories of the colonial period, deliberately emphasizing their European origins to place themselves on equal footing with the newcomers, who often rather stridently insisted on their own cultural and racial superiority. The US conquest brought mostly Protestant settlers from as far as Ohio but also German Jews, Irish Catholics, and other nationalities and faiths.[16] Some, like the Polish Jewish settler Luis Gold, learned Spanish. He or his family apparently took some pride in this accomplishment, for when he died of typhoid thirty years later in Santa Fe, this was inscribed in his obituary: "He learned perfect Spanish, had many Spanish customs, had many acquaintances among the Spanish American families of the territory and was most considerate of his fellow businessmen."[17] His headstone, along with others from the late nineteenth century (as in figs. 7.1 and 7.2), suggest the diverse origins of the area's newcomers.

Not all arrivals shared Luis Gold's desire to integrate into local life, however, and as the migrants sought to understand and define New Mexican society, their racial ideology frequently collided with the reality of their new home. A prominent example comes from the Secretary of the Territory of New Mexico (1853–54), William W. H. Davis, who reflects in *El Gringo* that "The great mass of the population are very dark, and can not claim to be more than one fourth or one eighth part Spanish. The intermixture between the peasantry and the native tribes of Indians is yet carried on, and there is no present hope of the people improving in color."[18] Contemporary congressional debates, newspaper articles, and other sources disparaged New Mexico's people, correlating moral

Figure 7.1 1885 gravestone of Alex Greenleaf Goold of Liverpool, England, Fairview Cemetery, Santa Fe, New Mexico. Photo courtesy of Suzanne Stamatov, PhD.

Figure 7.2 1880 gravestone of Luis Gold of Poland with Masonic symbol, Fairview Cemetery, Santa Fe, New Mexico. Courtesy Suzanne Stamatov, PhD.

character, intelligence, and the ability to govern with race. "Mexicans" received lower wages than those identified as "Americans," and many people lost their economic security along with their land.[19] These outsiders typically declared the New Mexican population deficient in all categories; the only thing they found the locals to possess in abundance was superstition and religious "fanaticism."

After 1880 the railroads' expansion brought additional newcomers to New Mexico, including more Anglos as well as European (predominantly German, Irish, and Italian) and to a lesser extent, Asian immigrants seeking their fortunes in mining and other industries. African Americans arrived in smaller numbers, totaling only sixteen hundred by the year 1900.[20] In this same year, the territory had 195,310 residents, of whom 7 percent were Native Americans (primarily Pueblo Indians), and about 50 percent "Anglos." This represented exponential growth, from about 1,500 to 100,000 Anglos in the space of fifty years.[21] The small "Spanish" elite—approximately 5 percent of the Hispanic population, according to Charles Montgomery—and poor Hispanics remained divided by wealth; however, both chafed against increasing European American incursions in political and economic life.[22] Deena González estimates that by 1880, 90 percent of Santa Fe's "Mexican" population had lost its land to the interlopers.[23]

Though New Mexico had been part of Mexico for only a few short decades, the incoming settlers began to refer to the locals as "Mexicans." Ramón Gutiérrez interrogates the meaning of this semantic choice, which served to "signify a dominated population, stigmatized by defeat and subordination."[24] To the consternation of some recent arrivals, however, lighter-skinned "Mexicans" could undercut the triumphalist amalgamation of racism and nationalism so characteristic of this period, by passing as white. The danger of such subterfuge, however, only sharpened the compulsion to establish racial distinctions more neatly. Charles Montgomery argues, "the physical variations made it even more necessary to construct and constantly reinforce the idea of a fundamental racial divide."[25] Ironically, the inverse took place in the Northeastern United States in the last quarter of the nineteenth century, as waves of immigrants challenged the meaning of whiteness and demanded full citizenship even as African Americans were progressively disenfranchised and segregated. Thus, within territorial New Mexico, the colonized existed in a political limbo that left them twice-removed from power: they not only lacked full citizenship but increasingly found themselves excluded economically and politically within the land of their birth.

Given these circumstances, it is not surprising that some Hispanic New Mexicans asserted their whiteness rather than be lumped together with the "Mexicans" whom Anglos deemed inferior. Though colonized, by emphasizing their Spanish heritage, these elites resolutely laid claim to whiteness and its attendant privileges. As they asserted this identity, they also found it expedient to distinguish themselves from nonwhite groups, including Indians and African Americans. While clinging doggedly to Indian slavery, they wrestled with the question of African slavery, which was very much intertwined with that of statehood. Having previously supported abolition, in 1859 some elite New Mexicans embraced a harsh slave code that included a ban on marriages between even free blacks and whites.[26] Though this short-lived legislation was largely a political ploy, it hints at a hardening of racial lines just a decade after the US conquest that is especially noteworthy given a history of relative indifference on the subject of intermixing, and the extremely small population of African Americans in the territory.[27] To secure their tenuous position in the new racial hierarchy, some New Mexicans found it advantageous to define themselves at least in part in contrast to other ethnic groups. Laura Gómez reasons that "Mexican elites' defense of the system of Indian slavery constituted resistance to American hegemony, but also capitulation to American white supremacy."[28]

Boosters of New Mexican migration and tourism soon employed this same language of white supremacy. Established in 1880, the Bureau of Immigration promoted settlement in New Mexico by characterizing the territory as "biracial": full of the descendants of Spanish conquistadors and civilized Pueblo peoples.[29] The growing use of "Spanish" and "Spanish-American" to describe the population made the cause of statehood more palatable by downplaying the majority population's mixed-race heritage. This emphasis on the Spanish (and therefore "white") past anticipated New Mexican statehood, as political parties "adopted the new rhetoric for public reference to all Hispanos," while still privately referring to people as "Mexicans."[30] Whitening the New Mexican population, however, came at a price. Though New Mexico attained statehood in 1912, it was 1924 before the federal government granted US citizenship to Native Americans. New Mexico, however, denied its Pueblo Indian population the right to vote until 1948.

Burial Practices in the Colonial and Mexican Periods

Though long excluded from full citizenship, New Mexicans (Hispanics and Indians) remained the dominant population group in terms of sheer numbers until 1910. This demographic reality combined with their faith helps to explain the somewhat unique nature of New Mexican burial practices. Officially Roman Catholic and intolerant of other faiths in both the Spanish (1598–1821) and Mexican periods (1821–48), New Mexicans enjoyed a long history of burying their dead exclusively in Roman Catholic burial grounds. Only in exceptional cases did Catholics deviate from this practice. Unless suspected of heresy or suicide, burial within sacred ground was the right of the faithful and the duty of survivors. In fact, even suicides might be given the benefit of the doubt and receive burial in sanctified ground had they expressed remorse prior to dying. Typically, parishioners received burial within twenty-four hours of death in their parish church or its adjacent churchyard or "camposanto" (literally, "holy field"). Since Pueblo peoples lived in their ancestral settlements, this meant interment within their respective parish churches. Even those possessing the lowest social status—Comanches, Utes, Apaches and other captives who lived and served in households as criados or slaves—found burial within the faith and within sacred ground, so long as they had been baptized. In fact, captives—especially males, according to David Brugge's research on the Navajos—often married into local society, and were no longer identified by a tribal point of origin upon burial.[31]

Archival and archaeological evidence strongly suggests that New Mexicans did not segregate their dead by race or ethnicity in the eighteenth or nineteenth centuries. Social and economic status might well determine one's final resting place, however, as indicated in Fray Andrés García's 1768 diagram of the church of Santa Cruz de la Cañada, which stipulates different burial costs according to one's proximity to the altar. For merely two pesos, a loved one might receive interment in the graveyard outside the church entrance or just within the church doors. Divided into thirds, burial costs within the nave ranged from two to eight pesos, increasing in cost as one approached the main altar. The sanctuary—the space immediately around this main altar—remained reserved for priests. Generally, the most coveted spots were those closest to the church's sacred images, but the desire to appear humble before God inspired others to seek the most modest burial location such as a doorway, where parishioners would trample their remains as they walked over the threshold.[32]

Notwithstanding the social hierarchy implicit in the Santa Cruz diagram, New Mexican burial practices remained remarkably democratic through much of the nineteenth century, as foundlings, servants, officers, Indians, coyotes, Spaniards, and others shared the space beneath the parish church. In 1786, for example, Juan Miguel Martin, an adult identified as a coyote and servant ("criado") in the household of "Spaniards" Antonio Martin and María Ignacia Gonzales, received burial within the Santa Cruz church. A few weeks later, the "Spanish" Antonia Trujillo buried her two "natural children"—i.e., children of an unknown (presumably unnamed) father—here. In January of the following year, Antonio Martin joined his deceased servant/slave beneath the same church floor. This relatively egalitarian approach did little to sustain the church coffers, however. One of the region's few diocesan (or secular) priests in 1800 concluded that "churches have no money because the *vecinos* [here used to signify "Spaniards"] are buried in the same manner as the Indians."[33] Burial registers affirm this concern. Santa Fe's residents in the late eighteenth century paid on average only five pesos for interment just inside the church entrance; by 1801 the average amount for a burial actually had fallen to three pesos in the area closest to the doorway.[34] The parish of San Felipe de Neri in Albuquerque accepted as little as a bottle of wine or a pound of wax for interment, and in 1818 most burials recorded there only yielded a single peso.[35]

While payment in kind had the sanction of tradition, it did not please the incoming secular clergy. Almost immediately upon settling into his post at Santa Cruz in April 1821, Cura Manuel Rada sent a detailed report to the bishop decrying the sad state of record-keeping and complete lack of funds in the parish coffers. He complained that mismanagement combined with the fact that none of the parishioners paid in cash had placed the parish in financial straits. Furthermore, everyone wanted to bury their dead in the church. To Rada's consternation, even for a privileged burial within the church in 1821, parishioners paid a maximum of four pesos.[36] In other words, the religious charged only a fraction of the amount set forth in the *arancel* or fee schedule. Probably in response to the vicar's efforts, at some point prior to 1831 the costs for burial in the nave doubled, as is faintly visible in the Santa Cruz church plan. Though the erstwhile governor, visitors, and in time numerous Anglo traders criticized the schedule of fees and accused the clergy of greed and overcharging, the evidence suggests that New Mexicans actually underpaid for funerals and burials. A regression analysis of Albuquerque, Santa Fe, and Santa Cruz burial records demonstrates that over the years 1730–1850, people actually were spending less on burial.

Despite the disparity between the arancel and actual charges, the priests' fees frequently provoked discord in the late eighteenth and early nineteenth centuries. In the wake of the devastating smallpox epidemic of 1780–81 and the resultant loss of Pueblo lives, missionaries became increasingly dependent on the Hispanic population for economic support. The arrival of the secular clergy exacerbated the situation, as they tried to undermine customary practices. While parishioners had always found reasons to grumble, their grievances with the Franciscans typically had centered on issues of incompetence and failure to say masses or administer the last rites.[37] In contrast, the diocesan clergy who arrived in New Mexico in the early nineteenth century more commonly earned people's enmity for trying to adhere to a fee schedule that for much of the colonial period had been largely ignored. Santa Cruz parishioners wasted little time in lodging a complaint against their first secular priest, Cura Juan José Lombide, whom they accused of shamelessly extorting goods in payment for burial of the town's most destitute. In one instance, the priest had wrested twelve pesos from a poor widow; on another occasion, he exacted a *colcha* or coverlet in payment for his burial of a little girl.[38] When it came to finances, parishioners took issue with the diocesan clergy more often than not due to the priests' adherence to the fee schedule, rather than their avariciousness as claimed by some US traders and settlers.

New Mexico developed its own elite, but its eighteenth- and early nineteenth-century burial geography suggests that people on the northern frontier lived in a more egalitarian and socially mobile society than their peers residing in central Mexico.[39] Although a clear caste/class hierarchy existed, a fair degree of social mobility prevailed, fueled in part by the need for soldiers and settlers but also by high rates of *mestizaje* or racial mixing, which, according to Antonio José Rios-Bustamante, meant that "anywhere from 70 to 80 percent of the population of Albuquerque were mestizo in fact, if not in convention by 1790."[40] Certainly, New Mexico's hierarchy remained far more elastic than that of either Bourbon Spain or central Mexico, where only elites and confraternity members in good standing could hope for interment within the church. Although the higher costs associated with burial in a chapel or in the section closest to the main altar kept these spots out of reach for many New Mexicans, burial somewhere within the parish church was a prerogative for most throughout the colonial and part of the Mexican periods. Made relatively affordable by a barter economy and sympathetic Franciscans, almost 90 percent of people specifically requested burial within the church in their testaments.[41] Parish burial books substantiate the wills, revealing that, for most of the colonial period, approximately 95 percent of the dead did indeed repose beneath the church.[42] Colonial burial registers for the Pueblos of Picurís, San Juan, Santa Clara, Nambé, and Cochití all corroborate these findings, demonstrating that upwards of 90 percent of Pueblo burials also took place within the Pueblos' churches. In the first decade of the nineteenth century, for example, Fray Teodoro Alcina buried all Santa Clara Pueblo residents, Chama vecinos, and Ute captives within the church, notwithstanding a deadly 1805 measles epidemic.[43]

In some parishes, Ute or Navajo slaves along with the indigent were more likely to receive interment in the churchyard than within the church; however, this was not necessarily or even exclusively a question of race or ethnicity but also one of cost and who was paying for the funeral and burial. Even so, in the three Spanish villas, the burial registers identify 25 percent of those buried within the churches as Plains Indians—primarily Apaches, Navajos, and Utes— compared with 17 percent of those buried in the cemetery.[44] Thus, even slaves received interment within the church. Furthermore, no evidence suggests that they were buried in distinct sections of either the church or cemetery or otherwise segregated in any way.

Even the poor often found a final resting place within the church floors, for priests had to bury their "wretched parishioners" free of charge. The fee schedule, too, made allowances for economic realities, by establishing burial and funeral costs that differed by race. Indians, mulattos, and other non-Spaniards paid the least. Though the fee schedule seems to have been ignored for the most part, most families paid something for interment, even if on credit. Even the poor could usually string together enough chiles or onions to pay for a parent's or child's burial.[45] Though "he did not make a will because he had nothing," for example, Estanislado Chávez was buried in the second section of Albuquerque's parish church in 1819.[46] Parish account books make clear that many parishioners paid only part of the fee at the time of burial and owed the remainder to the parish coffers; thus, those with few resources during a hard winter could wait until the next harvest to pay.

In 1833 Bishop José Antonio Laureano de Zubiría established a new arancel, which seems to have more accurately reflected New Mexican realities than the previous century-old one.[47] Though still pegged to the silver peso, costs fell and the bishop recognized the right of parishioners to pay either in cash or the equivalent due to the province's lack of specie. The bishop fixed burial prices at one to six pesos, depending on location within the church. One would incur additional charges for frills like the use of a high cross, a cope, an incensory, or the ringing of bells at the burial. As late as 1848, adult parishioners in Albuquerque paid an average of only one peso for burial, with burials of eight pesos or more exceptional.[48]

Burial Reforms and Resistance

Official doctrine regarding burial grounds, however, had already shifted by the last quarter of the eighteenth century, when the Spanish Crown banned the burial of cadavers inside and adjacent to churches and ordered the construction of cemeteries outside of towns. Contending that subfloor burials endangered public health, the king and his successors repeatedly instructed their subjects to bury cadavers only in well-ventilated cemeteries, to be established at a distance from population centers. Shifting interment from churches to suburban or rural cemeteries, while potentially democratizing burial, also restricted the authority of parishes and localities and threatened to undermine popular piety. Spanish and later Mexican authorities repeatedly legislated and disseminated the reforms, each new decree underscoring the ineffectualness of earlier legislation. Though decades passed before any New Mexican communities constructed true suburban cemeteries, priests in many settlements finally responded to the 1819 legislation with at least selective obedience. After 1820 burial registers demonstrate a shift in favor of churchyard burials. Increasingly, when clergy did bury someone within the church, the dead seemed to hold claim to some social standing or wealth.

This shift was the source of friction in San Juan Pueblo, where the reforms underscored ethnic and class tensions already heightened by economic and demographic growth favoring the Hispanic population.[49] Located just north of Santa Cruz, about two hundred Tewa Indians called San Juan home in the early nineteenth century, and approximately seventeen hundred españoles lived nearby.[50] Dissatisfied with what they saw as their priest's selective application of the law, San Juan *alcalde* José Manuel Archuleta and two other community members in 1821 signed a petition addressed to the region's highest civil author- ity, Commander General Alejo García Conde.[51] The complainants alleged that Fray Mariano José Sánchez Vergara, who had served in different New Mexican missions since 1794, only buried the community's poor outside of the church while continuing to inter wealthy residents inside. The authors poignantly asked: "Whence is it decreed that he who is poor shall cease to love the temple?" Further arguing that the cemetery had been frozen for six months and that the ground was therefore impenetrable, they implored García Conde to remedy the situa- tion in favor of religion and peace in the community.[52] The Commander General forwarded the complaints to the Custos, the Franciscan superior. Judicial pro- ceedings began the following year, and three of San Juan's leaders came forward to enumerate the community's problems with the friar, which included physical abuses. They claimed that he refused to bury Indians inside the church "because they do not pay," and only allowed vecinos [here suggesting ethnicity rather than civil status] the privilege of church burial.[53] Unfortunately, Sánchez Vergara, like his predecessors, left only vague entries in the parish burial registers, and it is therefore impossible to determine where the truth lay regarding burials.

The San Juan case highlights broader changes taking place in New Mexico. Even prior to the formal abolition of their protected status shortly before inde- pendence, New Mexico's Pueblos found themselves increasingly at odds with the rapidly growing Spanish vecino population, which used legal and illegal means to gain access to Pueblo lands. In addition to their grievances against the friar, San Juan's leadership expressed concern over threats to reduce Pueblo landholdings and increase the first fruits they had to pay. Though the subsequent proceedings remain silent on these points, concentrating instead on the alleged abuse, land and economic issues most certainly triggered tensions in the community. As Ross Frank's work demonstrates, conflicts between vecinos and Pueblos rose in the late eighteenth and early nineteenth centuries, and many legal proceedings after 1810 stemmed from land disputes between Pueblos and encroaching veci- nos.[54] Even the subtext of the clash with the friar appears economic and social in nature: the Indians contended that the vecinos received preferential treatment, and the priest shamed the Indians before the vecino congregation.

Notwithstanding the apparent tensions between vecinos and Pueblos, San Juan Pueblo enlisted the assistance of a sympathetic vecino to travel to Durango, Mexico, and appeal to the bishop on its behalf. Ignacio Madrid, selected in part because he knew the way to Durango, claimed familiarity with both the civil and ecclesiastical hierarchies and agreed to help the Pueblo navigate the legal system. San Juan's leadership contended they had no other recourse, having been left "orphaned" since the death of the former *protector de indios*, the crown-appointed official who defended the interests of Indian communities in Spanish courts.[55] Actually, this was only part of the story. In reality, the protector to whom the Indians referred had died a few years earlier, but his replacement probably did not sympathize with San Juan's plight, for Ignacio Sánchez Vergara was the despised friar's brother. According to San Juan's complaint, Sánchez Vergara the protector did not defend the Pueblo's interests. Perhaps he did not even believe in the need for the post to which he had been named; he had once argued that the Indians of New Mexico no longer needed special status before the law, having already "emerged from their minority."[56]

Lacking a protector to represent their interests, and claiming only a limited knowledge of Spanish and the law, San Juan's leadership had little choice but to turn to an intermediary to access the legal system. Once able to do so, their complaints were taken seriously and duly investigated. The following year, San Juan's leaders succeeded in ridding themselves of the friar. He moved on to a new post in Abiquiú (a genízaro settlement), where in short order several citizens accused the Franciscan of numerous "tyrannies," including leaving the dead unburied up to three days.[57] In addition to demonstrating vecino–Pueblo tensions in this period, the San Juan case presages the more general social stratification that would become increasingly evident in New Mexican mortuary practices in ensuing years.

About a decade later, some of these same divisions impelled some to take up arms in the Chimayó Rebellion, which inflamed communities across northern New Mexico. Proclaiming their faith in God and their devotion to Christ, rebels violently threatened their parish priests as summer 1837 drew to a close. In Santa Cruz de la Cañada, the pious insurgents jabbed a gun in Cura Fernando Ortiz's back and ordered him to inter a corpse beneath the parish church. Taos rebels pledged to kill Cura Antonio José Martínez if he tried to prevent their burying a body in the chapel of St. Francis.[58] Although not strictly about burials, like contemporaneous cemetery rebellions in Guatemala and Brazil, the uprising in New Mexico's Río Arriba, the district including Santa Fe northward, conflated political, economic, and religious grievances.[59] Three to six thousand people united in their opposition to "godlessness," taxation, the centralist constitution or "Departmental Plan," and the recent arrival of a new governor and military commander from Mexico, Colonel Albino Pérez.[60]

Enjoying widespread support among New Mexico's economically disadvantaged Pueblo, coyote, and genízaro populations, the bloody insurrection resulted in the murder of the governor and his entire cabinet—eighteen people in all—before the rebels' final defeat in January of the following year. "More than anything else," argues historian Andrés Reséndez, "the specter of such a caste war galvanized a powerful counterrevolutionary movement," resulting in exceptional unity on the part of civil and religious authorities, who invoked nationalist and Catholic rhetoric as they quashed the revolt.[61] Reséndez observes that the governor and his cabinet were "white Hispanics of the highest social standing, whereas the men carrying out the executions were overwhelmingly Indian."[62] Thus the 1837 rebellion expressed tensions among New Mexico's population that had been brewing for some time, and which would increasingly surface in burial geography.

Despite earlier failed efforts to effect change, the 1819 decree banning church burials signaled a jarring break from custom. It undermined traditional burial practices that comforted the faithful, who believed burying the dead in proximity to relics and images of the saints hastened the soul's release from purgatory. For over one hundred years, Santa Cruz had interred most of its dead within the parish church; in fact, only two burials had taken place in the *campo santo* (literally "holy field" or churchyard) in the years before Bishop Castañiza's orders arrived in 1821.[63] In the same month that the decree arrived, the once meticulous Cura Juan Tomás Terrazas became sloppy in recording burial location; suddenly, he was vague in his notations or did not note burial location at all. This silence lasted for a short time even after Vicar Juan Manuel de Jesús Rada replaced Terrazas the following month. Though perhaps deliberately oblique in his citations, Terrazas in time reconciled himself—if not his parishioners—to the changes. With the charitable burial in May 1821 of a free mulatta, María Ramona, the parish began to bury its dead in the churchyard.[64] Underscoring his personal commitment to the reforms, Vicar Rada even informed the parish's majordomo in writing that there were to be no exceptions to cemetery burial, regardless of social status.[65]

After just four years, however, opposition replaced obedience. In 1825 the *ayuntamiento* or town council of Santa Cruz made a last-ditch effort to end the practice of burying their dead in the cemetery. Four years after Spain's rule had ended and one year after Mexico wrote its constitution, the ayuntamiento questioned the validity of the burial reforms. Optimistic that independence or perhaps the new constitution had nullified them, the town's leadership said that the parish had been most "discontent and disconsolate" since the ban on church burials. The townspeople had not buried even a single corpse in the church floor in four years and five months. Yet only with "pain in our hearts" did the townsfolk obediently bury their dead in the cemetery; this anguish impelled the ayuntamiento to ask Vicar Rada for permission to revert to traditional burial practices.[66]

Notwithstanding the reference to the town's sorrow, the ayuntamiento firmly grounded its case in reason and hygiene, a language they hoped would resonate with the ecclesiastical hierarchy that comprised their real audience. Reassuring

Rada that "few people die in New Mexico," and "little or no pestilence is seen here due to the natural health of the country," the council informed the parish priest of the adversity they had encountered in adhering to the reforms.[67] The layer of ice covering the ground during the six months of winter impeded outdoor burials, so only with the greatest trouble could the community dig graves. Forced to work outdoors in the harsh climate, the reforms actually jeopardized the health of the unfortunate gravediggers, whose tools sometimes even broke due to the severe cold. Finally, turning the very logic of the legislation against itself, the ayuntamiento maintained that because of these difficulties, corpses lay unburied for long periods of time; here resided the real public health danger. Powerless to grant an exception to legislation that he perhaps found equally odious, Rada forwarded the community's concerns to his superiors in the cathedral chapter of Durango. The pragmatic and legalistic response tersely affirmed the law.[68]

Shortly after Santa Cruz's failed appeal, Bishop Castañiza sent Visitor General Agustín Fernández de San Vicente to New Mexico in 1826. After secularizing the parishes of Abiquiú, Belén, Taos, San Juan, and El Vado, Fernández de San Vicente disclosed that it was "foremost among my duties . . . to see to the establishment of ventilated cemeteries throughout this territory, which has been repeatedly ordered."[69] He sent a circular reminding all the parishes of the changes. While referring only vaguely to "the ills" that the government sought to avoid with this legislation, by now it had to be crystal clear precisely what these words meant. The key difference this time was that Fernández de San Vicente was not content to settle for halting church burials and interring the dead in graveyards contiguous to churches, a tactic that some communities had used to sidestep the real issue. He actually expected parishes to construct cemeteries outside the town limits and cease burying any of the dead within settlements.

The bishop's renewed interest in the reforms and Fernández de San Vicente's efforts ultimately resulted in changes across New Mexico, though some people continued trying to evade them. In some cases they enjoyed short-term success, but the combination of legislation, more careful oversight from Durango, and time gradually wore away at resistant priests and their parishioners.[70] The variety of resistance and reasons proffered speaks to the diversity and the creativity of New Mexicans, who chafed against the effort to segregate the living and the dead. Placed in the difficult position of implementing the unpopular and income-threatening legislation, many clergy—both secular and regular—undoubtedly found themselves torn as well. In general, however, it appears that, despite their much smaller numbers, the secular clergy led the way in implementing the reforms. Though the crown had pushed for burial reform since the late eighteenth century, only with the introduction of the secular clergy—who took control in these key Spanish settlements—did New Mexican mortuary practices noticeably change.

In the late 1820s through the 1840s, secular clergy replaced the dying Franciscans and served in predominantly Spanish settlements.[71] Most of these men came from northern Mexico, including New Mexico. Trained at the seminary in Durango, Mexico, they may have been exposed to new ideas of piety and hygiene during their education. Considerably younger than the aging Franciscans who remained in New Mexico, these priests may have been less married to the traditional ways, and in any case must have felt some loyalty to the bishops—Bishop Castañiza and later Bishop Zubiría—who ordained them and who wholeheartedly supported the reforms. The diocesan clergy arrived in New Mexico under the authority of the bishop of Durango, in contrast to the Spanish-born Franciscans, who had historically resisted Durango's control.[72] Aghast at what they perceived as the physical and moral deterioration of many communities, they assumed responsibility for revitalizing their parishes. They commissioned artisans to create more acceptable representations of the saints, instituted needed building repairs, and put doors on the confessionals.[73] The secular clergy did not confine their restorative efforts to the physical structures of the church but also demonstrated concern with New Mexicans' moral laxity, which they corrected in some cases through more careful oversight and instruction, establishing primary schools or becoming involved in politics.[74]

That the diocesan clergy served in many instances as the impetus for obedience to the twenty-year-old burial reforms is apparent in the case of Albuquerque, which illustrates the general trend. Fray Ambrosio Guerra had ministered to Albuquerque's parishioners for over thirty years, with only a few interruptions. He consistently interred the dead within the church dedicated to San Felipe Neri, dutifully noting in the sacramental records where in the church floor they lay and whether or not they had received the last rites. He favored the transept for the burial of foundlings and other children, regardless of their ethnicity and their parents' ability to pay. He only occasionally buried people in the campo santo, though some charity cases wound up there. Sometimes he identified these people as Utes or Comanches, but frequently he did not mention ethnicity, suggesting by this omission that they were of Spanish descent. After Fray Ambrosio Guerra was relocated to Sandia Pueblo at the end of 1817, his successor, Cura José Francisco Leyva y Rosas, almost overnight began to use the churchyard for virtually all interments.

Though the sudden break with tradition probably generated discontent in the parish, the documents do not provide any hint of dissent until a decade later, when the Fernández de San Vicente circular arrived in 1826. Leyva had returned again to San Felipe Neri by now, and he wrote for advice to Cura José Luis Rodríguez of Santa Fe. Though his letter to Rodríguez does not survive, we can surmise his concerns from the response he received. Rodríguez emphatically instructed Leyva to follow the official position on cemeteries expressed in the Fernández de San Vicente circular. He told Leyva to conform to the regulations as soon as possible, and directed him to communicate to his parishioners the reforms' many benefits:

> It is necessary that you place yourself in accord with this illustrious constitutional government, and that you rush to take the measures you see as prudent in order to expedite compliance with the circular promulgated by this government on May 10th. If you encounter any difficulties, it is your duty as parish priest to smooth out these difficulties through your prudent exhortations to your parishioners, making them see the benefits that all will enjoy with the continuation of the campo santo in a ventilated site.[75]

As parish priest, he reminded Leyva, it was his responsibility to eliminate opposition and make sure that the reforms succeeded in their principal goal of "protecting the towns from corruption."[76] Just as under Spanish rule, priests represented the front line of promoting the transformation in burial geography after independence. Since people had to walk through the churchyards to enter the church, merely burying the dead in the churchyard did not alleviate official concerns.

The Mexican government added to the considerable volume of legislation on the topic of subfloor burials by issuing yet another circular, which reached New Mexico by July 1833. Though the notice targeted a practice not even available locally—that of burying children inside religious communities—it reveals that despite the erosion of parish priests' authority in the late colonial period and the anticlericalism of the liberals who then held power, the state still relied on clerical authority to promote its agenda. The government instructed priests to redouble their efforts so as to protect the public welfare and ensure the proper respect due the places of worship. Liberal Vice President Valentín Gómez Farías, himself a medical doctor, demanded that all ecclesiastical and civil authorities enforce existing religious and civil laws with greater zeal, or else risk cholera and the other epidemics plaguing Cuba.[77] Despite the cholera epidemic's arrival in Mexico that same year and the ongoing promulgation of decrees and circulars emphasizing the importance of the "new" regulations, not just New Mexicans but rural mestizo communities and Indian towns in Mexico continued to oppose burial reform.[78]

While available to only a minority of people, burial in a private chapel or in a chapel that had no resident priest allowed some to circumvent the mandates. Private and public chapels proliferated in New Mexico in this period, spurred as much by economic growth as by population growth.[79] Sometimes family chapels offered a final resting place, but in most cases community chapels served the purpose in areas lacking a permanent clerical presence. In some cases, priests who buried their parish dead obediently in the campo santo, when going elsewhere in their jurisdiction had no problem burying the dead in a chapel. Thus in rural areas like Tomé and Alameda, near Albuquerque but far enough away to have their own chapels, the traditional burial ways endured after 1819 and the worlds of the living and dead remained more integrated.[80]

Although he possessed several private chapels, one of Santa Fe's most generous church benefactors had given so much to the parish church that he felt entitled to burial within its chapel dedicated to Saint Joseph, or San José.[81] In 1797 Bishop Olivares had granted merchant-rancher Antonio José Ortiz and his family members the right to burial within the chapel in gratitude for Ortiz's considerable philanthropy.[82] Ortiz personally had assumed responsibility for the parish church's rebuilding, which included significant renovation as well as a roof, bell towers, cemetery walls, a room for the chapel of the Third Order, and a graveyard.[83] As for the San José chapel, Ortiz had cleaned and decorated it "exclusively with the objective that my body and that of my spouse, my children and all my family, be interred therein."[84] Ortiz's complaint years later centered on the priest's insistence that Ortiz pay for his and his family's interment. Contending that this violated the agreement he had reached with the bishop, Ortiz's letter demonstrates the role that wealth and social influence would increasingly play in securing a coveted subfloor burial. Both he and his wife did finally receive church burials, though not per the terms of the 1797 agreement. His family buried Ortiz's corpse below the altar of the Rosario chapel in 1806.[85] A few years later, his wife, Rosa Bustamante, was buried beneath the altar of the chapel dedicated to the Virgin of Guadalupe, which adjoined their home on San Francisco Street.[86] Clearly, wealth and status could mitigate the law, which at this time forbade any exceptions to the burial reform.

Even people of lesser means continued to prefer the traditional burial within the church well into the 1840s. While survivors were not always able to honor their loved one's dying wishes, the baroque ideal of church burial endured through much of the Mexican period regardless of gender, urban versus rural residency, and season of the year. Notwithstanding the growing contact with outsiders after the 1821 opening of the Santa Fe Trail and the ongoing process of parish secularization, most people still sought burial as close as possible to the altar or in a favorite chapel. By the 1830s most of the population had to be well aware of the growing impossibility of fulfilling such requests. Still, their wills testify to the enduring resonance of the ideal and corroborate studies suggesting that New Mexico in this period experienced a heightened religiosity.[87] In communities without a resident priest, or where the priest was temporarily absent, parishioners quietly resisted the reforms by burying the dead independently, within the church.[88] Gradually, however, the new ways began to insert themselves in people's wills. Surviving wills show that from 1826 to 1850, about one-third of people asked that they be buried in a cemetery, a significant increase from earlier decades. Though almost half of testators still elected inter-ment within their parish church through at least the 1850s, burial registers show a shift away from church burial after 1819.[89]

By the middle of the Mexican period, then, New Mexico had a two-tiered burial system in place.[90] Though still without true rural cemeteries, after the funeral mass people quickly exiled the dead from the church. The parish priest made exceptions for the approximately 15 percent of people who could pay, though, at least through the early Territorial period. But even in rural commu-nities like Sapelló, near Las Vegas, burial inside the church was now reserved for those who could afford the twenty-five-peso minimum.[91] Increasingly, the living segregated the dead: first, by moving them to the space outside the walls of the church, and in time, by moving all burials outside of the settlements themselves.

Segregating the Dead

Even as they established new cemeteries in response to changing laws, shifting burial expectations, and population expansion, segregation did not emerge as a concern in the Mexican period. The Mexican Constitution in 1824 affirmed the Roman Catholic faith as the nation's official religion; however, foreign traders and others who died within Mexican boundaries also required burial and there-fore the Ministerio de Relaciones Interiores y Exteriores (Ministry of Interior and Foreign Relations) deemed important separate cemeteries for non-Catho-lics.[92] Still, as the 1820s and 1830s wore on, New Mexicans made little progress on the long-required "suburban" cemeteries, and no records mention anything resembling a public or nondenominational cemetery. Communities made and collected adobe bricks for walls for new suburban Catholic cemeteries, but con-struction seems to have limped along at best. The historical record is very thin on these processes, but in surviving documents, concerns surface over bricklay-ers and the pace of construction rather than segregating the dead.[93]

In Santa Fe, the new suburban cemetery finally built was probably the same one that construction crews unwittingly unearthed in 1997, 2003, and 2005. In each case, the Museum of New Mexico's Office of Archaeological Studies exam-ined the human remains that the backhoes had uncovered. In 2003 and 2005, they studied the complete or partial remains of more than thirty-eight indi-viduals from a ridge north of the central plaza, a site they named "La Garita Camposanto."[94] Archaeologists established that the earliest burials dated to the 1830s or 1840s, suggesting that this may have been the site of the city's first "sub-urban" Catholic cemetery, referenced in an 1833 document by Bishop Zubiría.[95] Archaeologists determined that some of the remains were Caucasian, but with-out DNA testing they could not determine race and ethnicity for the majority of the remains, which belonged to children.[96] Based on the limited evidence, the only suggestion of segregation in the cemetery was that of children from adults, common to the period.[97]

Since the beginning of the reform movement, enforcement had been selective, contingent on local conditions, the inclination of the parish priest, and, to a lesser degree, the social status of the dead. Once New Mexico was in US control, the latter became a more significant factor as cost assumed greater importance, with the sanction of the church hierarchy. After the US occupation, Bishop Zubiría and, later, Bishop Jean-Baptiste Lamy confirmed that for the price of twenty-five pesos, parishioners could receive burial within the church, essentially negating the reforms enacted in the Spanish and Mexican periods.[98] By this time more than a generation had passed since their implementation, so of the few individuals who could afford a twenty-five-peso burial, even fewer elected one.[99] In Albuquerque the only interment inside the church in 1848 was that of Isabel Luján, who died at age seventy-eight. Her burial cost twenty-five pesos, considerably more than the average cost of one to two pesos.[100] In 1852 the executors of the estate of Manuel Roybal and his wife María Manuela Trujillo paid twenty-five pesos for their burial in the church of Our Lady of Guadalupe in Pojoaque.[101] Though race and ethnicity had not segregated the dead, wealth now did.

The "La Garita" cemetery fell out of public memory and out of use within a few decades, but by 1853 the Masons and Santa Fe's two lodges of the International Order of Odd Fellows had purchased land to establish a cemetery. These recently established fraternal orders set aside one parcel of land within this shared cemetery to inter "strangers" or nonmembers for $10 or in some cases, for free as a form of charity. In the United States, the International Order of Odd Fellows had established itself as a male-only, white-only institution, and in that respect, these cemeteries were racially segregated by definition.[102] Correspondence between the two Santa Fe lodges indicates considerable discord on the strangers' section, which the Paradise Lodge insisted was reserved only for someone known to be "a respectable citizen or any of his relatives of respectability in the community or the body of a respectable female." Equating female respectability with sexual modesty, Paradise Lodge maintained that prostitutes and women "having the character of prostitutes, by which term those females living in an illicit connexion [sic] with a man without being lawfully married to him" could not receive interment here.[103]

This pronounced concern with women's chastity underscores Pablo Mitchell's characterization of this era in New Mexican history as relying upon discourses of sexuality to help "produce whiteness and sustain claims to white privilege."[104] Surprisingly, in this case the Montezuma Lodge broke from this propensity and condemned the Paradise Lodge, calling upon it to consider the true charity the Order should exemplify, and asserting:

Among others, two females have been interred in this ground set apart for the stranger. This circumstance seems to have wrought up in our brethren of Paradise Lodge this unseemly, uncharitable, and bigoted horror. Who are they? Or who are we? To say that this body or that body is more respectable than another, when the breath of life has departed from it. When the spirit has gone to be judged by the God who gave it—what is left of all, each, any of us, but dust, and only dust, who shall apply[.] the words of preference or respectability over one heap of dust of the earth more than another? In the grave we are all equal.[105]

The Montezuma Lodge decried the Paradise Lodge's bigotry against two women "spurned from the so-called holy ground of their church by beings in all things as culpable as themselves." The early date of this discussion—1856—and a concurrent reference in the local newspaper affirm that these women were Hispanic Catholics, now segregated not by their faith, but by public appraisal of their characters.

The Paradise Lodge's lack of charity caused a significant rift between the two lodges, but it is unclear whether the Montezuma Lodge's charity included other racial and ethnic groups as well as immodest Spanish women. Since African Americans could not join the whites-only establishments, they formed their own Masonic and Odd Fellows lodges by the 1880s. In 1883, the first Colored Odd Fellows Lodge in Santa Fe celebrated its three-year anniversary at an event which was "crowded with the best people in the city." W. W. Tate addressed the large audience of members and nonmembers, providing first a general history of the "secret beneficial society." Most interestingly, the Ohio-educated restaurateur in his speech attempted to clarify the difference between the "colored" and white orders, in the end concluding that they were "essentially the same" in their objectives. The newspaper's summary of his speech may well be the first reference to overt segregation in Santa Fe.[106] A decade later, Tate, "a colored man well known and esteemed all over New Mexico," was interred by the "colored" Masons of Santa Fe following his death of pneumonia. Tate had been born free in Virginia in 1830, and migrated to Santa Fe in 1862 after some time in Ohio. He belonged to both the Colored Masons and the Colored Odd Fellows, and his life's trajectory is in many respects the quintessential story of New Mexico's growing newcomer population in the Territorial period, even though his social prominence and his burial were demarcated by his race.[107]

As more foreigners settled in New Mexico, the need for new, nonsectarian cemeteries became a greater concern. As early as 1856, the *Santa Fe Weekly Gazette* proposed the sale of subscriptions to create a nondenominational cemetery, citing the Catholic church's refusal to bury "those females who died with the reputation of having lived a life of variance with one of virtuous chastity." Given the Odd Fellows' acrimonious debate over the burial of two such women,

Figure 7.3 1902 gravestone of Buffalo Soldier Isaac Jackson, Fairview Cemetery, Albuquerque, New Mexico. Courtesy of Christine Taute.

the city could not rely on the fraternal orders' charity, either. Underscoring the intersection of colonization and bodily control, the article concluded with the caution that "the morals of a people cannot be made perfected in a day, and some allowance should be made for our Mexican population, who are yet under the influences of customs that have remained unaltered for ages past."[108] To be worthy of full citizenship and integration into the nation, New Mexico's predominantly Hispanic and Indian population had to behave respectably; even dead bodies were subject to scrutiny.

Despite the need for a nondenominational, independent burial ground that would allow for any of the city's dead to find a resting place, it was not until 1884 that Santa Fe established Fairview Cemetery (in fact, the cemetery's oldest headstone dates to 1862, revealing a much earlier, if informal, genesis).[109] Its early records do not indicate any formal segregation of any kind, and the historic burial records make no note or race, religion or other identifiers.[110]

As in Santa Fe, in Albuquerque the Mexican period saw little headway in the construction of suburban cemeteries, despite the bishop's detailed instructions.[111] Albuquerque's leadership remained in a perpetual state of planning, it appears, and the question remained as to who would build the cemetery. Someone proposed in 1849 that the community employ its most impoverished members—who would likely have to be buried free of charge in the new cemetery—to build it, thereby preventing them from becoming burdens on the parish church.[112] What came of this project ultimately remains unclear, for the city records are silent on the question. It appears that the first true suburban cem-

Figure 7.4 View of historic Fairview Cemetery's "Colored" Section, Albuquerque, New Mexico. Courtesy of Christine Taute.

etery in Albuquerque may have been the Catholic cemetery named for Santa Barbara, inaugurated with its first interment in 1870, a response to the lack of space in the parish cemetery of San Felipe de Neri.[113]

A decade later, in 1882 local businessmen formed the Albuquerque Cemetery Association and established Fairview Cemetery at a site on the outskirts of the city where residents had already been burying their dead without official sanction.[114] Though the original cemetery plan appears to have been lost, a visit today reveals both religious and ethnic segregation. Distinct sections for members of different faiths (Jewish, B'nai B'rith) existed by the turn of the century. Groups including the International Order of Odd Fellows, Masons, Elks Club, and Woodmen of the World likewise established their own sections over time to provide for their members. In 1884 the Presbyterian Home Mission Board established an Indian section for children who died while at its boarding school, the Albuquerque Indian School. Rather than the product of legal mandates, these distinct sections were the creation of individual religious, fraternal, and other groups that purchased areas within the cemetery to guarantee their members a dignified resting place.

Notwithstanding the visible vestiges of segregation, the historian for Fairview Cemetery, Susan Schwartz, cites numerous examples of interments that defy ethnic and/or racial segregation. She contends that African Americans were buried throughout the cemetery beginning in 1886, when barber Abraham Alexander was interred in a five-dollar plot. In 1902 a "Colored" section appears in the cemetery records, and some individuals found a spot here, including former Buffalo Soldier and city jailor Isaac Jackson, whose headstone (see fig. 7.3) is among the few remaining.[115] A review of Albuquerque historic newspapers offers no mention of the creation of the Colored section, and Schwartz's expansive database of approximately twelve thousand burial records suggests no consistent pattern of racial segregation. In fact, she contends that the Colored section, pictured as it appears today in fig. 7.4, is somewhat underpopulated.[116] When the Atchison, Topeka and Santa Fe Railway cut through New Mexico in the 1880s, it bought and distributed plots in Fairview to its white, African American, Japanese, Chinese, and Indian employees. They received burial in their own section, segregated by virtue of their employment. The complex and nuanced nature of burial geography here, as elsewhere in northern New Mexico, suggests that New Mexico retained a somewhat fluid sense of identity and social hierarchy relative to the rest of the United States.

Conclusion

For the colonial and Mexican periods, burial registers indicate that the population beneath New Mexico's earthen church floors was fairly representative of the settlements themselves, a mixture of Spaniards, Indians, and mestizos even in the "Spanish" towns; we may attribute the relative fluidity of late nineteenth-century mortuary practices, then, to this legacy. Of course, for hundreds of years, New Mexico's residents were officially Catholic, and no call for any kind of segregation emerged in what was a heterogeneous society unified—officially, at least—by devotion to a single faith. At the nexus of faith and law, in this most intimate and intensely personal of matters, it took considerable ecclesiastical and civil effort to change New Mexican burial customs from traditional church burials to "suburban" cemetery interment. By the second half of the nineteenth century, however, socioeconomic segregation seeped into mortuary practices, primarily as a result of burial reforms that had placed the desired church burials out of reach for most. Some New Mexicans would request burial within the church as late as the 1890s, but for most Catholics the baroque concern with burial in proximity to the saints dissipated over the generations, especially as Catholic cemeteries sprouted up in the dry landscapes on the fringes of settlements. Relegated to the desolate outskirts of growing cities, all but the wealthiest of the dead were now segregated from the living.

As more and more newcomers came to New Mexico in the second half of the nineteenth century, each group of migrants brought with it its own sense of social/racial hierarchy and accompanying taxonomy. Catholics and non-Catholics, chaste and unchaste women, Odd Fellows and Masons: each time someone identified as part of one group or another—or was identified by survivors as one

Figure 7.5 View of Fairview Cemetery, Santa Fe, New Mexico. Courtesy of Suzanne Stamatov, PhD.

or the other—the sorting of the dead began. Assurance of a proper burial most certainly motivated many to enlist in the burgeoning fraternal orders. Others clung to their faith communities. In either case, group membership undoubtedly reassured those who had wandered far from their places of birth and sought a new life in northern New Mexico. Lacking the deep roots and family ties that they had left behind, the migrant minority could rest assured that their fellow Odd Fellows would tend their graves in this distant land. Thus, the same group solidarity that informed someone's social life defined the location and boundaries of their interment. As statehood became less elusive, racial segregation did appear in New Mexico, as suggested by the presence of separate lodges for African American Odd Fellows and Masons in Santa Fe by 1880, and a "Colored" section in Albuquerque's Fairview Cemetery in 1902. Like the Catholic burial records, New Mexico's public cemeteries that maintained records either did not indicate the race of the deceased, or buried the dead without regard to race, however, suggesting at most a halfhearted sort of racial segregation in northern New Mexico at the turn of the century.

Not surprisingly, when looking at the places to which the living consigned the dead and segregated them on the fringes of towns, the former differences are today often imperceptible. Though some of the new cemeteries had ambitious designs to rival those found in the Northeast, the high desert climate made rural cemeteries and garden cemeteries costly and challenging to sustain. Roads and public works projects cut through other cemeteries over the course of the twentieth century. Population growth and urban sprawl mean that formerly peripheral sites now rest in the crosshairs of interstates. Dedicated volunteers struggle to maintain these places sanctified by the dead from all walks of life, and the segregation that persists is largely one of neglect or forgetting.

Notes

The quotation in the chapter title comes from 1856 correspondence from Montezuma Lodge No. 1 of the International Order of Odd Fellows in Santa Fe, cited below. Portions of this chapter have been previously published as part of *Death and Dying in New Mexico* (Albuquerque: University of New Mexico Press, 2007). I am grateful to the University of New Mexico Press for granting permission to publish this material here in a new context. Thank you also to Suzanne Stamatov for her comments on a draft of this chapter as well as her photographs. I am also most grateful for the photos, documents, and insights shared by Susan Schwartz, Christina Taute, and Barbara Fix.

1. For the sake of brevity, I use "Anglo-American" and "European American" rather interchangeably, while recognizing that this shorthand, like the blanket term "Hispanics," belies the diversity within each group.

2. Sabrina M. Sanchez, "In the Name of the Father, the Governor, and 'A-1 Good Men': Performing Gender and Statehood in Territorial New Mexico, 1880–1912" (Diss., University of California at Santa Cruz, 2013), 5.

3. Many scholars have written about the ideas underpinning Anglo superiority and New Mexico's reluctant admittance as a state, but most recently the work of William S. Kiser is particularly detailed and insightful; see Kiser, "The Politics of Slavery and Social Hierarchies in Colonial, Mexican and Territorial New Mexico," *New Mexico Historical Review* 92:3 (Summer 2017): 283–309; quote, 301.

4. Alicia Tjarks estimates another five thousand people in the jurisdiction of El Paso at this time. Alicia V. Tjarks, "Demographic, Ethnic and Occupational Structure of New Mexico, 1790," *The Americas* 35 (1978): 45–88. Per the conventions outlined by Fray Angelico Chavez, I use the title "Fray" or "Father" to refer to the Franciscans and the title "Cura" or "Padre" to refer to the secular clergy of Durango. Fray Angélico Chávez, *Archives of the Archdiocese of Santa Fe, 1678–1900* (Washington, DC: Academy of American Franciscan History, 1957), 5.

5. Ross Frank, *From Settler to Citizen: New Mexican Economic Development and the Creation of a Vecino Society, 1750–1820* (Berkeley: University of California Press, 2000), 47–48.

6. Furthermore, many documents identified people not by whether they were "español" or "indio," but by their belonging to a particular community. Though the term "vecino/a" suggests non-Indian, settler status for much of the colonial period, by the late colonial period the meaning of the word was more inclusive, and even non-Spaniards might assume this designation. Even today, some New Mexicans identify themselves as "Spanish." Historian Charles Montgomery has written an insightful study of this and other elements of New Mexico's construction of a Spanish past in *The Spanish Redemption: Heritage, Power, and Loss on New Mexico's Upper Rio Grande* (Berkeley: University of California Press, 2002). His discussion of race and the struggle for statehood is especially cogent (63–88).

7. John M. Nieto-Phillips, *The Language of Blood: The Making of Spanish-American Identity in New Mexico, 1880s–1930s* (Albuquerque: University of New Mexico Press, 2004), 38.

8. See Alexandra Minna Stern, "From Mestizophilia to Biotypology: Racialization and Science in Mexico, 1920–1960," in *Race and Nation in Modern Latin America*, ed. Nancy P.

Appelbaum, Anne S. Macpherson, and Karin Alejandra Rosemblatt (Chapel Hill: University of North Carolina Press, 2003), 187–210.

9. Olivia Gall, "Mexican Long-Living Mestizophilia versus a Democracy Open to Diversity," in *Latin American and Caribbean Ethnic Studies* 8:3 (2013): 280–303. DOI: 10.1080/17442222.2013.797212. Notwithstanding this noble philosophizing, whites remained at the helm, and nineteenth-century Mexico "belonged politically, economically, and culturally to the few." Claudio Lomnitz-Adler, *Exits from the Labyrinth: Culture and Ideology in the Mexican National Space* (Berkeley: University of California Press, 1992), 277.

10. María Elena Martínez, *Genealogical Fictions: Limpieza de Sangre, Religion, and Gender in Colonial Mexico* (Stanford: Stanford University Press, 2008), 95.

11. A *villa* was a chartered municipality with some stature, smaller than a *ciudad* and larger than a *pueblo*. For a concise discussion of settlement patterns, see Marc Simmons, "Settlement Patterns and Village Plans in Colonial New Mexico," in *New Spain's Far Northern Frontier*, ed. David J. Weber (Albuquerque: University of New Mexico Press, 1979), 97–115.

12. James F. Brooks, *Captives and Cousins: Slavery, Kinship, and Community in the Southwest Borderlands* (Chapel Hill: University of North Carolina Press, 2002), 125. Enrique Lamadrid and Moisés Gonzáles, who are working on a volume titled *Genízaro Nation*, state in an interview with KUNM that fully one-third of the New Mexican population was genízaro by the late eighteenth century. See Cristina Baccin, "Genízaro Nation," January 8, 2017, http://kunm.org/post/gen-zaro-nation.

13. See Andrés Reséndez, *The Other Slavery: The Uncovered Story of Indian Enslavement in America* (New York: Houghton Mifflin Harcourt, 2016).

14. A recent article points to the challenges of uncovering this past, even with DNA analysis. Simon Romero, "Indian Slavery Once Thrived in New Mexico. Latinos Are Finding Family Ties to It." *New York Times*, January 28, 2018, https://www.nytimes.com/2018/01/28/us/indian-slaves-genizaros.html.

15. See Kiser, "The Politics of Slavery," 288–90.

16. In this early period, a few newcomers married into local society. In her seminal study, Deena González considers the economic, political, and social aspects of the conquest on New Mexico's women. Deena González, *Refusing the Favor: The Spanish-Mexican Women of Santa Fe, 1820–1880* (New York: Oxford University Press, 2001).

17. Obituary at https://www.findagrave.com/memorial/48249527/luis-gold. See also: Corinne P. Sze, "Fairview Cemetery History," http://www.fairviewcemeterysantafe.org/history/.

18. William W. H. Davis, *El Gringo; or New Mexico and Her People* (New York: Harper and Bros., 1857), 216.

19. González, *Refusing the Favor*, chapter 2, offers a thoughtful discussion of this as it pertained to women in particular.

20. Even as late as 1920, African Americans represented less than 2 percent of the territory's population. Pablo Mitchell, "Bodies on Borders: African Americans, Penitentes, and Social Order in the Southwest," in *Race, Religion, Region*, ed. Fay Botham and Sara M. Patterson (Tucson: University of Arizona Press, 2006), 89–100.

21. Mitchell, "Bodies on Borders," 90.

22. Montgomery, *The Spanish Redemption*, 7–10.

23. González, *Refusing the Favor*, 10.

24. Ramón Gutiérrez, "Hispanic Identities in the Southwestern United States," in *Race and Classification: The Case of Mexican America*, ed. Ilona Katzew and Susan Deans-Smith (Stanford: Stanford University Press, 2009), 183.

25. Montgomery, *The Spanish Redemption*, 9.

26. Mark Stegmaier, "A Law That Would Make Caligula Blush: New Mexico Territory's Unique Slave Code, 1859–1861," in *African American History in New Mexico: Portraits from Five Hundred Years*, ed. Bruce A. Glasrud (Albuquerque: University of New Mexico Press, 2013), 56–84.

27. Laura Gómez, *Manifest Destinies: The Making of the Mexican American Race* (New York: New York University Press, 2007), 102–3.

28. Gómez, *Manifest Destinies*, 109.

29. Nieto-Phillips, *The Language of Blood*, 73–74, 119–21.

30. Montgomery, *The Spanish Redemption*, 86.

31. David M. Brugge, *Navajos in the Catholic Church Records of New Mexico*, 1694–1875 (Santa Fe: School for Advanced Research Press, 1968 and 1985), 119.

32. The plan is in the Archives of the Archdiocese of Santa Fe, Book of Accounts Book XXV Santa Cruz, 1768. Interested readers may see it in my *Death and Dying in New Mexico* (Albuquerque: University of New Mexico Press, 2007), 86, which could not be reprinted for this publication.

33. José María Vibián de Ortega to Francisco Gabriel de Olivares y Benito, Santa Fe, June 19, 1800, Archivo Histórico del Arzobispado de Durango, New Mexico State Library, Southwest Collection [hereafter AHAD, followed by microfilm reel and frame numbers in parentheses] (203/798–799).

34. See Santa Fe Burial Books in AASF, reel 40. José María Vibián de Ortega to bishop [Francisco Gabriel de Olivares y Benito], Santa Fe, June 19, 1801, AHAD (206/624–625). This document appears to be a copy of the bishop's circular made first by Ortega and then by Fray Francisco de Hozio and sent to the bishop in 1802 to confirm receipt of the circular. Compared to the price demanded by the *arancel*, the price exacted by parish priests was consistently lower, regardless of the service. The *arancel* required two pesos in cash for the bells to be rung at a funeral, but in reality, people only paid one peso (in goods) to sacristans for this service. José Vibián de Ortega to Pedro Bautista Pino, Santa Fe, March 4, 1801, Archives of the Archdiocese of Santa Fe [hereafter AASF, followed by collection name and microfilm reel and frame in parentheses], Loose Documents, Mission, 1801, #6 (53/343–344).

35. Albuquerque Accounts Book B-XXII, 1818–1861, AASF, Accounts, reel 45.

36. The only difference between a four-peso burial and a two-peso burial in Santa Cruz was probably the location of the burial within the church, for like the four-peso burial, a two-peso burial included high cross, mass, office of the dead, and cope. Rada was recently arrived from Sonora and his discontent with the status quo in Santa Cruz indicates that even as far removed from the viceregal capital as Sonora, funerary customs were in keeping with the Spanish norm. Though Rada claims here that there was no graveyard, he is probably referring to the fact that there was no true "ventilated" cemetery. Manuel Rada to bishop, Santa Cruz de la Cañada, April 30, 1821, AHAD (246/235–241).

37. Yalom mistakenly credits the Jesuits with missionizing New Mexico. Marilyn Yalom, *The American Resting Place* (New York: Houghton Mifflin, 2008), 201. I take issue with Yalom's generalization regarding Spanish missionaries in the Southwest using markers for whites but not for Indians (11); though perhaps accurate for some missions, this was not the case in New Mexico, which seems to have used no grave markers beyond the church itself. Given that New Mexico was the most populous of the Spanish settlements in what became the US Southwest, this generalization is inaccurate.

38. Juan José Ornelas to Bishop of Durango, Santa Cruz de la Cañada, n.d., AHAD (231/761–763). According to Chávez, Lombide served in Santa Cruz from January 1802 to November 1803.

39. See, for example, Alicia V. Tjarks, "Evolución urbana de Texas durante el siglo XVIII," *Revista de Indias* 33–34 (1973–74): 605–36. See also Alicia V. Tjarks, "Comparative Demographic Analysis of Texas, 1777–1793," *Southwestern Historical Quarterly* 77 (January 1974), 291–338, and "Demographic, Ethnic and Occupational Structure," 45–88; and Ana María Alonso, *Thread of Blood: Colonialism, Revolution, and Gender on Mexico's Northern Frontier* (Tucson: University of Arizona Press, 1995), 54–55.

40. Antonio José Rios-Bustamante, "New Mexico in the Eighteenth Century: Life, Labor and Trade in la Villa de San Felipe de Albuquerque, 1706–1790," *Aztlán* 7 (1976): 357–89.

41. Eighty-eight percent of testators specifically asked for a church burial from 1704–1821. This figure is based on my examination of all extant wills (183) from the period. A shift takes place after independence, and from 1830–49 only one-third of testators requested church burials while fully 24 percent requested a cemetery burial (the remainder left the decision up to their heirs or made no mention of burial location at all). The 251 wills that survive for the period 1704–1849 are in the manuscript collections of the Center for Southwest Research at the University of New Mexico [hereafter cited as CSWR], the New Mexico State Records Center and Archives [hereafter NMSRCA], and the microfilmed Spanish Archives of New Mexico [hereafter SANM] I and II.

42. This figure is based on careful analysis of the burial records from Albuquerque, Santa Fe, and Santa Cruz. All burial books examined are located in the AASF, reels 34–43.

43. Santa Clara Burial Book, AASF, reel 38, f. 548–571.

44. Priests only occasionally recorded the dead's ethnicity. This figure is based on analysis of the approximately six hundred cases (of more than two thousand considered), where the burial registers identified individuals as belonging to a particular tribe or Pueblo or indicated that someone was "Spanish" or a "vecino."

45. Narcisco Gardarilla to Máximo Jesús de Irigoyen, quoting José Antonio de Zubiría to vicarages of Parral and Chihuahua, Durango October 3, 1836, Catholic Archives of Texas, Various Spanish and Mexican Photostats, 101.47.

46. Albuquerque Burial Book, December 9, 1819, AASF (34/445).

47. Arancel of José Antonio Zubiría, Albuquerque, August 9, 1833, AASF Accounts (45/690–694).

48. In the eighteenth and early nineteenth centuries, New Mexican funerary rituals on the whole tended to be far less elaborate and less entangled with reinforcing social hierarchies than those in central Mexico, where the most coveted church burial cost upwards of one hundred times an artisan's daily wage. Pamela Voekel, *Alone Before God: Death and the Origins of Mexican Modernity* (Durham, NC: Duke University Press, 2002), 107.

49. See Frank, *From Settler to Citizen*, chapters 4–5. Since 2005 San Juan Pueblo officially has been renamed its pre-Spanish name, *Ohkay Owingeh*.

50. Population figures for San Juan appear in John L. Kessell, *The Missions of New Mexico since 1776* (Albuquerque: University of New Mexico Press, 1980), 91.

51. The alcalde was the chief executive in a village or town.

52. José Manuel Archuleta et. al. to Alejo García Conde, San Juan de los Caballeros, October 11, 1821, Twitchell 1367, SANM I (6/1712–1713). See also *WPA Translations of the Spanish Archives of New Mexico*, vol. 21, 123–24.

53. Complaint of Indians of San Juan Against Fray Manuel Sánchez Vergara; Request for Outside Protector, January 1-March 18, 1822, Mexican Archives of New Mexico [hereafter, MANM], (1/1184–1198). When giving his testimony, Sánchez Vergara freely admitted to the charges of corporal punishment, contending its occasional necessity. He also acknowledged

preaching against the worship of rocks and feathers, claiming that the Indians venerated them as gods, not being true Christians at all.

54. Frank, *From Settler to Citizen*, 201–5.

55. See Charles R. Cutter, *The Protector de Indios in Colonial New Mexico, 1659–1821* (Albuquerque: University of New Mexico Press, 1986).

56. This opinion is referenced in a document from the Junta Provincial dated February 21, 1821. Cutter, *The Protector de Indios*, 100. Appointed to the post by the Audiencia of Guadalajara in 1817, Sánchez Vergara served as protector until a royal decree in 1821 abolished the office shortly before independence.

57. Rafael Trujillo and Miguel García to Governor [Facundo Melgares], Abiquiú, September 1822, MANM (1/1110–1111). A newly available collection of parish registers for Abiquiú promises to shed light on burial practices in this community during the period in question: http://manitos.net/2019/11/11/discovering-and-recovering-abiquius-lost-archive/.

58. In both communities, at least one burial appears to have taken place under these conditions, though the burial registers are silent or vague for these months in Taos and Santa Cruz. Fernando Ortiz to Bishop José Antonio de Zubiría, Santa Cruz, October 8, 1837, Archivo General de la Nación, Mexico [hereafter cited as AGN]-Justicia, tomo 138, leg. 48, 162–63, copy in Bancroft Library, University of California at Berkeley; Antonio José Martínez to Bishop José Antonio de Zubiría, Taos, September 25, 1837, AGN-Justicia, tomo 138, leg. 48, 166–68, copy in Bancroft Library, University of California at Berkeley, translation in Janet Lecompte, *Rebellion in Río Arriba, 1837* (Albuquerque: University of New Mexico Press, 1985), 123–34. These events and the precursors of the revolt are discussed in detail in Andrés Reséndez, *Changing National Identities at the Frontier: Texas and New Mexico, 1800–1850* (Cambridge: Cambridge University Press, 2005). See also Angélico Chávez, *But Time and Chance: The Story of Padre Martínez of Taos, 1793–1867* (Santa Fe: Sunstone Press, 1981), 55. For a general discussion of the revolt, see David J. Weber, *The Mexican Frontier, 1821–1846: The American Southwest under Mexico* (Albuquerque: University of New Mexico Press, 1982), 261–66.

59. For Guatemala, see Douglass Sullivan-González, *Piety, Power, and Politics: Religion and Nation Formation in Guatemala, 1821–1871* (Pittsburgh: University of Pittsburgh Press, 1998), chapter 3; and Greg Grandin, *The Blood of Guatemala: A History of Race and Nation* (Durham, NC: Duke University Press, 2000), chapter 3. On Brazil, see João José Reis, *Death Is a Festival: Funeral Rites and Rebellion in Nineteenth-Century Brazil*, trans. H. Sabrina Gledhill (Chapel Hill: University of North Carolina Press, 2003).

60. Reséndez, *Changing National Identities*, 183.

61. Reséndez, *Changing National Identities*, 188.

62. Reséndez, *Changing National Identities*, 180. Most Pueblos in both the Río Arriba and the Río Abajo supported the rebellion, as did many Plains Indians. See also James F. Brooks, *Captives and Cousins*, 273–80.

63. Both of these cemetery burials were of infants; from a review of ninety-three total burials, 1819–March 1821. The letter from Santa Cruz, dated August 1825, notes that the decree had arrived four years and five months prior, or March 1821. Ayuntamiento of Santa Cruz de la Cañada to Manuel de Jesús Rada, Santa Cruz de la Cañada, August 28, 1825, AASF Loose Documents, Mission (54/692–694). Burial book of Santa Cruz de la Cañada, AASF, reel 34.

64. Burial book of Santa Cruz de la Cañada, AASF (39/694).

65. Ramón Frega(?) to Manuel Rada, Santa Cruz, June 10, 1821, AASF, Santa Cruz Patentes (50/15–16). Rada became New Mexico's representative to the 1829 Congress.

66. Ayuntamiento of Santa Cruz de la Cañada to Manuel de Jesús Rada, Santa Cruz de la Cañada, August 28, 1825, AASF Loose Documents, Mission (54/692–694). It is unclear why the

town waited so long after independence to write their petition. It may be that this was not the first attempt, or that new leadership in the ayuntamiento spearheaded this effort.

67. Ayuntamiento of Santa Cruz de la Cañada to Manuel de Jesús Rada, Santa Cruz de la Cañada, August 28, 1825, AASF (54/692–694).

68. Agustín Fernández de San Vicente to ayuntamiento of Santa Cruz de la Cañada, Santa Fe, July 1, 1826, AASF, Loose Documents, Mission, 1825, n. 10 (54/692–697).

69. Agustín Fernández de San Vicente to priests and ministers of New Mexico, Santa Fe, May 10, 1826, AASF, Patentes, LXIX-92 (48/144) and AASF, Loose Documents, Mission, 1826, n. 25 (54/783).

70. After the death of Bishop Castañiza in 1825, no bishop served Durango for six years. Vacancies became common throughout Mexico due to a conflict between the Vatican and the Mexican government, and by 1829 Mexico had no bishops whatsoever. José Ignacio Gallegos, *Historia de la Iglesia en Durango* (México, DF: Editorial Jus, 1969), 257; Weber, *The Mexican Frontier*, 70.

71. There were four or five [Wright says four, Martínez says five] secular priests in New Mexico by 1821; this number increased to eight by 1829, and eleven in 1846. Jerome J. Martínez y Alíre, "The Influence of the Roman Catholic Church in New Mexico under Mexican Administration: 1821–1848," in *Four Hundred Years of Faith: Seeds of Struggle, Harvest of Faith: A History of the Catholic Church in New Mexico* (Santa Fe: Archdiocese of Santa Fe, 1998), 329–44.

72. See Jim Norris, *After "the Year Eighty": The Demise of Franciscan Power in Spanish New Mexico* (Albuquerque: University of New Mexico Press, 2000), 136–39.

73. The activities of Cura Leyva in Albuquerque and Cura Rada in Santa Cruz are especially noteworthy.

74. It should be noted that the secular clergy did not confine themselves to criticizing the Franciscans, and on occasion pointed out the weaknesses of other priests as well. See, for example, Francisco Leyva's critique of Father Madariaga. José Francisco Leyva to Vicar General [Don Juan Rafael Rascón], San Miguel del Vado, February 18, 1831, AHAD (515/732–734). Cura Rada established a primary school in Santa Cruz, for example. Relación de Meritos y Servicios del Pbro. Manuel de Jesús Rada, Durango, May 25, 1831, AHAD (269/537–541).

75. José Luis Rodríguez to José Francisco Leyva, Santa Fe, June 10, 1826, AASF, Loose Documents, Mission, 1826, n. 11 (54/753–754).

76. José Luis Rodríguez to José Francisco Leyva, Santa Fe, June 10, 1826, AASF, Loose Documents, Mission, 1826, n. 11 (54/753–754). See also José Luis Rodríguez to José Francisco Leyva, Santa Fe, June 10, 1826, AASF, Accounts (45/603–604).

77. Gómez Farías exercised considerable authority given President Santa Anna's abandonment of Mexico City, and he implemented a wide-ranging program of liberal reforms for a time. Vice President [Valentín Gómez Farías] to José Antonio Laureano de Zubiría to the parishes of New Mexico, Mexico City, April 23, 1833, AASF, Patentes (49/255–256).

78. Voekel, "Scent and Sensibility," 386. William B. Taylor's work on rural Guadalajara demonstrates that despite changing elite conceptions, popular pious practices remained as strong as ever at the turn of the century. William B. Taylor, *Magistrates of the Sacred: Priests and Parishioners in Eighteenth-Century Mexico* (Stanford: Stanford University Press, 1996), 299.

79. The 1826 Fernández de San Vicente visitation is replete with authorizations for the construction of private and public chapels and oratories. Likewise, Frank counted over thirty licenses for new churches and chapels in the 1833 visitation of Bishop Don José Antonio de Zubiría. Frank, *From Settler to Citizen*, 182.

80. Private chapels, which had not been specifically mentioned in any decree from either the crown or the Mexican government, finally came under attack, too. In 1841 burials in private chapels in Belén raised the ire of some church officials. Reminding Belén's residents that the church had "considerable moral force" at its disposable to ensure compliance with its precepts,

Cura José de Jesús Luján of Santa Fe warned that burial inside chapels must immediately cease. Rafael Ortiz to José de Jesús Luján, Santa Fe, June 22, 1841, AASF, Accounts Book C-1 (46/871–872). In Summer 2018, a three-year excavation at Belén's historic church began, promising new insights into nineteenth-century mortuary practices. Julia M. Dendinger, "The Excavation at Nuestra Señora de Belen," *Valencia County News-Bulletin*, August 8, 2018, http://www.news-bulletin.com/news/features/the-excavation-of-nuestra-se-ora-de-belen/article_c4f153b0-9b2e-11e8-885e-af6a85b22e9c.html.

81. Art historian Felipe Mirabal has identified four chapels belonging to Ortiz: 1) Our Lady of Guadalupe in Ortiz's rancho of San Antonio in Pojoaque; 2) Our Lady of Guadalupe at his home in Santa Fe; 3) Our Lady of the Rosary chapel in the parish church of Santa Fe; and 4) the freestanding Sanctuary of Our Lady of Guadalupe, Santa Fe. Felipe Mirabal to Martina Will, private correspondence, July 1999.

82. Bruce Ellis, *Bishop Lamy's Santa Fe Cathedral* (Albuquerque: University of New Mexico Press, 1985), 61. Ellis here cites documents that have reportedly been lost in the interim since José D. Sena translated and published them in "The Chapel of Don Antonio José Ortiz," *New Mexico Historical Review* 13:4 (October 1938): 347–59. Incidentally, Ortiz's devotion and connections to the church were such that his grandson, Santiago Baca y Ortiz, was a seminarian and a page in the household of Bishop Olivares. Never ordained, he eventually became the first governor of the immense Department of Durango. Felipe Mirabal to Martina Will, private correspondence, July 1999. For a detailed genealogy of the Ortiz family, see Virginia Olmsted, *The Ortiz Family of New Mexico: The First Six Generations* (n.p., 1978), and Nancy Ligon de Ita, *The Ortiz Family of New Mexico* (n.p., 1998). Both unpublished works are available at the Center for Southwest Research, Zimmerman Library, University of New Mexico.

83. Based on the plan of the parish church, it is likely that Ortiz had paid for both the large cemetery's repairs and the small "sementerito" adjacent to the Third Order's chapel.

84. Antonio José Ortiz to Francisco Gabriel de Olivares y Benito, Santa Fe, November 16, 1805, AHAD (212/415–416). See also Kessell, *The Missions of New Mexico Since 1776*, 37.

85. Ligon de Ita, *The Ortiz Family*, 15. The entry in the Santa Fe Burial Book, August 13, 1806, AASF (40/504), does not specify burial location.

86. Ligon de Ita, *The Ortiz Family*, 15. As with her husband's burial, the entry in the Santa Fe Burial Book, August 16, 1814, AASF (40/572), does not specify burial location.

87. Weigle and others have noted as evidence of this heightened religiosity increased santo production, significant church construction, and "the resurgence of severe penitential activities." Marta Weigle, *Brothers of Light, Brothers of Blood: The Pentitentes of the Southwest* (Albuquerque: University of New Mexico Press, 1976; reprint, Santa Fe: Ancient City Press, 1989), 37.

88. See, for example, Picurís Burial Book, April 22, 1830, AASF (36/1225).

89. There were many inconsistencies among priests in recording entries. The parish burial books from Santa Cruz de la Cañada and Santa Fe, for example, only occasionally provide information on burial location, with priests and friars alike noting simply "ecclesiastical burial" in many entries. It is therefore impossible to make broad, comprehensive comparisons of burial practices over time due to the lack of uniformity in burial books. Only in Albuquerque were the records for select years more complete, including (to varying degrees, depending on the priest in charge) the deceased's name, ethnicity, age, burial location, and funeral arrangements. Albuquerque burial books examined are located in AASF, reel 34. The parish included the populations of Alameda to the north and Tomé to the south, and therefore some of these burials actually took place within the churches or cemeteries of these communities.

90. According to Jordan, subfloor burials continued in Texas for these same reasons of wealth and status. Terry G. Jordan, *Texas Graveyards: A Cultural Legacy* (Austin: University of Texas Press, 1982), 66.

91. Sapelló is thirteen miles north of Las Vegas, New Mexico. Smaller communities like Sapelló might still allow subfloor burials, but the price was considerable: the cost for burial in the nave of the church was twenty-five to fifty pesos. For merely six pesos, one could be buried in the cemetery in front of the same church. See burial accounts in the Libro de Fábrica, 1860–71, Sapelló, AASF Loose Docs., Diocesan, 1860 n. 29 (57/148–165).

92. Ministerio de Relaciones Interiores y Exteriores, July 7, 1824, AGN, Ayuntamientos, vol. 3, exp. 1.

93. Proceedings of the Ayuntamiento of Santa Cruz de la Cañada, Santa Cruz, May 28, 1826, CSWR Sender Coll. (1/523) and Communication from Governor Antonio Narbona to Alcalde Constitucional of Santa Cruz de la Cañada, July 3, 1826, CSWR Sender Coll. (1/535–537). Governor José Antonio Cháves to Santa Fe Ayuntamiento, Santa Fe, June 18, 1830 (MANM 10/930–933), and Ayuntamiento of Santa Fe to Governor José Antonio Cháves, Santa Fe, June 18, 1830 (MANM 10/656–658). See also Cabildo records, Santa Fe, March 30, 1833, CSWR, MSS 76 BC, box 1, fol. 1.

94. H. Wolcott Toll, Nancy J. Akins, Natasha Williamson, Matthew Barbour, and Glenna Dean, *La Garita Camposanto: Work at a Forgotten Cemetery Under Kearny Road, Santa Fe, New Mexico, 2003 and 2005* (Santa Fe: Museum of New Mexico, New Mexico Office of Archaeological Studies, Archaeology Note 358, 2006). According to the Archdiocese of Santa Fe, the archives contain no evidence of any cemetery or church in the area; however, an 1846 map indicates the presence of both. Julie Ann Grimm, "Emergency Money Will Be Used to Pay for Excavation," *Santa Fe New Mexican*, October 17, 2003, B3; John Arnold, "City Funds Cemetery Research," *Albuquerque Journal*, October 17, 2003, A1.

95. Visitation of Bishop José Antonio Laureano de Zubiría y Escalante, Santa Fe, October 18, 1833, NMSCRA, Microfilm of Zubiría Visitation (1 reel), 47r-48v.

96. A 1997 excavation discovered remains of five Caucasian and Hispanic adults from the Territorial period at Kearny Road (which the report spells "Kearney"). See Eric G. Ozolins, Vincent H. Stefan, and J. F. Powell, "A Bioarchaeological Analysis of the Human Remains Recovered from LA120430, the Kearney Road Site, Santa Fe, New Mexico," in *The 124 Kearney Road Burials (LA 120430): Report on the Human Remains Recovered from a Water Meter Excavation near Downtown Santa Fe, New Mexico*, by Stephen S. Post, Nancy Hanks, Eric G. Ozolins, Vincent H. Stefan, and Joseph F. Powell (Santa Fe: Museum of New Mexico, Office of Archaeological Studies, Archaeology Note 248, 1998), 39–48. The predominance of children's burials at the adjacent site, identified a decade later as "La Garita," made biological affinity difficult to determine on the basis of osteology alone, and no DNA was performed to make this determination. See Nancy J. Akins, "Kearny Road Human Remains," in *La Garita Camposanto: Work at a Forgotten Cemetery under Kearny Road, Santa Fe, New Mexico, 2003 and 2005*, by H. Wolcott Toll, Nancy J. Akins, Natasha Williamson, Matthew Barbour, and Glenna Dean (Santa Fe: Museum of New Mexico Press, 2006), 37–68.

97. Toll, *La Garita Camposanto*, 67.

98. Bishop Jean-Baptiste Lamy to Cura José de Jesús Lujan, Santa Fe, July 4, 1855, AASF Loose Documents, Diocesan (56/402–403).

99. Zubiría made it clear that these funds from subfloor burials were to be kept separate and used for repairs of the church and its decorations. Only one person was interred in the church in the period 1850–53. José Antonio Laureano de Zubiría, September 17, 1850, Santa Cruz de la Cañada Burial Book, AASF (39/1127–1128).

100. Albuquerque Burial Book, January 17, 1848, AASF (34/901).

101. Settlement of the estate of Manuel Ruival and his wife María Manuela Trujillo, Jacona area, December 2, 1852, NMSRCA, Frank Romero Papers, box 1, fol. 2.

102. African Americans established their own lodges beginning in the 1840s. See "A Historical Study" from the Davis Lodge, http://davislodge.org/wp-content/uploads/20131103AHistor

icalStudy.pdf, accessed December 8, 2017. Santa Fe's first "Colored Lodge" of Odd Fellows cel-ebrated its third anniversary in 1883. Further research is needed on this institution's history in New Mexico. *Daily New Mexican*, October 14, 1883.

103. Thanks to Barbara Fix, who kindly shared her transcription of this document, which is housed at the Odd Fellows Hall, and to Alysia Abbott, who alerted me to the document. Letter to Montezuma Lodge No. 1, International Order of Odd Fellows from Paradise Lodge No. 2, International Order of Odd Fellows, January 26, 1856, in personal communication to author from Barbara Fix, Santa Fe, New Mexico, December 2, 2017.

104. Pablo Mitchell, *Coyote Nation: Sexuality, Race, and Conquest in Modernizing New Mexico, 1880–1920* (Chicago: University of Chicago Press, 2005), 180.

105. Transcription of letter to Paradise Lodge No. 2, International Order of Odd Fellows from Montezuma Lodge No. 1, International Order of Odd Fellows, Santa Fe, New Mexico, April 5, 1856, in personal communication to author from Barbara Fix, Santa Fe, New Mexico, December 2, 2017.

106. "Odd Fellows' Anniversary," *Daily New Mexican*, October 14, 1883.

107. *Santa Fe Daily New Mexican*, January 12 and January 17, 1894. *Chronicling America: Historic American Newspapers.* Library of Congress. See https://chroniclingamerica.loc.gov/lccn/sn84020631/1894-01-17/ed-1/seq-4/.

108. *Santa Fe Weekly Gazette*, March 1, 1856, http://chroniclingamerica.loc.gov/lccn/sn88071075/1856-03-01/ed-1/seq-2.pdf.

109. "A History of Fairview Cemetery," extracted from *Bulletin of the Historic Santa Fe Foundation*, 12:1 (April 1984), http://www.fairviewcemeterysantafe.org/history/history-short-version/. See also Corinne P. Sze, "Fairview Cemetery History," http://www.fairviewcemetery-santafe.org/history/.

110. Fairview Cemetery Collection, Minute Book Board of Directors, 1884–1930, NMSCRCA. Private communication with Michael Mulligan, president, Fairview Cemetery Preservation Association, December 13, 2017, and with David Mason, vice president, Fairview Cemetery Preservation Association, December 17, 2017.

111. José Antonio Zubiría, Arancel, San Felipe de Neri de Albuquerque, August 9, 1833, AASF, Accounts (45/690–694).

112. Manuel Gallegos et al., October 15, 1849, Albuquerque, AASF, Accounts (45/798–800). Commander General of the Provincias Internas Pedro de Nava had suggested to the king that criminal labor be used for cemetery construction as early as 1796. King of Spain [Carlos IV] to Bishop of Durango [Francisco Gabriel de Olivares y Benito], San Lorenzo, December 1, 1798, AHAD II (110/179–183).

113. The first recorded burial in Santa Barbara Cemetery was that of Rafael Apodaca on March 8, 1870. Book C, "Libro de defunciones de la Parroquia de Albuquerque desde Octubre 1859 a Diciembre 1891," AASF roll 96A, no frame number. Many thanks to Brian Graney for this citation. The Jesuit-built Santa Barbara Cemetery is now part of Mt. Calvary Cemetery and continues to be under the care of the Catholic Church. Carol J. Condie, "The Cemeteries of Albuquerque, Bernalillo County and Parts of Sandoval and Valencia Counties," unpublished report to the City of Albuquerque, August 1999, 13.

114. Elaine D. Briseño, "Cemeteries, Like Albuquerque's Fairview, Tell a Community Story," *Albuquerque Journal*, August 28, 2016, 32.

115. Personal communication with Susan Schwartz, November 17, 2017. Although his head-stone remains in the cemetery, Schwartz believes vandals moved it away from the actual grave. Personal communication with Susan Schwartz, August 17, 2018.

116. Personal communication with Susan Schwartz, December 8, 2017. Marc Simmons observes that Albuquerque's Fairview Cemetery maintained segregated burials until "about

1962," suggesting that the "Colored" section established in 1902 signaled a shift that took firm root over the course of the twentieth century. He does not cite a source for this date, however, and has not had access to the trove of historic burial records that Schwartz is presently compiling into a database, and which she states do *not* support a history of segregation in Fairview Cemetery. Marc Simmons, "New Mexico Embraced Early Tradition of Racial Tolerance," *New Mexican*, January 19, 2013, A-5.

Bibliography

ARCHIVES

Archives of the Archdiocese of Santa Fe (AASF), Santa Fe, NM
Archivo General de la Nación, México (AGN), México, DF
Archivo Histórico del Arzobispado de Durango (AHAD), New Mexico State Library, Southwest Collection (microfilm holdings), Las Cruces, NM
Catholic Archives of Texas, Austin, TX
Center for Southwest Research (CSWR), University of New Mexico, Albuquerque, NM
Mexican Archives of New Mexico (MANM)
New Mexico State Record Center and Archives (NMSRCA), Santa Fe, NM
Spanish Archives of New Mexico (SANM), Series I and Series II

SOURCES

Alonso, Ana María. *Thread of Blood: Colonialism, Revolution, and Gender on Mexico's Northern Frontier*. Tucson: University of Arizona Press, 1995.
Arnold, John. "City Funds Cemetery Research." *Albuquerque Journal*, October 17, 2003.
Baccin, Cristina. "Genízaro Nation." January 8, 2017. http://kunm.org/post/gen-zaro-nation.
Briseño, Elaine D. "Cemeteries, Like Albuquerque's Fairview, Tell a Community Story." *Albuquerque Journal*, August 28, 2016.
Brooks, James F. *Captives and Cousins: Slavery, Kinship, and Community in the Southwest Borderlands*. Chapel Hill: University of North Carolina Press, 2002.
Brugge, David M. *Navajos in the Catholic Church Records of New Mexico, 1694–1875*. Santa Fe: School for Advanced Research Press, 1968 and 1985.
Chávez, Fray Angélico. *Archives of the Archdiocese of Santa Fe, 1678–1900*. Washington, DC: Academy of American Franciscan History, 1959.
Chávez, Fray Angélico. *But Time and Chance: The Story of Padre Martínez of Taos, 1793–1867*. Santa Fe: Sunstone Press, 1981.
Condie, Carol J. "The Cemeteries of Albuquerque, Bernalillo County and Parts of Sandoval and Valencia Counties." Unpublished report to the City of Albuquerque, 1999.
Crocker, Edward C. "Excavations at Santuario de Guadalupe Interim Reports: The Iconography." Santa Fe: City of Santa Fe, 1991.
Cutter, Charles Ross. *The Protector de Indios in Colonial New Mexico, 1659–1821*. Albuquerque: University of New Mexico Press, 1986.
Davis, W. W. H. *El Gringo; or New Mexico and Her People*. New York: Harper and Bros., 1857. Reprint, Lincoln: University of Nebraska Press, Bison Books, 1982.
Dendinger, Julia M. "The Excavation at Nuestra Señora de Belen." *Valencia County News-Bulletin*, August 8, 2018. http://www.news-bulletin.com/news/features/

the-excavation-of-nuestra-se-ora-de-belen/article_c4f153b0-9b2e-11e8-885e-af6a85b22e9c
.html.

Domínguez, Francisco Atanasio. *The Missions of New Mexico, 1776. A Description By Fray
Francisco Atanasio Domínguez With Other Contemporary Documents*. Edited and translated
by Eleanor B. Adams and Fray Angélico Chávez. Albuquerque: University of New Mexico
Press, 1956.

Ellis, Bruce. *Bishop Lamy's Santa Fe Cathedral*. Albuquerque: University of New Mexico Press,
1985.

Frank, Ross. *From Settler to Citizen: New Mexican Economic Development and the Creation of a
Vecino Society, 1750–1820*. Berkeley: University of California Press, 2000.

Frazer, Robert. *New Mexico in 1850: A Military View*. Norman: University of Oklahoma Press,
1968.

French, Stanley. "The Cemetery as Cultural Institution: The Establishment of Mount Auburn
and the 'Rural Cemetery' Movement." *American Quarterly* 26 (March 1974): 37–59.

Gall, Olivia. "Mexican Long-Living Mestizophilia versus a Democracy Open to Diversity." *Latin
American and Caribbean Ethnic Studies* 8:3 (2013): 280–303. https://doi.org/10.1080/174422
22.2013.797212.

Gallegos, José Ignacio. *Historia de la iglesia en Durango*. México, DF: Editorial Jus, 1969.

Gómez, Laura. *Manifest Destinies: The Making of the Mexican American Race*. New York: New
York University Press, 2007.

González, Deena J. *Refusing the Favor: The Spanish-Mexican Women of Santa Fe, 1820–1880*.
New York: Oxford University Press, 1999.

Grandin, Greg. *The Blood of Guatemala: A History of Race and Nation*. Durham, NC: Duke
University Press, 2000.

Gregg, Josiah. *Commerce of the Prairies*. 1844. Norman: University of Oklahoma Press, 1954.

Grimm, Julie Ann. "Emergency Money Will Be Used to Pay for Excavation." *Santa Fe New
Mexican*, October 17, 2003.

Gutiérrez, Ramón. "Hispanic Identities in the Southwestern United States." In *Race and Classification: The Case of Mexican America*, ed. Ilona Katzew and Susan Deans-Smith. Stanford:
Stanford University Press, 2009.

"A History of Fairview Cemetery." *Bulletin of the Historic Santa Fe Foundation* 12:1 (April 1984).
http://www.fairviewcemeterysantafe.org/history/history-short-version/.

Jordan, Terry G. *Texas Graveyards: A Cultural Legacy*. Austin: University of Texas Press, 1982.

Kessell, John L. *The Missions of New Mexico Since 1776*. Albuquerque: University of New
Mexico Press, 1980.

Kingsbury, John M. *Trading in Santa Fe: John M. Kingsbury's Correspondence with James Josiah
Webb, 1853–1861*. Jane Lenz Elder and David J. Weber, editors. Dallas: Southern Methodist
University Press, 1996.

Kiser, William S. "The Politics of Slavery and Social Hierarchies in Colonial, Mexican and Territorial New Mexico." *New Mexico Historical Review* 92:3 (2017): 283–309.

Lecompte, Janet. *Rebellion in the Río Arriba, 1837*. Albuquerque: University of New Mexico
Press, 1985.

Ligon de Ita, Nancy. *The Ortiz Family of New Mexico*. N.p., 1998.

Lomnitz-Adler, Claudio. *Exits from the Labyrinth: Culture and Ideology in the Mexican
National Space*. Berkeley: University of California Press, 1992.

Martínez, María Elena. *Genealogical Fictions: Limpieza de Sangre, Religion, and Gender in Colonial Mexico*. Stanford: Stanford University Press, 2008.

Martínez y Alíre, Jerome J. "The Influence of the Roman Catholic Church in New Mexico
under Mexican Administration: 1821–1848." In *Four Hundred Years of Faith: Seeds of*

Struggle, Harvest of Faith: A History of the Catholic Church in New Mexico. Santa Fe: Archdiocese of Santa Fe, 1998.

Mitchell, Pablo. "Bodies on Borders: African Americans, Penitentes, and Social Order in the Southwest." In *Race, Religion, Region,* ed. Fay Botham and Sara M. Patterson. Tucson: University of Arizona Press, 2006.

Mitchell, Pablo. *Coyote Nation: Sexuality, Race, and Conquest in Modernizing New Mexico, 1880–1920.* Chicago: University of Chicago Press, 2005.

Montgomery, Charles. *The Spanish Redemption: Heritage, Power, and Loss on New Mexico's Upper Rio Grande.* Berkeley: University of California Press, 2002.

Nieto-Phillips, John M. *The Language of Blood: The Making of Spanish-American Identity in New Mexico, 1880s–1930s.* Albuquerque: University of New Mexico Press, 2004.

Norris, Jim. *After "the Year Eighty": The Demise of Franciscan Power in Spanish New Mexico.* Albuquerque: University of New Mexico Press, 2000.

Olmsted, Virginia Langham. *The Ortiz Family of New Mexico: The First Six Generations.* N.p., 1978.

Ozolins, Eric G., Vincent H. Stefan, and J. F. Powell. "A Bioarchaeological Analysis of the Human Remains Recovered from LA120430, the Kearney Road Site, Santa Fe, New Mexico." In *The 124 Kearney Road Burials (LA 120430): Report on the Human Remains Recovered from a Water Meter Excavation near Downtown Santa Fe, New Mexico,* by Stephen S. Post, Nancy Hanks, Eric G. Ozolins, Vincent H. Stefan, and Joseph F. Powell. Santa Fe: Museum of New Mexico, Office of Archaeological Studies, Archaeology Note 248, 1998.

Reis, João José. *Death Is a Festival: Funeral Rites and Rebellion in Nineteenth-Century Brazil.* Translated by H. Sabrina Gledhill. Chapel Hill: University of North Carolina Press, 2003.

Reséndez, Andrés. *Changing National Identities at the Frontier: Texas and New Mexico, 1800–1850.* Cambridge: Cambridge University Press, 2004.

Reséndez, Andrés. *The Other Slavery: The Uncovered Story of Indian Enslavement in America.* New York: Houghton Mifflin Harcourt, 2016.

Rios-Bustamante, Antonio José. "New Mexico in the Eighteenth Century: Life, Labor and Trade in la Villa de San Felipe de Albuquerque, 1706–1790." *Aztlán* 7 (1976): 357–89.

Romero, Simon. "Indian Slavery Once Thrived in New Mexico. Latinos Are Finding Family Ties to It." *New York Times,* January 28, 2018. https://www.nytimes.com/2018/01/28/us/indian-slaves-genizaros.html.

Sanchez, Sabrina M. "In the Name of the Father, the Governor, and 'A-1 Good Men': Performing Gender and Statehood in Territorial New Mexico, 1880–1912." Diss., University of California at Santa Cruz, 2013.

Sena, José D. "The Chapel of Don Antonio José Oritz." *New Mexico Historical Review* 13:4 (1938): 347–59.

Simmons, Marc. "New Mexico Embraced Early Tradition of Racial Tolerance." *New Mexican,* January 19, 2013.

Simmons, Marc. "Settlement Patterns and Village Plans in Colonial New Mexico." In *New Spain's Far Northern Frontier,* edited by David J. Weber. Albuquerque: University of New Mexico Press, 1979.

Stegmaier, Mark. "A Law That Would Make Caligula Blush: New Mexico Territory's Unique Slave Code, 1859–1861." In *African American History in New Mexico: Portraits from Five Hundred Years.* Ed. Bruce A. Glasrud, 56–84. Albuquerque: University of New Mexico Press, 2013.

Stern, Alexandra Minna. "From Mestizophilia to Biotypology: Racialization and Science in Mexico, 1920–1960." In *Race and Nation in Modern Latin America,* ed. Nancy P. Appelbaum, Anne S. Macpherson, and Karin Alejandra Rosemblatt. Chapel Hill: University of North Carolina Press, 2003.

Sullivan-González, Douglass. *Piety, Power, and Politics: Religion and Nation Formation in Guatemala, 1821–1871*. Pittsburgh: University of Pittsburgh Press, 1998.

Sze, Corinne P. "Fairview Cemetery History." http://newmexicohistory.org/people/fairview-cemetery-santa-fe.

Taylor, William B. *Magistrates of the Sacred: Priests and Parishioners in Eighteenth-Century Mexico*. Stanford: Stanford University Press, 1996.

Tjarks, Alicia V. "Comparative Demographic Analysis of Texas, 1777–1793." *Southwestern Historical Quarterly* 77 (1974): 291–338.

Tjarks, Alicia V. "Demographic, Ethnic and Occupational Structure of New Mexico, 1790." *The Americas* 35 (1978): 45–88.

Tjarks, Alicia V. "Evolución urbana de Texas durante el siglo XVIII." *Revista de Indias* 33–34 (1973–74): 605–36.

Toll, H. Wolcott, Nancy J. Akins, Natasha Williamson, Matthew Barbour, and Glenna Dean. *La Garita Camposanto: Work at a Forgotten Cemetery Under Kearny Road, Santa Fe, New Mexico, 2003 and 2005*. Santa Fe: Museum of New Mexico, New Mexico Office of Archaeological Studies, Archaeology Note 358, 2006.

Voekel, Pamela. *Alone before God: Death and the Origins of Mexican Modernity*. Durham, NC: Duke University Press, 2002.

Voekel, Pamela. "Scent and Sensibility: Pungency and Piety in the Making of the *Gente Sensata*, Mexico, 1640–1850." Diss., University of Texas at Austin, 1997.

Weber, David J. *The Mexican Frontier, 1821–1846: The American Southwest under Mexico*. Albuquerque: University of New Mexico Press, 1982.

Weigle, Marta. *Brothers of Light, Brothers of Blood: The Penitentes of the Southwest*. Albuquerque: University of New Mexico Press, 1976. Reprint, Santa Fe: Ancient City Press, 1989.

Will de Chaparro, Martina. *Death and Dying in New Mexico*. Albuquerque: University of New Mexico Press, 2007.

Yalom, Marilyn. *The American Resting Place*. New York: Houghton Mifflin, 2008.

Chapter Eight

Family, Religion, and Relocations: Arab American Burial Practices

—ROSINA HASSOUN

Arab American history is not well known outside of Arab American circles. If Arabs or Arab Americans were seen at all in film and TV depictions before 9/11, it was stereotypically as "belly dancers, billionaires (oil-rich sheiks), Bedouins, or bombers (terrorists) in movies."[1] After 9/11, the leading Hollywood image of Arabs has been quite exclusively as terrorists. While the first Arabic speakers in the Americas arrived with the early Spanish explorers and with North Africans brought to the United States as slaves,[2] the first significant modern Arab migration to the United States began in the 1880s. Although there is a large gap between the US Census count of 1.2 million versus the estimated 3.5 million Arab Americans,[3] Arab Americans represent a small but growing ethnic population in the United States.

There has been no previous research on Arab American burial patterns. This preliminary study examines the shifts and trends in burial practices that accompanied the different waves of Arab American immigration and their settlement patterns. Arabs migrated to the United States in three major waves: 1880–1924, 1952–65, and 1965–2001 (see table 8.1). Arab Americans have also experienced two exclusionary periods. In general, the broad burial patterns show a tendency to bury by religious subgroups (Catholic, Orthodox, Sunni, and Shi'a) either in separate sections of cemeteries or in separate cemeteries, with fewer return burials over time. As will be discussed, Arab Americans in general, with some exceptions like the existing ethnic enclaves in New York, Illinois, and Michigan, went from living and being buried in ethnic enclaves to more dispersed burials by separate religious denominations and religious divisions of Christianity and Islam. Muslim and Christian Arab Americans (see below) appear to have

Table 8.1: Waves of Arab American Immigration

Wave	Dates	Demographics	Burial patterns
First wave	1880–1924	Predominantly Syrian/Lebanese Christians, some Yemenis, a few Palestinians, small number of Levantine Muslims	Many sojourners, others living and dying in ethnic enclaves, migrant Yemeni workers, subsequent spread of communities and cemeteries, and some remains returned to countries of origin
First exclusionary period	1924–1952	Exclusion from the US of "Turks from Asia" and other non–Northern European immigrants	First generation born in US, expansion of ethnic churches, building of mosques, increased separation in burials
Second wave	1952–1965	More Muslims, more educated, brain drain immigrants, and refugees including Palestinians and Yemenis	Slowing but continued building of churches, decline in traditional church attendance, intermarriage and relocations begin
Third wave	1965–2016	More Muslims, brain drain immigrants, more refugees including Palestinians, Lebanese, Iraqis, and Syrians, more educated North Africans	More mosques being built, more Muslim cemeteries in suburbs, intermarriage and conversions to other denominations, and relocations scatter Christians more than Muslim Arab Americans
Second exclusionary period	2017–?	Travel bans exclude Syrians, Sudanese, and Libyans, harder in general for Arabs to get visas, and threat of end to family and friend immigration	Continuation of third wave issues. Fewer return burials. Inability to save relatives dying in wars

divergent patterns. As will be demonstrated, there is evidence that Arab Christian conversions away from their traditional denominations, greater intermarriage with non-Arabs, and mobility for work are increasingly separating Arab Christian families. At the same time, as Arab Muslim communities become more established, they are building more Muslim cemeteries where their family members can be buried together. While most of the religions of Arab Americans (for both Christians and Muslims) forbid cremation, there are some cases that illustrate that people have violated their religious injunctions against cremation due to a desire to have loved ones buried back in their countries of origin and with the rest of their families. The changes in immigration laws appear to have influenced burial patterns, specifically during the First Exclusionary Period (1924–52). There is considerable worry in Arab American communities about the current administration's desire to end family reunification that has been so much a part of Arab American immigration. So-called merit-based immigration laws would once again exclude large numbers of Arabs from immigrating to the United States and would also result in separating more families both in life and in death.

One complication that the study of Arab Americans presents for researchers is that Arab Americans are not a homogeneous group regarding their religion or country of origin. Arab Americans can be from Muslim or Christian backgrounds. This diversity of religion and country of origin appears to give rise to the different patterns of burial seen today in Arab American communities. The majority of Arab Americans are of Lebanese, Palestinian, Iraqi, Yemeni, or North African origin. Syrian/Lebanese Christians (so designated because they initially came from the Mount Lebanon area of Greater Syria that was under Ottoman rule prior to World War I) were then the largest segment of the Arab American population and remain so today.[4] People are sometimes surprised to learn that the majority of Arab Americans today are Christian Lebanese.

Some 200,000 Lebanese came to the United States between 1890 and 1915.[5] According to the historian Akram Khater,[6] so many mostly Christian villagers (approximately a third of the population of Mount Lebanon) left their Lebanese mountain villages to immigrate to the United States that the trajectory of the development of modern Lebanon was altered. Changes in Lebanon occurred due to the flows of Syrian/Lebanese, the financial remittances from the United States, and the impressions of American democracy. The composition of the first wave of Arab immigration had a profound influence on subsequent demographics and the development of Arab communities in the United States. Subsequent waves of Arab immigration increased the number of refugees and Muslims to the Arab American population, but today the Lebanese remain the largest Arab American subgroup. The increasing diversity in countries of origin and in the number of Muslim Arab Americans added more separation by religious subgroups.

Because a large body of previous research on Arab American burial patterns does not exist, the author employed a variety of historical and anthropological methods to acquire this perspective on Arab American burial patterns. In order to research Arab American burial patterns, the author of this chapter relied on scholarly articles on the history of Arab Americans, visited cemeteries in Michigan, spoke to priests and imams, searched the archives of the Arab American National Museum in Dearborn, Michigan, and used genealogical and cemetery websites to locate burial sites across the United States.[7] The cemeteries visited were all in Michigan. The evidence gathered from multiple sources for this research provides preliminary hypotheses and examples that will hopefully provide the foundation for future study. In some cases, all we have is anecdotal evidence. This work should inspire further investigation of this subject. Burial patterns can add ancillary evidence and enrich the historical record of populations. For example, the Arab American historical accounts state that Arabs returned in large numbers to Lebanon and Yemen during the first wave.[8] In scouring cemetery sites and records, there appears to be a scarcity of gravesites (less than would be expected if Arab Americans had not been returning either in life or after death via return burials).

Arab American patterns of burial appear to have shifted from living and being buried in ethnic urban enclaves during the early wave of immigration to a more religiously diverse population that buried according to religious groups in separate sections of cemeteries or in separate sectarian cemeteries during subsequent waves of immigration. These shifts in burial practices appear to have increased the separation of Arab Americans after death over time. The practice of living immigrants returning to or sending the remains of loved ones back to their countries of origin also appears to have changed over time.

Subsequent waves of Arab Americans contained increasing numbers of Muslims and immigrants from many more Arab countries. It is important to note that the religious diversity of Arab Americans is more complicated than the dichotomous designation of either Muslim or Christian. Arab Christians brought with them many Christian traditions and denominations. For example, many Arab Americans belong to the Eastern Uniate Churches like the Maronites and Melkites that have preserved their Aramaic/Syriac rites but are members of the Roman Catholic Church; other Arabs are Roman (Latin Rite) Catholics, Orthodox (mostly the Antiochian Greek or previously called Syrian Orthodox) Church, and some Protestants (including Anglicans). Note that the majority of Chaldeans and Assyrians in the United States do not usually identify as Arabs. They are Eastern Christian ethno-religious groups from Northern Iraq for whom Arabic may be a second language. The Muslim Arab Americans include Sunni, Shi'a, and a small number of Sufis and other smaller Muslim religious groups. There is also a small but significant number of Druze Arab Americans, as evidenced by the earliest Druze organization in Flint, Michigan.[9] We have recently seen the arrival of a tiny number of Yazidis, Mandeans, and other religious groups from Iraq.

Even if a person does not practice his or her religion, families prefer to be buried together. As will be seen, many of these religious groups bury either in a separate section or a separate cemetery for their practitioners. Early Arab Americans settled in ethnic enclaves (like Little Syria in New York), as did so many other immigrants that arrived in the late 1800s and early 1900s. Over time, that population has moved from the Manhattan area from Washington Street at Battery Park to above Rector Street, an area that partially included what would become the World Trade Center,[10] and more recently to Brooklyn. For example, today there is a concentration of Arab Americans (predominantly Palestinians and Yemenis) between 4th and 8th Avenues in the Bay Ridge neighborhood in Brooklyn.

Other Arab American ethnic enclaves like Dearborn, Michigan, remain, but the author's fieldwork indicates that they are increasingly burying their relatives in cemeteries in nearby suburbs. Also, as the United States became more mobile and Arab Americans spread across the country, some Arab American families have become separated. At the same time, Muslims are building new cemeteries. With these general patterns in mind, this article will explore the historical waves of Arab immigrants to the United States, focusing on the more recent changes in burial patterns. Table 8.1 provides an overview of the waves of Arab American immigration and the patterns of burials that represent that wave and time.[11]

Lastly, it is important to note some of the similarities and differences between Arab American funeral and burial practices. Traditionally, Christian and Muslim Arabs buried their dead quickly. Many Christian Arabs used to bury on the third day after the death in remembrance of the resurrection of Christ. Muslims in the Middle East prefer to bury on the same day the person dies before sunset, often in only a shroud. Both Muslim and Christian Arabs have visitations in the home of the grieving family. Friends and relatives bring food as gifts for the bereaved family. While it is the norm in ordinary daily settings to serve sweetened Arabic coffee to guests in the home in Levantine countries (Lebanon, Syria, Jordan, Iraq, and among the Palestinians) and in most Arab American homes, in the aftermath of a death of a relative only unsweetened (*kahwah saada*) is served. Consumption of desserts may also be avoided.

Both Christian and Muslim Arabs have commemorative services for the departed some weeks later. Most Eastern Christian Arabs usually commemorate the deceased after forty days, while Muslims usually commemorate after thirty days. None of the Eastern churches nor Islam condone cremation.[12] These are practices that have remained consistent since Arab Americans first immigrated to the United States, with the exception that the US bureaucracy usually does not allow same-day burials or burials without caskets. Many Arab families today delay burial so that distant family members have time to travel to the funeral. When the first Syrian/Lebanese began arriving in the United States in the late 1800s, they expected long ocean voyages across the Mediterranean Sea and the Atlantic Ocean. Letters took months to arrive. If someone passed away, family in their homeland would only find out much later.

The First Wave, 1880–1924

Historian Philip Hitti[13] wrote that Anthonius al-Bishalani was the first immigrant from what today is Lebanon to arrive in the United States in 1854. As
previously stated, the first significant wave of immigration from the Arab world
began when villagers from Mount Lebanon began arriving in the United States
in the 1880s. The major push factors sending them to the United States were
increasing population with resulting land scarcity for sons that did not inherit
family farms, changes in Ottoman tax laws that required cash payments, and
the collapse of the silk industry in Lebanon. Historian Fuad Khater[14] researched
and discussed the fact that while the majority of Lebanese that left Lebanon
were young men, a small but significant number of women who worked in the
silk factories before a silkworm plague devastated the industry purchased passage to the United States. Some of the pull factors were contact with Protestant
missionaries, tales of the enormous opportunities and wealth in the United
States, as well as educational opportunities.[15]

However, Suleiman[16] pointed out that before World War I, the majority of the
Syrian/Lebanese considered themselves sojourners. They came to the United
States to find work as door-to-door salespersons (peddlers) before the era of the
department store, in textiles, and other businesses. The role of the peddler was
essential to the early Syrian/Lebanese. However, it was not the sole type of work
done by Arab Americans. After passing through customs at Ellis Island, some of
the new Arab immigrants were met by relatives or suppliers willing to set them
up in the peddling networks for a percent of their profits.

The immigrants first settled in a tight-knit community in a New York City
enclave that came to be known as Little Syria. As the local area became satu-
rated with peddlers, Arabs searched for new areas to sell their goods or work in
other industries like textiles, like the scholar Khalil Sakakini, who found work
in a Boston area textile factory. As some of the peddlers that carried dry goods
in packs on their backs became wealthier, they could afford a horse and carriage
or afford to own their stores. Arab Americans began settling in other urban
areas up the East Coast and across the Midwest.[17]

In Michigan, Arab Americans found work in the early car factories, as did
the Yemeni in Henry Ford's Hamtramck and Dearborn factories.[18] The five-dol-
lar-a-day wages in the Ford factory attracted Yemenis and many other immigrants to Michigan. Chrysler and other early car manufacturers were also hir-
ing. A certain amount of the money made in peddling, working in factories, or
for other jobs like working for the railroads would be sent back home to villages in Mount Lebanon or Yemen to help their families back in the old country
pay their taxes and survive. However, until the end of World War I, at least a
third of the Syrian/Lebanese would return to their home country.[19] The mili-

tary service during World War I (see below), the restrictions on immigration of Arabs that were instituted after 1924 that isolated the Lebanese population in the United States, and the process of acculturation over time are factors that may have affected the first wave to settle permanently in the United States. But the Yemenis would make the decision to stay permanently in the United States much later than the Lebanese.

Most all of the Yemeni initially came only to work in the Ford factories would eventually return home to Yemen. After working grueling hours in some of the most difficult and dangerously jobs in the auto factories like shoveling coal into the furnaces, they would retire in the mountains and port cities of Yemen. However, they then would send their sons to work in the United States. The Yemenis were among the earliest Arab Muslims to form a community in the United States, but they were not the only Muslim Arabs who came to the United States during the first wave of significant Arab immigration.

During World War I, some 27,000 Syrian/Lebanese fought in uniform for the United States.[20] However, from 1915 to 1918, Lebanon and parts of Greater Syria experienced an extreme drought, a plague of locusts, and the wartime blockade of the port of Beirut that resulted in a half a million Lebanese dying of starvation. The Syrian/Lebanese collected money through churches and other charities to try to help people in their homeland. In the end, because Lebanon was under Turkish Ottoman rule, and the Ottomans found themselves invaded by Western forces during World War I, there were only a few things that could be done from the United States. Kahlil Gibran wrote heartbreaking poems about the deaths in his homeland of Lebanon. Some of the Syrian/Lebanese were pro-Ottoman and were hoping that the Ottoman Turks would remain in Lebanon. However, many more people in the Arab communities were anti-Ottoman. Some in the community were also pro-French, while others supported the United States intervening in the war against the Ottomans. Clashes over these issues erupted in the Arab American press and underground anti-Ottoman groups formed across the United States.[21] These differences of opinion often pitted Orthodox against Maronite, although the splits were not always strictly along religious lines.[22] Simultaneously, Orthodox and Maronite were beginning to bury separately. Following World War I, the Syrian/Lebanese began settling permanently in the United States. Then the United States passed the Immigration and Naturalization Act of 1924, which effectively closed the doors to non–Northern European immigrants to the United States.

However, the question is: what evidence of the burial patterns of the first wave remains? A hidden history of the United States is the number of immigrants of little or modest means that were buried in mass graves, unmarked graves, or pauper graves. Hart Island in New York contains one such mass grave, and the Boston South End Cemetery is another site where many immigrants were buried without headstones. There are Arabic inscriptions on some of the headstones in the Boston South End Cemetery, providing a clue that there may be other Arabic speakers buried in the mass graves there. It is likely that many Arab Americans may have been buried in these cemeteries in New York and Boston because of their proximity to those ethnic enclaves. The author was not able to find obituaries in the *New York Times* for any but the most prominent Arab Americans, and this is a trend seen in Dearborn as well, where death notices are not often placed in the newspapers. Family and friends are invited to funerals and burials that are often very soon after passing, especially in Muslim families.

Therefore, the problem of unmarked and mass graves necessitates a different approach to finding the earliest burial patterns of Arab American burials until if and when further research can be conducted. The author began by visiting the Woodmere Cemetery, which rests very near the Ford Rouge automobile factory in Dearborn, Michigan, as an anthropologist already familiar with the Arab American history and the local Arab population. Woodmere Cemetery contains some 190,000 graves and is one of the largest cemeteries in Michigan.[23] Many Detroit dignitaries such as David D. Buick, founder of Buick Motor Company, Henry L. Leland, founder of Cadillac and Lincoln car companies, and many other Detroit dignitaries are buried in Woodmere Cemetery.

If any of the early factory workers had died in accidents or if some of the early Dearborn Arabs had been buried in Woodmere, as one of the oldest and largest cemeteries in southwest Detroit/Dearborn this would logically be the place to begin a search. Today, the small Yemeni mosque sits across from a corner of Woodmere Cemetery. The mosque community bought that section of the cemetery. That section of the Woodmere cemetery appears to show an increase in number of people buried there since the 1970s, including recent burials. The purchase of the section in the Woodmere Cemetery and the increased burials there corresponds to the expansion of the Yemeni community in Dearborn and the settlement of Yemenis into another suburb of the Greater Metropolitan Detroit area in Hamtramck, Michigan. Although there is still a Yemeni enclave in the Southend area of Dearborn, Yemenis began moving into Hamtramck in the early to mid-1970s. A recent burial of a Yemeni from Hamtramck anecdotally indicates that some Hamtramck Yemenis are burying their family members in Dearborn at the Woodmere Cemetery. The Hamtramck burials may also explain the number of Bosnian and Bangladeshi Muslim burials within the Yemeni section of the cemetery, as Hamtramck is also home to a sizable and diverse Muslim population from other non-Arab nations. In this sense, this section of the Woodmere Cemetery appears to be more diverse than other cemeteries where Arab Americans predominate.

There are few if any grave sites in the Woodmere Cemetery that date to the first wave. By searching through other cemeteries in Dearborn and searching

Figure 8.1 Woodmere Cemetery Muslim section. The grave markers are modest and lie flat to the ground.

their online records, very few graves of first wave Arabs were found. This paucity of graves supports historians' claims that the Yemeni and others saw themselves as sojourners and some sent the bodies or remains of their loved ones back to be buried in their countries of origin. Anecdotal evidence from the *Mahjar* writers such as Gibran and Mokarzal (see below) suggests that Arab Americans who could afford the expense returned the bodies of deceased relatives to Lebanon to be interred with family in their country of origin.

A second method for discovering burial patterns of the first wave was to search for the graves and historical documents about the funerals and burials of prominent Arab Americans. The first large ethnic enclaves of Arab Americans were in New York and Boston, and these cities were disproportionately home to a significant number of writers and prominent Arab Americans at that time. Historical reports in newspapers point out where and how these prominent Arab immigrants were buried. Many of the most prominent Arab Americans of that era were the *Mahjar* writers. *Mahjar* refers to the place of migration. The *Mahjar* writers included Kahlil Gibran, the famous artist, poet, and author of the widely known book of poetry *The Prophet*. Gibran organized a group of writers, newspaper publishers, and poets that created a writer's group called the Pen Club or Pen League (*Ar-rabbitah al Kalimiyah*). The burials of these individuals may provide clues or hypotheses to broader general burial patterns. Kahlil Gibran (his birth name was Gibran Kahlil Gibran) immigrated in 1895 as a child with his mother, Kamila, to live in the South End of Boston,[24] a crowded, ethnically diverse area of mostly cold-water flats teeming with immigrants from many different countries. One section of the South End had a concentration of Syrian/Lebanese.

Gibran's mother immigrated to the United States with her children. She carried a heavy pack of trade goods through the more affluent streets of Boston to support her family. There are few accounts of other women Syrian/Lebanese peddlers from this era. While it is known that women who worked in the Lebanon silk industry in the late 1800s and early 1900s did occasionally migrate without a close male relative, these were non-normative events.[25]

The South End was also periodically struck by epidemics like measles and consumption, as it was called then (tuberculosis, TB). Gibran's bother Peter died of TB, as did one sister.[26] Gibran's mother died of cancer. The famous poet and artist's mother and sister are buried together in a grave with a single headstone in the Mount Benedict Cemetery in the Boston neighborhood of West Roxbury, Massachusetts.

Kahlil Gibran suffered from an unknown illness that took his life in 1931 at the age of forty-eight. As Gibran's flag-draped coffin processed through the streets of Boston, some of the people on the sidewalks dropped to their knees to honor the fallen poet.[27] His body was taken to New York and placed aboard a ship bound for Lebanon. Gibran was buried in the village of his birth, Besherri, with a long procession of Lebanese dignitaries accompanying the casket on its trip into the mountains. Today, there are several monuments and memorials in the United States dedicated to the memory of Kahlil Gibran, including the Gibran Memorial Garden in Washington, DC.

In examining the funerals and burials of the other members of the *Ar-rabit-tah al-Khalimiyya*, a number of these prominent Arab Americans were buried in their homeland. Some, like the writer Mikhail Naimy, returned (alive) to Lebanon. Another example of the Pen Club members was Na'um (sometimes transcribed as Naoum) Mokarzel, a Maronite Catholic, who was the publisher, editor, and founder of the largest and longest-published Arab American newspaper, *al Hoda* (The Guidance). Mokarzel immigrated from Lebanon in 1881 and lived in Little Syria in New York. Upon his passing in 1932, there was a large public funeral in New York, and his body was taken back to his village of Frieke in Lebanon.[28]

It appears that sizable numbers of Arab Americans returned to their countries of origin, and others who could afford the expense had their relatives' remains returned to their countries of origin. The cost of returning a loved one's remains to their homelands was prohibitive to many, and some of the early Arab

Americans violated their religious restrictions and chose cremation in order to have their loved ones' ashes buried in their home countries. Another prominent member of the *Mahjar* group was Ameen Rihani, writer, intellectual, and political activist.[29] Rihani's works include some books and *The Book of Khalid,* one of the first novels written by an Arab American. His many works are foundational in Arab American literature. Rihani died in 1940, and he was buried in his home village of Freike, Lebanon, after a bicycle accident there at age sixty-four. However, his American wife, artist Bertha Case, died at age ninety-one in 1970 and was cremated. Her ashes were buried next to his grave in Lebanon.[30] Cremation would have been a violation of Arab and Arab American religious norms, but she married into the community.

Most of the Arab Americans who were not wealthy, including the family members of Kahlil Gibran, were buried in one communal family grave or in tiny plots very close together. In addition, large numbers of those who arrived in America at the turn of the twentieth century from so many different countries and parts of the world, and who lived and died in impoverished ethnic enclaves like South End of Boston, may have been buried in pauper's cemeteries. There are so many stories of the early Arab Americans that remain unknown.

After World War I, a shift happened in most Arab immigrants' attitudes toward settling permanently in the United States.[31] The Arab sojourners began to think of themselves as Americans. Some of the reasons that there was a change in attitudes toward permanent settlement may have been military service, the isolation after 1924, and the length of time to acculturate in the United States.

The Immigration and Naturalization Act of 1924 closed nearly all immigration from the Middle East and North Africa to the United States. For more than thirty years until 1952, Arabs were largely excluded from immigration. The expected response was that more Arab Americans were born in the United States and more of the older Arab Americans were buried in the United States. At the same time, the establishment of new churches and mosques across the United States and the subsequent creation of religiously segregated cemeteries continued. The exclusion ended the first wave of Arab immigration.

The First Exclusionary Period, 1924–52

From 1948 until 1952, virtually all immigrants from non–Northern European countries were excluded from coming to the United States due to discriminatory US immigration policies. This restriction included people from the Middle East and North Africa. The United States went through a period of xenophobia. However, the Mount Lebanon area (what would become the modern state of Lebanon) was economically devastated after World War I. Syrian/Lebanese in the United States were desperate to bring relatives to the United States but were prevented from doing so.

At the same time, Arab Americans in the United States continued their spread into the Midwest, eventually reaching west to California and south into Texas.[32] The dispersion was marked by the growth and establishment of new Arab ethnic churches. The author of this chapter surveilled dozens of Melkite, Maronite, and Orthodox church websites in order to draw this conclusion.[33]

As the communities spread, they built new churches. The Syrian/Lebanese were looking for better opportunities for jobs. The Arabs continued looking for opportunities in peddling, factories, and a small number working for the railroads.[34] Small communities formed around Melkite, Maronite, and Orthodox churches.

Some of the first mosques in the United States were also built during the first exclusionary period as well. One such mosque stands out. Although there may have been other mosques built by or before 1929, the mosque built in Ross, North Dakota, vies for the title of the oldest mosque in the United States. However, it is unique in another way. The early Syrian/Lebanese, regardless of whether they were Christians or Muslims mostly originated from agricultural villages in the mountains and hillsides of Greater Syria.[35] Very few Arabs attempted farming after they immigrated to America; however, the Ross Muslim community is a significant exception. At first, the little farming community flourished. Children were born into these pioneering families, and the elderly were buried in one of the first exclusively Arab Muslim cemeteries in the country. The associated cemetery was named the Assyrian Moslem Cemetery.

The Ross community survived well into the second wave of Arab immigration. However, by the 1970s, the "Little Mosque on the Prairie" stood empty, and it was torn down.[36] The cemetery stood alone and silent for decades, cared for by descendants of the original Muslim community, many of whom had married Christians and moved to nearby towns. The current caretaker is a convert to Christianity who does not know if he will decide to be buried in the cemetery that he tends.[37] The mosque has been recently rebuilt, and it stands as a monument to the early Arab Muslims of Ross, Dakota.[38]

In the meantime, America's doors were closed to the Arab victims of World War II, including the Libyans, who had experienced the internment of their entire population in camps; a third of their population, some 80,000, had starved to death under Mussolini's Italian forces.[39] The doors of the United States remained closed to North Africans, as well as the Lebanese during and after World War II.

While new groups of Arabs sought unsuccessfully to find haven in the United States, Arab Americans who were already in the United States continued to thrive. Still, more churches established separate religious cemeteries. Just as it seemed that Arab Americans were spreading across the United States with the subsequent acculturation and assimilation pressures, the United States opened its door a crack to let in another wave of Arab immigrants.

Second Wave, 1952–65

In 1952 the United States again changed its immigration laws. But the doors of immigration were not flung wide open. Instead, they were opened cautiously with the use of a national-origin quota system under the Immigration and Nationality Act of 1952 (the McCarron-Walter Act).[40] The Middle East and North Africa received one of the lowest quotas. Western and Northern Europeans were still favored because the new quota system allowed for one-sixth of 1 percent of each nationality group in the United States in 1920 to provide the number of immigrants allowed into the United States. It is fortunate for Arab Americans that so many of the first wave of Syrian/Lebanese had arrived before 1920. Nevertheless, the Arab population in the United States in 1920 was relatively small in comparison to other ethnic populations.

When Arab Americans were once again allowed into the United States, the second wave contained significantly more Muslims and refugees. Some Palestinian Muslim and Christian refugees were able to immigrate to the United States during this period. Many of the Palestinian refugees had lost their homes in 1948. The father of the author of this chapter arrived in 1952 as a refugee. More Lebanese also arrived in this wave, including both Shi'a and Sunni Muslims. The second wave of Arab immigrants had a wider choice of cities, often in established Arab American communities in New York, the Midwest, and by the 1950s in larger cities in Texas and California.[41]

During the period from 1952 to 1965, the Middle East and Egypt experienced a wave of uprisings and anticolonial wars, such as the 1963 coup d'etat that deposed King Faisal in Iraq. Pan-Arabism under Gamal Abdul Nasser spread regionally.[42] The rise of the Baathist Parties in Iraq and Syria occurred and contributed to a brain drain from the MENA (Middle East and North Africa) due to purges of intellectuals and elites from some Arab countries, specifically Egypt and Iraq, who found their way to the United States.

As Arab countries gained independence from their previous colonial masters, the newly independent countries implemented public primary and secondary schools. More Arabs began obtaining college educations in American universities in the Middle East like the American University of Beirut.

Consequently, the second wave of Arab Americans was more educated than the first wave.[43] People who had experienced colonialism and anticolonial uprisings arrived in the United States during the civil rights movement. While a few

Arab American activists did participate in the civil rights movement, particularly the March to Freedom led by Dr. Martin Luther King Jr. down Woodward Avenue in Detroit, it must have been a sobering sight for the new immigrants who had just arrived from the turmoil in the MENA region to observe.

In the meantime, more Yemenis came to work in the factories in Michigan, and some to the fields in California. Some of the Yemenis began settling in the United States permanently for the first time. Men who had worked generationally in the Ford automobile factory in Dearborn began bringing their families to Dearborn after 1965.[44]

At the same time, families expanded, and the members of the Arab American population that had arrived in the early part of the first wave began passing away, including the *Mahjar* writers. The spread and expansion of ethnic Arab churches continued, but the pace of expansion slowed. Congregations grew, and new cemeteries were created that separated Christians by denominations (Melkite, Maronite, and Orthodox from other Christian denominations).

However, in the 1960s, the children of the first wave of Arab Americans became more mobile. Like so many other Americans, more affluent Arab Americans began moving to the suburbs. A demographic pattern was established where new immigrants settled in the well-established Arab ethnic enclaves like Dearborn, Michigan, and more affluent second-generation families moved to the suburbs. This pattern of movement would have consequences for the separation of families in burial plots, especially into the third wave. The early Arab Americans had sent for wives from their original villages, making the first wave of Arab Americans highly endogamous to group, even within families and with cousin marriages. Cousin marriages were seen as acceptable and even preferable. However, more marriages were occurring with non-Arabs, particularly among Arab Christians. As they married outside their group, the Christian Arabs began marrying outside of their ethnic denominations. It appears that more Arab American men, particularly Christians, married non-Arab women than Arab women marrying non-Arab men, but we do not have statistically sound data to support this observation. Exogamous marriage would have consequences for separating families at that time and after the next wave of Arab Americans arrived.

The Third Wave, 1965–2017

What has occurred regarding Arab immigration since 1965 is that even more Muslims and more refugees have come to the United States. In 1965 US immigration laws changed again. The doors of immigration were opened much wider. Under family reunification rules, family members were allowed to sponsor other family members. For Arab Americans, this was a blessing as the

United States again became a refuge for people from the MENA region seeking an escape from the wars and unrest in their region of origin. The wars sent minispasms of refugees and those escaping wars to the United States.

The Lebanese Civil War (1975–90) sent many Lebanese to the United States (mostly Muslims, including many Shi'a). The 1967 Arab-Israeli War sent another wave of Palestinian refugees, including a group of students from the West Bank who were studying in the United States and found themselves stranded and homeless. The Iran-Iraq War (1980–88) sent a limited number of Iraqis to the United States. Periodic brain drains from Iraq continued after the first Gulf War and the US invasion of 2003 and its aftermath. The first Gulf War sent more Iraqis to the United States, and the US government allowed some three thousand Iraqi refugees in per year after the war.

After the first Gulf War, the Office of Refugee Resettlement attempted to scatter the Iraqis across the United States to places like North Dakota, Arizona, and many other states so that they would be less visible. This strategy sent Iraqi refugees to areas of the country that had no social services, no Arabic speakers to help them, no ethnic churches or mosques, and no ethnic cemeteries. Eventually, they made their way to areas of the country, like areas of California and Michigan, that had Arab social service agencies and established communities that could help them adjust to life in the United States. The author worked with a major Michigan Arab social service organization as the Iraqi influx began from other states.

This most recent wave of Arab Americans also saw a small but significant number of immigrants (in relation to the number of Arab Americans) come from North African Arabic-speaking countries like Egypt, Tunisia, Algeria, and Morocco. This miniwave of North African immigrants were young and well-educated, mostly college graduates, seeking opportunity.

When the tragedy of 9/11 befell the United States, few people realized that there were a small number of Arab Americans in the towers and on the planes that died and were innocent victims. Some years ago, the author met an Arab American whose nephew had died in the plane that hit the Pentagon. While there is a myth that large numbers of Arab and Muslim Americans celebrated the tragedy, in reality something else happened. In Dearborn, large numbers of refugees and victims of war were re-traumatized by what they witnessed that day. ACCESS, the Arab Community Center for Economic and Social Services, had to open three additional emergency trauma centers for Arab Americans suffering from PTSD attacks as a result of the towers and the plane crashes they witnessed on television. They had come to escape the violence of the Middle East, and it had followed them to the United States.

However, before and after 9/11, new arrivals came to settle with relatives and friends, and Arab American communities continued to move from urban areas to suburbs. The number of new churches and mosques continued to increase slowly.

At the same time, many of the existing churches began to face problems. The Arab Eastern Christian churches tell the story of a problem maintaining their congregations. Arab American intermarriage appears to be reaching its highest numbers, and this may mean that families are no longer as able to be buried in family groupings as in the past. For example, some Orthodox churches in America are restricting non-Orthodox from being buried with their relatives (note: most religious cemeteries restrict to their denomination). For example, in one Orthodox cemetery, non-Orthodox spouses are allowed, but non-Orthodox grandchildren cannot be buried with their families (this often equates to the second generation born in the United States). Therefore, changes in religious affiliation result in separation in burial in these cases. Relocation for jobs and intermarriage with other groups may also mean separation of families after death. Multiple cases of Arab ethnic churches, as indicated by their web pages, write that they are suffering from the relocations of parish members for job opportunities and from conversions to the Latin churches, evangelicals, and other Christian denominations. Religiosity may also be declining among Arab American Christians.

The situation for Arab American Muslims appears to be different. According to the 2018 Pew Research Center findings, only 26 percent of Muslims in the United States are Arab American. While the Arab ethnic churches have experienced a decline in attendance and parishioners in the last few decades, the number of mosques has quietly continued to increase. Along with this trend of more mosques is a trend toward the opening of Muslim sections in mixed cemeteries and new exclusively Muslim cemeteries.

In the Dearborn area, that has both Sunni and Shi'a Arab Americans, there appears to be occurring a separation by Muslim division. The Islamic Memorial Cemetery in Westland, just outside of Dearborn, has become a majority Shi'a cemetery. While the author of this chapter has seen significant grave decorations with plastic or real flowers and occasionally photos at specific Sunni and Shi'a graves, it is known in the Dearborn Shi'a population that whole families will spend substantial time visiting with family members at the grave sites. Families have placed memorial benches near the grave sites of their relatives specifically for visiting, something that is rarely done by Sunni Muslims.

As these shifts in burial patterns of Arab Americans occurs, the settlement patterns of Arab Americans today reflect their historical movements. As in the past, they tend to live in urban areas. Today, Arab Americans are found in all states, but they have significant concentrations in ten: California, Michigan, New York, Florida, New Jersey, Illinois, Texas, Ohio, Massachusetts, and Pennsylvania.[45] Dearborn, Michigan (a suburb of Detroit), still has the most densely concentrated population of Arab Americans. Dearborn, Brooklyn, New York, and other towns still have Arab American ethnic enclaves. However, more significant numbers of Arab Americans now live in the suburbs.

Arab Americans today have higher average incomes and higher average education levels than the average American. The Arab American rate of entrepreneurship is also higher than that of the average American. Lebanese Americans have the highest incomes of all the Arab Americans, and they constitute the majority of Arab Americans.[46] Regardless if they were refugees, recent arrivals, or long-term residents of America, Arab Americans have worked hard and succeeded in this country despite having to overcome many obstacles including stereotyping, discrimination, and their past traumas.

The third wave of Arab Americans contained more Muslims and more refugees than the first two waves of immigrants. Arab American settlement patterns also changed. As Arab Americans moved to the suburbs, their places of worship and their places of burial did, too. Also, some of the ethnic enclaves have filled their local cemeteries, and they have sought out cemeteries in neighboring suburbs as their cities expanded into suburbia. One such example is that some of the Dearborn, Michigan Arab community are now burying in places like the nearby Plymouth township. Some of these trends appear to be continuing. According to community members, there is only one company today in Dearborn that arranges for the transportation of deceased family members back to their countries of origin. The practice of return burials seems to be limited only to recent immigrants, and now happens infrequently. Because of new travel bans, there are new restrictions on the travel of certain groups of Arabs to the United States. The restrictions have limited family reunifications. People cannot come and go as they once were able to do. The travel restrictions may also affect return burials.

Second Exclusionary Period, 2017–?

In 2016, the United States elected Donald Trump president. Among his first acts as president were a series of attempted travel bans against selected Muslim-majority countries, most of which are Arab countries. Mr. Trump declared that he wanted a complete ban on all Muslims coming to the United States. The courts stopped his first efforts, but eventually, the ban on individuals coming from several Muslim countries, as well as North Korea and Venezuela, was upheld by the Supreme Court.[47] These restrictions initiated the beginning of the second exclusionary period for Arab Americans.

Even before Trump became president, he spoke of putting an end to family-reunification immigration and Muslim bans. Since coming to office, Trump has attempted to fulfill these campaign promises. After two unsuccessful attempts, President Trump's administration succeeded in banning travel from Yemen, Somalia, Syria, Libya, and Sudan, which are all Arab countries, as well as the non-Arab countries of Iran, North Korea, and Venezuela.[48]

Somalia is a member of the Arab League for political reasons, but most Somalis do not identify as Arab. Arabic is their religious language, as most Somalis are Muslim. Their country of origin was torn by civil wars. Minneapolis has a sizable Somali population. They are now banned from bringing their family members to the United States.

In Yemen, the Houthi Shi'a uprising sparked an intervention by the Saudi Arabian Sunni rulers that became a full-fledged war. With an outbreak of cholera that is the worst in modern times and widespread famine in Yemen, the United Nations declared that Yemen now faces an enormous humanitarian crisis. Dearborn and Hamtramck, Michigan, have sizable Yemeni populations. Yemenis have worked in American car factories in Michigan since at least 1904.[49] At present, Yemeni Americans can do nothing to bring their relatives out of that war; US policy prevents them.

The war in Syria that started as an Arab Spring uprising is a continuing disaster that has sent millions of Syrians fleeing Syria. Syrian refugees are also blocked from coming to the United States. As of April 2018, the United States had allowed only eleven Syria refugees into the United States (forty-four since the last fiscal year in October 2017) on waivers of the travel ban.[50]

People from these selected Muslim-majority countries that are torn by civil wars and that have populations that are traumatized by war, often with thousands of internally displaced persons, are now denied haven in America. Arab Americans who have family members in harm's way are desperate to save them. Having personal friends and students from families with relatives in Syria and Yemen, the author of this chapter has seen, heard, and felt the anguish of people in this situation. Part of that anguish is not knowing the fate of relatives, especially those killed in the fighting and whether their family members received proper burials.

The demise of family-reunification immigration will be harmful to the Arab American community, as it is to countless other ethnicities in the United States. What the proposed shift in immigration policy to a so-called merit system will do is to separate more people permanently in life, as well as after death. We can only hope for a day when such policies are reversed. In the meantime, a large segment of Arab Americans is experiencing the second exclusionary period of immigration to the United States. Arab Americans survived the first exclusionary period, and they and their culture continue to thrive and diversify in the United States despite the restrictions.

Arab American Burial Trends and Implications

In conclusion, Arab American burial patterns show distinct trends and changes over time that were heavily influenced by changes in immigration laws in the United States. The first wave of largely Syrian/Lebanese Christian and the first Yemeni immigrants saw themselves as sojourners. They tended to return in life and return their deceased family members to their countries of origin when they could afford to do so. Other members of the first wave may have been buried in pauper mass graves or buried with multiple members of their family in a single grave. Sill other cemeteries from this era in the United States may have yet to be discovered. So strong was the desired to be buried with kin that some Arab immigrants had their deceased family members (both Muslim and Christian) cremated against their religious norms to be able to have them buried back in their countries of origin, specifically in Lebanon.

Attitudes toward remaining in the United States changed after World War I with a number of Arab Americans who fought in the war. The Immigration and Naturalization Act of 1924 severely curtailed Arab immigration. While new Arab immigrants were not arriving, the generation born after the first wave began spreading out across the United States. During this exclusionary period, Arab Americans began spreading from the East Coast across the Midwest in search of cities in which to peddle their wares door to door and for other jobs. As new Lebanese Melkite, Maronite, and Orthodox churches were established, some new denominational cemeteries and sections of cemeteries were established.

This trend of expanding communities to major urban centers continued well into the second wave of Arab immigration from 1952 until 1962. This wave of Arab Americans included more Lebanese, but it was also more Muslim, included more refugees, and was more educated than the first wave of immigrants.[51] Church and mosque communities began to expand throughout most of this period, and separate cemeteries and separate areas of cemeteries by Arab subgroup and by religious affiliations were established. These trends continued toward the end of Arab immigration for the second wave and into the third wave. The third wave ended in 2017 when new exclusionary immigration policies were enacted. The Arab ethnic churches saw more intermarriage with non-Arabs and conversions away from the traditional churches, as well as young people moving for work.

There is a strong trend for Arab American Muslims to establish their own cemeteries and sections in cemeteries, as seen in the first Arab Muslim cemeteries such as the community in North Dakota, to the separate Muslim section in Woodmere Cemetery in metropolitan Detroit, to the newer cemeteries in nearby suburbs outside of the large ethnic enclaves, for example near Dearborn, Michigan.

Of the two trends now present in Arab American communities, the first is to build new religiously segregated cemeteries, seen mostly in Muslim communities. The second trend, for both Muslims and Christian Arab Americans, is that their cemeteries are spreading into new suburbs away from the traditional ethnic enclaves like Dearborn when the older cemeteries become full. With younger generations leaving for job opportunities, we see two more recent conflicting burial patterns. On the one hand, more families are being buried with others of their religious faith (particularly with new Muslim cemeteries); on the other hand, intermarriage and relocation means more Arab Americans (particularly Christians) are being buried apart.

With over one hundred years of Arab Americans living and dying in the United States, Arab Americans are deeply rooted in the United States. Arab Americans fought beside other Americans in all the wars since and including World War I. While Arab Americans are a small but significant segment of the population of the United States, they have contributed to the fabric of America through their work, entrepreneurship and high regard for education. There is much additional work that is needed to expand upon this preliminary research.

Notes

1. Jack Shaheen, *Reel Bad Arabs: How Hollywood Vilifies a People*, 2nd ed. (New York: Olive Branch Press, 2009).

2. Estevanico, as the Spanish called him, or Mustafa Zemmouri was a Moroccan from the town of Azemour who was taken as a slave and participated in the expeditions of the Spanish explorers Navaez and Cabeza de Vaca following being brought to the Americas in 1527. He is considered both the first Arab American and the first African American. His story is featured at the Arab American National Museum in Dearborn. Michigan. See Richard A. Gordan, "Following Estevanico: The Influential Presence of an African Slave in Sixteenth-Century New World Historiography," *Colonial Latin American* 15, no. 2 (December 2006): 183–206.

3. The American Community Survey 2006–2010, conducted by the US Census, estimates the number of Arab Americans at only 1.5 million. https://www.census.gov/library/publications/2013/acs/acsbr10-20.html. According to the US Census, the number of Arab Americans has doubled since the 1990s. Immigration and birth rates do not appear to account for this rapid increase, and the Arab American leadership questions the Census numbers as serious undercounts. Arab Americans are not an official minority. The Census numbers are based on self-identification. After 9/11, the US Census provided information to the US Department of Homeland Security on country of origin to the smallest census unit. The US Census told the Arab American community that they did this to place signage in local airports with the appropriate dialects. However, written Arabic, especially signs, are written in a universally understood script. This event was only the second time in US history that this level of detail was provided by the Census Bureau to another agency. The first time this was done was just before

the internment of the Japanese in World War II. This event, as well as Islamophobia, Arabo-phobia, and hate crimes may be influencing Arab identification on the Census. To compensate for this, the Arab American Institute obtains Arab American demographics from the well-established Zogby International Poll to provide estimates that use polls and other proprietorial sources of information to supplement the Census numbers. The Census also does not provide information on religion. For these reasons, all the demographic statistics provided about Arab Americans are estimates. The data provided is the best available under the circumstances. The Arab American Institute, using the Zogby data, estimates that there are currently 3.5 million Arab Americans.

4. Barbara C. Aswad and Barbara Bilgé, *Family and Gender among American Muslims: Issues Facing Middle Eastern Immigrants and Their Descendants* (Philadelphia: Temple University Press, 1996).

5. Akram F. Khater, *Inventing Home: Emigration, Gender, and the Middle Class in Lebanon, 1870–1920* (Berkeley: University of California Press, 2001).

6. Khater, *Inventing Home.*

7. Genealogical online databases and cemetery websites were used to direct the author to the gravesites and cemeteries where the individuals were buried. These sources provided valuable clues to the burial sites of these early Arab American immigrants. Biographies and autobiographies provided supplementary information.

8. Michael Suleiman, *Arabs in America: Building a New Future* (Philadelphia: Temple University Press, 1999).

9. Hani J. Bawardi, "Arab American Political Organizations from 1915 to 1951: Assessing Transnational Political Consciousness and the Development of Arab American Identity" (diss., Wayne State University 2009); Hani J. Bawardi, *The Making of Arab Americans: From Syrian Nationalism to U.S. Citizenship* (Austin: University of Texas Press, 2014).

10. For a more extensive description of Little Syria, see Gregory Orfalea, *Before the Flames: A Quest for the History of Arab Americans*, 1st ed. (Austin: University of Texas Press, 1988).

11. Rosina J. Hassoun, *Arab Americans in Michigan* (East Lansing: Michigan State University Press, 2005).

12. Adnan Hammad, Rashid Kysia, Raja Rabah, Rosina Hassoun, and Michael Connelly, "Guide to Arab Culture: Health Care Delivery to the Arab American Community," 1999, http://naama.com/pdf/arab-american-culture-health-care.pdf.

13. Philip Khuri Hitti, *The Syrians in America* (Piscataway, NJ: Gorgias Press, 1924).

14. Khater, *Inventing Home.*

15. Suleiman, *Arabs in America.*

16. Suleiman, *Arabs in America.*

17. Alixa Naff, *Becoming American: The Early Arab Immigrant Experience* (Carbondale: Southern Illinois University Press, 1993).

18. Sameer Y. Abraham and Nabeel Abraham, *Arabs in the New World: Studies on Arab-American Communities* (Detroit, MI: Wayne State University, Center for Urban Studies, 1983).

19. See the introduction to Suleiman, *Arabs in America.*

20. Suleiman, *Arabs in America.*

21. See Bawardi, *The Making of Arab Americans*, for a more detailed perspective.

22. Bawardi, *The Making of Arab Americans*, 2014.

23. Gail D. Hershenzon, *Detroit's Woodmere Cemetery* (Charleston, SC: Arcadia Publishing, 2006).

24. Jean Gibran and Kahlil Gibran, *Kahlil Gibran: His Life and World*, rev. ed. (Northampton, NA: Interlink Publishing Group, 1998).

25. Khater, *Inventing Home*.

26. Gibran and Gibran, *Kahlil Gibran: His Life and World*.

27. Gibran and Gibran, *Kahlil Gibran: His Life and World*.

28. Linda K. Jacobs, *Strangers in the West: The Syrian Colony of New York City, 1880–1900* (New York: Kalimah Press, 2015).

29. Nijmeh Hajjar, *The Politics and Poetics of Ameen Rihani: The Humanist Ideology of an Arab-American Intellectual and Activist* (London: Taurus Academic Studies, 2010).

30. Hajjar, *The Politics and Poetics of Ameen Rihani*.

31. Suleiman, *Arabs in America*.

32. Suleiman, *Arabs in America*.

33. Selected church websites: Melkite: http://www.catholic-hierarchy.org/diocese/dneme.html and https://melkite.org/ (includes a parish locator); Maronite: http://www.stmaron.org/spirituality/online-articles/the-maronites-in-the-united-states/ (has a history of Maronite churches in the United States, including the spread of the Maronite churches in the United States); Syrian/Antiochian Orthodox: http://syrianorthodoxchurch.org/2010/05/the-syrian-church-in-north-america/ (also has a history of the church and of the expansion of the Orthodox churches that are predominantly Arab American).

34. Hassoun, *Arab Americans in Michigan*.

35. Hitti, *The Syrians in America*; Hassoun, *Arab Americans in Michigan*.

36. Tessa Torgeson, "Little Mosque on the Prairie," *High Plains Reader*, Fargo, North Dakota, August 2, 2016, http://hpr1.com/index.php/feature/culture/little-mosque-on-the-prairie.

37. Torgeson, "Little Mosque on the Prairie."

38. Torgeson, "Little Mosque on the Prairie."

39. Ilan Pappé, *The Modern Middle East* (London: Routledge, 2005), 26.

40. See https://history.state.gov/milestones/1945-1952/immigration-act.

41. Suleiman, *Arabs in America*.

42. George Antonius, *The Arab Awakening: The Story of the Arab National Movement* (New York: Capricorn Books, 1946).

43. Suleiman, *Arabs in America*.

44. Abraham and Abraham, *Arabs in the New World*.

45. Hassoun, *Arab Americans in Michigan*.

46. S. El-Badry, "Arab American Demographics," *Arab American Market*, http://www.allied-media.com/Arab-American/Arab/american/Demographics.htm. 2009.

47. Rick Gladstone and Satoshi Sugiyama, "Trump's Travel Ban: How It Works and Who Is Affected," *New York Times*, July 1, 2018, https://www.nytimes.com/2018/07/01/world/americas/travel-ban-trump-how-it-works.html.

48. Gladstone and Sugiyama, "Trump's Travel Ban."

49. Hassoun, *Arab Americans in Michigan*.

50. Laura Koran, "US Admitted Just 44 Syrian Refugees in Last 6 Months." CNN, April 18, 2018, https://www.cnn.com/2018/04/18/politics/us-syria-refugees/index.html.

51. Suleiman, *Arabs in America*.

Bibliography

Abraham, Sameer Y., and Nabeel Abraham. *Arabs in the New World: Studies on Arab-American Communities*. Detroit, MI: Wayne State University, Center for Urban Studies, 1983.

"A Miserable Year in Brooklyn: Khalil Sakakini in America, 1907–1908." The Institute for Palestine Studies, n.d. Accessed September 15, 2018. http://www.palestine-studies.org/jq/fulltext/77994.

Antonius, George. *The Arab Awakening: The Story of the Arab National Movement*. New York: Capricorn Books, 1946.

Aswad, Barbara C., and Barbara Bilgé. *Family and Gender among American Muslims: Issues Facing Middle Eastern Immigrants and Their Descendants*. Philadelphia: Temple University Press, 1996.

Bawardi, Hani J. 2009. "Arab American Political Organizations from 1915 to 1951: Assessing Transnational Political Consciousness and the Development of Arab American Identity." Diss., Wayne State University.

Bawardi, Hani J. *The Making of Arab Americans: From Syrian Nationalism to U.S. Citizenship*. Austin: University of Texas Press, 2014.

Cainkar, Louise. *Homeland Insecurity: The Arab American and Muslim American Experience after 9/11*. New York: Russell Sage Foundation, 2009.

El-Badry, S. "Arab American Demographics." *Arab American Market*, 2009. http://www.allied -media.com/Arab-American/Arab/american/Demographics.htm.

Gibran, Jean, and Kahlil Gibran. *Kahlil Gibran: His Life and World*. Rev. ed. Northampton, MA: Interlink Publishing Group, 1998.

Gladstone, Rick, and Satoshi Sugiyama. "Trump's Travel Ban: How It Works and Who Is Affected." *New York Times*, July 1, 2018. https://www.nytimes.com/2018/07/01/world/ameri cas/travel-ban-trump-how-it-works.html.

Hammad, Adnan, Rashid Kysia, Raja Rabah, Rosina Hassoun, and Michael Connelly. "Guide to Arab Culture: Health Care Delivery to the Arab American Community." 1999. http:// naama.com/pdf/arab-american-culture-health-care.pdf.

Hassoun, Rosina J. *Arab Americans in Michigan*. East Lansing: Michigan State University Press, 2005.

Hershenzon, Gail D. *Detroit's Woodmere Cemetery*. Charleston, SC: Arcadia Publishing, 2006.

Hitti, Philip Khuri. *The Syrians in America*. Piscataway, NJ: Gorgias Press, 1924.

Hajjar, Nijmeh. *The Politics and Poetics of Ameen Rihani: The Humanist Ideology of an Arab-American Intellectual and Activist*. London: Taurus Academic Studies, 2010.

Jacobs, Linda K. *Strangers in the West: The Syrian Colony of New York City, 1880–1900*. New York: Kalimah Press, 2015.

Khater, Akram F. *Inventing Home: Emigration, Gender, and the Middle Class in Lebanon, 1870–1920*. New ed. Berkeley: University of California Press, 2001.

Koran, Laura. 2018. "US Admitted Just 44 Syrian Refugees in Last 6 Months." CNN, April 18, 2018. https://www.cnn.com/2018/04/18/politics/us-syria-refugees/index.html.

Naff, Alixa. *Becoming American: The Early Arab Immigrant Experience*. Carbondale: Southern Illinois University Press, 1993.

Orfalea, Gregory. *Before the Flames: A Quest for the History of Arab Americans*. 1st ed. Austin: University of Texas Press, 1988.

Rihani, Albert. *Where to Find Ameen Rihani*. Beirut: Arab Institute for Research and Publications, 1979.

Shaheen, Jack. *Reel Bad Arabs: How Hollywood Vilifies a People*. 2nd ed. New York: Olive Branch Press, 2009.

Suleiman, Michael. *Arabs in America: Building a New Future*. Philadelphia: Temple University Press, 1999.

Torgeson, Tessa. 2016. "Little Mosque on the Prairie." *High Plains Reader*, Fargo, North Dakota, August 2, 2016. http://hpr1.com/index.php/feature/culture/little-mosque-on-the-prairie.

Contributors

Allan Amanik is an assistant professor of Judaic studies at Brooklyn College of the City University of New York. His research interests include American Jewish history, immigration, gender, and social welfare policy in the United States. He is author of *Dust to Dust: A History of Jewish Death and Burial in New York* (New York University Press, 2019).

Kelly B. Arehart received her PhD from the College of William and Mary in 2014. She served as the manager of interpretation and visitor services at the George Washington Foundation and is currently a research historian for the Colonial Williamsburg Foundation. She lives in Williamsburg, Virginia, with her husband and her collection of embalming textbooks.

Sue Fawn Chung is professor emerita in the Department of History at the University of Nevada, Las Vegas, specializing in Chinese and Chinese American history. She received her master's from Harvard University and her doctorate from University of California, Berkeley. She is advisor emerita for National Trust for Historic Preservation. She has written several books: *The Chinese in Nevada* (2011), *In Pursuit of Gold: Chinese Miners and Merchants in the American West* (2011 Carolyn Bancroft Award), and *Chinese in the Woods: Logging and Lumbering in the American West* (2015). She has published several book chapters: "Tracking Some Central Pacific Railroad Workers and Their Accomplishments," in *Chinese Railroad Workers in North America: Recovery and Representation* (2018); "Beyond Railroad Work: Chinese Contributions to the Development of Winnemucca and Elko, Nevada," in *The Chinese and the Iron Road* (Stanford University Press, 2019); "Chinese Exclusion, the First Bureau of Immigration, and the 1905 Special Chinese Census, 1892–1906," in *Chinese America: History and Perspective 2018* (Chinese Historical Society of America, 2019).

Kami Fletcher is an associate professor of American and African American history at Albright College, researching slave and autonomous African American burial grounds, African American male and female undertakers, and African American public mourning rituals. She is the author of "Real Business: Maryland's First Black Cemetery Journey's into the Enterprise of Death, 1807–1920" (*Thanatological Studies*, April 2015). She holds a PhD in history from Morgan State University. She serves on the international editorial board for *Mortality: Promoting the Interdisciplinary Study of Death and Dying*; is associate network member for Interdisciplinary Death & Culture Research (DaCNet) at University of York; and is president of the Collective for Radical Death Studies. For more, visit her website at www.kamifletcher.weebly.com and/or contact her on Twitter using @kamifletcher36.

Rosina Hassoun is an associate professor of anthropology at Saginaw Valley State University. She holds a PhD from the University of Florida, Gainesville, in anthropology and an MS and BS from Texas A&M University in biology and zoology. She is the author of *Arab Americans in Michigan* (Michigan State University Press, 2005) as well as author of numerous articles and book chapters. She served on the editorial board of the *Michigan Historical Review* from 2012 until 2018. Her areas of interest are acculturation, health disparities, chronic illnesses, environmental health, Arab diasporas, refugees, and immigrants. Her work has entailed examining historical patterns of Arab American immigration. She has conducted community participatory and health research in Arab and Chaldean American communities in Michigan and Ohio.

James S. Pula is a professor of history at Purdue University Northwest specializing in immigration studies and nineteenth-century US history. He is the author and editor of over twenty books and more than one hundred other works, including the recent *Immigration and Immigrant Communities (1790–2016)* from Grey House Publishing (2017). He served as editor-in-chief of *The Polish American Encyclopedia*, which the American Library Association selected as one of the best reference sources of the year. He was three times awarded the Oskar Halecki Prize for his research publications. Among his other recognitions are the Mieczysław Haiman Award for scholarly achievement; the Distinguished Service Award from the American Council for Polish Culture; the Rudewicz Medal for scholarly research; the Tadeusz Kościuszko Medal from Polonica Technica; the Gambrinus Prize in History from the Milwaukee County Historical Society; and the Officer's Cross of the Order of Merit of the Republic of Poland.

Jeffrey E. Smith is a professor of history at Lindenwood University and editor of *The Confluence*, a regional studies journal in a magazine format. He is author of *The Rural Cemetery Movement: Places of Paradox in Nineteenth-Century America* (Lexington Books, 2017) and *William Clark: Explorer and Diplomat* (Truman State University Press, 2016) for fifth-grade readers. Smith holds a PhD in history from the University of Akron, an MFA in museology from Syracuse University, and a BA from Mount Union College. He was the first recipient of the President's Scholar-Teacher Award at Lindenwood in 2008.

Martina Will de Chaparro, PhD, is a former associate professor of history at Texas Woman's University, and the author of numerous articles and the book *Death and Dying in New Mexico* (University of New Mexico Press, 2007). She has edited journal articles and reviewed journal and book manuscripts for several publishers and is coeditor of *Death and Dying in Spanish Colonial America* (University of Arizona Press, 2011). She earned her PhD from the University of New Mexico, her MA in Latin American studies from the University of California, San Diego, and her BA in history and German from the University of Virginia. Currently, she is the president of HISTORIAS, a Denver-based consulting firm specializing in historical research and writing and nonprofit fundraising (www.historiasllc.com).

Index

Page numbers in **bold** refer to figures and tables.

Syrian/Lebanese, 249, 251, 252–53, 256, 258–59, 265
Sze Yup (Siyi), **86**
Szwajnos family, gravestone of, 70, **70**

Taishan County, Guangdong, China, 87–88, 100, 110, 111
Taishan district association, 95, 106
tang (Chinese association), 91, 93, 94, 104, 111
Taos, New Mexico, 221, 223
taste-making, 10, 188
Tate, W. W., 229
Temple Emanu-El, New York, New York, 15, 20–22, 25, 31n40
temporary burial, 9, 102, 107
Terrazas, Juan Tomás, 222
Tewa, 220
Thomas Cooper Society, **139**
Tombstone, Arizona, 108
Tomé, New Mexico, 226
Tom Kim Yung, 95
tong. See tang
Tonopah, Nevada, 108
trees: as memorials, 196; in Polish cemeteries, 53, 55, **58**, 59, **59**, **60**
Truckee, California, 91–92
Trujillo, Antonia, 216
Trujillo, María Manuela, 228
Trump, Donald, 263–64
Tuman, Józef, gravestone of, 65–66, **66**, **68**
Tuman, Marya, gravestone of, 65–66, **66**, **68**
Tung Wah Hospital, Hong Kong, 100–101

undertakers, 148, 167, 186, 187; African American, 151, 152; Jewish, 18
Union Cemetery, Bakersfield, California, 107–8
Union Pacific Railroad, 90
United Daughters of Ruth Beneficial Society, **139**, 140, 143, 146
United Textile Workers of America, 49
universalism, 8, 22, 28
unmarked graves, 86, 169, 172, 253–54
UPRR (Union Pacific Railroad), 90
urban development, 19, 112–13, 164, 165, 234
US Census, 266n3
Utes, 212, 216, 218, 224

Valhalla Cemetery, St. Louis, Missouri, 99
vecinos, 210, 216, 218, 220, 234n6
Vernon, Christopher, 161
Victoria, British Columbia, Canada, 106
Viet, Richard, 161
Virginia, 187
visitations, 251
Viskočil, Anna, gravestone of, 40, **40**
Viskočil, Jan, gravestone of, 40, **40**

Wagner, Georgiana, 169
Wah, Gue Gim, 114
wakes, 48–49, 63, 71
Walker, Joel J., 198
Wallis, Thomas, 194
Ware, Sam, 138
Warren, Idaho, 108
Warren, Nelly "Aunt Nelly," 169, 176; headstone of, **168**
Washington Mission Conference, 147
Washington State, **88**
Wesleyan Cemetery, St. Louis, Missouri, 166
Western Sanitary Commission, 167
whiteness, 11, 209, 214
white supremacy, 6, 7, 88, 133, 146, 150, 212, 215
Wilson, Lewis, 174, 176; gravestone of, **173**
"Witaj, Królowo nieba" ("Hail Queen of Heaven"), 50, 64
Wong Halgson, 95
Wong Hun, gravestone of, **99**
Wong Joe (Zhou) Shee, gravestone of, **99**
Wong You, 97
Woodlawn Cemetery, Dayton, Ohio, 199
Woodlawn Memorial Park, Colma, California, 115
Woodmere Cemetery, Dearborn, Michigan, 254–55, 265
working class, 10, 62, 63; cemetery sections for, 196, 197
World War I, 252–53, 257, 265
Wu Yunian (Ing Hay), 108
Wyrobisz, Andrzej, 78n69

xenophobia, 6, 24, 257

Yalom, Marilyn, 5
Yanghe (Young Wo), **86**
Yanner, Keith, 162–63

CPSIA information can be obtained
at www.ICGtesting.com
Printed in the USA
LVHW091700110221
679070LV00008B/1670

9 781496 827890